Archaeology in the Environs of Roman York: Excavations 1976–2005

By Patrick Ottaway

Published for the York Archaeological Trust by the
Council for British Archaeology

2011

Contents

List of Figures

List of Tables

Volume 6 Fascicule 2

Archaeology in the Environs of Roman York: Excavations 1976–2005

By Patrick Ottaway

Key words: cemeteries, ditches, field systems, roads, Roman, suburbs, York

Introduction

This fascicule in Volume 6 of *The Archaeology of York* (*AY*), dedicated to Roman extramural settlement and roads, brings together the results of some 50 excavations and watching briefs by York Archaeological Trust. They were conducted largely during the years 1987–2005, but also included are some earlier sites such as 16–22 Coppergate, excavated in 1976–81. The sites were located at almost every point of the compass in an area encircled by the city ring road (A64 and A1237) and lay, for the most part, up to c.3.5km from the city centre. For the purposes of this report the sites have been grouped into seven zones as shown in Fig.54. The sites vary in size and scope. Some such as 16–22 Coppergate and 14–20 Blossom Street were relatively substantial excavations; others were small scale and would not necessarily be worthy of publication in their own right. Taken together, however, the sites in this publication make a very important contribution to the study of the history and topography of the Roman settlement at York.

A history of Roman York by the author of this fascicule (Ottaway 2004) serves as a general introduction to the subject, but the following section summarises particular aspects by way of an introduction to the archaeological work described below.

Roman York: an introduction

Setting

The Roman Ninth Legion *Hispana* is thought to have arrived in York (*Eburacum* or *Eboracum*) on the banks of the River Ouse in about AD 71 to found a fortress which would act as a base for the conquest of the north of Britain ordered by the Emperor Vespasian (69–79). However, there is now some evidence, principally from the 9 Blake Street site in the *praetentura*, for activity earlier than the establishment of the fortress (*AY* 3/4, 308–10). This may have been connected with the campaigns of Governor Vettius Bolanus (68–71) during which, as Tacitus tells us (*Histories* III, 45; trans. Ireland 1996, 77-8), the Romans had to rescue the Queen Cartimandua of the Brigantes from her former consort

Venutius. It is not intended to discuss the evidence for the earliest Roman military incursions in the York region in any detail here, but the subject has recently been re-examined by Peter Wilson (2009).

York stands at a point where the River Ouse cuts through a glacial moraine which runs more or less east–west across the Vale of York. Whereas much of the York area lies at c.5–15m OD, the moraine rises in places to 30m OD or slightly more (Fig.55). In addition, the Roman fortress stands on a slightly elevated plateau on the north-east bank of the River Ouse and is protected on its south-east side by the River Foss which approaches the city

113

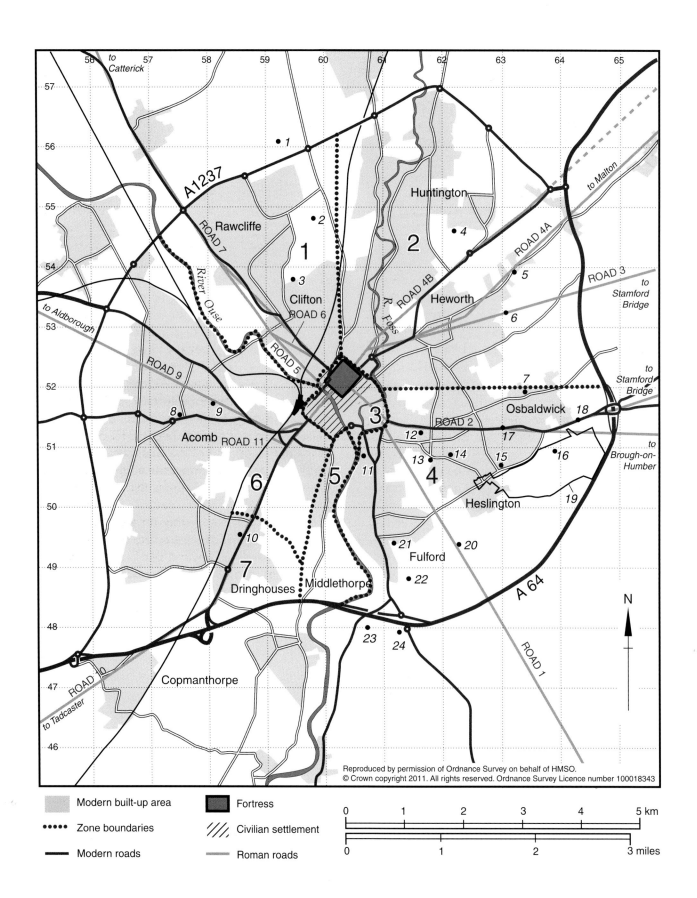

Modern built-up area

Fortress

●●●●● Zone boundaries

/// Civilian settlement

Modern roads

Roman roads

| 0 | 1 | 2 | 3 | 4 | 5 km |

| 0 | 1 | 2 | 3 miles |

N

from the north. York was chosen by the Romans for its strategic value derived from its location in the centre of the lowland zone between the Pennines to the west and Wolds to the east. In addition, the moraine provided a land route running across the low-lying and, in places, frequently flooded Vale of York, a route which had been exploited since the Bronze Age (RCHMY **3**, xxvii–xxviii). York lay at the junction of this land route with the River Ouse near its tidal head and at a point where it could easily be crossed. The Ouse provided a navigable route, via the Humber estuary, to the east coast and North Sea some 60km distant.

The solid geology of the York area is Triassic Sandstone, but this is overlain by drift deposits, largely warp and lacustrine clay. There is also boulder clay, and sand and gravel on the moraine, and alluvium in the river valleys (British Geological Survey 1983).

The course and width of the rivers at York in Roman times are not entirely clear, but the course of the Ouse has probably not changed a great deal, although it is now narrower due to encroachment of the banks, largely in medieval and later times. However, the Foss has been greatly affected by the creation of the King's Fish Pool in the 11th century and canalisation in more recent times. The elevated position of the fortress in the surrounding landscape is not so apparent today as it would probably have been in Roman times since the valleys of the Ouse and Foss have been filled in

by occupation material over the centuries and the river level has clearly risen by perhaps as much as 3m. The Ouse is no longer tidal and the average summer river level of c.5m OD has been artificially maintained since the mid-18th century by Naburn Lock downstream from the city (Radley and Simms 1970).

On the south-west bank of the Ouse, where the principal Roman civilian settlement was to emerge, ground level in the valley bottom was several metres lower than in the fortress. A reconstructed cross-section of the Ouse valley is shown in Fig.56 which is based on levels taken in a number of excavations on or close to its line, beginning at Bar Lane at the south-west end, near to the city walls at Micklegate Bar, and running up to Wellington Row near the Ouse crossing where the main road from the south-west (RCHMY **1**, 3; Road 10) was sectioned. Reference is made on the figure to a 'limestone surface' which dates to c.160 and was probably associated with creation of a causeway for a bridge over the river. The level at the north-east end of the cross-section is based on that at the 9 Blake Street site in the fortress (*AY* 3/4). The cross-section shows that on the south-west bank of the Ouse the natural ground surface is level or only rises slightly for a distance of up to c.100m from the river bank, but then rises quite sharply for c.150m. Beyond Bar Lane the ground levels off or dips away slightly towards the line of the present city walls which are thought to correspond to a Roman defensive circuit (see below).

Fig. 54   *York showing the location of the Roman fortress, principal civilian settlements, roads, other archaeological sites in relation to the extramural zones, and modern settlement and roads*

1. *Rawcliffe Moor*	13. *Green Dykes*
2. *Bootham Stray Roman camps*	14. *Heslington Hill*
3. *Water Lane, Clifton*	15. *Field Lane, Heslington (burials)*
4. *Huntington South Moor Roman camps*	16. *Kimberlow Hill*
5. *Ryethorpe Grange Farm*	17. *Gallows Hill*
6. *Apple Tree Farm, Heworth*	18. *Grimston Bar*
7. *Osbaldwick*	19. *Heslington East*
8. *Front Street, Acomb*	20. *Germany Beck (Roman road)*
9. *Severus Hills, Acomb*	21. *St Oswald's School, Fulford*
10. *Starting Gate, Dringhouses*	22. *Germany Beck evaluation*
11. *Fishergate House/Blue Bridge Lane*	23. *Lingcroft Farm, Naburn*
12. *Former D.C. Cook Garage, Hull Road*	24. *A19/A64 interchange (burial)*

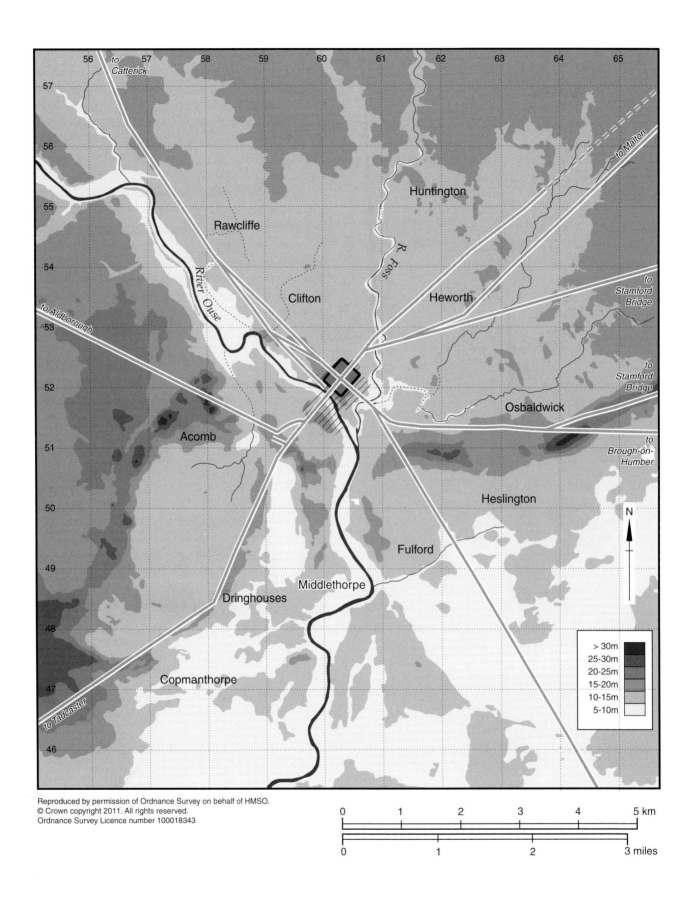

Fig. 55   *Relief map of York with principal Roman roads*

Late prehistory

Before the Roman conquest York lay within the territory of the Brigantes who occupied much of northern Britain except for land in east Yorkshire which is thought to have belonged to the Parisi named in Ptolemy's *Geography* of the 2nd century AD (Jones and Mattingly 1990, 19, map 2.4). A boundary between the two peoples may have been formed by the River Derwent, c.11km east of York. There is as yet no evidence that there were any late prehistoric settlements or related field systems in what is now the urban area of York when the Roman army arrived. The soldiers would probably have encountered a meadowland scene not unlike that on the rural reaches of the Ouse today. Research on the well-preserved organic material, including plant remains and snail shells, from recent excavations suggests a mixture of woodland scrub and cleared agricultural land (*AY* 14/6, 386–7). An absence of settlement may be due to the prevailing clay of the drift deposits which is usually thought to have been unsuitable for early arable agriculture. However, the remains of late Iron Age roundhouses and a probable field system have been found on clay at Rawcliffe Moor, c.4.5km north of the city (Fig.54, 1). Any areas of well-drained land would, presumably, have been far more attractive to the late Iron Age farmer and on the south-facing slope of the moraine c.3km east of the centre of York, at Heslington East, an extensive mid–late Iron Age field system and settlement site was excavated by YAT in 2007–8 (Fig.54, 19). At Lingcroft Farm, Naburn, c.5km to the south of the city, a similar site on glacial sand has been excavated by Bradford University (Fig.54, 23; Jones 1988; Jones 1990).

The Roman fortress

The fortress at York was to become one of three permanently garrisoned in Britain during the Roman period. It occupied c.20ha and adopted the usual playing-card-shaped plan with its corners more or less at the cardinal points (Fig.54). An outline plan of the streets and principal buildings of the early fortress has been established and it clearly faced south-west towards the Ouse (*AY* 3/3, 202–9). Before AD 120 the Ninth Legion had departed and was replaced as the garrison in about that year by the Sixth *Victrix* which remained in York until the end of the Roman period. The fortress became a base for renewed campaigns in the north in the years 208–11 during the reign of the Emperor Septimius Severus who was to die here. In 306 the Emperor Constantius I also died in York while on campaign. The development of the fortress layout and buildings from the late 1st century onwards has been studied in detail elsewhere (*AY* 3/1–4; Phillips and Heywood 1995). One need say no more here other than to suggest that the varying degree to which supply of the Roman army in York generated wealth locally probably had an important bearing on the rapid growth of settled areas at York from the early 2nd–early 3rd centuries and then their slow subsequent contraction. Both processes are clearly implied by many of the excavations described below.

Civilian settlement

In addition to its role as a military base, York also became the site of an important civilian settlement of urban character. One part of this settlement grew up on the north-east bank of the Ouse, outside the fortress. Some of the excavations in this fascicule (Zones 1–3) were located in this settlement, thought by the Royal Commission on Historical Monuments for England (RCHME; RCHMY **1**, xxxiv–xxxv) to have had its origins as *canabae* – a term meaning 'the booths' which has been used elsewhere to denote a settlement under direct military control, housing, as RCHME put it, 'the motley crowd of tradesmen and purveyors wont to gather about any large military force'. RCHME also supposed that this settlement would have formed part of the *territorium legionis*, a potentially very extensive area of land around York managed directly by the army for supply purposes (*ibid.*, xxxiv–xxxv). There is as yet, however, no evidence either for the use of the term *canabae* at York or for the extent of any *territorium*.

Growth of the settlement on both banks of the Ouse was particularly rapid in the third quarter of the 2nd century, represented by new streets and buildings both private and public. The latter included, north-east of the Ouse, temples dedicated to Hercules and a local deity coupled with the imperial *numen* (RCHMY **1**, xxxv). South-west of the Ouse public buildings included a substantial bath house at 1–9 Micklegate, a large reception hall – possibly part of another bath house – located near the city walls by Station Road (*ibid.*, 55–6),

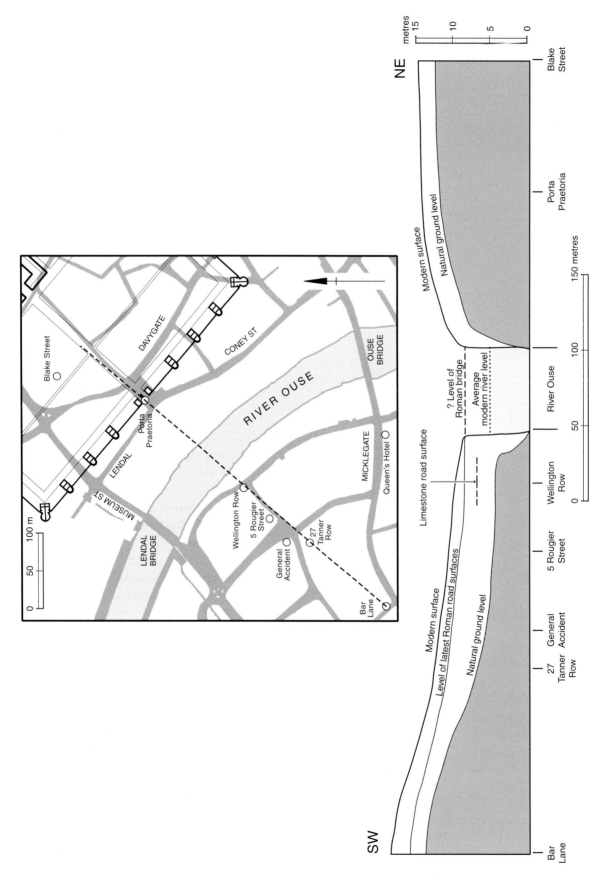

Fig. 56   Simplified cross-section across York (with location plan) along the line of the main Roman road from the south-west and fortress via praetoria, showing approximate ground and river levels in the Roman period

and temples to the gods Mithras (*ibid.*, 120–1) and Serapis (*ibid.*, 53–4). In addition, there is plenty of evidence on both banks of the Ouse for the laying of drains and provision of a water supply with pipes and wells.

In the early 3rd century, probably in the reign of Caracalla (211–17), York was made capital of the province of *Britannia Inferior* (Lower Britain), on the division of *Britannia* into two. The civilian settlement probably acquired the honorific status of *colonia* at the same time, although this is not attested until the year 237, the date of an altar dedicated at Bordeaux by a *sevir* of the *coloniae* of both York and Lincoln (*ibid.*, xxxvi). The term *colonia* has often been used to refer solely to the Roman civilian settlement south-west of the Ouse, largely because of the discovery of the inscribed sarcophagi of a *decurion* of the *colonia*, and of a *sevir augustalis* and his wife in the adjacent cemetery to the north-west (*ibid.*, xxxvi). This settlement has usually been defined by the medieval defences which are thought to correspond to a Roman defensive circuit. By analogy with the defences of the fortress on its north-west and north-east sides, which lie below a medieval earthen rampart capped by the city walls, this is certainly possible, although a Roman wall below the medieval rampart south-west of the Ouse has been located in only three places, all to the west of Micklegate Bar (RCHMY **1**, xxvii). In any event, there is no good reason to suppose that the principal settled areas north-east of the Ouse did not also enjoy *colonia* status, although where any boundaries to the *colonia* may have lain, whether north-east or south-west of the river, remains unknown.

Late Roman York

In the late Roman period York as fortress and provincial capital retained a unique status recognised not only by the visit of Constantius I in 306 but also, perhaps, by the acclamation here of his son Constantine (the Great) as his successor. In addition, York was the seat of a bishop by the early 4th century when a certain Eborius attended the Council of Arles in 314. York may also have been the base of a senior army officer referred to in the *Notitia Dignitatum* as the *Dux Britanniarum* (Duke of the Britains). However, York did not develop into a major late Roman provincial capital along the lines of Arles or Trier or even perhaps London. This

may to some extent be due to a reduced permanent garrison following changes made to the organisation of the Roman army such that large bases near the frontiers were no longer required. However, some refurbishment of the fortress defences, buildings and streets can be ascribed to the early–mid-4th century, although the end of the century presents us with a picture of derelict buildings and abandoned infrastructure. The civilian settlements appear to have experienced a period of prosperity in the late 3rd–mid-4th centuries with, for example, construction and expansion of town houses, some appointed with fine mosaic pavements. A gradual decline in population, however, seems to have followed after the mid-century, represented again by abandoned, and even demolished, buildings and a deterioration in standards of street maintenance.

The extramural areas

For the purposes of *The Archaeology of York* the term extramural is taken to refer to areas within a radius of c.3.5km from the city centre, lying outside the defences of the legionary fortress north-east of the Ouse, and the assumed defences, as defined above, of the town south-west of the Ouse (Fig.54). It should be noted, however, that the date at which any defences were established is unknown, although it would almost certainly have been by the early 3rd century. In the early years of Roman York, settlement south-west of the Ouse, within the area later enclosed by any defences, may have had no status distinct from what subsequently became extramural and so for this period the concept of 'extramural' as defined by *The Archaeology of York* may not be strictly meaningful. However, the Roman archaeology of the town encompassed by the presumed defences is not discussed in detail in this publication, but will be found in Volume 4 of *The Archaeology of York*.

Because of their number and wide distribution, the sites considered in this fascicule have provided a valuable, if sometimes frustratingly incomplete, insight into the development of the Roman extramural areas. As a result it builds substantially on the work reported in the first fascicule in this volume (hereafter *AY* 6/1). Of particular importance in what follows is the work in two areas. The first is on the Foss banks (Zone 3; Fig.54) and in particular the site of 16–22 Coppergate where a large area in a hitherto largely unexplored zone south-east of the fortress was examined. The second is on Blossom Street and The Mount (Zone 6) where excavations were concerned with the main Roman approach road to York from the south-west and land use immediately adjacent to it.

Important components of the Roman landscape in all the extramural areas, especially within c.1km of the fortress and civilian settlements, are the cemeteries (Fig.57). In *The Archaeology of York* Roman cemeteries will be considered in detail in Volume 5, but a number of sites with burials are reported on

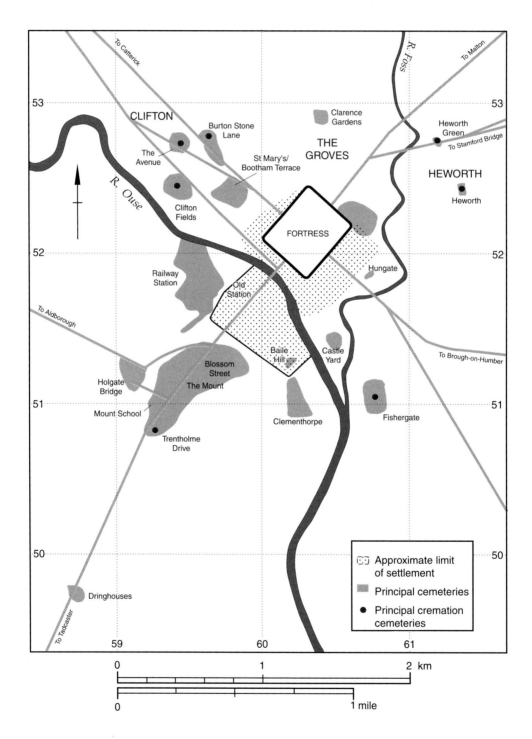

Fig. 57 *Location of the principal cemetery zones of Roman York*

120

in this fascicule inasmuch as they relate to patterns of settlement and land use. Summary information on the human remains is given as appropriate, derived from reports by Professor Don Brothwell, Simon Mays (16–22 Coppergate), Gill Stroud (35–41 Blossom Street), and Katie Tucker (3 and 6 Driffield Terrace).

Research into the extramural areas of Roman York has, until recently, rather lagged behind that concerned with the fortress and settlement south-west of the Ouse. *Eburacum* (RCHMY **1**), the great compendium of finds and structures in Roman York, published in 1962 by RCHME, provided a description of the main Roman approach roads to York (pp.1–3) which is still largely valid, although more recent work, most of it reported either in *AY* 6/1 (pp.84–101) or in this fascicule, has made important additions and amendments. The principal cemetery zones have been revealed over the last 300 years or so and have yielded a large number of burials, although until the late 20th century they had usually been recorded in ad hoc investigations by local antiquaries rather than by systematic archaeological excavation. As far as other forms of activity and settlement are concerned, RCHME was able to refer to only a small number of discoveries, few of which had been made in formal excavations (RCHMY **1**, 58–65).

A great step forward in knowledge was made in 1986 with the publication of *AY* 6/1, which reported on important excavations conducted to modern standards at a number of extramural sites including 39–41 Coney Street (late 1st- to 2nd-century timber granaries and riverside street), 21–33 Aldwark (streets and a 4th-century house) and Clementhorpe (3rd-century terracing and house with 4th-century additions). Since 1986 the pace of investigation has quickened, in part because of changes in the way the local authority planning process now treats archaeology. Since c.1990 the City of York has demanded a routine archaeological evaluation of all development sites in archaeologically sensitive areas in a much more comprehensive manner than hitherto – hence the numerous small investigations included in this fascicule. In some cases the city requires work over and above evaluation, leading to a formal publication. Sites in Roman extramural areas treated in this way include the former D.C. Cook garage site in Lawrence Street (Evans

2004); Huntington South Moor (Johnson 2005), The Starting Gate, Dringhouses (McComish 2006), excavated by YAT. A short summary of The Starting Gate is included below and reference will be made in discussion to the other sites.

Another feature of the current environment in which archaeology is conducted in York is that developers are free to employ contractors of their own choosing. This has meant that excavations in the York area are no longer solely conducted by York Archaeological Trust. In the extramural zone there have been a number of excavations by other organisations in recent years. It has not been possible to include them in this publication, but reference will be made to them where relevant in the discussion sections, based for the most part on publications or reports lodged with the City of York Sites and Monuments Record.

Organisation of this fascicule

The site reports in this fascicule are organised according to their location in one of seven zones (Fig.54) as follows:

North-east of the Ouse
1. North-west of the fortress
2. North-east of and immediately east of the fortress
3. South-east of the fortress and east of the Foss (within the medieval walls)
4. East of the Ouse and Foss (outside the medieval walls)

South-west of the Ouse
5. Bishopthorpe Road area
6. Blossom Street and The Mount area
7. Dringhouses

The text on each zone has an introduction followed by site reports which describe the stratigraphy and structures, and also give a summary of the pottery and small finds. Pottery for sites excavated in the years up to and including 1990, and selectively until 1992, has been considered in *AY* 16/8, and references to that publication are given here. Reports on pottery not published in *AY* 16/8 will appear in future fascicules of *AY* 16. Reports on the small finds will appear in future fascicules in *AY* 17. Richard Brickstock has undertaken an unpublished survey of Roman coins from York excavated up to c.1990. The animal bones and other biological material from most of the sites have been examined and any significant data are referred to. The work was undertaken either by the Environmental Archaeology Unit at York University or Palaeoecology Research Services, Durham.

Each section is concluded with a discussion which adopts, as far as possible, a set order beginning with natural topography and Roman roads, followed by land use and settlement in the late 1st–mid-3rd centuries (corresponding to Ceramic Periods [CP] 1–3 in *AY* 16/8), followed by burials, and concluding with land use and settlement in the late Roman period (CP 4 in *AY* 16/8). The fasci- cule concludes with a general discussion of Roman activity and settlement at York with particular reference to the extramural areas, but including reference, where relevant, to the fortress and principal civilian settlements, on the one hand, and areas further afield in the York region, on the other.

The post-Roman archaeology of sites described below will be published in future fascicules in Volumes 8–11 of *The Archaeology of York*.

Sites excavated in York usually have a Yorkshire Museum accession code of the form 19xx.xx. Summary information on sites excavated by York Archaeological Trust can be found on www. yorkarchaeology.co.uk by following prompts for the gazetteer.

Key to excavation plans

— ·· — ·· — ·· — ··	Limit of excavation	Clay			Occupation deposits
— · — · — · — · —	Limit of intrusion	Clay sand			Ash
- - - - - - - - - -	Limit of context	Clay silt			Cobbles
▲ — — — — — — ▲	Line of section	Burnt clay			Mortar
		Silt			Peat

Zone 1: North-west of the fortress

Introduction *(Figs 54, 58)*

Extramural Zone 1 encompasses an area north-east of the River Ouse extending for a distance of c.3km north-west of the legionary fortress (Fig.54, Fig.58). The zone is crossed by three major Roman roads which approach York from the north-west (RCHMY 1, 2–3; Roads 5–7; pp.95–7, *AY* 6/1). The line of Road 5, which probably originated in Catterick (*Cataractonium*), was traced by RCHME on the basis of parish boundaries, but it was also exposed in Water End in 1893 and in St Peter's School in 1954. It appears to have headed towards the Roman bridge over the Ouse, bypassing the fortress. Road 6 linked Road 5 with the north-west gate (*porta principalis dextra*) of the fortress. Close to the junction of Queen Anne's Road and Bootham (see below report on 108–110 Bootham, pp.140–42), Road 6 joined Road 7 and adopted the line now followed by Bootham. Road 7 may have diverged from Road 5 somewhere north-west of Clifton and then adopted the line now followed by Clifton and Bootham as far as its junction with Road 6.

A feature of this zone about which there has been a certain amount of speculation, but on the basis of little hard evidence, is an 'annexe' or 'fortified enclosure' on the north-west side of the fortress (RCHMY 1, 45–7). In the 19th century a wall on a north-east/south-west alignment was exposed in two places under Marygate near the junction with Bootham at its north-east end (Fig.58, 13). The wall was recorded standing 1.2m high and the top lay 0.90m below the modern level. Although deemed Roman, it is quite possible that this wall is the same as that seen in 1996 under and earlier than the St Mary's Abbey precinct wall a little to the south-west of Tower C (1996.168), which appeared to be 12th century. RCHME suggested that the south-west side of the proposed annexe was formed by a substantial Roman wall on a north-west/south-east alignment, continuing the alignment of the south-west fortress defences, which was found c.95m north-west of the west corner of the fortress in excavations by G.F. Wilmott in 1956–7 (RCHMY 1, 47, fig.35, a; Fig.58, 17). It was reported as being over 2.5m thick and surviving to a height of over 0.60m, and was thought to have been demolished when the overlying south

wall of the south aisle of St Mary's Abbey church was built. Within the proposed annexe Roman discoveries include those by Miller in 1928 in the garden of King's Manor House (c.SE60015224 – not as given in RCHMY 1; Fig.58, 15). A street running north-west/south-east, building remains and occupation deposits were found (unpublished, but see RCHMY 1, 47). Another possible street or cobbled surface was found in a YAT training excavation near the junction of Marygate and Bootham (Fig.58, 12). Excavations by G.F. Wilmott in 1951–3 took place in the cloister walk, west of the modern path from the Museum to the Abbey Gatehouse (Fig.58, 16). Although not fully published (but see Gentil 1988 and summaries in Wilmott 1952–3; Wilmott 1953–4; RCHMY 1, 61), it appears that the earliest phase was a timber structure, aligned north-west/south-east, thought to be late 1st–early 2nd century. This was succeeded by a cobbled floor and then the remains of a stone building thought to be early 3rd century, succeeded in turn by a street on a north-west/south-east alignment dated after c.260. In the final phase there was a cobbled surface associated with 4th-century pottery.

In Monaghan's survey of the Roman pottery from York (*AY* 16/8, 1096–7) some late 1st-century material came to light from the cloister walk site, but insufficient to support claims of a focus of pre-Flavian occupation made by Wilmott (1953–4) and revived by Cool (1998) on the basis of a small number of glass sherds which have a pre-Flavian origin.

In conclusion, the idea of a fortress annexe in the area of St Mary's Abbey appears hard to sustain at present, but there is some evidence for an important area of settlement north-west of the fortress which existed throughout the Roman period about which one would like to know a good deal more.

The so-called annexe area apart, knowledge of Roman activity in Zone 1 north-west of the fortress has hitherto been largely confined to burials (Fig.57). The nearest burial to the fortress appears to be a late 1st- to early 2nd-century cremation from the Art

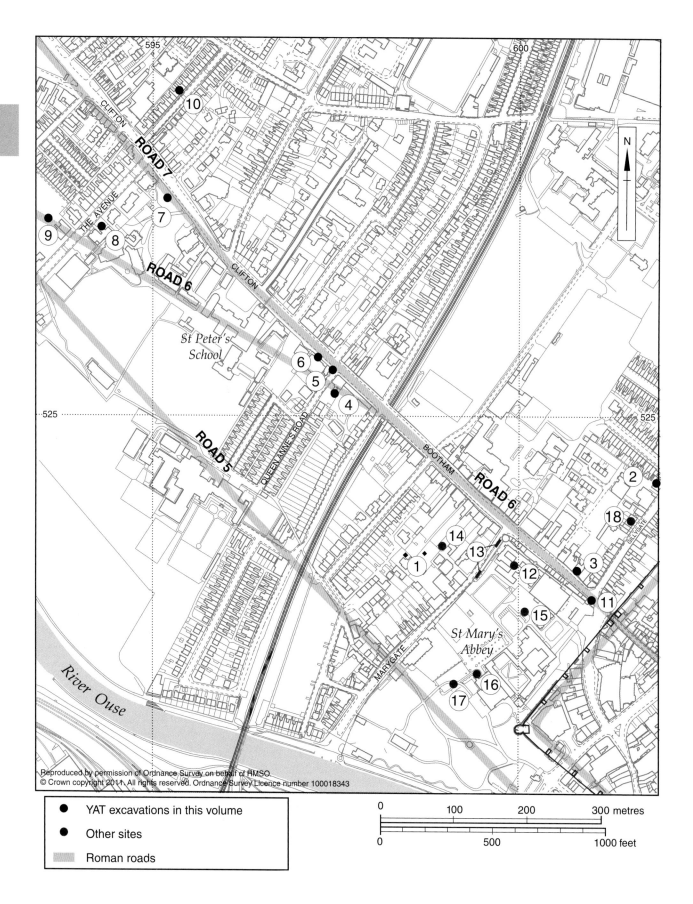

● YAT excavations in this volume

● Other sites

▨ Roman roads

0   100   200   300 metres

0   500   1000 feet

Gallery, Exhibition Square, c.75m north-west of the north-west gate (RCHMY **1**, 72) – and inside the proposed annexe. It is likely, however, that cemeteries came to line the main roads for a distance of up to 1km from the fortress with particularly important areas known at St Mary's/Bootham Terrace, Clifton Fields, The Avenue and Clifton/Burton Stone Lane (*ibid.*, 72–6), while individual and small groups of burials were, on occasions, made in outlying areas. Other evidence for Roman activity in Zone 1 reported in RCHMY **1** is confined to three small-scale observations of occupation debris, and one of a building with a tessellated pavement at St Olave's School, Clifton (*ibid.*, 65). Since its publication, small-scale excavations have taken place, in 1964, at 52 Bootham which revealed a cobbled surface and possible ditch containing pottery largely of the late 1st–early 2nd century (Keen 1965; *AY* 16/8, 1097; Fig.58, 14), and, in 1972, at 31–7 Gillygate (Fig.58, 18; pp.49–53, *AY* 6/1) which produced traces of a timber building, a cobbled surface and pits. The pottery from Gillygate, much of it residual in its context, was largely of the late 1st–early 3rd centuries, with a particular emphasis on the late 1st–early 2nd (*AY* 16/8, 1097). In 1972 also, some evidence for Roman structures and other activity was revealed, but not recorded in detail, in the bases of medieval and later cut features at 6–28/21–7 Union Terrace (*AY* 11/1, 12–13), 200m north-west of the fortress. Residual pottery of 1st- to 4th-century date was recorded, with a particular emphasis on the 3rd century (*AY* 16/8, 1097).

On the north-west edge of the zone under discussion, on Bootham Stray, there are two Roman camps (Fig.54, 2; RCHMY **1**, 46–7; Stephens and Ware 1995; Welfare and Swan 1995, 135–6). They are probably two of the 'seven or eight of different sizes' referred to in Francis Drake's *Eboracum* of 1736. Their form and size suggests a late 1st – 2nd century date and they may have been contemporary with two similar camps on Huntington South Moor which are probably Hadrianic (Fig.54, 4; Johnson 2005).

21–23 Bootham

In a watching brief on construction work at 21–23 Bootham (SE60085229) in 1991 cobbles were recorded at depth of 2.10m (Fig.58, 3). They presumably represent the Roman approach road from the north-west (RCHMY **1**, Road 6) which is followed by Bootham in this area. The cobbles were overlain by an olive-grey deposit containing Roman pottery.

A watching brief in 1992 on the corner of Bootham and Gillygate (SE60105226; Fig.58,11;) also recorded cobbles at a similar depth.

Records for these sites are stored under the Yorkshire Museum accession codes 1991.1025 and 1992.175.

45–57 Gillygate

Introduction

In April 1992 an evaluation excavation was undertaken at 45–57 Gillygate (SE59945245; Fig.58, 2; Fig.59, Fig.63), under the supervision of D. T. Evans, to a brief prepared by the Principal Archaeologist for City of York Council. The work took

Fig. 58 *(facing page)   Zone 1: location of sites described in this fascicule (1–11) and other sites (12–18)*

1. 26–28 Marygate (1992)

2. 45–57 Gillygate (1992)

3. 21–23 Bootham (1991)

4. 108–110 Bootham (2003)

5. 3 Clifton (1994)

6. 5–9 Clifton (1994)

7. St Peter's School, Clifton (1999)

8. Wentworth House, The Avenue (1999)

9. 12–13 The Avenue (2000)

10. 21–23 Avenue Terrace (2000)

11. CCTV Pit, Bootham/Gillygate (1992)

12. St Mary's Abbey (2005)

13. Walls on Marygate

14. 52 Bootham (1964)

15. King's Manor House (1928)

16. St Mary's Abbey (1951–3)

17. St Mary's Abbey church nave south aisle (1956–7)

18. 31–37 Gillygate (1972)

Fig. 59   *45–57 Gillygate: site location. Red line represents the Roman fortress defences*

place in advance of the construction of town houses on the Gillygate street frontage. At the time of excavation the site was a garage forecourt. The brief called for a single trench, 6 x 4m, to be excavated to a depth of 1.5m. It was laid out adjacent to the street with the long axis at right angles to Gillygate.

The finds and site records are currently stored with York Archaeological Trust under the Yorkshire Museum accession code 1992.8.

This report is based on the site evaluation report by D. T. Evans.

The excavation

After mechanical clearance of modern concrete, archaeological deposits were encountered c.0.30m below modern ground level (c.15.4m OD) and excavation by hand began. Due to weather conditions and other circumstances, the entire trench could not be taken down to the specified depth of 1.5m, but this was achieved in most of the south-west quadrant and provided a complete sequence through the deposits.

Natural orange-brown clay was encountered at c.14m OD and it was capped by another natural layer, c.0.2m thick, of coarse white sand. These deposits were only observed in the bases of the deeper cut features. Some 0.2m of deposits overlying the sand were not excavated. They were, however, seen in the sides of features such as ditch 1093 and appeared to be grey silts. The earliest deposit recorded, although not excavated, was a build up of mid-brown clayey sandy silt (1094).

Before the excavated sequence is described, it may be noted that a summary report on the pottery comments that most of it belonged to the early 2nd century (*AY* 16/8, 1098). There was, however, sufficient later material to justify the revised dating given below.

Ditches 1093 and 1078 (*Figs 60 and 63*)

Cut into 1094 was a ditch (1093) running approximately north-west/south-east across the entire trench. This was a substantial feature c.1.40m wide and c.0.80m deep. It contained three fill layers, the earliest being a dark grey, silty sandy clay deposit (1091), succeeded by an orange-brown silty sandy

clay (1084), and then a greyish-brown sandy silt (1083). Pottery from these deposits suggested that the ditch became disused and was backfilled in the late 2nd or early 3rd century. As the ditch was silting up a brown, slightly clayey sandy silt (1089) was building up to the north of it. This could not be directly related to the ditch because of a later cut. Pottery from 1089 was probably 2nd century. A shallow cut (1087) of unknown function lay 0.40m north of ditch 1093. It may have run parallel to 1093. The fill was a yellowish-brown clay (1086).

Overlying 1086 and 1089 was a spread of greyish-brown clayey silt (1085) over which lay a deposit of stony, sandy, silty clay (1077). The latter contained a

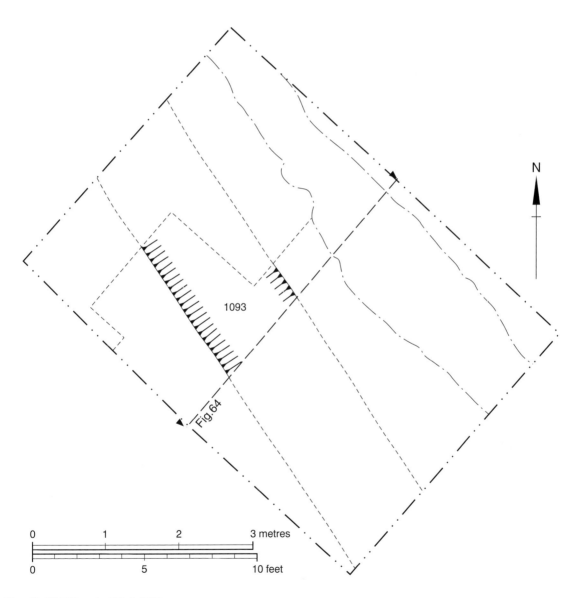

Fig. 60   *45–57 Gillygate: Ditch 1093*

fragment of a glass pillar-moulded bowl (sf89) dated to the late 1st century. Contemporary but to the south of ditch 1093 and overlying it was a deposit of grey silt (1079) which contained a fragment of a glass cylindrical bottle (sf86) which was dated late 1st–the first quarter of the 2nd century.

Cutting through 1077 and 1079 was a ditch (1078) c.0.82m wide and c.0.55m deep, aligned approximately north-west/south-east on the same line as 1093 and presumably intended to replace it. Ditch 1078 had steep sides and an almost flat base. Seven infill layers were recorded, the earliest being a brown, slightly clayey sandy deposit (1076) succeeded, in turn, by brown and white hardpan (1092), a light greyish-brown sandy deposit (1090), a dark greyish-brown silty clay deposit (1088), a mixture of orange ash and charcoal (1074), a greyish-brown stony sandy silty clay (1081) and a dark greyish-brown deposit (1069).

Overlying and slumped into the top of ditch 1078 was a mixture of a dark brown, clayey deposit and pale white-yellow mortar (1068). In it was found the majority of the lower body and all of the base of a large, light green, tubular-rimmed bowl of Flavian date (sf82). Hilary Cool comments that this is noteworthy because it is very unusual to find such large fragments of vessel glass on Roman domestic sites. Other glass fragments date to the late 1st–mid-2nd

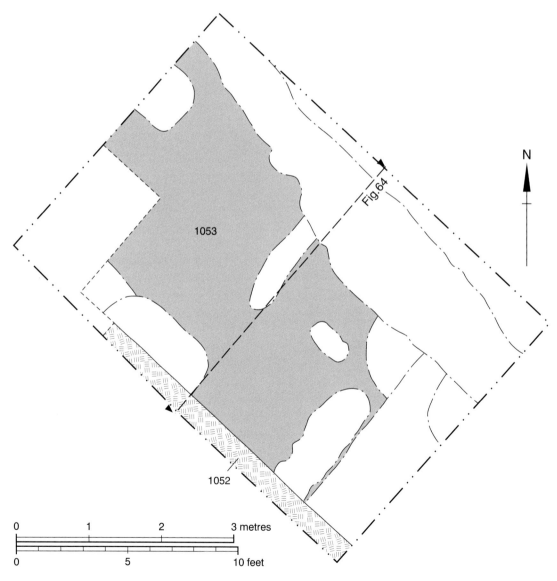

Fig. 61   *45–57 Gillygate: Deposit 1053*

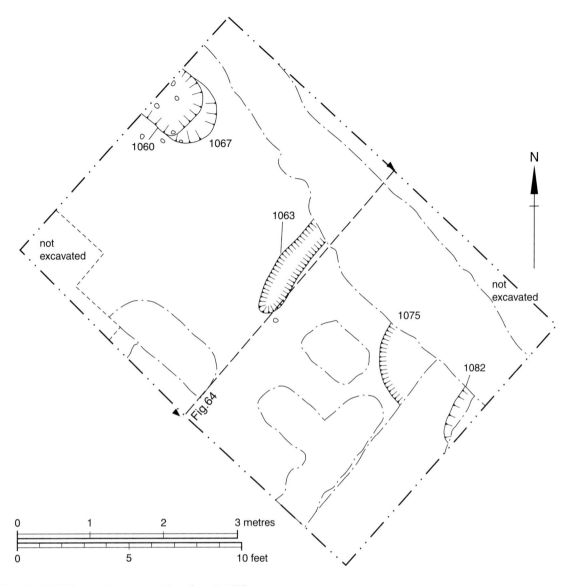

Fig. 62   *45–57 Gillygate: Features cut into deposit 1053*

century. Immediately above 1068 was a build-up layer of dark grey silt (1061).

Pottery from layers described here, later than ditch 1093 deposits, are dated to either the late 2nd or the early 3rd century, although there is earlier residual material.

Deposit 1053 and later features *(Figs 61–4)*

Above 1061 was an extensive spread of a dark orange-brown sandy deposit (1053) containing many small to medium-sized cobbles. It may have been laid to level off the site and fill the slumping caused by ditches 1093 and 1078. Deposit 1053

varied in thickness from c.0.40m over the slumping to less than 0.05m where slumping had not occurred. On the south side of 1053, but not clearly related to it in stratigraphic terms, and aligned north-west/ south-east was a band of orange-brown clay (1052) containing some large (up to 0.25m across) blocks of limestone. This may have been a foundation for the wall of a timber building. Pottery suggested that this phase of activity dates, once again, to the late 2nd–early 3rd century.

A series of cuts penetrated 1052 and 1053, some of which may be Roman while others were clearly medieval. Those which contained only Roman pottery included a slot of unknown function (1063),

Fig. 63 45–57 Gillygate: view south-east of the site as fully excavated, with ditch 1093 in centre (scale 1m)

1

aligned north-west/south-east, 0.40m wide and 0.20m deep, with steeply sloping sides and a flat base. It had a fill of greyish-brown silty clay (1062). Its north-western end had been cut away by a later intrusion; the southern terminal was roughly rounded. At the north-western end of the site was a pit of possible oval shape (1060/1067), lying partly beyond the trench edge, at least 0.80m across and 0.55m deep. It had steep sides and a flat base. The fill of the pit, a mid-grey, sandy clayey silt (1066), contained a large amount of animal bone indicating that it was used for rubbish disposal. Pottery from 1066 suggested a late 2nd-century or early 3rd-century date.

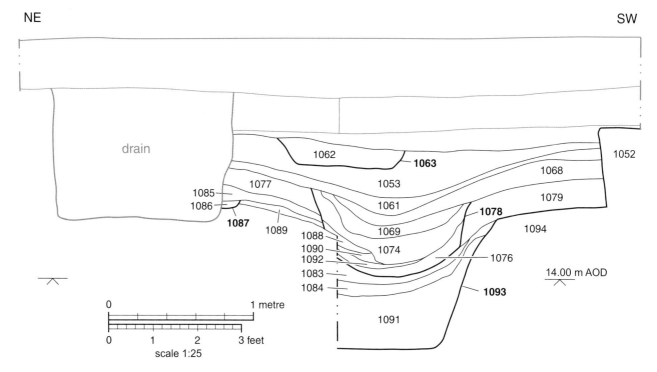

Fig. 64 45–57 Gillygate: Section across ditches 1078 and 1093

130

At the south-eastern end of the site was a cut (1075) which had probably been circular in plan, but most of it had been removed by later features. It was quite shallow, c.0.10m deep, and was filled with a grey sandy clayey silt (1073) which was dated to the 3rd century on the pottery evidence. Further southeast was the south-west part of another probable pit (1082), also largely removed by later features. The fill was a dark grey slightly silty clay (1082) and the feature was dated to the 3rd century or later.

No deposits from this site were dated to the 4th century.

Post-Roman

There was no evidence, artefactual or otherwise, of any Anglian or Anglo-Scandinavian activity. Deposits and features of the medieval period were numerous and generally well preserved.

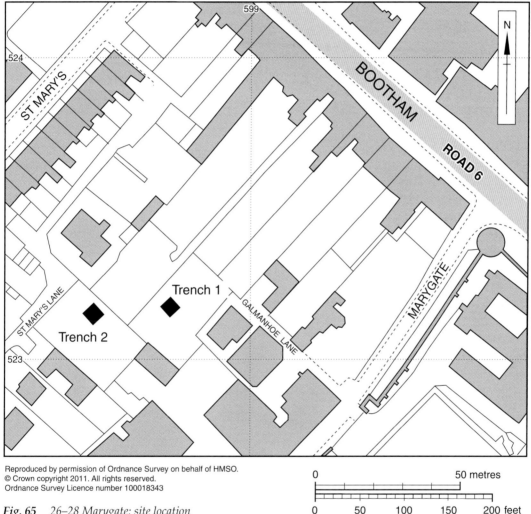

Fig. 65   *26–28 Marygate: site location*

26–28 Marygate

Introduction

In May–June 1992 an archaeological excavation was carried out, under the supervision of Mark Whyman, on land behind 26–8 Marygate (SE 59885232; Fig.58, 1; Fig.65) and in a small, walled enclosure adjacent to St Mary's Lane. The excavation consisted of two 5 x 5m trenches, one at each location as required by the archaeological brief provided by the the Principal Archaeologist for City of York Council. The work was conducted in response to a proposed residential development comprising three houses with freestanding garages. Both trenches were located on open ground which behind 26–8 Marygate (Trench 1) was partly overgrown and partly used as a car park; the St Mary's Lane enclosure contained a small orchard (Trench 2). In terms of Roman topography the site lies c.100m south-west of the main road approaching York from the north-west (RCHMY **1**, 3; Road 6) and c.250m north-west of the legionary fortress.

The finds and site records are currently lodged with the York Archaeological Trust under the Trust and Yorkshire Museum accession code 1992.11. This report has been compiled using a site evaluation report by Mark Whyman.

The excavation

Initial clearance of both trenches was carried out using a mechanical excavator. From a modern ground surface at c.15.1m OD, c.1.5m of homogeneous soil was removed from Trench 1 before deposits thought to be of archaeological significance were encountered. The modern ground surface in the vicinity of Trench 2, was approximately 1m below that of Trench 1 c.20m to the east. A brick wall aligned north-east/south-west separated the blocks of land in which the excavations were located and demarcated the change in ground level. In Trench 2 almost 2m of homogeneous overburden was removed before stratified archaeological deposits were reached at a level of c.12m OD in the north-western part of the trench and at c.11.6m in the

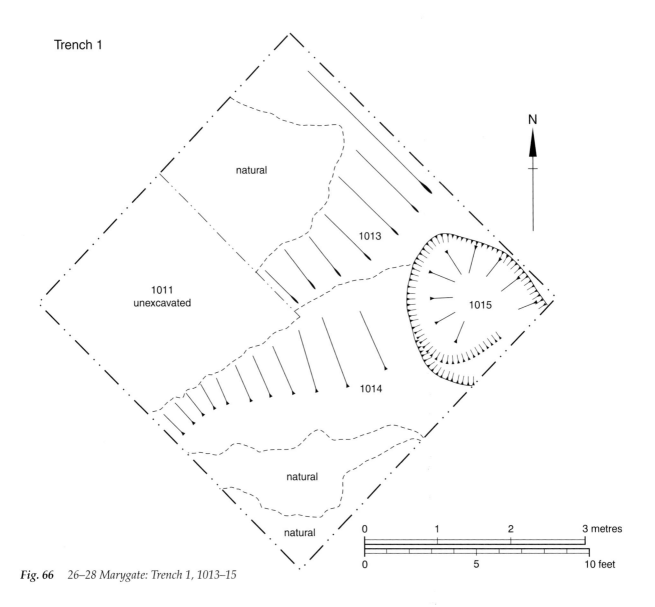

Fig. 66   *26–28 Marygate: Trench 1, 1013–15*

south-eastern part. Natural ground level appears to fall sharply by at least 1.5m from north-east to south-west between Trench 1 and Trench 2.

Trench 1 *(Figs 66–7)*

Natural orange clay was encountered at 13.5m OD in the southern corner of the trench. Further north, this gave way to disturbed natural while in the north-eastern part of the site natural took the form of sand.

The earliest archaeological deposits included 1014, orange sandy clay mixed with a small amount of grey-brown silt. It extended over much of the south-eastern part of the site, but was not fully excavated. In the northern part of the trench 1014 was overlain by 1013, dark grey-brown clayey sand mottled with

patches of dark red sandy clay. Pottery from these deposits dates them to the late 2nd century.

In the north-east corner of the trench, cutting 1013 and 1014, was 1015, a pit, roughly oval in plan, c.1.8m wide with a maximum depth of c.0.7m. Unfortunately inundation by rising groundwater made it impossible to excavate the feature fully. The backfill excavated was 1012, a grey-brown silty clay containing cobbles and fragments of limestone, sandstone, brick and tile.

Pit 1015 was overlain by 1010, a dark brown-grey sandy clay deposit, which was restricted to the eastern corner of the trench. Overlying 1013 was 1011, grey-brown silty clay, which extended over the much of the western half of the trench; it

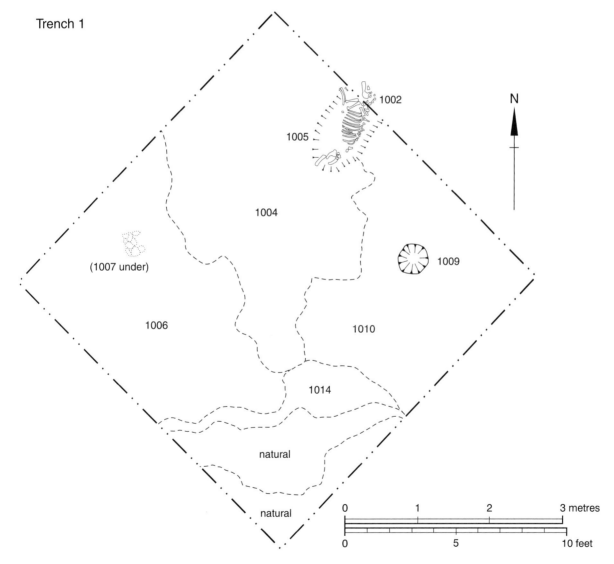

Trench 1

Fig. 67   26–28 Marygate: Trench 1, 1009–10

was not fully excavated. Deposits 1010–11 largely levelled up a ground surface which had previously sloped down from south-east to north-west. Pottery from these deposits dated to the later 3rd or 4th centuries. 1010 contained a bone pin (sf87).

Deposit1010 was cut by 1009, a small post-hole, roughly circular in plan with a diameter of c.0.40m and depth of c.0.30m. Its fill was 1008, a dark brown-grey clay deposit. A cluster of cobbles and fragments of limestone, sandstone and tile (1007) in the western part of the trench was possibly packing material for a post.

Layers 1004 and 1006, which overlay 1007 and 1011, were deposits of homogeneous dark brown-grey clay which covered most of the western half of the site. They contained some medieval pottery. Later archaeology included a post-medieval pig burial (1002).

Trench 2 *(Figs 68–72)*

The trench was not fully excavated, but natural orange clay was encountered in the eastern part of the trench where it was seen to be cut by the edge of a probable pit (2053). Contexts above this cut, but only partly excavated, were an extensive charred layer (2034; Fig.68) and an overlying clay deposit (2047; Fig.69), both of which appeared to be sinking into the earlier pit.

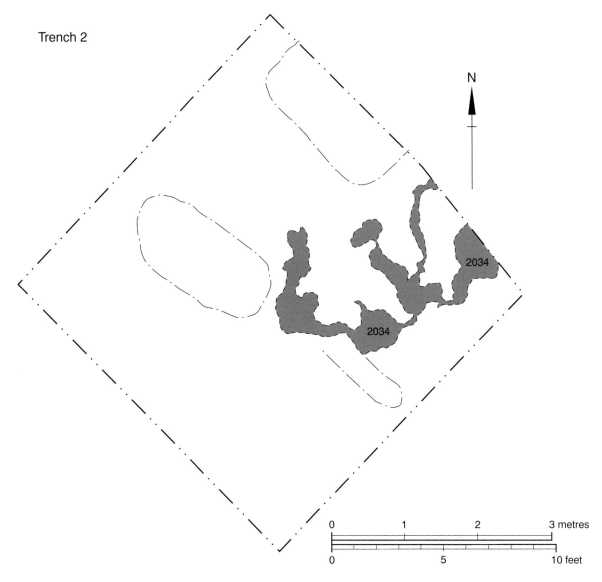

Fig. 68   *26–28 Marygate: Trench 2, charred deposit 2034*

134

The charred deposit (2034) was exposed over much of the north-east quarter of the trench. It was clearly more extensive, however, remaining covered by the unexcavated parts of 2047 in the north-eastern and south-western parts of the trench. The deposit contained iron nails, fragments of burnt daub, tiles and fragments of sandstone slab, laid flat with their edges overlapping, possibly debris from a collapsed roof. Pottery dates 2034 to the mid–late 2nd century.

2047 (overlying 2034) was an extensive deposit of orange-brown silty clay containing large fragments of pottery and tile, and more flat slabs of sandstone, as well as cobbles. Varying between c.0.10m and c.0.25m in thickness, 2047 brought the ground surface near level across the whole of the trench. The animal bones from 2047 included the incomplete remains of two terrier-sized dogs and a single humerus from a third individual. The pottery dates 2047 to the mid-3rd century (*AY* 16/8, 1097).

Overlying 2047 was 2035 (Fig.70), a small concentration of cobbles and fragments of limestone, sandstone, pottery and tile, c.0.70 x c.0.30m, located close to the south-western edge of the excavation. Immediately to the south-east was a near-complete Dales-type ware vessel (2036) set upright in a small pit (2038), perhaps for votive purposes.

In the southern corner of the trench 2047 was succeeded by 2042–4 (Fig.70). 2044 was a deposit of dark greyish-brown silty clay, 10–50mm in depth. It contained frequent flecks of charcoal and tile, as well as some cobbles, fragments of limestone and sandstone and lumps of pinkish clay. To the

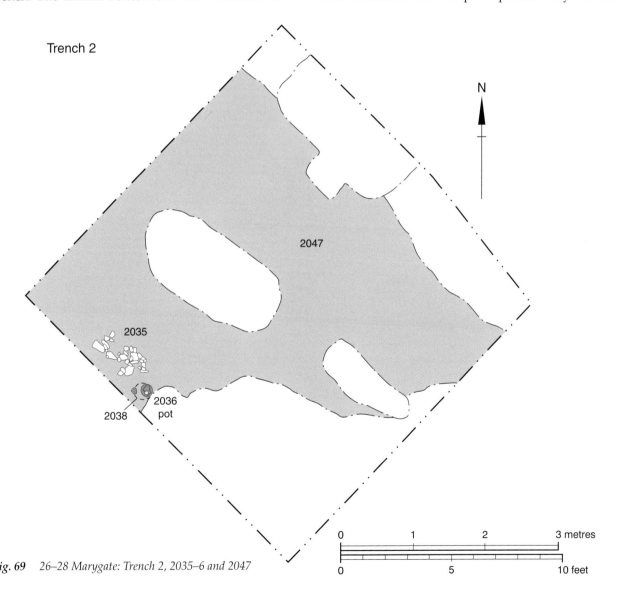

Fig. 69   *26–28 Marygate: Trench 2, 2035–6 and 2047*

135

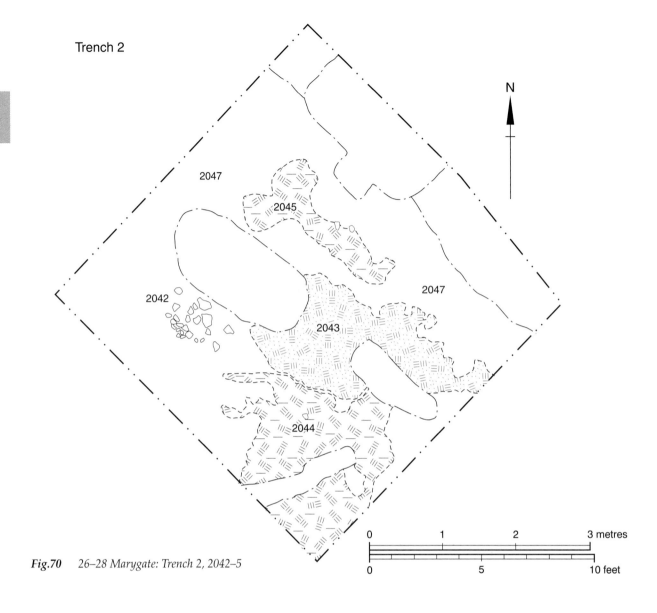

Trench 2

N

0   1   2   3 metres

0   5   10 feet

Fig.70   *26–28 Marygate: Trench 2, 2042–5*

north was 2043, a pinkish-orange, slightly sandy clay with patches of dark grey-brown sandy silt, containing occasional cobbles and fragments of limestone, sandstone and tile. To the north again was 2045 (Fig.70), similar to 2044, an orange clay mixed with dark grey-brown silty clay, containing flecks of brick, charcoal and mortar, as well as a few cobbles and fragments of stone. Probably contemporary was 2042, a spread of limestone, sandstone, brick and tile fragments with mortar and occasional cobbles. These deposits may be dated after c.225.

In the northern part of the trench, overlying the northern extremity of 2047, were 2041 (Fig.71) and 2046 (not illustrated), small deposits of grey-brown

sandy silt containing a few pebbles and fragments of limestone, sandstone and tile. 2046 produced two bone pins (sfs88 and 245) and a jet pin (sf89).

In the centre of the trench 2043 was overlain by 2025, an orange-brown clayey deposit incorporating patches of orange-brown clay and brownish silt as well as cobbles, pebbles and occasional flecks of charcoal (Fig.71). Deposit 2045 was succeeded by 2014, fragments of brick, tile, limestone, sandstone and mortar.

Contexts 2014, 2025, 2041 and 2046 are dated by pottery to after c.250.

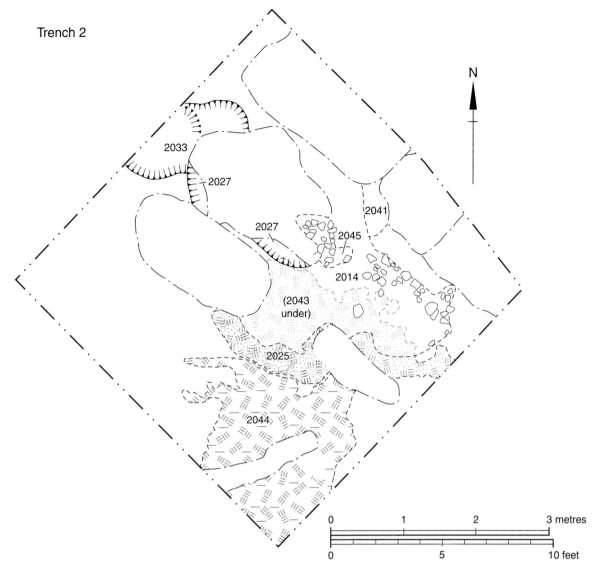

Trench 2

N

1

Fig.71   *26–28 Marygate: Trench 2, 2011, 2014, 2025, 2027, 2033, 2052*

Shallow features *(Fig.71)*

Deposits in the trench were now cut by two shallow intercutting features. A cut (2033), oval-shaped in plan with steep sides and a flat base, was filled with 2028, a grey-brown slightly sandy silt with lenses of orange sand containing fragments of tile and flecks of charcoal. The bones of a frog (*Rana temporaria*) appeared in a soil sample. On its south-eastern side this feature was cut by 2027, subcircular in plan with a flat base (truncated by a later intrusion), filled with 2022, a grey-brown clay silt with occasional lenses of charcoal and patches of orange clay. These two features appeared to be the kind of

irregular, amorphous holes which might result from the uprooting of bushes or small trees.

Above the fill layer 2022 and extending over a considerable area in the western half of the trench was 2021, a dark grey-brown clayey silt containing fragments of limestone, sandstone, brick and tile (Fig.72). Amongst the animal bone from the deposit was a small dog skull which appeared to have skinning marks along the crests of the frontal bone. In deposit samples herring (*Clupea harengus*) and salmonid vertebrae were recovered, in addition to several scales from grayling (*Thymallus thymallus*) or perch (*Perca fluviatilis*). 2021 and 2028 contained pottery dated after c.250.

The burials *(Fig.72)*

In the centre of the trench deposit 2021 was cut by 2039, a grave cut with rounded ends, steep sides and a flat base, aligned north-west/south-east. It contained an extended, supine adult skeleton (2030) with its head to the north-west. The grave was filled with 2024, a grey-brown clayey silt containing fragments of sandstone, limestone, brick, tile, charcoal and shell. Nails and iron objects found along the length of the body indicated that it was coffined.

Deposit 2024 also produced two bone pins (sfs18 and 96) and a fragment of gold (sf194); the records do not show whether or not these objects were grave goods. A mandible and maxilla of the field vole (*Microtus agrestis*) were present in a deposit sample from 2024.

Found on the north-east side of the trench was another grave cut (2040), like 2039 aligned north-west/south-east, which was rectangular in plan and had steep sides and a flat base. It contained an extended, supine adult skeleton (2029) with its head to the north-west and slightly flexed at the knees. A coffin is suggested by the presence of nails around the skeleton. Overlying the bones was 2023, lenses of orange silt and redeposited orange clay. This was

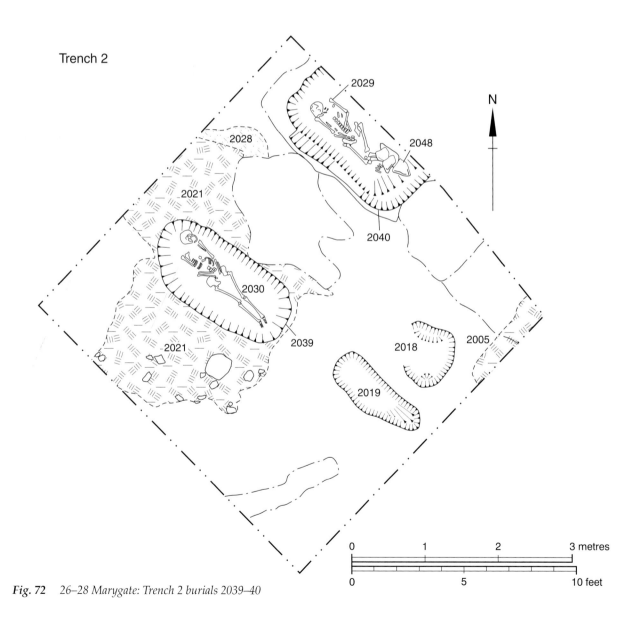

Fig. 72   *26–28 Marygate: Trench 2 burials 2039–40*

succeeded by 2032, a slightly greyish-brown clayey silt. There were then three overlapping flat stone slabs (2048), one of limestone and two of sandstone, which rested on the lower legs of the skeleton. The grave was completely filled by 2020, a grey slightly sandy silt. It produced three bone objects: a counter (sf146), a point (sf147) and a pin (sf240), and a jet bead (sf241); again it is not clear if they were deliberately deposited. A fragment of a large pig radius from this context, although heavily butchered, may have come from a wild boar.

South-east of grave 2039 was a shallow linear cut (2019) aligned north-west/south-east and measuring c.1.40 x c.0.50m. The fill, 2016, was a slightly sandy grey silt containing cobbles, fragments of limestone and sandstone and lumps of orange-brown clay. It is possible that this feature was a grave subsequently truncated by later activity such as to leave no trace of the body.

Contemporary with the two graves, near the south-east edge of the trench, was 2018, a shallow (c.0.15m deep) cut with rounded corners, measuring c.0.80 x 0.80m, with vertical sides. It was filled with 2017, a deposit of light grey silt, incorporating cobbles and occasional lumps of bright orange clay.

Grave 2040 was cut by 2013, a shallow (c.0.20m deep) cut in the north corner of the trench. It was roughly rectangular in plan with rounded corners, measuring c.0.80 x 0.70m, with steep/vertical sides and a flat base. The fill was 2012, a mid-grey silt containing cobbles. Over grave 2039 in the centre of the trench was 2003, an extensive layer of mid–light grey-brown clayey silt incorporating fragments of tile and limestone, and large sherds of pottery which date the layer to after c.280. The graves may probably, therefore, be assigned to the later 3rd century.

Layers 2003 and 2012 were cut by 2011, an extremely irregular feature which may again have resulted from the removal of a bush or small tree. The fills of 2011 were 2026, a dark grey silty clay incorporating bands of orange sand, which produced a bone pin (sf20), and 2015, a grey clayey silt with fragments of limestone, sandstone, brick, tile and mortar. It is possible that any removal of a bush or tree was carried out to accommodate another burial because cut into the top of 2011 was 2002, an ill-defined grave on a north-west/south-east alignment. Of the skeleton only the torso, pelvis and upper parts of the femurs survived, but the head had clearly lain to the north-west. (This later part of the sequence is not illustrated.)

Also cut into 2015 was 2009, a post-hole square in plan with vertical sides and a flat base, measuring c.0.60 x c.0.40m and c.0.35m deep, filled with 2010, a grey slightly sandy silt, 2008, a light brown-grey silt incorporating a few tile fragments, and 2007, a light brown silt also containing tile fragments, some of which were medieval.

Layers 2002 and 2015 were the latest features in the excavated sequence. All subsequent strata were removed mechanically.

Based on Monaghan's comments on the pottery assemblage as a whole it appears there was little evidence for activity before the early–mid-3rd century or after the end of the 3rd century in either trench (*AY* 16/8, 1097).

108–110 Bootham

Introduction

In March 2003 York Archaeological Trust carried out an archaeological evaluation, supervised by Jane McComish, at the Bedford Hotel, 108–110 Bootham (SE59755254; Fig.58,4; Fig.73). The site lay immediately to the south of Bootham, in a car park to the rear of the hotel measuring c.30 x 19m, and sloped from 15.57m OD at the northern side to 14.93m OD at the southern side.

The work involved the excavation of two small trenches. Trench 1 measured 2.1 x 1.8m and was excavated to a maximum depth of 2.34m OD. Trench 2 measured 2.1 x 2.2m and was excavated to a depth of 1.6m OD.

The work was carried out on behalf of Blueroom Properties to a brief prepared by the Principal Archaeologist for City of York Council. This report has been based on a site evaluation report by Jane McComish. The site records and finds are currently stored by York Archaeological Trust under the Yorkshire Museum accession code 2003.250.

The excavation

The uppermost 1.5m of deposits in Trench 1 and 1.6m of deposits in Trench 2 were excavated using a machine under close archaeological supervision. The remaining deposits were excavated by hand.

Trench 1 *(Fig.74)*

Natural was not encountered, excavation finishing at a Roman road surface which covered the entire trench. This was RCHME's Road 6 as it approached the junction with Road 7, itself approaching from the north-west. The surface was composed of compacted pebbles up to 30mm across and occasional cobbles up to 0.10 x 0.05m in size, in a matrix of orange gritty sand (1024). A probable repair was represented by a deposit of compacted pink-red clay with occasional grey patches and occasional cobbles up to 0.05m in diameter (1023). Above this was another road make-up deposit (1022) of compacted pebbles, up to 0.05m across, and occasional cobbles, up to 0.05 x 0.08m, in a matrix of orange gritty sand. Within this deposit there was a

patch of compacted red clay on the north-eastern side of the trench and a patch of clean, yellow, coarse-grained sand against the north-western side. These may also have represented patching or repairs to the road surface.

Above 1022 was a compact deposit (1021) of dark brown sandy clayey silt with charcoal flecks and numerous medium to large cobbles up to 0.2 x 0.2m in size, but averaging 0.1 x 0.1m. Amongst the finds were two grey ware sherds, probably 2nd century, and a human tibia shaft fragment. This deposit may have been a final road make up of poorer quality than the earlier ones and it may be noted that it sloped down to the south-west as one would expect on a road running north-west/south-east.

Above 1021 was a build up of homogeneous deposits (1017–20) which contained mixed, often abraded, finds of Roman and medieval date.

Trench 2 *(not illustrated)*

Natural was encountered at the base of the trench (12.9m OD) and consisted of moderately compacted rounded and sub-rounded gravels in a silty sand matrix (2014). This was cut by a substantial ditch (2016) on a north-west/south-east alignment of which the south-west side was located, but north-eastern side lay beyond the trench edge. The ditch could not be fully bottomed for considerations of safety, but it was in excess of 2m wide and 0.55m deep. The original profile of the south-western edge was difficult to determine as natural had slumped into the cut forming the earliest deposit recorded (2015). This was a mid-brown to yellow silty sand with mid-brown mottling containing cobbles c.0.3 x 0.1m and occasional sandstone fragments. This was overlain by 2013, a soft mid-grey clayey silt with frequent charcoal flecks containing occasional tile and sandstone fragments. In addition to twelve Roman pottery sherds of probable 2nd-century date, there was also a hand-made rim sherd in a calcareous fabric similar to calcite-gritted ware, but in a form thought to be Anglo-Saxon. A deposit sample produced a small amount of charcoal, almost all of which comprised

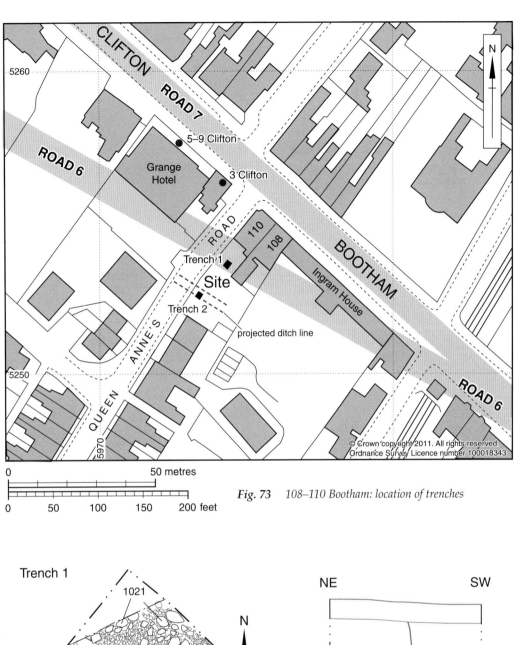

0   50 metres

0   50   100   150   200 feet

Fig. 73   *108–110 Bootham: location of trenches*

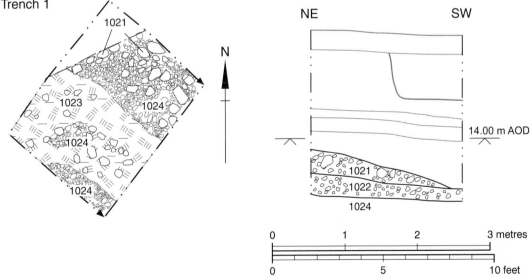

Fig. 74   *108–110 Bootham: Trench 1, plan (left) and north-west-facing section*

twig fragments of heather (*Calluna vulgaris*). This suggests the burning of peat or turves in the area, a well-known means of heating in the Roman period (see *AY* 14/6, 413–14).

Over 2013 there was, as in Trench 1, a post-Roman build up of homogeneous material (2012), a mid-brown-grey clayey sandy silt with occasional sandstone fragments, roughly 1m in thickness. This was succeeded by post-Roman deposits and features.

3 Clifton

An articulated human skeleton was discovered during underpinning of the external walls of 3 Clifton (SE59745256; Fig.58, 5) on 28 March 1994. The finds and records are stored under the Yorkshire Museum accession code YORYM : 1994.1780.

A trench had been dug on the south-east side of the property to a depth of 1.90m. The skeleton was found at the base of the trench c.0.30m below the property wall. It was removed and the area cleaned for recording. No grave cut was visible and the remains lay on the surface of an orange-brown, sandy clay natural deposit under c.0.16m of dark grey silty clay. Deposits above this consisted of concrete and brickwork. The skeleton was aligned north-east/south-west and a coin of Constantine I (AD 330–35) was discovered directly under the bones.

The skull and much of the spine of the skeleton were missing and the remainder was in poor condition, but it was probably a female of around 13 years of age.

The burial had originally lain immediately north-west of the junction of Roman approach roads 6 and 7.

The Grange Hotel, 5–9 Clifton

In June 1994 a watching brief was carried out by R. Marwood on the north-east side of The Grange Hotel, Clifton during building work (SE59735256; Fig.58, 6). This was intended to expose two walled light wells for the basement, which were to be removed, and to construct an external staircase to service a restaurant. In an area c.4.10 x 1.80m material was removed to a depth of 2.10m below modern ground level. At a depth of c.2.05m a prone human skeleton (1006; Fig.75) of a male, aged 24–30 years,

was found lying on the surface of the orange-brown clay natural (1005). No grave cut was recorded, but the skeleton lay on a north-west/south-east alignment, with its head to the south-east, more or less parallel to the main Roman approach road from the north-west which is followed today by Bootham (RCHMY 1, 3; Road 7).

Fig. 75   *5–9 Clifton: the burial (lower legs and feet were recovered under the wall at the bottom). Scale 0.50m*

Above the skeleton was a deposit, c.0.10m thick, of light brown sandy clay (1004) which was succeeded by a dark grey silty deposit (1003), 0.20m thick, which contained several sherds of 2nd-century pottery. The surface of 1003 lay at a depth of 1.80m below modern ground level. Above this was the backfilling of a World War II air raid shelter.

All site records are stored under the Yorkshire Museum accession code YORYM : 1994.1812.

St Peter's School

Introduction

Between 4 and 22 October 1999 York Archaeological Trust carried out an archaeological watching brief, supervised by Bryan Antoni, in the grounds of St Peter's School, Clifton (SE59525279; Fig.58, 7; Figs 76–7). The work was carried out at the request of St Peter's School and was undertaken during the excavation of a service trench for the installation of a fibre-optic cable for the computing department, located in a former residence known as The Rise. The trench was approximately 0.50m wide, up to 0.40m deep, and it ran from the school entrance for a distance of some 45m to The Rise at its north-west end. In 1947 a rubbish pit of mid-2nd-century date sealed by a floor deposit of the late 2nd century

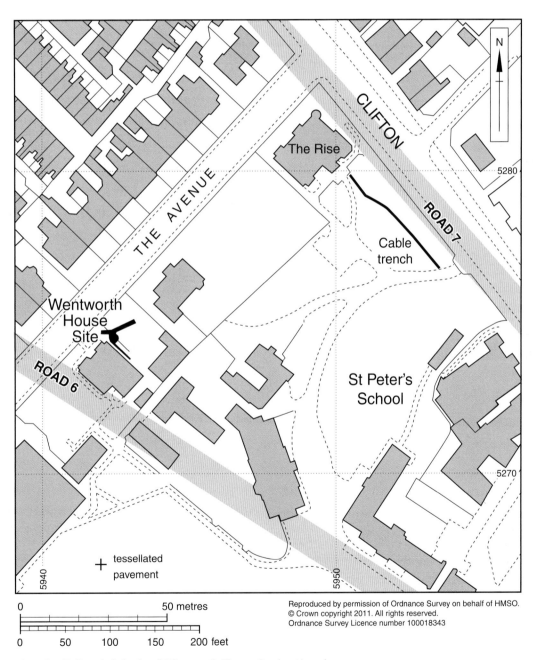

Reproduced by permission of Ordnance Survey on behalf of HMSO.
© Crown copyright 2011. All rights reserved.
Ordnance Survey Licence number 100018343

Fig. 76 *St Peter's School and Wentworth House sites location plan*

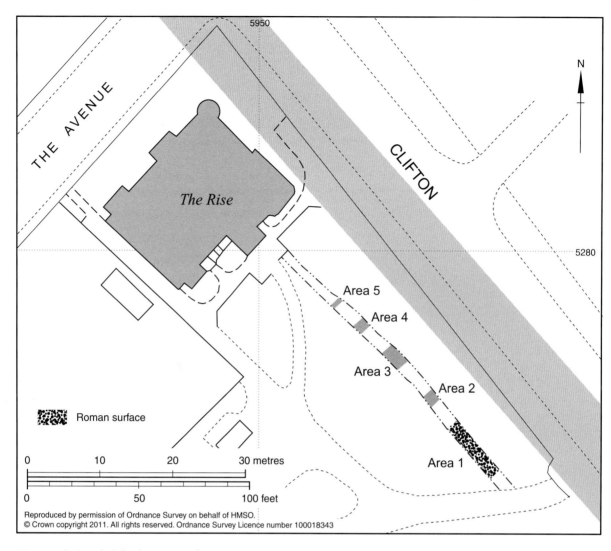

Fig. 77 *St Peter's School: Location of Areas 1–5*

was found near The Rise on the corner of The Avenue and Clifton (RCHMY **1**, 65). South of Road 6 a Roman tessellated pavement and other building debris was found in 1813 (*ibid.*) (Fig.75).

Initially the cable trench was mechanically excavated to a maximum depth of c.0.35m. The discovery of a Roman cobbled surface at the south-eastern end of the trench (Figs 77–80) prompted the hand excavation of several small areas (1–5), up to 0.75m deep, along its length. These were intended to ascertain the extent and nature of the surface, to determine its alignment, and to recover dating evidence. Modern ground

level lay between 14.07m OD (Area 5) and 14.40m OD (Area 1).

The narrowness of the cable trench rendered interpretation of the deposits and features that were encountered difficult; a fuller understanding could only be gained by further archaeological excavation. With the exception of Areas 1–5, all of the remaining ground-works were carried out by a tracked mini-digger.

The artefacts and site records are currently stored with York Archaeological Trust under the Yorkshire Museum accession code YORYM : 1999.1066.

The watching brief

Area 1 (Figs 78–80)

The earliest feature encountered in Area 1 was an irregular surface made up of compacted cobbles and pebbles (211), at least c.9.20m long, which in the south-eastern 2m of the area recorded became a patchy deposit of compacted coarse sand and fine gravel. The deposit could not be recorded in detail in the south-eastern 1.80m of the trench as it ran beneath recently installed cable ducts. However, the surface clearly extended beyond the south-east, north-east and south-western limits of the trench. There was a noticeable fall in the surface level of 211, from 13.99m OD at the south-east end to 13.65m OD at its north-west end. On its north-western side 211 lay below a deposit (221) of brown-orange clay sand with gravel and pebbles.

Cut into the centre of surface 211 was a shallow irregular north-east/south-west aligned slot (226) defined by a lack of cobbling rather than by being

a deliberate cut. Located 0.80m to the north-west of slot 226, and also cut into 211, was another shallow feature defined by a lack of cobbles (225). It was noted that the metalling of 211, in the area around 225, was composed of smaller more compacted cobbles than elsewhere.

Above 211 and 221 was a deposit (223) of light brown-orange clay sand, 0.14m thick, with occasional inclusions of limestone and charcoal flecks, and pebbles. Above both 223 and context 225, was a deposit (222) of light to mid-orange-brown silt sand, up to 0.10m thick, with inclusions of charcoal flecks and cobbles. Above 222 was a deposit (205), 0.08m thick, with an uneven surface, of small to medium-sized cobbles and pebbles in orange-brown silt sand, with occasional inclusions of thin limestone slabs, cobbles and charcoal flecks. This deposit may have originally continued further to the south-east

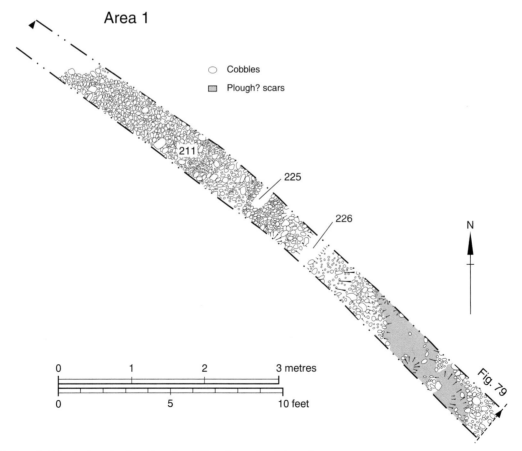

Fig. 78   *St Peter's School: Area 1, plan of surface 221 and associated deposits*

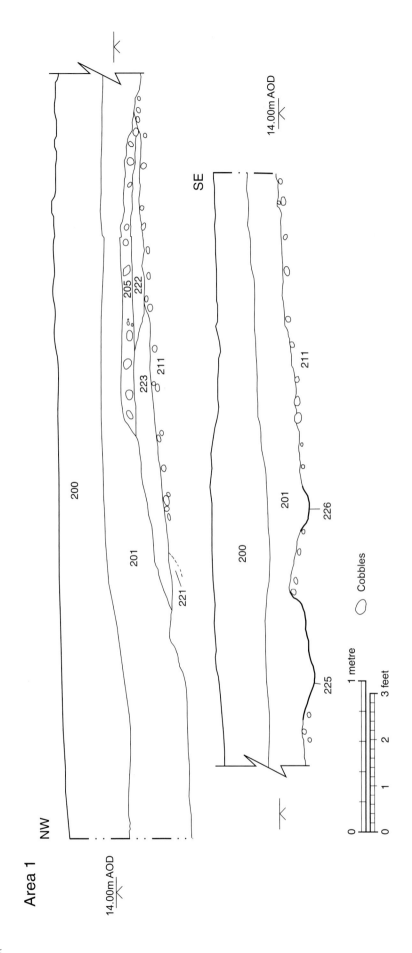

Fig.79 *St Peter's School: Area 1, south-west-facing section*

sherds, mainly of 2nd- to 3rd-century date, but also medieval sherds. Overlying 201 was the topsoil of the gardens of St Peter's School (200).

Area 2 *(Fig.81)*

Area 2 was located c.5m to the north-west of Area 1 and was 1.20m long. It was mechanically excavated to a depth of 0.40m before being hand excavated for a further 0.12m, to 13.43m OD. The earliest deposit observed (210), but not excavated, was a sparse spread of cobbles and small pebbles. Above this was a 0.34m thick deposit of yellowish-brown sand silt (209) with occasional charcoal flecks, pebbles, limestone fragments and mortar flecks. This was sealed by up to 0.20m of deposit 201 (see Area 1 above) beneath the topsoil (200) below the lawn of St Peter's School.

Fig.80 *St Peter's School, Clifton: view south-east of the cobbled surface in Area 1 (scale 0.50m)*

than was recorded, but had been removed by later ploughing. The evidence for ploughing was a series of parallel north–south-aligned shallow scars in the surface of 211 (Fig.78).

Deposit 205 and the plough scars were overlain by 201, orange to reddish-brown sandy silty clay with occasional cobbles and pebbles. This varied in thickness from 0.40m at the north-west end of Area 1 to 0.18m at the south-east end. Deposit 201 produced a copper-alloy coin (sf10) of the House of Constantine (AD 330–35), and 84 very small

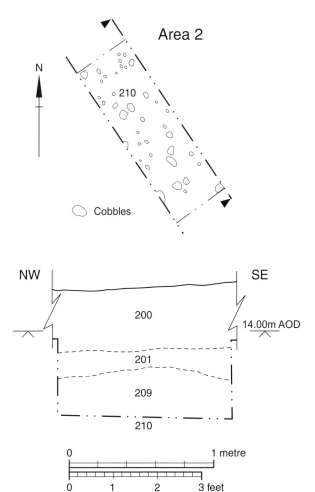

Fig. 81 *St Peter's School: Area 2, plan and south-west-facing section*

147

Area 3 *(Fig.82)*

Area 3 was located 8m to the north-west of Area 2 and was 3.72m long. It was mechanically excavated to a depth of 0.40m before being hand excavated for a further 0.34m (13.50m OD).

The sequence begins with 220, a mid-greyish-brown sand silt. This was overlain by a cobbled surface make up (219), consisting of cobbles in grey silt sand with occasional limestone and tile fragments, of which only a small area survived. 219 was cut by 224, a linear feature, perhaps a ditch, aligned north-east/south-west which was excavated to a depth of 0.22m. 224 was backfilled with a deposit numbered 201 on account of its similarity to 201 in Areas 1

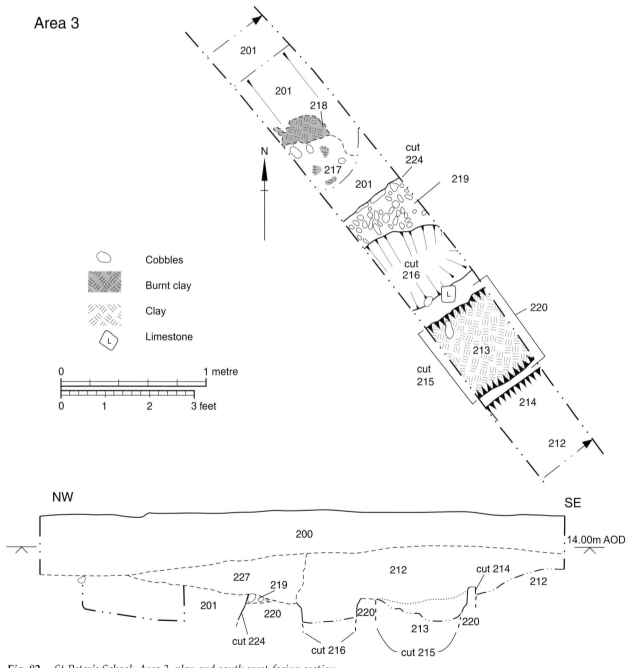

Fig. 82   *St Peter's School: Area 3, plan and south-west-facing section*

and 2 (see above). This was overlain by deposit 218, an orange-red burnt clay with occasional charcoal flecks. Above this was a deposit (217) of brown silt sand with occasional cobbles, burnt clay patches and charcoal flecks. The cobbled surface 219 was cut, on its north-east side, by a pit or ditch (216) excavated to a depth of 0.14m, which was aligned north-east/south-west and was 0.54m wide.

Context 220 was cut by features 214 and 215, aligned north-east/south-west. Feature 214, probably a ditch, extended beyond the south-east limit of the hand-excavated area. The fill layer (212) was not excavated. Feature 215 was 0.60m wide and was excavated to a depth of 0.10m; the fill (213) was a stiff clay. Above 212 and also overlying 213 in 215, and filling cut 216, was deposit 212, a loose grey-brown cindery deposit with slag. This deposit was similar to 227, to the north-west, an orange-brown silt sand with occasional charcoal flecks and small to medium pebbles. Overlying 212 and 227 was 200, a 0.40m thick deposit of topsoil under the modern turf.

Area 4 *(Fig.83)*

Area 4, 1.60m long, was located 6m to the north-west of Area 3. It was mechanically excavated to a depth of 0.31m before hand excavation to a depth of 0.76m.

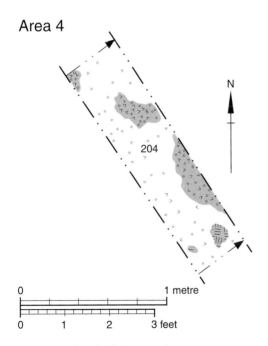

Fig. 83 *St Peter's School: Area 4, plan*

The earliest deposit observed, but not excavated, was a pale brown sandy silt (204) with frequent charcoal-rich ash patches, occasional small to medium burnt clay patches and small patches of yellow burnt matter. Above this was a deposit (203), 0.13m thick, of pale to mid-greyish-brown sandy silt with occasional inclusions of charcoal and mortar flecks, and small patches of yellow clay. It produced one or two sherds of Anglian pottery as well as twenty 2nd- to 3rd-century Roman sherds. This was overlain by 202, presumed to be Anglian or later, and then a 0.28m thick build up of plough soil (201) which was sealed by a 0.29m thick layer of topsoil and turf (200).

Area 5 *(Fig.84)*

Area 5, 1m long, was located 5m to the north-west of Area 4. It was machine excavated to a depth of 0.32m, before being hand excavated to a depth of 0.73m (13.33m OD).

The earliest deposit observed (208), but not exca-vated, was a light brown sandy silt with flecks and fragments of charcoal, occasional light grey ash flecks and cinder. Cleaning produced five 2nd- to 3rd-century Roman sherds. Above 208 was a 0.33m thick build up of deposit 201 (see Area 1 above) which had been cut by a shallow pit (207) of post-Roman date containing two sherds of Anglian pottery. This was sealed by the top soil and turf (200), 0.40m thick.

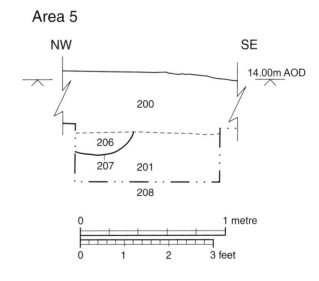

Fig. 84 *St Peter's School: Area 5, south-west-facing section*

Wentworth House, The Avenue, Clifton

Introduction

In September–October 1999 an archaeological excavation, supervised by Bryan Antoni, was undertaken on land that had served as the car park to Wentworth House, The Avenue, Clifton (SE59435275; Fig.58, 8; Figs 76 and 85). The site was situated c.100m to the south-west of the junction of The Avenue with Clifton and within a known Roman cemetery zone (centred on SE59545272; RCHMY **1**, 74–5) close to Road 6.

The work was undertaken at the request of St Peter's School and was instigated by the discovery of a human burial by the site contractors, Wm Birch & Son, during the excavation of an external drain trench for a new hall of residence for St Olave's School. The initial cursory archaeological inspection of the sides of the drain trench revealed that several inhumation burials had been cut into by the groundworks. The new hall of residence was attached to the north-east wall of Wentworth House and had been almost completed prior to the commencement of the excavation of the external drain trenches. As the area covered by the development was not initially the subject of any archaeological condition in the planning process, the excavation of the foundation trenches and related services was not observed.

Before the discovery of the inhumations the trenches had been excavated mechanically. When it became obvious that the trenches ran through

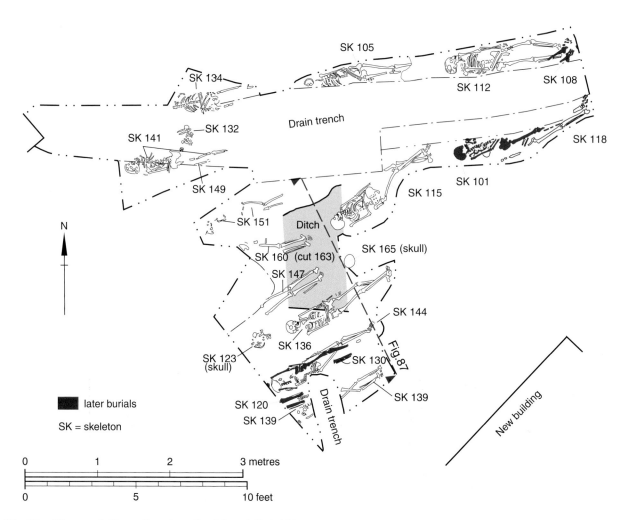

Fig. 85 *Wentworth House: Location of burials and ditch 163*

a cemetery, excavation was continued by hand, employing archaeological techniques for recording both the unexcavated drain trenches and the burials around the areas already machined away. In the event a roughly L-shaped area, with a northern arm running east–west, and a southern arm running north–south, with highly irregular edges was examined. Cutting through the northern arm on an east–west alignment was the mechanically excavated drain trench in which no archaeological remains survived.

Twenty burials in varying states of completeness were recorded, including several located outside the threatened area which were overlying those in the path of the drain runs. Any burials which were not threatened by the groundworks were left in situ.

The artefacts and site records are currently stored with York Archaeological Trust under the Yorkshire Museum accession code YORYM : 1999.952.

The Excavation (Figs 86–87)

The natural (128), a mid-orange-yellow clayey sand, was recorded sloping down from north (14.31m OD) to south (14.16m OD). The earliest archaeological feature was a ditch (163) aligned roughly east–west, 1.36m wide and 0.48m deep, with gently sloping sides and a rounded base (Fig.86). The southern edge of the ditch cut was c.0.15m lower than the northern edge, a difference which corresponded to the fall from north to south in the level of the natural.

The backfill of ditch 163 was a light to mid-brown, fine-grained sand silt with occasional inclusions of cobbles and charcoal flecks (162). Overlying this was a deposit (125), 0.18m thick in the western part of the excavation, rising to 0.37m in the southern part, of pale greyish-brown sand silt with occasional fragments of limestone and charcoal flecks. While deposit 125 was accumulating, the site became a cemetery. It is assumed that the graves were cut through 125, but their backfill layers were very similar to it and so this was difficult to determine in every case, as was the exact size and shape of the grave cuts. In some cases no grave cut could be identified at all. The cemetery probably dates to the mid-4th century, although the only dating evidence for this is a coin (sf1) dated AD 330–47, from grave 107, which appears to have come from the backfill around Skeleton 105 and not to have been a deliberately deposited grave good.

In spite of the irregular shape and disturbed nature of the area available for investigation, the site at Wentworth House has provided a valuable sample of human remains from one of York's Roman cemeteries. The sample is, moreover, the first from the cemetery centred on what is now The Avenue, Clifton, to be recorded using modern scientific techniques.

A certain amount of disturbance caused by intercutting of graves had taken place in the Roman period and a considerable amount of disturbance had occurred in modern times. As a result there was a quantity of disarticulated human bone from

Fig. 86   *Wentworth House, The Avenue: view east of the section of ditch 163 (scale 0.50m)*

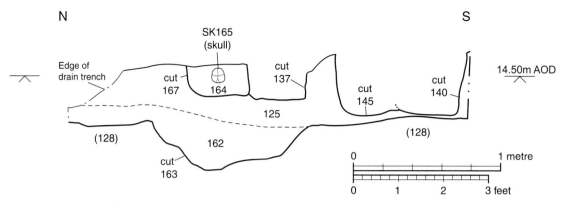

Fig. 87 Wentworth House: west-facing section

the site as a whole and deposit 125 contained some disarticulated fragments, including three skulls (contexts 153–4 and 158) and various long bones (contexts 155–7). The state of preservation of the surviving bones was usually poor, probably due largely to soil conditions and the effect of compaction by the overlying driveway.

The graves appear to have been in regular, roughly parallel rows and there was only a limited amount of intercutting of earlier burials by later (shown in red on Fig.85). The alignment of the graves lay between a near exact east–west and near exact east-north-east/west-south-west. The heads of the skeletons lay at the western ends of the graves. Amongst those graves for which alignment could be determined with any accuracy there appear to be two groups. Four skeletons (105, 112, 134, 141) on the north side of the site were aligned such that the head end was c.8–12° south of west–east, whilst eight skeletons south of the modern drain trench were aligned such that the head end was c.23–39° south of west–east. Although there is no stratigraphic evidence, it is possible that the difference between the groups is a chronological phenomenon, the four northern

skeletons being buried when the ditch alignment still had some influence on the layout of the cemetery. However, after a while, it may be suggested, this influence was lost and the cemetery then expanded over and to the south of it. As a result interments of this second phase adopted a new alignment less close to true east–west, but closer to being at right angles to the line of approach road 6.

All the skeletons appear to have been supine and extended, although their arm positions varied. In spite of the unfavourable ground conditions it was possible to determine that, with four exceptions, all the burials were of adults; of the few exceptions one (151) was of a child of c.10 years, and three could not be aged. Sex attribution was possible in up to nine cases, with three skeletons being deemed male, one possibly male, and five possibly or probably female. A summary of the burials appears in Table 1. Further details will appear in *AY* 5/1.

Because of levelling down of the area and other disturbance in modern times there was no evidence for any post-Roman activity at Wentworth House until the construction of the St Olave's School buildings.

Table 1 Summary of Wentworth House burials

Grave No.	Skeleton No.	Alignment: degrees south of west–east	Age	Sex
103	101	23	Adult 35+	
107	105	10	Adult	
110	108	–	Adult	f?
113	112	8	Adult	m
116	115	39	Adult	m
119	118	11	Adult	f?
122	120	–	Adult	
–	123	–	Adult 45+	m?
131	130	26	Adult (or Juvenile)	f?
–	132	–	Adult	
–	134	12	–	
137	136	29	Adult	m
140	139	32	Adult	
–	141	10	Adult 25+	
145	144	27	Adult	
148	147	32	Adult	f?
–	149	–	–	
152	151	23	Child c.10	
161	160	–	Adult	f?
–	165	–	–	

12–13 The Avenue

In December 2000 a brief evaluation excavation, supervised by Mark Johnson, took place in the grounds of Clifton Preparatory School at 12–13 The Avenue (SE59385274; Fig.58, 9; Fig.94). The site lay on or very close to the line of approach road 6.

The work was undertaken on behalf Barratt, York, to a brief prepared by the City of York Council and involved inspection of three mechanically excavated test pits and hand excavation of three trial trenches (to a depth of 1.5m below modern level). The former produced no evidence for Roman activity. The latter produced no certain Roman strata, but a few Roman finds testified to activity in the area.

The artefacts and site records are currently stored with York Archaeological Trust prior to deposition with the Yorkshire Museum under the accession code YORYM : 2000.4287.

Trench 2 *(Fig.89)*

Natural red-brown sandy clay (2003) was encountered at 13.39m OD, 0.30m below modern ground level. It was overlain by 2002, a thin spread of cobbles unevenly distributed in yellow-brown clayey silty sand. The only find from 2002 was a Roman tile fragment suggesting the deposit may be Roman but it was not obviously a road-related

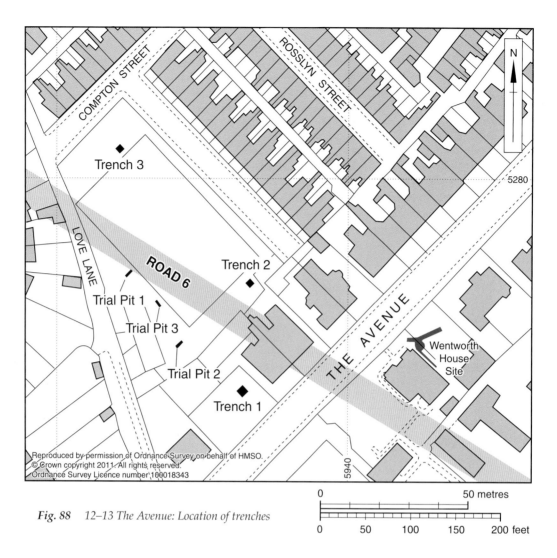

Fig. 88 *12–13 The Avenue: Location of trenches*

0   50 metres

0   50   100   150   200 feet

Trench 2

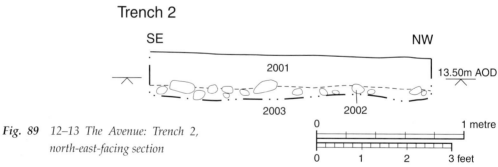

Fig. 89 *12–13 The Avenue: Trench 2,*
north-east-facing section

deposit. Context 2002 was overlain by grey-brown silt (2001) which produced a little Roman and later pottery.

Trench 3

Excavation reached a depth of c.1.40m (10.17m OD) below modern ground level where a pale yellow-brown silty sand was encountered (3006). As little of this deposit fell within the 1.50m depth limit, a further 0.28m was excavated in the north corner of the trench and a sherd of Roman pottery and fragments of tile were recovered. It is suggested that 3006 was alluvial in origin, perhaps created by flooding of the Bur Dyke, a water course which ran roughly north–south immediately west of the site.

21–23 Avenue Terrace

On 11 August 2000 YAT was contacted by North Yorkshire Police with a report of the discovery of human bones by a resident of Avenue Terrace, Clifton. Four bones had been recovered from a spoil tip outside Nos 21–23 (SE59545292; Fig.58, 10), created during digging of a gas main trench running the length of the street. On examination natural orange-brown clay was observed at a depth of c.1.25m below modern level. Above this were clayey silty deposits, 0.70m thick, but no grave cut was seen. In view of the Roman cemeteries known in the region the bones are likely to be Roman.

The archive has the Yorkshire Museum accession code YORYM : 2000.587.

Water Lane, Clifton

Introduction

In September 1997 an archaeological evaluation, supervised by D. T. Evans, was undertaken on land adjacent to Water Lane, Clifton (SE59405390; Fig.54, 3; Fig.90) in advance of development by Harrison Construction Ltd of Malton. The site lies c.3km north-west of the city centre in an area where there has been very little archaeological investigation except for the two Roman camps on Bootham Stray c.1km to the north-east (Fig.54, 2; RCHMY **1**, 47; Stephens and Ware 1995). The site was roughly rectangular, c.290 x 175m, and existed as rough pasture divided into three main areas by field boundaries formed by ditches and hedges. The modern ground surface in the north-western half of the site was fairly level (13.10–13.40m OD) but the south-eastern half sloped gently down to the Bur Dyke which runs on an east-north-east/west-south-west line at this point. The modern surface adjacent to Trench 14 was at 11.70m OD.

In the first phase of work a geophysical survey of approximately half the site was undertaken by GeoQuest. This was followed by excavation of sixteen trenches opened by machine in which hand excavation of a sample of the features and deposits was undertaken.

In the event the geophysical survey, employing magnetometry, revealed little of archaeological interest and so the trenches were positioned to ensure the area was examined as comprehensively as possible. However, only Trenches 7 and 9 produced Roman archaeology; in the others were features of medieval and modern date.

The artefacts and site records are currently stored with York Archaeological Trust prior to deposition with the Yorkshire Museum under the accession code YORYM : 1997.95.

Trench 7

Trench 7 measured 52m (north-east/south-west) x 2m. Natural, yellow-orange sand, was encountered at a depth of c.0.70m below modern ground level. Cut into natural was a large ditch (7021), aligned north–south which was c.3.2m wide and c.0.85m deep (Figs 91–93). The primary filling (7020) was mixed light grey to orange-brown sand. The ditch was then recut (7019) on the same alignment, but its width was reduced to c.1.8m and its depth to c.0.75m. At the base there was a distinct slot with near vertical sides, 0.10m wide and 0.13m deep. The slot was filled with a mix of cream-white sand, pale grey sand and orange-brown clay (7018). Above this was 7017, a light to mid-grey silty sand in which six 1st- to 3rd-century sherds of Roman pottery were found. This deposit was succeeded by 7016, a pale orange-brown slightly clayey sand with patches of grey sandy silt which produced three sherds of 1st- to 3rd-century Roman pottery.

Also cut into natural at the south-west end of trench was a gully on a north-west/south-east

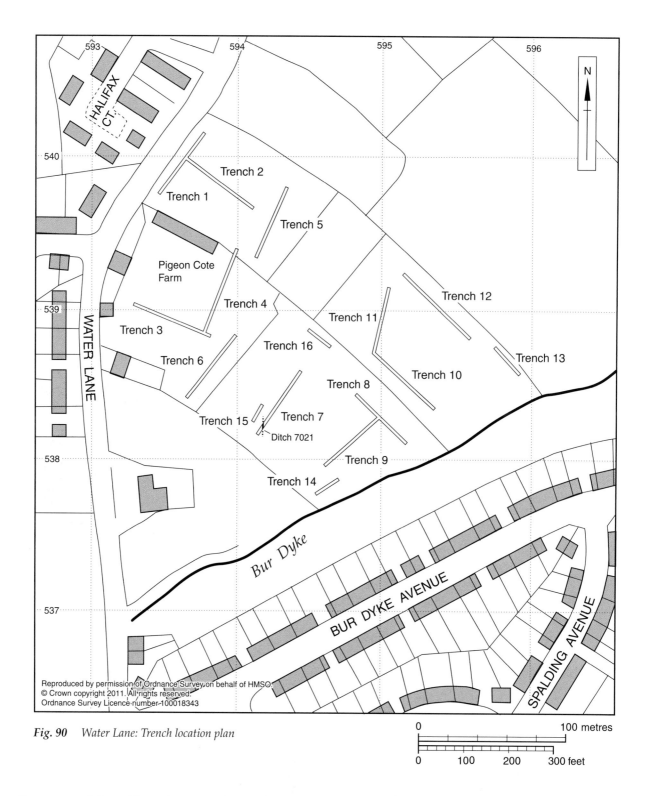

Fig. 90 *Water Lane: Trench location plan*

alignment, c.1.8m wide and c.0.15m deep, of which only the north-western half was excavated. The fill was 7008, a light brownish-grey silty sand which produced no finds.

These two features were sealed by a deposit of greyish-brown silty sand, 0.40m thick (7002). This was cut by modern field drains which were overlain by deposits of recent origin (7001).

Trench 9

Trench 9 lay to the south-east of Trench 7 and measured 48m (north-east/south-west) x 2m.

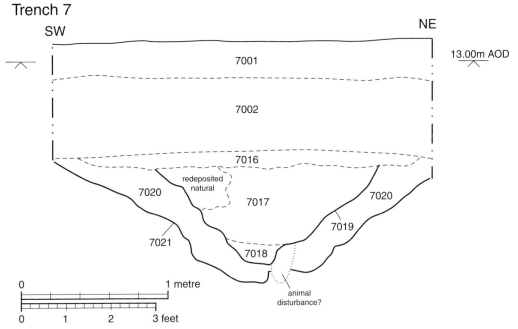

Trench 7

SW

NE

13.00m AOD

7001

7002

7016

redeposited
natural

7020

7017

7020

7021

7019

7018

animal
disturbance?

0   1 metre

0   1   2   3 feet

Fig. 91   *Water Lane: Section of ditch 7021*

Natural sand (9007) was encountered at a depth of 0.90m below modern ground level. Overlying natural at the south-west end of the trench was a small spread of a few small to medium-sized cobbles in a matrix of greyish-brown sand and gravel (9004). On its north-east side the cobbles appear to have been cut by a linear feature which was, unfortunately, not excavated. It appeared to be c.3m wide and filled with blue-grey clay, grey clayey sand and pale grey-brown sand (9003). Cleaning produced seven pot sherds of 1st- to 3rd-century date. Sealing 9003–4 was a deposit of mid-grey-brown silty sand (9002) c.0.55m thick. This was cut by modern field drains which were sealed by deposits of recent origin.

Fig.92   *Water Lane, Clifton: view east of ditch 7021 (vertical scale 0.50m, horizontal scale 1m)*

Fig.93   *Water Lane, Clifton: view north-east of section through ditch 7021 (scale 0.50m)*

157

Zone 1: Discussion

Roads

A useful recent addition to knowledge of the main Roman approach roads to York in Zone 1 is the location of Road 6 and the roadside ditch to the south-west of it at 108–10 Bootham. The road can now be shown to run a little to the west of the line proposed by RCHME. It is possible that the cobbled surface recorded in Area 1 at St Peter's School was a road, but unfortunately it was not fully exposed and so its character and function could not be conclusively determined (see below for further discussion).

Land use and settlement in the late 1st–mid-3rd century

In general terms excavations and observations in Zone 1, both described above and recorded elsewhere, suggest activity of one sort or another throughout this period. However, apart from the St Mary's Abbey area (see above) evidence for structures is sparse, although post-holes at 31 Gillygate and a possible wall footing at 45–57 Gillygate suggest the existence of timber structures immediately outside the fortress, at least in the late 2nd–early 3rd centuries. Building debris from 26–8 Marygate suggests structures in the vicinity of that site, perhaps of the early–mid-3rd century. On the line of the main Roman road from the north-west (Road 7) there was a hint of structures at the St Peter's School site although little can be made of the diverse range of deposits and features recorded but not fully excavated. The cobbled surface in Area 1 has been suggested above as a possible road, but perhaps a yard associated with buildings alongside the road is more likely. In Area 3 there was a fragmentary cobbled surface (219), apparently on a north-east/south-west alignment, i.e. at 90° to the main road, which may have been a path or a yard. Other features in Area 3 are on the same alignment, but may not be Roman. However, deposits such as 217–18, containing burnt clay, and 204, containing charcoal, ash and burnt clay in Area 4, may also indicate the presence of Roman structures in the vicinity. This evidence may be set alongside the discoveries made in 1947 on the corner of The Avenue and Clifton (RCHMY **1**, 65). Some sort of ribbon development along Road 7 would not be surprising.

In addition to traces of buildings, evidence for activity in Zone 1 also took the form of ditches for land division and/or drainage. At 52 Bootham the feature, not fully excavated, referred to as containing late 1st- to early 2nd-century pottery was probably a ditch on a north-west/south-east alignment (Keen 1965). At 45–57 Gillygate there were two phases of a ditch on a north-west/south-east alignment which were probably both late 2nd–early 3rd century. In terms of their alignment, which follows that of one of the main axes of the legionary fortress and that of the approach road from the north-west, and of their date, these ditches are similar to those on many other sites in the extramural zones at York (see discussion of ditches pp.370-71).

Ditches were recorded at both Wentworth House and Water Lane, at the north-western limits of the zone, neither of which adopted the alignment of the main axes of the fortress, being close to east–west and north–south respectively. Perhaps these sites were far enough away from the fortress to escape the discipline governing alignment in areas closer in or were subject to some more local constraint.

The Water Lane ditch, c.3.2m wide and c.0.85m deep, was more substantial than most of the ditches recorded in the extramural zones and its unusual size may indicate some distinct function. The site lies c.1km south-west of the Roman camps on Bootham Stray, one of which has its principal axis aligned near to north–south, and it is just possible that the Water Lane ditch belonged to another camp, although it is wider than those recorded nearby at Bootham Stray and also at Huntington South Moor, typically 1.4m wide and 1.1m deep. The 'ankle-breaker' slot recorded in the recut of the ditch is sometimes seen as a military feature, but, as will be seen below (p.371), it occurs on other sites in York where there was no apparent military involvement. It is just possible that a camp of a size comparable to the others, c.130 x 80m, could have existed on the site and not been identified, especially if the unexcavated feature in Trench 9 was a ditch comparable to that in Trench 7 returning on an east–west line.

Burials

The investigations described above add a small amount to knowledge of cemeteries north-west of the fortress. The burials at 3 Clifton and 5–9 Clifton cannot be dated exactly, but extend the area alongside the main Roman road from the north-west in which graves may be expected beyond the corner of Clifton and Queen Anne's Road. The discovery of human remains in Avenue Terrace suggests another area which has not previously been included in Roman York's north-western cemeteries. The three inhumations at 26–8 Marygate also occurred in an area in which burials were not previously known. They probably date to the late 3rd century and it may be significant, firstly, that they were located as much as c.90m from the main Roman road, suggesting that land nearer to it was already occupied by earlier burials or buildings. Secondly, it may be significant that the Marygate burials are only c.200m from the fortress as there is some indication that whereas in the late 1st and 2nd centuries cemeteries were often sited at a respectable distance from the fortress or other settled areas (see p.368 for further discussion), in the 3rd–4th centuries vacant ground nearer in was, on occasions, being claimed for burial. Having said this, the Wentworth House burials at a site c.0.9km from the fortress were probably early–mid-4th century, although it is possible they derive not from the main Roman civilian settlement but from a community living nearby, perhaps the ribbon development along the main approach road from the north-west alluded to above. The burials appeared to have been laid out in a regular manner comparable to the so-called 'managed cemeteries' of the 4th century identified by Charles Thomas (1981, 232). Similar regularity can be seen, south-west of the Ouse, in the 4th-century cemetery (Phase 4) at 35–41 Blossom Street (pp.305–308).

Land use and settlement in the late Roman period

Apart from burials, there is little evidence for activity in Zone 1 in the late 3rd–4th centuries except in the St Mary's Abbey grounds (see above). No pottery assemblages of Ceramic Period 4 (280–410) in the zone were recorded in *AY* 16/8.

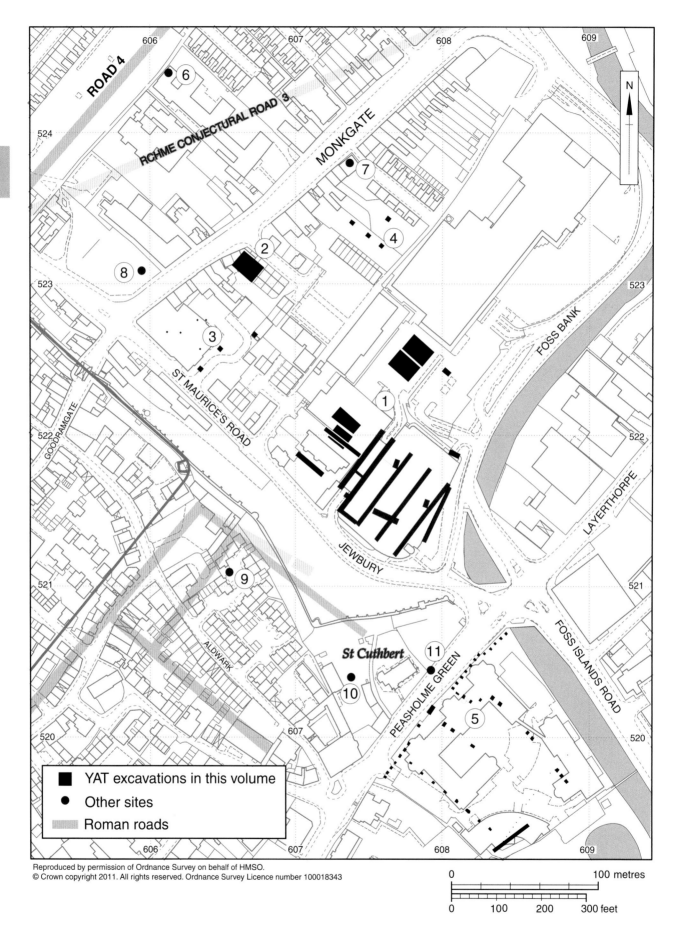

ROAD 4

606

RCHME CONJECTURAL ROAD 3

MONKGATE

524

6

7

4

2

8

523

523

3

ST MAURICE'S ROAD

1

FOSS BANK

GOODRAMGATE

522

522

LAYERTHORPE

521

9

JEWBURY

521

ALDWARK

St Cuthbert

11

10

PEASHOLME GREEN

5

FOSS ISLANDS ROAD

520

607

520

606

607

608

609

■ YAT excavations in this volume

● Other sites

Roman roads

0   100 metres

0   100   200   300 feet

2

Zone 2: North-east and immediately east of the fortress

Introduction *(Figs 54, 94)*

Extramural Zone 2 lies north-east and east of the Roman fortress, but what follows is principally concerned with sites within c.250m of the fortress. As noted in the introduction, the legionary fortress stands on a slightly raised plateau between the Foss and Ouse, and land immediately to the north-east is at a similar level, but to the east and south-east of the fortress the modern ground level drops towards the Foss. It is suggested by investigations at Peasholme Green, described below, that this drop was more pronounced in Roman times when river level was clearly lower than it is today (see above p.115).

The two principal excavations described below took place on sites within and adjacent to the premises of the former County Hospital – one adjacent to Foss Bank and the other to Monkgate (Fig.94,1–2). In addition, work on three smaller sites is reported.

Roman activity previously recorded in this zone includes Roman roads approaching York from Malton and Stamford Bridge (Fig.54; RCHMY 1,1–2; Roads 3–4; pp.91–3, *AY* 6/1) and minor roads in the Aldwark area close to the fortress (pp.36–40, *AY* 6/1). Scattered Roman burials have been recorded adjacent to Peasholme Green, Layerthorpe, Monkgate and Lord Mayor's Walk (RCHMY 1, 71–2), and a single burial was found at 21–33 Aldwark (p.36, *AY* 6/1). Some Roman strata and a burial were excavated in small trenches at the School Dental Clinic on the north-west side of Monkgate (Fig.94,6; YEG 1967; YEG 1968; Radley 1968, 118). At St Maurice's Newbiggin (1972.17; Fig.94,8) excavations in 1972 reputedly encountered Roman strata in a restricted area, but the site records do not lend themselves to easy interrogation.

East of the east corner of the fortress evidence for the manufacture of pottery and tiles has been found since the early 19th century when William Hargrove recorded seeing 'at the depth of about five feet great quantities of ashes and charcoal intermixed with human bones and broken urns, *paterae* etc' – as well as the wall of a Roman building – under the north aisle of St Cuthbert's church and in its graveyard to the north (Hargrove 1818, II, part 2, 346–7). In 1970–2 a small excavation by York Excavation Group located ash, fired clay, kiln debris, pottery waste and tiles in the former Borthwick Institute grounds (Fig.94, 10) to the south-west of St Cuthbert's (King 1975). At 21–33 Aldwark, 60m south-east of the east corner of the fortress (Fig.94, 9), further kiln debris and wasters were found in contexts of early 3rd-century date where they were possibly used as hardcore for a street (pp.39–40, *AY* 6/1; *AY* 16/8, 1068–71). In Peasholme Green itself excavations by MAP revealed a series of deposits of ash, pot, tile and kiln debris in which the layers tipped down at about 45° from horizontal towards the south-east, presumably reflecting the natural fall of the land towards the Foss (Fig.94, 11; MAP 1996a, 14; MAP 1998, 14–15).

Cremation burials in this zone have been found in small cemeteries at Heworth and Heworth Green, and inhumations at Clarence Gardens near the junction of Haxby and Wigginton Roads (RCHMY 1, 70–1). Further afield, adjacent to Road 3, two burials in stone coffins and evidence for another in a lead coffin, along with an early 2nd-century

Fig. 94 (facing page)   Zone 2: location of sites described in this fascicule (1–5) and other sites (6–11)

1. County Hospital: Foss Bank (1982–3)
2. County Hospital: Monkgate (1982–3)
3. Monkgate/St Maurice's Road (1987) and 2 St Maurice's Road (1992)
4. 40–48 Monkgate (2005)
5. Peasholme Green (1990–1)

6. School Dental Clinic (1966)
7. 52 Monkgate (1995)
8. St Maurice's Newbiggin (1972)
9. 21–33 Aldwark (1972–3)
10. Borthwick Institute (1970–2)
11. Peasholme Green (1995)

cremation, were found at Apple Tree Farm (Fig.54, 6; Wenham 1968a, 50–7).

At a distance of c.2.75km north-east of the fortress, at Huntington South Moor (Fig.54, 4), two camps similar to those on Bootham Stray were identified by English Heritage from aerial photography in 2002. One of them was completely excavated in 2002–3 by YAT (Johnson 2005) and the second was evaluated by MAP in 2002.

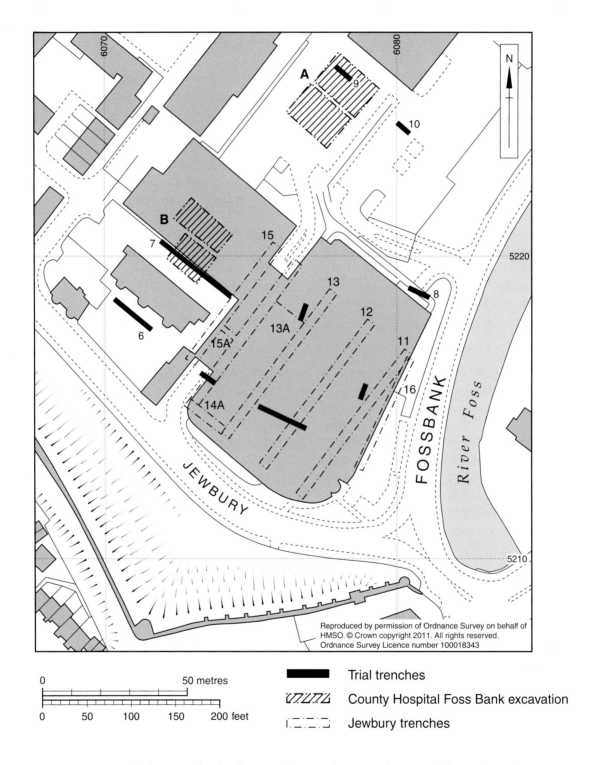

▬▬	Trial trenches
▨▨▨	County Hospital Foss Bank excavation
⌐·−·−⌐	Jewbury trenches

0   50 metres
0   50   100   150   200 feet

Fig. 95 County Hospital, Foss Bank: Plan showing all excavated areas in relation to the former hospital

County Hospital, Foss Bank

A programme of trial excavations, supervised by Patrick Ottaway, was conducted in February–March 1982 in what was then the Jewbury/Fossbank car park and the grounds of the former County Hospital (Fig.94, 1; Fig.95). The principal objective was to locate the medieval Jewish cemetery, which documentary sources suggested lay in the area, and to examine the nature of any Roman activity to the north-east of the legionary fortress. The cemetery was located and in 1983 a major project was undertaken to excavate it fully (*AY* 12/2). This report is concerned with Roman archaeology in the Trial Trenches 6–10 and the subsequent larger scale excavation in summer 1982 directed by Percival Turnbull. In both cases the excavation was undertaken by participants in a STEP programme funded by the Manpower Services Commission.

Records and finds from the trial excavations are stored under the Yorkshire Museum accession code 1982.5 and those from the main excavation under the code 1982.10.

The trial trenches (Fig.95)

Trial Trenches 6–10 were excavated mechanically to the level of natural.

Trench 6 (22.5 x 1.5m) lay between the former nurses' home and the street Jewbury. Natural clay was encountered at 10.70m OD, a depth of 2.10m below modern ground level. The earliest deposits (626 and 632), c.0.30m thick, contained a few sherds of Roman pottery. They were cut by medieval pits.

Trench 7 (29.80 x 1.5m) lay to the north-east of the former nurses' home and was later incorporated in the southern trench of Area B in the main excavation (see below). Natural sandy clay was encountered at 10.70m OD, a depth of 1.30m below modern ground level. Cut into natural, c.3.50m from the north-west end of the trench, was a ditch (707) running north-east/south-west. It had sloping sides and a flat bottom, and was 0.50m wide and 0.20m deep. The backfill (708) was a grey-brown silty deposit. This feature was recorded as 0125 in the northern trench of Area B in the main excavation (see below). A further 0.80m to the south-east was a second, parallel ditch (740) with a wide U-shaped cross-section profile, 0.35m deep and 1.50m wide. The backfill (741) was a light grey silty deposit. This was recorded as 0055/0139 in the southern trench of Area B in the main excavation (see below). A further 1.60m to the south-east was another feature with steep sloping sides (709), thought to be a ditch. It was 0.70m wide and excavated to a depth of 0.20m, but not bottomed. The backfill was 710. It does not appear to have been recorded in the main excavation. In addition, some later pits, probably medieval, were observed cut from a higher level than those features already referred to.

Trench 8 (7 x 1.50m) was dug immediately north-east of the car park boundary and north-west of Foss Bank. Natural light brown sandy clay was located at a depth of 2.10m below modern ground level. Above this was c.0.85m of a dark brown silty deposit, but there were no archaeological features and no finds other than modern material were recovered.

Trench 9 (6.80 x 1.5m) was dug north-east of the then hospital tennis court. Natural clay was encountered at 11.50m OD, a depth of c.0.90m below modern ground level. Immediately over natural was a deposit (903) of brown sandy clay with occasional pebbles 55mm thick. It was cut by a ditch (904) running north-west/south-east which was c.1.80m wide and c.1m deep with sloping sides and a flat bottom. The backfill (905) was a grey silty deposit with cobbles and pebbles; it contained two samian and ten other Roman sherds. The feature was overlain by a deposit (902) 0.40m thick. Ditch 904 was re-excavated in the northern trench of Area A in the main excavation as 1033 (see below).

Trench 10 (4.90 x 1.5m) was dug 21.30m south-east of Trench 9. Natural clay was encountered at 11.30m OD, a depth of c.1m below modern level. Immediately over natural was a light yellow-brown sandy deposit (1005) c.0.20m thick. It was succeeded by a dark brown sandy deposit 0.50m thick (1003).

The main excavation

Excavations took place in two areas (A and B) to the south-east of the former County Hospital.

Area A

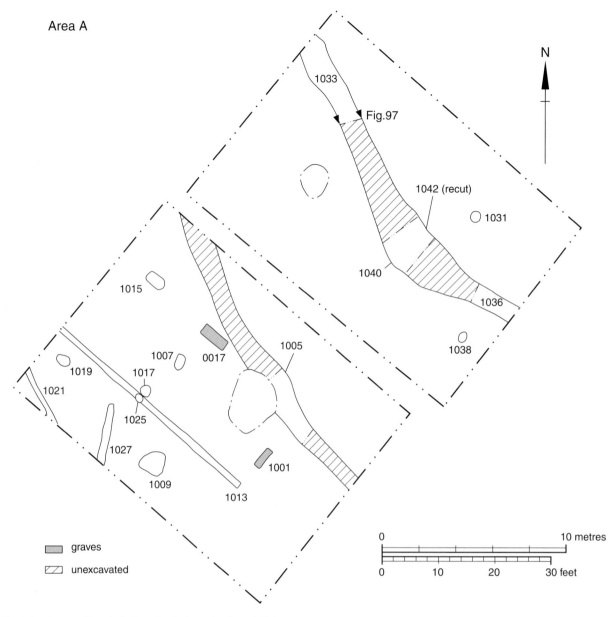

Fig. 96 *County Hospital, Foss Bank: Area A: plan of all features*

In each area there were two trenches and in total an area c.2750m² was examined. Area A's northern trench, which encompassed Trial Trench 9, measured 18m (north-west/south-east) x 13.50m. There was c.0.50m of overburden on the north-east side and natural was encountered at c.11.70m OD. This was a stiff yellow clay containing pebbles and cobbles. The southern trench measured 18m north-west/south-east by 11.20m and natural occurred at c.11.60m OD. In Area B the northern trench measured c.17.90 x 10.30m. The southern

trench, which included most of the north-western half of Trial Trench 7, measured 13m north-west/ south-east by 10.80m. Natural was encountered at c.11.40m OD. There was c.1.50m of overburden on the south-west side of the southern trench.

Removal of overburden in both areas, usually to the level of natural, was effected by machine.

In the absence of much in the way of either vertical stratigraphy or closely datable artefacts it is difficult to establish a clear phasing for the site. The archaeological features may, however, be discussed under three group headings:

1. Linear features which do not observe a north-east/south-west or north-west/south-east alignment and other features cut into natural. Some of these features may be medieval, but in the absence of finds they cannot be dated.
2. Linear features on a north-east/south-west or north-west/south-east alignment.
3. Pit cuts, graves and grave-related features which post-date features in 1 and 2.

The archaeology of the each trench will be described in group order starting from the north and indicating stratigraphic relationships where they existed.

Area A *(Fig.96)*

Northern trench

Group 1

There were two post-holes on a north–south line. Post-hole 1031, 0.60m in diameter and 0.20m deep, was backfilled with 1032, a dark grey-brown deposit. Post-hole 1038, near the south corner of the trench, was 0.45 in diameter and 0.59m deep. The backfill was 1039, also a dark grey-brown deposit. As a north–south line is not usually one adopted by Roman features these post-holes may be medieval.

Group 2

The ditch (904) excavated in Trial Trench 9 was traced running roughly north-west/south-east across the whole trench and was shown to curve and to become narrower and shallower towards the south-east. The stretch in the trial trench was re-excavated in the north-western part of the trench as 1033 and was shown once again to be 1.8m wide, up to 1m deep and to have a V-shaped profile (Fig.97). The fill (1034) was a dark grey-brown silt deposit. In the centre of the trench another stretch was excavated and there appeared to be two phases. The earlier (1040) was backfilled with 1041, a dark grey-brown deposit. This was largely cut away by the recut (1042) which was 2m wide and 0.80m deep, and backfilled with 1043, a dark grey-brown

deposit. Another stretch of the ditch was excavated on the south-east side of the trench as 1036, where it was no more than 1.20m wide and 0.30m deep. The fill of this stretch (1037) was again a dark grey-brown deposit.

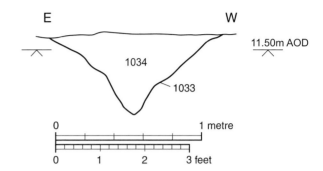

Fig. 97   *County Hospital, Foss Bank: Area A north, section of ditch 1033*

Southern trench

Group 1

Running into the south-west edge of the trench was a gully or small ditch (1027) on a near north–south alignment for c.3.2m. It was up to 0.45m wide and 0.37m deep, and was backfilled with 1028, a dark grey clayey deposit with frequent charcoal flecks.

Near the centre of the trench and cut by ditch 1013 (see below) were two small features, possibly post-holes. 1025, originally of diameter 0.20m and depth 0.30m, was backfilled with 1026, dark grey clay. Immediately to the north-east, 1017, 0.60m wide and 0.35m deep, was backfilled with 1018, a dark yellow-orange clay in which a bone offcut (sf72) was found. These post-holes could have been contemporary with three other features. 1007 was a possible post-hole, oval in plan, 0.80 x 0.50m and 0.25m deep which was backfilled with 1008, a dark grey clay deposit. Near the north-west edge of the trench and south-west of ditch 1013 was a post-hole (1019) of diameter 0.66m and depth 0.58m which was backfilled with 1020, a dark grey clay deposit. In the centre of the trench, near the south-west side was a pit (1009) rounded in plan with vertical sides, of diameter 1.20m and depth 0.60m. It was backfilled with 1010, a dark yellow-orange clay.

Group 2

A ditch (1005) curving in a similar manner and roughly parallel to 1033/1036/1040 in the northern trench and c.9.50m to the south-west was found running from near the north corner to the south-east trench edge for c.16m. It had gently sloping sides and a rounded base, and was c.1.40m wide and 0.55m deep. The backfill (1006) was a dark grey clayey deposit.

Cutting across the west corner of the trench was a shallow gully (1021) which ran north-north-west/south-south-east for c.3m. It was 0.20m wide and 0.15m deep, and was backfilled with 1022, a dark grey clayey deposit.

Group 3

Another small ditch or gully (1013), two graves and a small pit should probably be considered together as part of a single episode of land use in view of their symmetrical relationship to one another. As Fig.96 shows, these features are unlikely to have existed at the same time as the curving ditch 1005, and are probably later, hence their appear-

Grave 1001

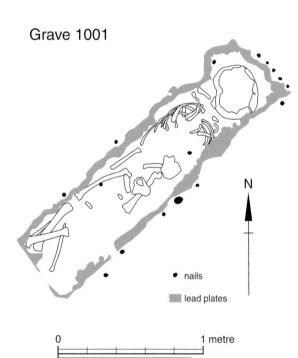

nails

lead plates

0   1 metre

0   1   2   3 feet

Fig. 98   *County Hospital, Foss Bank: Area A south, plan of grave 1001*

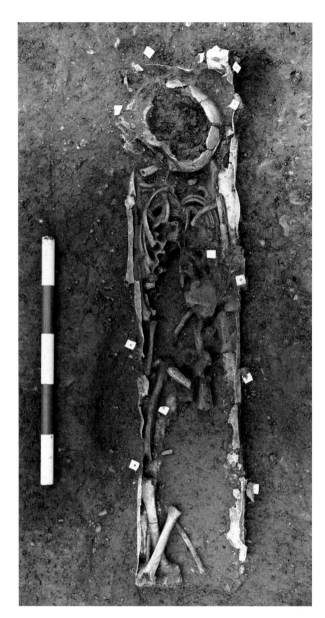

Fig. 99   *County Hospital, Foss Bank, Area A, view north-east of grave 1001: infant buried in a wooden coffin lined with lead sheets (scale 0.50m)*

ance under the Group 3 heading, although the ditch could have removed a feature forming the north-east corner of the cemetery plot suggested below (discussion pp.192–5). The few sherds of pottery from 1005 appear to be 2nd century while the graves are probably 3rd century.

Ditch or gully 1013 was a very shallow feature, 0.40m wide and no more than 0.20m deep, which ran on a north-west/south-east line for 12.80m from the north-west trench edge. Its backfill (1014) was a dark yellow-orange clay deposit in which a

Fig.100 *County Hospital, Foss Bank: Area B, view north-east, southern trench in foreground, showing ditch 0055 on the left and ditch 0020 in the centre (scale 2m)*

2nd-century stamped mortarium (*AY* 16/8, 931, *3361*) was found. Parallel to 1013, at a distance of c.5.25m to the north-east, was grave 0017. It was rectangular in plan, 1.60m long and 0.65m wide. The fill (0114) contained a skeleton in poor condition of which the head was missing, but it had lain at the north-west end of the grave; the lower left leg was also missing. In line with this grave c.3m to the north-west was a small pit (1015) also aligned north-west/south-east, and oval in plan with its long axis measuring 1.12m. It was 0.14m deep and the backfill (1016), was a dark grey sandy clay. At 90° to 0017 and 1013, and in line with the south-east end of the latter, lay grave 1001 on a north-east/south-west alignment (Fig.98; Fig.99). This was rectangular in plan and measured 1.20 x 0.38m with a depth of c.0.12m. It contained an infant skeleton buried in a nailed wooden coffin to the inner sides of which (but not to the base) were nailed (sfs73–88) a number of small lead sheets (sf89). The cut also contained two incomplete pots, a dish and jar, dated to the 3rd century (*AY* 16/8, 1095). The backfill of

the grave (1003/4) was a pale yellow sandy clay. It is possible that post-hole 1007 described above also formed part of this group of features as it lay approximately mid-way between 0017 and 1013.

Area B *(Figs 100–101)*

Northern trench *(Figs 102–5)*

Group 1

A shallow curving gully (0104) was found near the north-east corner (Fig.104). It was 3.50m long, 0.60m wide and 0.15m deep, and was cut by ditch 0115 (see below). The fill (0105), was a mid-grey sandy silt which produced a coin dated to AD 270 (sf59) which is difficult to explain except as an intrusive find. It is possible that this feature represents remains of part of a circular structure, but it does not reappear in the southern trench as one would expect, although three possible post-holes 0026, 0087–88 might have been associated features.

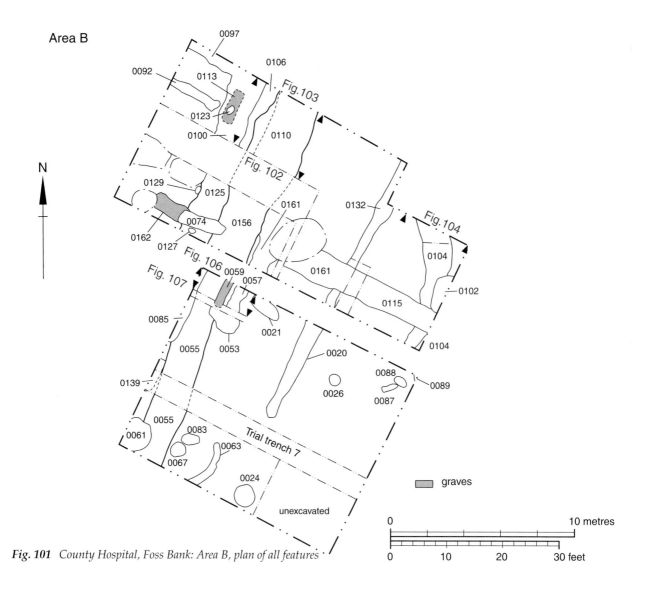

Fig. 101 *County Hospital, Foss Bank: Area B, plan of all features*

Group 2

Running across the centre of the trench on a north-east/south-west alignment was a ditch 0110 (north-east half)/0156 (south-west half), c.1.90–2.40m wide and up to 0.90m deep with a flat base. The backfill of 0110 was 0146, a dark grey silt, which was overlain by 0122, a grey sandy deposit with occasional pebbles. As 0156 the ditch was backfilled with 0157, a grey silty clay deposit in which a mid–late 2nd-century stamped samian base (*AY* 16/8, *3578*) was found. A recut of the north-eastern half of the ditch (0148) was 1m wide and 0.90m deep, and had steep sloping sides (Figs 102,103). The backfill layers were 0121, a layer of large cobbles, sealed by 0120, a dark grey deposit with occasional pebbles and cobbles, which was sealed in turn by 0111, a mid-brown sandy deposit with patches of orange sand.

Cutting into fill layer 0146 on the north-west side of 0110 was a shallow ditch, 0106, 0.80m wide and 0.35m deep, which ran north-west/south-east for 1.90m from the north-east trench edge. The backfill was 0107, dark grey silty deposit in which a bead (sf58) was found. The feature could not be traced south-west of an unexcavated baulk in the centre of the trench.

North-west of ditch 0106 was another ditch (north-east: 0097/0100; south-west: 0125). At its south-west end it was 0.80m north-west of 0110/1056 (measured south-east edge to north-west edge), but it curved away slightly from the latter to the north-west as it ran towards the north-east end of the trench. Ditch 0097/0100/0125 had

168

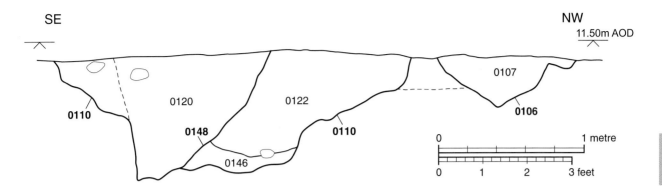

Fig. 102 County Hospital, Foss Bank: Area B north, section of central baulk, north-east side

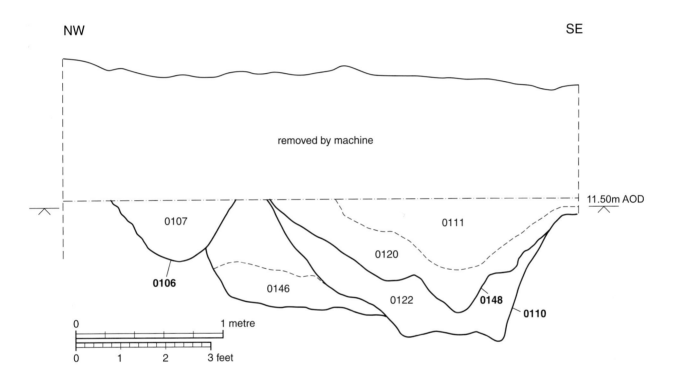

Fig. 103 County Hospital, Foss Bank: Area B north, section along north-east edge

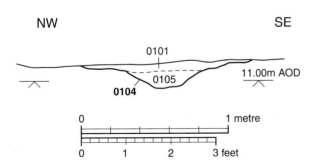

Fig. 104 County Hospital, Foss Bank: Area B north, section of gully 0104

gently sloping sides and a rounded base and was up to 1.80m wide and 1.35m deep, although at the north-east end (as 0097) it became c.1.40m wide and no more than 0.50m deep before it returned to the north-west.

Apparently cut into the base of the ditch before it was infilled were two post-holes (0123 and 0127). They were probably contemporary with 0129, cut into the north-west side of the ditch, as the three are more or less in a straight line. The distance from 0123 to 0129 was 4.40m and from 0129 to 0127 was

169

Fig. 105 *County Hospital, Foss Bank: Area B, northern trench, view south-east; ditches 0110/0156 and 0100/0125 run from left to right (scale 2m)*

2.20m; this regularity argues for another in the unexcavated area between 0123 and 0129. 0123 and 0129 had a diameter of 0.40m and 0127 a diameter of 0.30m. 0123 was filled with 0124, fine dark grey silt in which a bovine skull was found. 0127 was filled with 0128, a dark grey silty deposit, and 0129, 0.48 deep, was filled with 0130, a dark grey silty deposit containing some large cobbles.

As ditch 0100 the infill was 0099, a mid-brown deposit, in which an inscribed tile (sf62) and a

stamped tile (sf64) were found. As 0097 the infill was 0098, again a mid-brown deposit, in which three stamped samian bases were found (*AY* 16/8, *3466*, dated c.160–200; *3604*, dated c.100–20; and *3643*, dated c.160–200). As 0125 the infill of the ditch was 0126, a grey-brown deposit in which a pottery candleholder (sf67) was found.

Near the north corner of the trench and emerging from its north-west edge was a gully (0092) 0.45m wide and 0.25m deep, which ran on a north-west/

south-east line for 2.90m coming to a rounded end just before reaching ditch 0097/0100/0125. The backfill (0093) was a dark grey deposit.

Another ditch running north-east/south-west, c.5m south-east of 0110/0156, was 0132 which was c.0.50–0.80m wide and no more than 0.40m deep. The south-east side of this shallow feature sloped less sharply than the north-west side and the base was rounded. 0132 continued to the south-west in the southern trench as 0020 (see below). The fill of 0132 was 0131, light grey sandy silt. Ditch 0132 was cut at 90° by 0115/0161, a shallow ditch with a rounded base, on a north-west/south-east line, 2m wide and 0.25m deep, which ran for 10m. At its north-west end 0161 appeared to return to the south-west into a continuation of ditch 0057 recorded in the southern area (see below). 0115 was filled with 0112, a dark grey deposit with frequent cobbles and pebbles, in which were found a fragment of pipe clay figurine (sf60) and a stamped tile (sf69). As 0161 the ditch was filled with 0151, dark brown clay deposit, which was sealed by 0158, a light brown-orange clay.

Group 3

Found in no perceptible cut in fill layer 0099 of ditch 0097/0100/0125 in the north-eastern half of the trench was the skeleton (0113) of a female aged 13–15 years. She had been buried prone and lay on a north-east/south-west alignment, the head to the south-west. The skull had rolled over to face west, the arms were slightly akimbo, the hands were under the pelvis and the legs were slightly flexed. The grave lay above post-hole 0123 (see above) and it is possible that the bovine skull found in it actually relates to the grave, forming an offering of a ritual nature.

Close to the south-west edge of the trench, near the south-west corner was grave 0162 which had a rectangular cut c.1.90m long, on a north-west/south-east alignment. It contained a poorly preserved skeleton, with its head to the north-west; the presence of iron nails suggests it had been buried in a wooden coffin. The backfill was 0163, a grey deposit. Above the cut for the coffin the grave cut widened out to become roughly oval with sloping sides. The backfill of this upper part was 0155, a light grey-brown sandy deposit with frequent charcoal. The south-east end of the grave and ditch 0097/0100/0125 were cut by

an elongated oval feature (0074) with its longer axis, which measured 2.50m, on a north-west/south-east line. It was 0.60m wide and 0.55m deep, and back-filled with 0075, a black silty deposit with abundant charcoal flecks. There were no finds, but the alignment suggests a Roman date.

Fill 0151 of ditch 0115/0161 was cut on its north-east side against the south-east edge of the trench by 0102, a pit lying mostly beyond the south-east trench edge. The backfill of the pit was 0103, a dark deposit which was excavated to a depth of 0.40m but not bottomed. The ditch was also cut by a medieval pit (0160).

Although the trench was machine cleared to natural in most parts, in the north-west corner a thin layer of greenish sandy clay with many tile frag-ments, frequent charcoal flecks and pebbles and cobbles (0012/0013) was excavated over features in that area including 0097. The deposit contained Roman pottery including a stamped samian base (*AY 16/8, 3714,* mid-2nd century) and a near complete pot (sf53). In addition, two coins (sf23, Vespasian, AD 77–8, and sf25, AD 154–5), a ring (sf24) and a bone pin (sf52) were found. On the east side of the trench a layer (0101) of dark grey sandy deposit was excavated above features 0102 and 0104.

Southern trench *(Figs 101, 106–7)*

Group 1

0063 which emerged from the centre of the south-west trench edge was a curving gully c.2.50m long, 0.38m wide and 0.10m deep. The backfill (0066) was a light grey sandy silt which contained no finds. It is just possible that this feature represents the remains of a circular structure. If this were the case, its diameter would have been c.4.60m.

West of 0063, near the south-west edge of the trench, were two small pits. 0067 was rounded in plan with diameter 0.80m and depth 0.48m. Its backfill (0068) was a dark grey silty clay. 0083 was a shallow pit roughly oval in plan, 0.35m deep, with its longer axis east–west measuring 1.10m. Its backfill (0084) was a light brown clay.

Two features were cut by the Group 2 ditch 0134 or its major re-cut 0055 (see below). 0136/0138 was

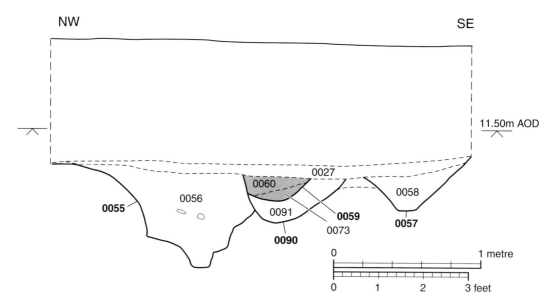

Fig. 106 *County Hospital, Foss Bank: Area B south, section along north-east edge in the north-east corner*

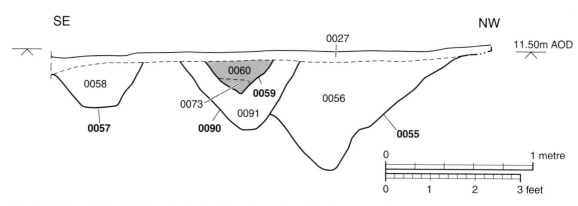

Fig. 107 *County Hospital, Foss Bank: Area B south, section of baulk near north-east corner, north-east side*

a shallow pit aligned north–south in which the fill (0137) of the surviving southern part contained two horse legs (not illustrated). 0139 was a pit, 0.55m deep, on the north-west side of the trench of which the backfill (0140) was a dark sandy clay.

Other features cut into natural include a shallow pit (0021), south-east of 0057 (see below) and close to the north-east trench edge. It was oval in plan, 0.35m deep, with the longer axis, measuring 1.70m, aligned north-west/south-east. Its backfill was 0044, a dark grey sandy clay deposit.

In the east corner of the trench there were three shallow cuts, possibly post-holes (0087–9). 0088 was c.0.50m in diameter and 0.40m deep and was backfilled with 0078, a mid-brown-grey silty clay

deposit. The feature was cut by 0087, 0.8 x 0.3m and 0.15m deep, backfilled with 0080, an orange-brown sandy silty deposit with frequent sandstone. 0089 lay largely beyond the trench edge, but was 0.30m deep and backfilled with 0082, a dark brown clay deposit. Between these features and ditch 0020 to the north-west was another possible post-hole (0026), rounded in plan with diameter 0.60m and 0.12m deep. The fill (0030) was a mid-brown sandy deposit. If not related to 0104 (see above) these four post-holes may originally have belonged to a row on a near east–west alignment which may, in turn, indicate that they are post-Roman.

Close to the south-west edge of the trench and south-east of gully 0063 was a pit (0024), rounded in plan with diameter 1.10m and depth 0.60m. Its backfill (0040) was a dark grey silty deposit in which antler (sf27) and worked bone (sf50) were found.

Group 2

0134 was the earliest of a sequence of ditch cuts on a north-east/south-west alignment which formed a continuation to the south-west of ditch 0156 in the northern trench. The cut (0134) was recorded at the south-west end of the trench, and had been largely obliterated by the re-cut 0055, but it had a flat base and was c.1.60m wide and 0.60m deep. The backfill (0135) was a grey-brown clayey deposit.

The ditch re-cut (0055), which was recorded in Trial Trench 7 as 740 (see above), ran the width of the trench from north-east to south-west. It was up to 1.80m wide and 0.60–0.70m deep with gently sloping sides which appear to have stepped into a near vertical-sided slot at the bottom. 0055 was infilled with 0056, a dark grey clay in which a stamped samian base (*AY* 16/8, *3530*, dated 65–95)

was found along with a copper-alloy belt fitting (sf54) and a pin (sf57).

0055 was re-cut on its south-east side by a narrow ditch (0090) located at the north-east end of the trench (Fig.107). 0090 was 0.30m deep and 0.65m wide with a rounded base. The backfill was 0091, a silty deposit.

Another short length of ditch (0057), 0.60m wide and 0.30m deep, running for 1.50m north-east/south-west was found at the north-east end of the trench, 0.20m to the south-east of 0055 (with which there was no stratigraphic relationship). It had a flat base and its fill was 0058, a clayey deposit.

Ditch 0020, on a north-east/south-west alignment, c.1m wide and 0.52m deep, was a continuation of 0132 found in the northern trench and ran from the north-east trench edge for 5.60m to a rounded end near the centre of this southern trench. Measured centre to centre 0020 was 5.72m south-

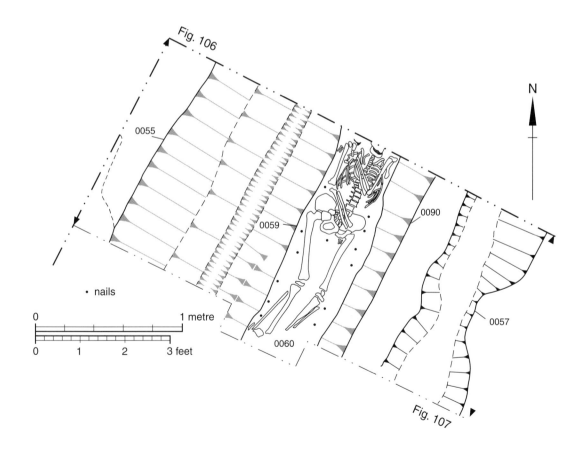

Fig. 108 *County Hospital, Foss Bank: Area B south, plan of grave 0059*

east of ditch cut 0055. The backfill deposits were 0045 (= 0046–50, 0052), dark brown clayey deposit, and above it 0028 (=0029, 0042–3, 0051), a mid-brown clayey deposit in which a possible ballista ball (sf46) was found.

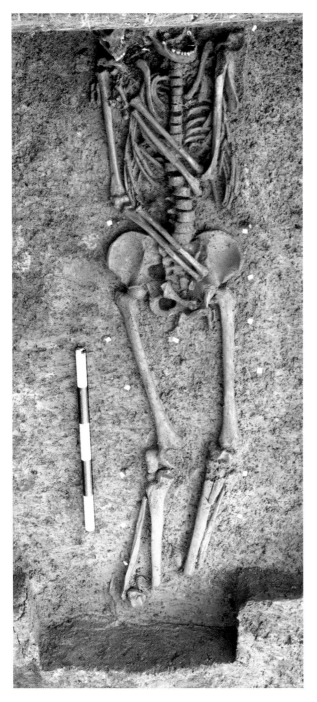

Fig.109 *County Hospital, Foss Bank: view north-east of the skeleton in grave 0059 (scale 0.50m)*

Group 3

Ditch fill layer 0091 was cut by a grave (0059) aligned north-east/south-west (Fig.108; Fig.109). Neither end of the cut was found, the north-east end lying beyond the trench edge, but as it survived it was c.1.60m long, 0.50m wide, and 0.15m deep. The earliest fill layer was 0073, orange clay and yellow sand, and above it within fill layer 0060 was a skeleton, probably of a female 13–15 years of age, originally buried in a nailed wooden coffin with the head to the north-east, the right arm across the pelvis and the left arm reaching up to the right shoulder. The lower parts of the legs were missing.

Both 0055 and 0057 and possibly grave 0059 were cut by a shallow pit (0053), oval in plan with its longer axis measuring 1.80m. The backfill (0054) was brown sandy soil with frequent charcoal flecks.

At its south-west end ditch 0055 was cut by a pit (0061). It was rounded in plan, of diameter 1.60m and 0.40m deep. The backfill (0062) was a dark brown silty clay deposit with frequent charcoal flecks.

0085 was a shallow pit on the north-west side of the trench, near its north-east end, and north-west of 0055 which it cut. The feature was 2.70m long, but most of it lay beyond the trench edge. The backfill (0086) was a dark grey clay deposit.

In the east corner of the trench cuts 0087–9 were overlain by a thin deposit (0010/0015) c.0.10–0.15m deep of clean grey clay which was left in situ after machining on the south-eastern side of the trench. 0010 was cut by two graves (0116–17) lying on a north-east/south-west alignment, head to the south-west, which were thought to be medieval and are probably outliers from the Jewish cemetery to the south-east. Near the south-west edge of the trench, near the south corner, under the ramp left for access, was grave 0118 also on a north-east/south-west alignment which may be another outlier from the Jewish cemetery.

On the north-west side of the trench 0027, a dark grey soil, was left in situ after machine clearance. The deposit contained a stamped samian base (*AY* 16/8, *3504*, dated 135–60).

County Hospital, Monkgate

Introduction

An excavation, directed by Amanda Clarke, took place from November 1982–March 1983 on a site on Monkgate (SE606552320; Figs 110–11). It was located on the south-east side of the street in an area now occupied by 30a–b Monkgate and 1–8 Monkgate Cloisters, and previously by the Outpatient Department of the County Hospital. The work took place in advance of development for housing by Wimpey Homes to whom the Trust is grateful for allowing access. The excavation was staffed by a team funded by the Manpower Services Commission. This report has been compiled from Amanda Clarke's site records and notes.

Finds and site records are stored at York Archaeological Trust under the Yorkshire Museum accession code 1982/3.19.

The excavation
(Figs 111–114)

The site consisted of an area c.18 x 13m. Mechanical clearance took place to a depth of c.0.85m below present ground level which is at c.13.20m OD and the site was then dug by hand to natural. This was a thick orange clay which occurred at c.11.70m OD, c.1.50m below modern level.

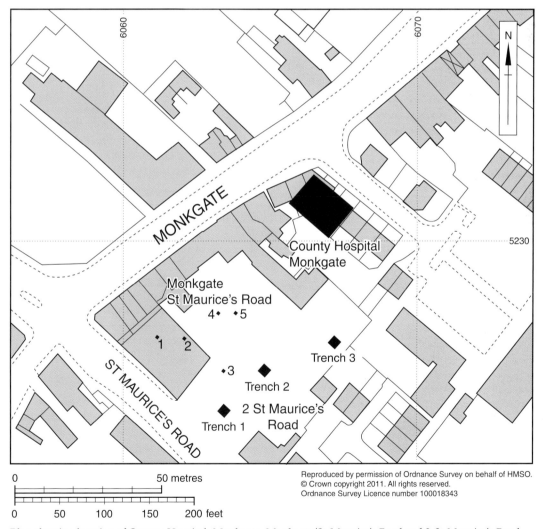

Fig.110 Plan showing location of County Hospital, Monkgate, Monkgate/St Maurice's Road and 2 St Maurice's Road

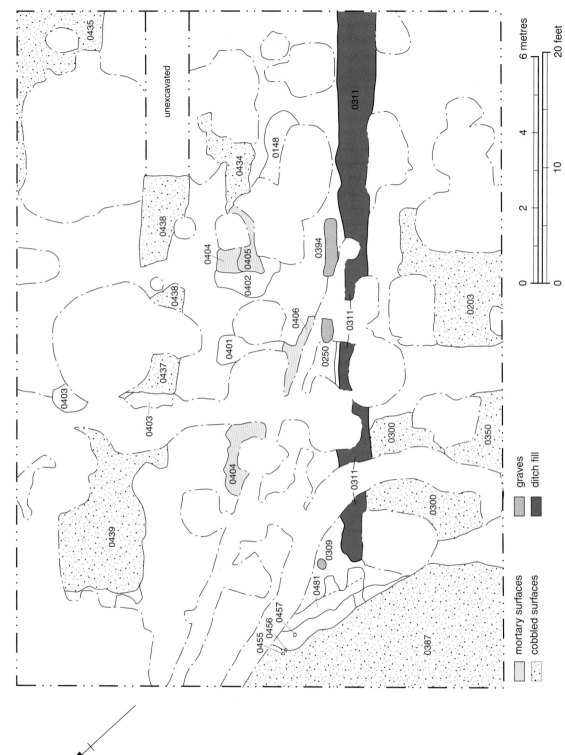

Fig. 111 County Hospital Monkgate: Plan of all Roman features

mortary surfaces

cobbled surfaces

graves

ditch fill

0435

unexcavated

0434

0148

0438

0404

0405

0402

0394

0311

0438

0406

0401

0250

0311

0203

0437

0403

0403

0404

0300

0350

0311

0439

0300

0309

0481

0457

0456

0455

0387

N

0   2   4   6 metres

0   10   20 feet

2

The earliest activity on the site can be dated to the Roman period and was represented by a number of deposits and features including cobbled surfaces and graves. Because of heavy disturbance by medieval and later pits, and the walls of the hospital, it was difficult to establish a clear stratigraphic sequence and the absence of substantial well-stratified finds assemblages prevents accurate dating of the discoveries.

Earliest deposits *(Fig.111)*

The earliest deposits (0462–4), which overlay natural in a number of areas, were 200–300mm thick and consisted of dark grey-brown silty material with occasional charcoal flecks, cobbles and pebbles (no plan survives). Overlying natural in the centre and north-eastern part of the trench there were small islands of dark grey-brown silty sand with a

few cobbles and mortar flecks (0401–3) heavily cut away by later features.

0401 was overlain by 0406, a small deposit of mortar and painted plaster. Nearby and overlying 0402, was 0404, a patch of mortar with occasional limestone fragments, overlain by 0405, white mortar with a few fragments of painted wall plaster.

The cobbled spreads *(Fig.111)*

In a number of areas of the site natural or the deposits referred to above were overlain by spreads of loosely packed cobbles. Near the north corner lay 0439; south-east of it lay a smaller spread (0437) and further to the south-east another (0438) which continued below an area left unexcavated as an access ramp. South-east of 0438 there was another small area of cobbles (0434) and another (0435)

Fig.112 *County Hospital, Monkgate: view north-east of site as fully excavated showing ditch 0311 near base running from right to left (scale 2m)*

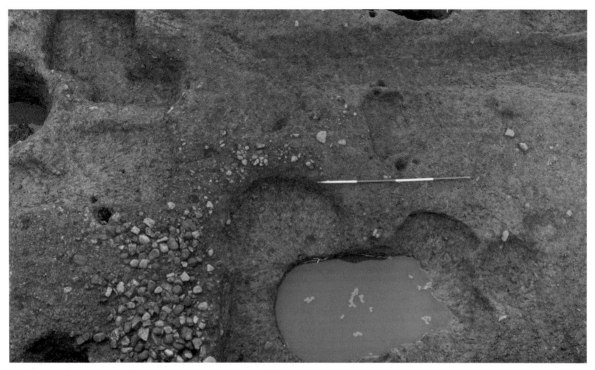

Fig. 113 *County Hospital, Monkgate: view north-east of the south-east corner of the site showing cobbles 0203 (lower left) and ditch 0311 (top, right to centre) (scale 2m)*

Fig. 114 *County Hospital, Monkgate: view north showing cobbles 0437 and 0439 (top). Scale 2m*

lay in the east corner of the trench. Taken together these deposits may make up a path or track running north-west/south-east, although they were extensively disturbed by later features.

Sloping down towards the west corner of the site there was a deposit (0387) measuring up to 8m north–south and 3.2m east–west, of tightly packed cobbles on average smaller than those in the deposits described above. This may, again, have been part of a path or track, in this case perhaps on a north-east/south-west or north–south alignment. A silver denarius of Delmatius (sf174) dated to 335–7 was found on the surface, although it cannot be taken to date the feature. The cobbles were cut by two stake-holes (0455–6) and a third (0457) lay immediately to the south-east. All were round in plan. 0455 was 0.07m in diameter and 0.37m deep, 0456 was 0.10m in diameter and 0.10m deep, and 0457 was 0.15m in diameter and 0.20m deep.

South-east of 0387 was a deposit of small cobbles (0300) less tightly packed than those in 0387, which was separated from a similar deposit (0350) further to the south-east by a modern drain trench (0211). South-east of 0350 lay 0203, a deposit of cobbles similar to those in the north-eastern part of the trench.

The burials *(Figs 111, 115–116)*

Three Roman inhumation burials were found lying on a north-west/south-east line near the centre of the trench. The best preserved was 0394, in a grave with a roughly rectangular cut, 1.50m long, 0.35m wide and 0.10m deep, and only slightly disturbed at the north-west end (Fig.115). The head of the skeleton (0396) lay at the north-west end and the backfill was 0395, a grey-brown deposit. About 1m to the north-west of this grave lay 0250 which had been substantially disturbed such that the cut was hard to identify clearly, and the legs and other parts of the skeleton were missing (Fig.116). Almost 6m further to the north-west a human skull (0309) was found which is presumably all that survives of a third, and very heavily disturbed, burial.

Other Roman features *(Fig.111)*

A shallow ditch (0311) with a U-shaped profile, c.1m wide and up to 0.33m deep, on a north-west/

south-east line lay immediately to the south-west of the line of graves referred to above and cut cobbled layer 0300. Although heavily cut away by later features the ditch appears to have run most of the length of the trench and may have defined the

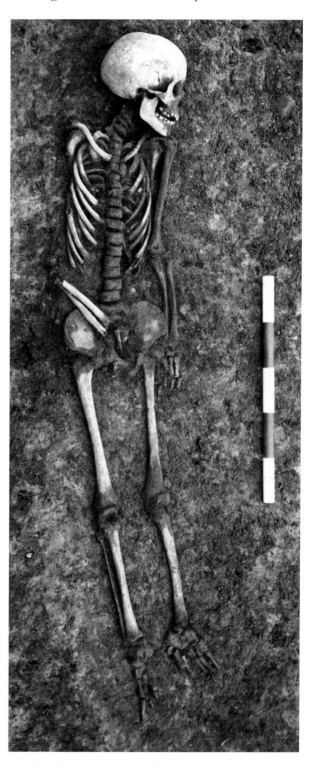

Fig. 115 County Hospital, Monkgate: view north-east of burial 0394 (scale 0.50m)

south-west side of a cemetery area. The fill layers of the south-eastern part of the ditch were 0312, a grey-brown clayey deposit with occasional charcoal flecks, and 0313, a dark yellow-brown clayey deposit. In the north-western part the fill was 0389, a deep–mid-brown silty deposit. At its north-west end this ditch terminated immediately before the south end of a shallow gully (0481) which ran for 2m north–south along the east edge of the cobbled layer 0387. This may indicate that the ditch, gully and cobbles were contemporary features. Gully 0481 was 0.40m wide and 0.27 deep, and the fill was a mid-yellow-brown silty deposit (0480).

Other features included a shallow oval scoop (0148) located near the central north-west/south-east axis of the trench and close to its south-east end. The scoop measured 1.52 x 0.44m and was 0.06m deep. The fill was 0188, a brown silty sandy deposit.

Dating

Only 76 stratified Roman sherds were found on the site, but they were largely 2nd- to early 3rd-century in date and resembled the assemblage from the Foss Bank site in character (*AY* 16/8, 1096).

Post-Roman

In undisturbed areas the layers and features described above were overlain by a dark deposit containing pottery dated up to the 12th–13th century.

Monkgate/St Maurice's Road

Five mechanically dug 1m square test pits were observed by Patrick Ottaway on 2 February 1987 on a site on the corner of Monkgate and St Maurice's Road (SE60645227; Fig.94, 3; Fig.110), entered through Nos 20–26 St Maurice's Road, then the premises of 'Hire-it' plant hire. Pit 1 was in an open yard and the others were within the standing buildings. The work was undertaken at the request of D.A.C. Wood, consulting engineer, and Tom Adams Design Associates.

Finds and records are stored under the Yorkshire Museum accession code 1987.2.

Fig. 116 *County Hospital, Monkgate: view north-west of burial 0250 (scale 0.50m)*

The only Roman archaeology was recorded in pit 1. Natural clay lay at a depth of c.2m below modern ground level and overlying it was a deposit c.0.10m thick of mixed brown clayey material in which two sherds of Roman pottery were found. Above this was a dark grey-brown silty deposit and then the modern yard surface. In the other trenches natural occurred at depths of 1.50m (pit 5), 2m (pits 2 and 4) and 2.50m (pit 3) below the building floor. In pits 2, 3 and 5 any Roman strata had probably been largely removed by medieval pits; in pit 4 natural was overlain by a grey silty deposit from which no finds were recovered.

2 St Maurice's Road

In June 1992 two weeks of evaluation excavation, supervised by Jane Lilley, took place at 2 St Maurice's Road (Fig.94, 3; Fig.110) on behalf of the developer, Mr C.A. Bird, following a brief issued by York City Council. Three small trenches were excavated on a north-east/south-west line, the south-westernmost (Trench 1) being c.33m north-east of the line of the Roman fortress defences. This report has been compiled using Jane Lilley's site evaluation report.

Finds and site records are stored under the YAT and Yorkshire Museum accession code 1992.12.

A summary description of the pottery from the site appears in *AY* 16/8 (p.1094). Over two-thirds of the c.260 Roman sherds came from Trench 2. Analysis confirmed that there was probably some 2nd- to 3rd-century activity in the area, but the features described below are probably late 3rd–early 4th century.

Trench 1 (*Fig.117*)

Trench 1 measured 3 x 2.40m. Natural was not reached, the earliest archaeological deposits being encountered at 12.86–13.20m OD, c.1.40–1.70m below modern ground level.

No record was made of the unexcavated deposits at the base of the trench. The earliest excavated deposits on the north-western side of the trench were 1023, mortar, overlain by 1022, sandy silt. The earliest deposit on the north-eastern side of the trench was 1021, silty clay (not on Fig.117). These three deposits contained 3rd-century pottery. They were cut by a ditch (1024) aligned north-east/south-west which had steep sides, a flat bottom, and measured 0.60m wide and 0.25m deep. Along both sides of the base was a series of iron nails pointing inwards suggesting a wooden lining which, in turn, suggests that the feature was used for drainage. The backfill was 1026, a grey silty deposit. The ditch was recut as 1020, up to 0.7m wide and 0.25m deep. It was filled with 1019, a silty clay containing late 3rd-century pottery. The ditch and its recut

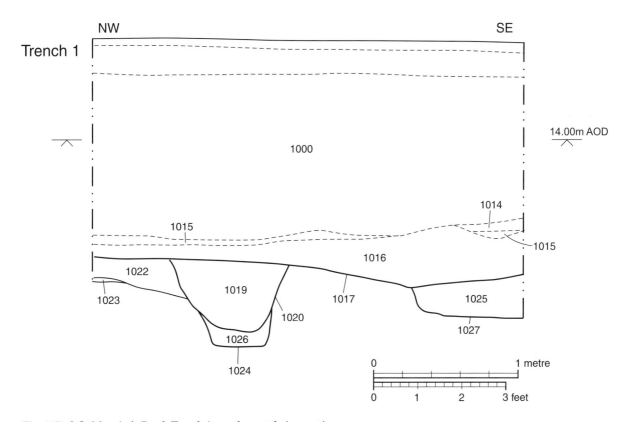

Fig. 117 2 St Maurice's Road: Trench 1: south-west-facing section

occurred at the same stratigraphic level as 1027, a shallow pit, subrectangular in plan, 0.7m wide and 0.25m deep, in the east corner of the trench. It was backfilled with 1025, silty clay containing pottery of late 3rd-century date.

Near the north-east side of the trench the ditch fill 1019 was cut by 1017, a shallow gully running north-west/south-east. The north-eastern side was beyond the trench edge, but as excavated the feature was 1.60m wide and 0.30m deep and had a flat base. The backfill layers were 1016, clay which contained mortar, tile and tesserae and a bronze brooch (sf3), and above this 1015, a mix of clay and sandy silt with tile and limestone fragments. Both deposits contained late 3rd-century pottery and 1015 produced a coin of Postumus (AD 259–68; sf7). A post-hole (1013) was cut into 1015 which was 0.24m in diameter and 90mm deep. It was filled with 1006.

Subsequently there was a build up of sandy clay silts (1001–5, 1007–12 and 1014) in total 0.10m thick and containing a mixture of Roman and later pottery. All material above these deposits was numbered 1000 and had been machined off. It included a 1.10m thick deposit of what appeared to be cultivated soil and above it was the car park make up.

Trench 2 *(Figs 118–120)*

Trench 2 measured 2.65 x 2.65m. Natural was not reached, the earliest deposit reached being 2017, a silty clay encountered at c.12.69m OD, c.1.60m below modern ground level. 2017 was unexcavated, although some 3rd-century pottery was recovered while cleaning its surface. In the northern half of the trench 2017 was cut by ditch 2015 running north-west/south-east of which the north-east

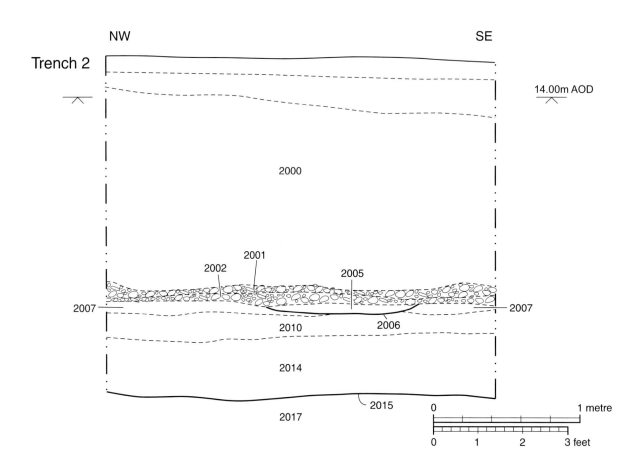

Fig. 118 2 St Maurice's Road: Trench 2, south-west-facing section

182

Fig. 119 *2 St Maurice's Road, Trench 2: view east of ditch 2015 (scale 1m)*

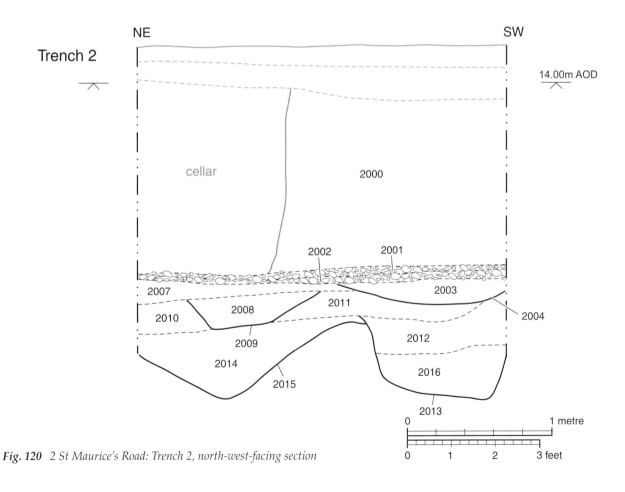

Fig. 120 *2 St Maurice's Road: Trench 2, north-west-facing section*

Fig. 121 *St Maurice's Road, Trench 2: view north-east of cobbled surface 2001 (scale 1m)*

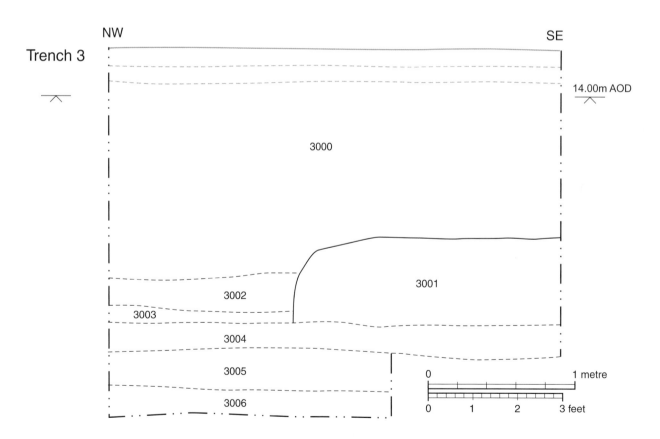

Fig. 122 *2 St Maurice's Road: Trench 3, north-east-facing section*

side was beyond the trench edge (Fig.119). It was at least 1.80m wide and 0.44m deep, and was filled with 2014, silty clay containing pottery dated to the later 3rd century and a bone pin (sf36). This feature was cut by a pit (2013) in the south corner of the trench, rectangular in plan, measuring 1 x 1m and 0.22m deep. The backfill was 2016, a clayey deposit, succeeded by 2012, silty clay. The ditch and pit were succeeded by 2011, in the centre of trench, and 2010 on its north side, both silty clays.

These deposits were cut by a ditch (2009) on the same line as 2015. 2009 was 1.20m wide and 0.40m deep, and backfilled by 2008, silty clay containing pottery dated to the 4th century and a bone pin (sf6). In the northern half of the trench above 2008 was 2007, a thin deposit of silty clay containing pot of the early 3rd century. 2007 was cut on the north-east edge of the trench by 2006, a very shallow feature, an irregular oval in plan, measuring 1 x 0.30m. It was filled with 2005, mixed sandy silty clay containing late 3rd-century pot. 2007 was cut in the south-western half of the trench by a shallow ditch (2004) c.1m wide, running north-west/south-east on the line of the earlier ditch 2013. 2004 was filled with 2003, silty clay with cobbles containing 3rd-century pottery. The trench was subsequently wholly given over to the make up of two successive cobbled surfaces, 2002 overlain by 2001 (Fig.121). Both layers had irregular surfaces and amongst the cobbles there were many animal bones, including a few cattle metapodials which showed signs of being worked. The pottery was late 3rd century and 2002 contained a coin of Tetricus I (AD 268–73; sf11). Material above 2001 was removed by machine and numbered 2000. It consisted of 1.20m of what appeared to be featureless silty clay which was cut by a cellar below the modern car park make up.

Trench 3 *(Fig.122)*

Natural sand containing pebbles (3005–6) was encountered at c.12.39m OD, c.2m below modern ground level. Above this was a deposit 0.20m thick (3004) of sand, silty clay and pebbles containing pottery of 2nd-century date and a human foetal humerus fragment. This was sealed by a deposit of silty clay removed in two spits (3002–3) containing 2nd- to 3rd-century Roman pot and two 11th- to 12th-century sherds in 3003. This deposit was cut by a trench for a modern concrete drain pipe (3001) which was succeeded by 3000, material removed by machine consisting of featureless silty clay 1.20m thick below the car park make up.

40–48 Monkgate

In November–December 2005 an evaluation excavation, supervised by D. T. Evans, took place on land to the rear of 40–48 Monkgate, York (SE 60765234, Fig.94, 4; Fig.123). The work was undertaken on behalf of Mack and Lawler, Builders Ltd of York to a brief for evaluation in advance of development from City of York Council. This consisted of the excavation of four trenches, each 3 x 3m, to a depth of 1.25m below modern level. In addition, eight boreholes were sunk against the south-west side of the property to determine the depth of deposits.

All records relating to this work are currently held by York Archaeological Trust under the Yorkshire Museum accession code YORYM : 2005.3204.

This report has been compiled from a site evaluation report by D. T. Evans and Ian Milsted (York Archaeological Trust Report 2006/13).

Roman archaeological remains occurred only in Trench 3.

Trench 3 *(Figs 124–5)*

Natural, a mottled clayey sand (3031), was located at c.11.9m OD, c.1.1m below modern ground level. Immediately overlying natural was a sequence of deposits, in total up to c.0.2m thick. The earliest was 3030, a grey sandy clayey silt with occasional cobbles and charcoal which was succeeded by 3037, a grey sandy silt below 3029, a light grey

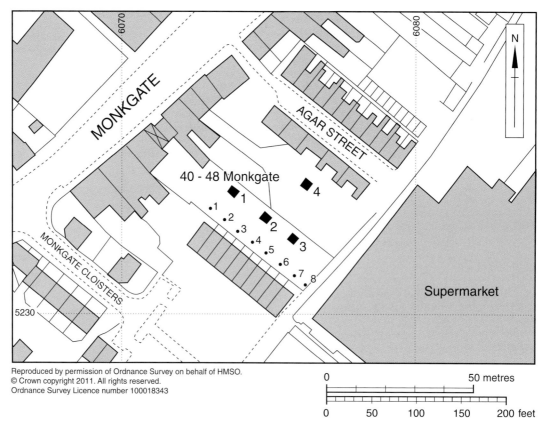

Fig.123 *40–48 Monkgate: Location of trenches*

sandy clayey silt. Also above natural in the north-corner of the trench was 3020, grey slightly sandy clayey silt. Above 3020 was 3004, a friable brownish-grey, clayey, sandy silt with occasional pebbles and charcoal, and above 3037 was 3036, brownish-grey clayey silt. 3029 was below 3028, greyish sandy clayey silt with occasional pebbles.

Cut into 3036 was a pit (3007), roughly circular in plan, of diameter c.1.3m, part of which lay beyond the south-east edge of the trench. The fill (3005) was a dark greyish-brown sandy silt with occasional cobbles. Excavation of the pit ceased at a depth of 0.3m. At a similar stratigraphic level in the west corner of the trench, but cut into 3028, was another pit (3015). Some 75% of 3015 lay beyond the trench edges, but it probably had a diameter of c.2m. Excavation ceased at a depth of c.0.40m. Five backfill layers were excavated, the earliest (3014) was a grey-brown silty, sandy clay with pebbles, cobbles, limestone fragments and mortar fragments. Over-lying this was 3013, a grey sand with moderate

patches of charcoal and occasional pebbles. Above 3013 was 3012 a mid-brown sandy silt with occasional pebbles and mortar, and above this was 3011, a mid-brown sandy silt with occasional charcoal, pebbles and limestone fragments. The uppermost deposit in the pit was 3026, grey-brown clayey silt with occasional pebbles.

Probably contemporary with pits 3007 and 3015 was 3019, a small ditch aligned north-west/south-east. After being traced for c.1.4m it appeared to taper to a terminal, although this had been cut away by a later feature (3010). Ditch 3019 was up to c.0.75m wide and 0.5m deep with quite steeply sloping sides. Four backfills were recorded, the lowest being 3018, a light grey silty sand with occasional charcoal and pebbles. Above this was 3017, a grey sandy silt with occasional charcoal and pebbles which lay below 3016, a brown silty clay with pebbles, small cobbles and occasional charcoal. The uppermost fill was 3027, grey-brown sandy clayey silt with occasional pebbles.

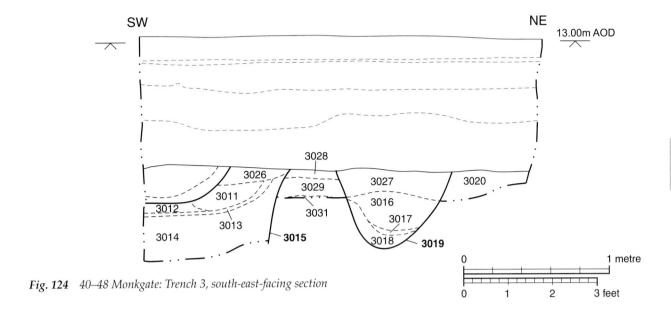

Fig. 124 40–48 Monkgate: Trench 3, south-east-facing section

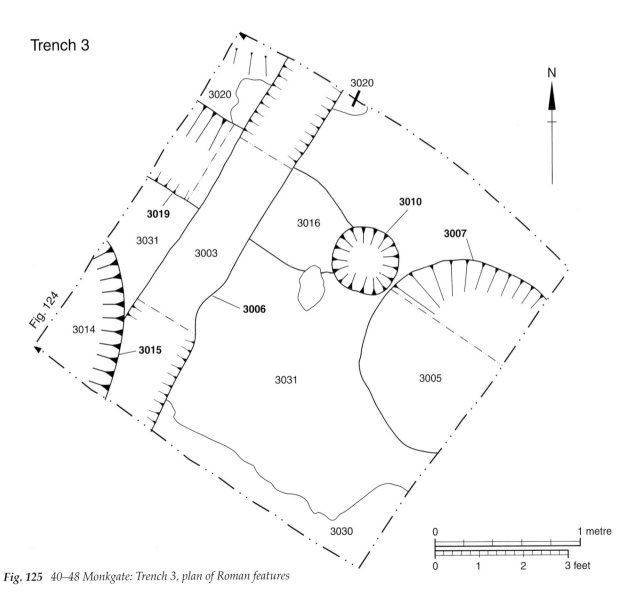

Fig. 125 40–48 Monkgate: Trench 3, plan of Roman features

Slightly later than features 3007, 3015 and 3019 were two roughly contemporary features, also thought to be Roman in date. Cut into ditch 3019 was a gully (3006) aligned north-east/south-west, 0.4–0.6m wide and up to 0.25m deep. It was filled with 3003, dark greyish-brown clayey silt with cobbles and occasional charcoal and mortar. Cutting the south-east end of 3019 was a post-hole (3010) c.0.3m deep. At the top it was circular with a diameter of c.0.45m but the base was square measuring 0.2 x 0.2m. It was filled with 3009, grey clayey sandy silt with large cobbles.

The pottery (c.70 sherds) from this sequence was all of late 2nd- to early 3rd-century date.

Next in the sequence were grey-brown deposits (3025, 3033–5) up to 0.35m thick which are thought to be post-Roman–medieval in date.

Peasholme Green

In 1990–1 York Archaeological Trust undertook three phases of evaluative excavation on a site on Peasholme Green (SE60775198–60855194; Fig.94, 5; Fig.126) formerly occupied by Adams Hydraulics. The work was undertaken on behalf of the Foss Development Corporation and followed briefs issued by York City Council.

Finds and records are stored under the Yorkshire Museum accession codes 1990.13 and 1991.13. This report was compiled by Patrick Ottaway from a draft by Niall Oakey.

Introduction

Phase 1

In October 1990 sixteen trenches were dug by machine (A1–7, B1–8 and C) to establish the depth and nature of surviving archaeological deposits. Subsequently, limited hand excavation was carried out to aid interpretation and dating. Trenches A1–7 each measured c.2 x 1.50m and (with the exception of A1) were positioned at 5m centres in a line as close to the modern street frontage as possible. Trench A2 was dug to a greater depth than the others in order to establish depth at which natural occurred. At right angles to Peasholme Green Trenches B1–8, also c.2 x 1.50m, were dug at 10m centres. Substantial disturbance from recently demolished brick buildings prevented deep excavation of Trenches B6 and B7, while deep brick foundations and unsafe conditions meant that observation of B5 could only be made from the surface. Trench C, 30 x 2m, was excavated at the south-eastern end of the site to a depth of 1.20m before a 10m length was shored and

a further 2.50m of material removed by machine. Detailed recording and limited hand excavation took place within a 5m length of this deeper area. The work was supervised by Niall Oakey.

Phase 2

The second phase of evaluative excavation was carried out in October–November 1990 under the supervision of Martin Brann. In order to establish the nature and depth of surviving archaeological deposits in the north-eastern third of the site 23 trenches were dug by machine. Subsequently, limited hand excavation was carried out to aid interpretation and dating. Trenches A15/D1 and A16–26 each c.2.50 x 2m were positioned at 5m centres in a line as close to the modern street frontage as possible. Trench A17 was dug to a greater depth than the others in order to establish the depth at which natural occurred. Trench A15/D1 was found to be located within a machine-pit lined with concrete and was not excavated. Trenches D2–12 were located to sample the deposits between the Peasholme Green frontage and the south-eastern boundary of the site. Their positions were determined by the need to avoid live services and reinforced machine mountings. Trench D5 could not be excavated because of the depth of concrete and rapid inflow of water.

On the south-east side of the site fifteen boreholes were positioned in a line running north-east/south-west to establish the depth of undisturbed natural and determine the sequence of archaeological deposits in an area believed to have been occupied in the medieval period by the King's

Fish Pool. The boreholes were drilled with a casing of 150mm diameter by Sub Soil Surveys Ltd of Manchester and an employee of York Archaeological Trust kept a record of the strata identified in the extracted soil cores. Borehole 8 could not be drilled because of the proximity of a standing wall.

Phase 3

The third phase of evaluation was carried out under the supervision of Rhona Finlayson during March–April 1991 on the central part of the site following the demolition of the remaining standing buildings. Three machine-dug trenches (E1–3), each 2 x 2m, were positioned on a north-west/south-east alignment in the north-western part of the site with the aim of plotting the profile of natural deposits. Two further trenches (F1–2) were opened adjacent to the Peasholme Green frontage. A machine was used to break concrete and remove modern material, but all subsequent excavation in these trenches was by hand. F1 measured 5 x 3m and was intended, firstly, to examine the extent and nature of medieval deposits adjacent to the street frontage and, secondly, to establish the nature and depth of any earlier archaeology. The trench was reduced to 2.75 x 1m once Roman levels had been reached. It was excavated to a depth of 4m below the modern ground level at which point natural was found. In Trench F2 excavation did not go below medieval deposits.

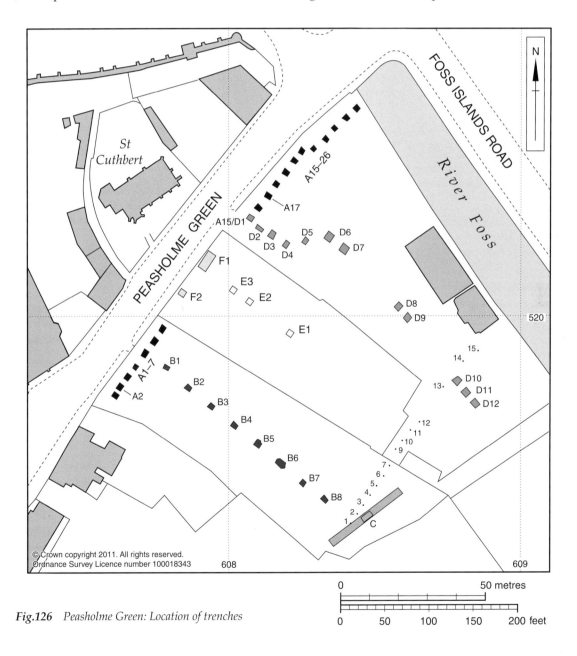

Fig.126 *Peasholme Green: Location of trenches*

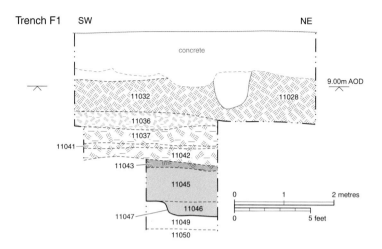

Trench F1   SW

NE

concrete

9.00m AOD

11032   11028

11036

11037

11041

11042

11043

11045

0   1   2 metres

11046

11047

0   5 feet

11049

11050

Fig.127 *Peasholme Green: Trench F1, south-east-facing section*

The natural ground level

Natural, a pale yellow-grey sand with pebbles, was encountered in only four of the trenches described above. It was at c.8m OD in Trench A2, at 6.14m OD in Trench F1 and at 5.52m OD in A17, c.25m further to the north-east. Finally, natural was encountered at 6.26m OD in E3, c.10m to the south-east of F1. Beyond E3 it is presumed that the natural level drops away sharply towards the River Foss. In the boreholes natural was located at between 3.30m and 4.80m OD, the level dropping towards the Foss. Except in an area perhaps c.15m wide along the street frontage it appears that much of the site was low lying and prone to flood in the Roman, Anglian and Anglo-Scandinavian periods before it was deliberately flooded to create the King's Fish Pool in the later 11th century.

The Roman archaeology

Roman strata were recorded in six trenches, but the principal focus of interest lay in Trench F1.

Trench A2 *(Not illustrated)*

Overlying natural a 0.50m thick layer of orange clay was excavated. Although it contained no finds,

it was similar to a deposit dated to the Roman period in Trench A17.

Trench A17 *(Not illustrated)*

Natural was overlain by an orange clayey deposit 0.75m thick (unnumbered). It contained Roman pottery of the early 2nd century and a large piece of human skull. This was sealed by a deposit 1.34m thick of silty clay which was very similar in nature to material found during the Phase 1 evaluation in many of the trenches along the Peasholme Green frontage and dated to the 10th–11th centuries, although no dating evidence was found in this material in Trench A17.

Trench F1 *(Fig.127)*

This was excavated to its full length (5m) and width (3m) to a depth of 1.8m and then reduced to a 2.75m long x 1m wide trench for another 0.75m, before being reduced again to a length of 1.5m and then excavated to natural (11050) at 6.14m OD. Above this was a build up, 0.60m thick, of silty sand (11049) and above it clayey silt (11048). These deposits contained no artefacts and may have been naturally formed. Into 11048 was cut a feature (11047), 0.80m deep, possibly a ditch running north-west/south-east of which only the south-western edge was located. The fill layers were organic clayey silts (11046 succeeded by 11045). 11046 contained few artefacts, but 11045 contained a wide range including glass fragments, a wooden object (sf357), a ballista ball (sf338) and a number of leather shoes (sfs335–7, 444–5) and leather offcuts (sfs345, 348–9, 351–2, 356, 360, 371, 449, 495). In addition, there were numerous cattle radii, probably disposed of after marrow extraction (cf. *AY* 15/2, 82). Other bones included seven dog skulls, and a human jaw and fibula. Deposit 11045 also produced a large assemblage of well-preserved insect and plant remains. The insects indicate damp or aquatic conditions. There were also grain pests and species which live in stable manure. Plant remains suggest the disposal of hay and straw, but there was also evidence for peat and domestic waste which included numerous nutlets of summer savory and fig seeds. Other plant remains of note were wild radishes and burdock, but there were no true aquatics and the assemblage suggests an environment of waste and cultivated ground. Deposit 11045 also produced a large group of pottery, largely Ebor ware dated c.200–25 (*AY* 16/8, 1075).

Deposit 11045 was overlain by a patchy cobbled surface (11044) which was at a level of 7.30m OD which corresponded to that of a surface make up (305) in Trench E3 (see below). Associated pottery was late 2nd–early 3rd century. Above the cobbles was c.0.20m of clayey silt with a high organic content (11043). A deposit sample produced a small quantity of well-preserved plant remains including seeds of rush, nettle and hemlock suggesting waste ground. A few insects were identified, mostly beetles which live in waterside mud, along with a few others which live by water. A few fragments of human bone were found in the deposit and the pottery was late 2nd–early 3rd century.

11043 was succeeded by up to 1m of deposits of silty clay interspersed with bands of orange clay some of which was burnt (11036–7, 11041–2). The deposits sloped down from north-west to south-east. All these deposits contained a large quantity of pottery, brick and tile including an example with a Sixth Legion stamp from 11037. The pottery was mainly mid-3rd century, including late forms of Ebor ware, and there

was a high proportion of wasters (*AY* 16/8, 1075). As there was little else in terms of pottery types it is likely these deposits originated as kiln refuse. In addition, early 3rd-century silver *denarii* were found in 11037 (sf319) and 11042 (sf331). Above 11036 the slope was levelled and the ground was raised by up to 0.50m by two thick clay deposits (11028/11032). They contained large quantities of pottery, brick and tile similar to the material in the deposits below.

Subsequent deposits and features were post-Roman.

Trench E1 *(Not illustrated)*

This was the south-easternmost of the three trenches dug behind the street frontage in the Phase 3 evaluation. Modern ground level lay at 9.70m OD and excavation reached a depth of c.5m OD. The lower 3.15m of deposits in the trench were silty clays (102–4), of which 103 contained late 2nd-century pot and 102 medieval pottery. Above 102 were modern deposits.

Trench E2 *(Not illustrated)*

Excavation reached a depth of c.5m OD and clayey silts (204–6) were found below 8.70m OD, i.e. 1m below modern level. The lowest deposit (206) contained Roman pottery of the early 3rd century.

Trench E3 *(Not illustrated)*

Natural (at 6.26m OD, 3.50m below modern level) was overlain by a deposit, 0.15m thick, of brown clay with charcoal and burnt clay (308) which contained late 1st-century pottery. Above this were a number of large limestone flags forming a surface at 6.36m OD. They were sealed by a deposit, 0.45m thick, of silty clay with lenses of black organic matter (307) which also contained late 1st-century pottery. This in turn was sealed by a deposit of clean clay (306) onto which a surface make up of compact cobbling (305) was laid at a level of 7.60m OD (see Trench F1 for same feature). Above this surface was a silty clay with lenses of organic matter (304) succeeded by a clayey silt (303) which contained pottery of mid-2nd- to 3rd-century date which was followed by a brown deposit (302) and then by modern deposits.

2

Zone 2: Discussion

Roads

Although the excavations in Zone 2 described above have nothing substantial to add to knowledge of major Roman roads in the area, some comment on their course and alignment is in order by way of background to the discussion of other topics (Fig.54). RCHME identified two approach roads to Roman York from the north-east (RCHMY 1, 1–2): Road 3 from Stamford Bridge and Road 4 thought to originate in Malton. It was proposed that the two roads joined at the point where Malton Road and Stockton Lane meet Heworth Green. The sighting of Road 3 nearest to York took place in 1959, c.2.5km north-east of the Roman fortress, just to the north of Apple Tree Farm, Heworth (SE63105310; Fig.54, 6; Wenham 1968a; Lawton 1997). The road line has also been traced on the surface for c.800m to the west and in fields to the east. Road 4 was recorded at Ryethorpe Grange Farm, also in 1959 (Fig.54, 5; Wenham 1968a, 45–50), c.3km north-east of the fortress. RCHME proposed that this road approached the city on a line slightly to the south of Stockton Lane and then adopted a line now taken by Heworth Green before joining Road 3. Three rather inexactly located sightings of metalling were thought by RCHME to represent the course of Road 3 between the north-east end of Monkgate and the fortress gate. However, an archaeological watching brief in 2005 (2005.402) on the corner of Monkgate and Penley's Grove Street on this line failed to locate any remains of a Roman road, although the ground was heavily disturbed by services. Immediately north-east of the Foss crossing the road was not located in excavations by FAS in 2004 at Heworth Croft on Heworth Green (Gustavsen 2004). A ditch found here was aligned north-east/south-west, but would not have respected the line of a Roman road followed by Heworth Green. It was, moreover, quite a shallow ditch (c.400mm deep) and unlikely to have been for roadside drainage.

Subsequent to the publication of *Eburacum* it was established that another Roman road approached the fortress from the north-east (p.91, *AY* 6/1). It was found at various locations south of the Foss off Huntington Road, Park Grove and Grove Terrace Lane. It is likely that this road also originated in Malton. On approaching York it might have adopted the straight line now followed by Malton Road and then, from the point where Malton Road turns south at its junction with Muncastergate headed across what is now Heworth golf course to a crossing over the River Foss. The possibility of this being an accurate projection was, perhaps, increased by the discovery in 2002 of two Roman camps on Huntington South Moor, Monk's Cross (Fig.54, 4) which lie only 350m north-west of Malton Road (Johnson 2005). Both camps had a principal axis on a similar alignment to the Malton Road and its proposed Roman forebear, i.e. north-east/south-west. It is now proposed to refer to the RCHME road, on the line of Stockton Lane, as Road 4A, and the road projected to run on the line of the Malton Road as Road 4B. In Fig.54, Roads 3 and 4A are shown meeting the road from Malton at a crossing of the Foss, although this must remain conjectural.

A final point on roads concerns the cobbled surfaces found at County Hospital, Monkgate. One possibility is that they formed a yard, perhaps for an adjacent building. Alternatively they may represent a minor road, perhaps giving access to a cemetery zone. Such a road would probably have had a north-west/south-east alignment and so would, perhaps, have joined the Roman road from the north-east (Road 4B) at right angles c.140m to the north-west of the site.

Land use in the late 1st–mid-3rd centuries

There were no certain structural remains on the sites in Zone 2 described above and they produced little in the way of building materials. This zone appears, therefore, to have been outside the settled area between the fortress and the Rivers Foss and Ouse (see Zone 3 below), although buildings may have existed along the main approach road from the north-east and close to the fortress defences.

An important aspect of the archaeology of Zone 2 described above is the ditches dug for land division and also perhaps for drainage. Dating evidence from their infilling and limited evidence for recutting suggests that these ditches were in use for quite a short period in the mid-2nd–early 3rd centuries. Only 2 St Maurice's Road produced ditches which appear to have been in use in the late Roman period.

The most complex pattern of ditches, along with other cut features, was found at County Hospital, Foss Bank. As noted, it was difficult to establish a coherent sequence encompassing all of them. The earliest were probably some of those in Group 1 including curving gullies 0104 in Area B north and 0063 in Area B south. Unfortunately insufficient survived to determine whether they were the eavesdrip gullies for small roundhouses, although this remains a possibility.

Other early features probably include the two roughly parallel curving ditches (1005 and 1033/1036/1040) on a north-west/south-east alignment in Area A which contained a small amount of early Roman pottery. It seems unlikely that the southern ditch can have existed at the same time as grave 0017 which appears to be a component of a group of features taking their alignment from the ditches in Group 2 in Area B.

Although some of the features on the Foss Bank site were probably earlier, the principal episode of activity was represented by ditches of the second half of the 2nd century, aligned north-east/south-west or north-west/south-east, apparently conforming to the alignment of the principal axes of the fortress and, perhaps, of the road (4B) from the north-east. A complex picture of cutting and recutting was recorded, especially in Area B where there was a major north-east/south-west ditch (0134/0055). Its line may have dictated those of the other, smaller, ditches in the area. Presumably they were not all in existence at the same time, although the only clear relationship among these 'secondary' ditches is that 0132 running north-east/south-west was cut by 0115 running north-west/south-east. The ditches in Area B at Foss Bank were probably silting up in the late 2nd century to judge by samian evidence, notably the stamped bases in the fill of ditch 0156 and ditch 0125 to north-west of 0156, and probably did not survive beyond the early 3rd century. After the infilling of the ditches any further activity on the site left little trace except for the burials of the 3rd century (see below).

What may be interpreted as part of the same system of land division as that at Foss Bank was found at 40–48 Monkgate and also at 52 Monkgate by MAP (1995) at each of which there was a ditch on a north-west/south-east alignment. At the former it was replaced a ditch on a north-east/south-west line. Elsewhere in Zone 2 at Peasholme Green a probable ditch, on a north-west/south-east line and again containing late 2nd- to early 3rd-century pottery was recorded in Trench F1.

This ditch in F1 was succeeded by remains of activity of a different character, although difficult to understand from such a small-scale excavation. After being infilled, the ditch was overlain by a cobbled surface which seems to have had only a brief existence before itself being overlain by a deposit of organic clayey silt, probably deposited in the early 3rd century. This was overlain in turn by deposits containing probable kiln waste which must derive from pottery and tile kilns thought to have been sited north-west of the present day street Peasholme Green, but east of the fortress. In view of the direction of the prevailing wind from the south-west this would be an entirely appropriate location for activity involving fire and noxious fumes. The most recent reviews of the evidence for kilns are by Monaghan (*AY* 16/8, 869–70) and by Swan and McBride (2002) who studied the pottery from the Peasholme Green site and the more substantial body of material excavated by MAP in a trench in Peasholme Green itself. Swan and McBride (2002, 193) identified three episodes of deposition reflecting peaks in production in the late 1st/ early 2nd century; the late 130s–140s (Hadrianic– early Antonine) and finally in the early 3rd century (Severan). It appears to be material from this last episode which was recorded in Trench F1.

Burials

The two County Hospital sites produced eight Roman inhumation burials (Table 2) to add to those previously recorded from the area noted above (p.161). In addition, a little disarticulated human bone was found in Trench F1 at Peasholme Green. Although dating and stratigraphic evidence is equivocal, the burials are likely to be early–mid-3rd century. There is as yet no evidence, however, for a major cemetery north-east of the fortress; rather it appears that there were scattered burials in small groups on vacant plots of land.

Further discussion of Roman burial practice will appear in *AY* 5, but a number of points related to the organisation of land for burials may be made here. At County Hospital, Foss Bank the five graves were aligned either north-east/south-west (3) or north-west/south-east (2) with heads to the north-east or north-west. In other words they were aligned on the earlier ditch system (and main fortress axes). Moreover graves 0113 and 0059 were both cut into the tops of ditches. This is a common phenomenon in the Roman period when ditches perhaps symbolised the liminal zone between life and death, although, alternatively, ditch fills may have attracted burials because they were easy to dig into.

Of particular interest as far as spatial organisation of burial is concerned is what appears to be a deliberately created plot at least 14m long (north-west/south-east) in Area A south. It consisted of a gully (1013), to which grave 0017 and pit 1015 to the north-west of the grave lay parallel (Fig.96). Grave 1001 lay at 90° to 0017 and 1013, opposite the south-east end of the latter. It may also be noted that, measured centre to centre, grave 0017 was 5.25m north-east of gully 1013. This converts almost exactly to 17.5 Roman feet (*pes monetalis* = 0.296m), a unit of measurement which occurs in many contexts, often doubled as 35 feet, in the layout of the Roman fortress (*AY* 3/3, 204).

In addition to the burials at County Hospital, Foss Bank, there are other features which may be contemporary with them (in Groups 1 and 3). Following the infilling of the main north-east/south-west ditch (0055) it was cut by two oval pits (0053 and 0074) on a north-west/south-east alignment, which are probably Roman. Another oval pit (0021) on the same alignment may well be contemporary. No indication of the function of these pits was gained from their infilling, but it is possible that they were empty grave pits similar to other examples at 35–41 Blossom Street (pp.291–308) in which the bones have deteriorated away to nothing or been removed subsequent to interment. In addition, pit 0085, which lies largely beyond the north-west trench edge and was cut into ditch 0055, may have been an unexcavated grave.

At County Hospital, Monkgate, two graves and a presumed third were aligned north-west/south-east and were found in a line, but because of later disturbance it is not clear if they were part of a larger cemetery. In any event the burials were probably dug to respect the ditch to the south-west (0311) which may have represented a cemetery boundary.

Table 2 Summary of Roman burials at the County Hospital sites

Site	No.	Alignment	Age	Sex	Remarks
Foss Bank A south	0017	NW–SE	Adult	—	
Foss Bank A south	1001	NE–SW	Infant	—	Lead coffin, 2 pots
Foss Bank B north	0113	NE–SW	13–15	f	Prone, in top of ditch
Foss Bank B north	0162	NW–SE	Adult	—	Coffin nails
Foss Bank B south	0059	NE–SW	13–15	f	In top of ditch
Monkgate	0394	NW–SE	—	—	
Monkgate	0250	NW–SE	—	—	Incomplete
Monkgate	0309	—	—	—	Skull only

Land use and settlement in the late Roman period

The only Zone 2 site to produce evidence for occupation or activity in the later 3rd–4th centuries was 2 St Maurice's Road where ditches in Trenches 1 and 2 may represent a late Roman development of the system of land division abandoned to the north-east. The significance of the cobbled surface in Trench 2 is not clear, but, taken together with the ditches may hint that late Roman activity in this Zone was confined to areas close to the fortress defences. Ditch 1024 appears to have had a wood lining, perhaps indicating a drainage function, and may be compared with a larger feature in which regularly spaced nails were found at Wellington Row, south-west of the Ouse, perhaps of much the same date, which was thought to carry a water supply (Ottaway 2004, 148). The County Hospital sites, 40–48 Monkgate and Peasholme Green produced little, if any, late Roman material and in the survey of pottery in *AY* 16/8 there are no sites north-east or immediately east of the fortress with material dated post-360 (Ceramic Period 4b), although the evidence of the mosaic at 21–33 Aldwark suggests 4th-century occupation here (Fig.94, 9; pp.40–2, *AY* 6/1), again close to the fortress defences.

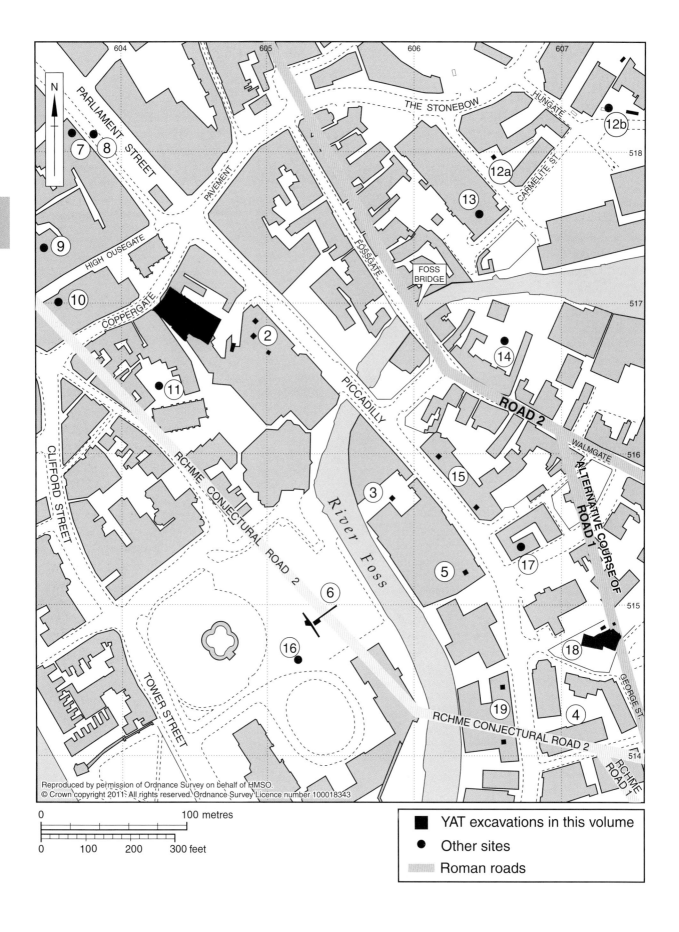

■	YAT excavations in this volume
●	Other sites
▨	Roman roads

Zone 3: South-east of the fortress and east of the Foss (within the medieval walls)

Introduction *(Figs 54, 128)*

Zone 3 encompasses an area south-east of the Roman fortress on both sides of the River Foss, including that part of the city enclosed by the Walmgate section of the medieval city walls (Fig.54). This is an area of great archaeological importance in which it has been shown that near the Foss and Ouse, in particular, there is a considerable depth of deposits, often well preserved by waterlogging. On the west side of the Foss this zone includes the large site at 16–22 Coppergate as well as smaller-scale sites at 22 Piccadilly and the Castle Car Park. On the east side of the Foss the zone includes a number of evaluation sites on Piccadilly.

All the sites in this zone reveal aspects of topographical development which have been influenced to a greater or lesser extent by the River Foss, and they have, in turn, shed light on the history of the river in the Roman period. This is a subject about which very little has hitherto been known, partly because of a lack of archaeological investigations and partly because great changes wrought in the river regime at various times in the past have rendered the Roman topography of the area impossible to determine in any detail from the modern layout. These changes include the damming of the Foss at Castle Mills in the late 11th century to create the King's Fish Pool. In addition, since the late 18th century the river has been canalised within artificial banks as it passes through the city to its junction with the Ouse at Blue Bridge. The only archaeological excavation,

hitherto, which has produced evidence for the Foss bank in Roman times took place at Garden Place, on the south side of Stonebow in 1950 (Fig.128, 13; Fig.160; Richardson 1959; RCHMY **1**, 64) a little to the north-east of Foss Bridge and c.90m north of the present day river.

The excavator of Garden Place suggested that a Roman wharf existed on the site which implied that the river ran north-east from Foss Bridge before curving away to the east, rather than curving directly to the east from the bridge as is the case today. Found adjacent to the north-west side of the proposed river course and aligned north-east/south-west, was a double row of timber piles, originally linked by horizontal timbers on its south-east side. North-west of the piles was a cobbled surface, also running north-east/south-west, and at its south-west end there was a small, but substantial, structure built of gritstone blocks up to 1.2m (five courses) high. Its longer axis was aligned approximately north-east/south-west and, although the north-east wall did not survive, the structure appeared to have measured c.7 x 4.57m and the walls were 1.5m thick. North-east of it was an area of large gritstone blocks, thought to be wharf-side paving. The function of the stone structure is unknown, but the RCHME suggested it was the base for a crane (for further discussion see below). Blocks of stone seen in trenches sunk by contractors to the south-west of the building suggested the presence of other structures in the vicinity.

Fig. 128 (facing page)   Zone 3: location of sites described in this fascicule (1–6) and other sites (7–19)

As far as Roman roads in Zone 3 are concerned, it was thought by RCHME that a road approaching from the east (RCHMY **1**, 1; Road 2) ran to a crossing over the River Foss from a junction with another approaching from the south-east (*ibid.*, Road 1) located at a point, east of the river, close to what is now George Street. From the river crossing it was proposed that the road headed north-westwards through what is now the castle precinct to a point where a road was recorded in 1959 at the junction of Spurriergate and High Ousegate (*ibid.*, 59). An apparent continuation to the north-west of this road, running along the north-east bank of the Ouse, was found in Area 2 at 39–41 Coney Street (p.14, *AY* 6/1).

It now seems clear that the layout of roads east of the Foss needs revision (see discussion below and discussion of Zone 4). In any event RCHME was unable to suggest a line by which roads from the east and south-east would have approached the south-east gate (*porta principalis sinistra*) of the fortress, although a continuation of Road 1 as seen at the Fulford golf course, c.3km to the south-east (Fig.54, 20), was more or less aligned on the gate.

The settlement in the area between the fortress and the Rivers Ouse and the Foss was, as noted above, thought by RCHME (RCHMY **1**, xxxiv–xxxv) to have originally been under military supervision (*canabae*). However, an inscribed tablet found in Nessgate bearing a dedication to Hercules (RIB 648; RCHMY **1**, 119) by two persons, apparently civilians and part of a corporate group of priests or magistrates, implies that at some stage the settlement acquired its autonomy. Other discoveries in the area imply buildings of urban character. Adjacent to the road at the junction of Spurriergate and High Ousegate, a group of structures was recorded in 1959, at least one of which was probably part of a bath house (*ibid.*, 59–61). Further limited excavation on the site by MAP in 2004, adjacent to Building ii of 1959, revealed a sequence beginning with deep pit of late 1st-century date succeeded by timber piles probably to support a structure represented by two phases of foundation trench (MAP 2005a). A little to the north-east two small observation trenches at 8 High Ousegate revealed a substantial wall of gritstone blocks running north-north-east/south-south-west alongside a cobbled surface, and a wall of limestone blocks (Fig.128, 9; pp.21–4, *AY*

6/1). At 11–13 Parliament Street walls on a north-east/south-west alignment were found, along with an altar dedicated to the *Genius Loci* (Fig.128, 7; pp.25–8, *AY* 6/1). A further stone wall aligned north-east/south-west was seen in a sewer trench in Parliament Street and a little to the south-east of it was a second wall on an east–west alignment (Fig.128, 8; pp.29–31, *AY* 6/1). Two ditches aligned north–south were also thought to be Roman.

RCHME records a number of other discoveries in the High Ousegate/Nessgate area (RCHMY **1**, 59) including a tablet from the former Midland Bank at the corner of High Ousegate and Nessgate bearing a dedication to the imperial *numen* and a goddess whose name begins IOV... (RIB 656; RCHMY **1**, 59, 119), along with walls and architectural fragments. Walls on a north-west/south-east alignment, two Ionic column capitals and two bases, possibly derived from the façade of a public building, were found at 25–27 High Ousegate in 1902–03 (Fig.128, 10; *ibid.*, 59). A mosaic pavement was found in 1871 immediately to the north of St Mary Castlegate (Fig.128, 11).

East of the Foss, south-east of Foss Bridge, a well dug in 1829 in the yard of what was then the Malt Shovel Inn (Fig.128, 14) located a timber and stone structure at a depth of c.9m which was interpreted by RCHME as a jetty (RCHMY **1**, 64–5). In 1938 in advance of the construction of the labour exchange, now the office of the Inland Revenue, in Piccadilly, two rows of rough stone columns c.1m (3 feet) high and 0.30–0.45m (1ft–1ft 6in) square were found (Fig.128, 17). Unfortunately no further information, for example, on the number of stones or on the depth at which they were found, is readily available. They were interpreted by RCHME (*ibid.*, 65) as part of a wharf, but it is clear from recent discoveries that this is unlikely. Finally, five pits containing late 1st- to 2nd-century pottery were found in 1973 at Leadmill Lane (Fig.161, 7; p.78, *AY* 6/1).

Roman burials in Zone 3 include two in coffins (one lead and one stone) found on Walmgate (RCHMY **1**, 70). In Castle Yard evidence was found for a late Roman cemetery in 1835 and again in 1956 (Fig.128, 16; Ramm 1958; RCHMY **1**, 67–8). Burials included three in stone sarcophagi, two of which were inscribed, one in a lead coffin and two more in wooden coffins.

16–22 Coppergate

by R.A. Hall, D.T. Evans and Patrick Ottaway

Introduction

In 1976–81 York Archaeological Trust carried out archaeological excavations, directed by R.A. Hall, at 16–22 Coppergate (SE60465168; Fig.128,1). In view of the paucity of information about the Roman settlement south-east of the fortress, as summarised above, the opportunity to excavate a large area of 1000m², c.160m from the fortress, was an important one. The broad academic research objectives underpinning the Coppergate excavation campaign included the discovery, firstly, of Roman activity and occupation, and, secondly, of whether and how this had influenced subsequent development of the area. These objectives required that at least part of the site be excavated down to the underlying natural (Fig.129). In the event, the excavations revealed that the Roman remains lay beneath a complex stratified sequence of the Anglo-Scandinavian and medieval periods (*AY* 8/4; *AY* 10/6).

A combination of practical, logistical, financial and operational considerations determined that the project objectives were initially met in 1980 through the examination of a discrete strip 7.5m wide across the modern street frontage. Coppergate today climbs perceptibly here from north-east to south-west to the crest of the natural interfluvial ridge utilised by the streets Nessgate and Castlegate. The gradient of the natural deposits, as revealed across the frontage of the excavation, was approximately 1 in 20. As this area had been sealed by a succession of buildings from c.900 onwards, it was less disturbed by medieval pit digging than were the medieval backyard areas. It transpired that a stratified sequence of Roman deposits up to 0.60m thick survived within this area, although later cut features had destroyed, seriously damaged or truncated elements in the Roman layout.

An extension to the period available for excavation allowed an area, 37 x 12m, at right angles to the modern street frontage on the south-western side of the site, to be completely excavated in 1981. As part of this exercise, and in order to test for the continuation of some linear features seen in the main part of the site, excavation was also taken down to

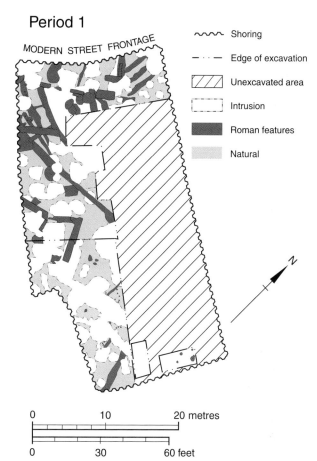

Period 1

MODERN STREET FRONTAGE

- ~~~~ Shoring
- — · — Edge of excavation
- ▨ Unexcavated area
- ⬚ Intrusion
- ▰ Roman features
- ▒ Natural

Fig. 129   *16–22 Coppergate: Plan showing extent of area excavated to Roman and natural deposits*

natural deposits in two small trenches immediately adjacent to the north-east (Fig.134, A and B). In the area on the south-western side of the site there was very little stratigraphy which could be attributed to the Roman period with any confidence. Here the Roman archaeology existed mainly as features cut into the natural and any Roman deposits above natural were, on average, only some 0.20–0.25m thick. In addition, the area was more heavily disturbed by later intrusions than that on the street frontage. The character of the Roman archaeology in the area on the south-western side of the site has made it difficult to link securely the structures and strata there with the more comprehensible stratification which survived across the street frontage, and most completely in the western corner.

Because of the nature of the stratification there were considerable difficulties in preparing a detailed interpretation of the Roman archaeology. Cut features of later date have severely depleted some Roman features, and split the surviving

199

stratification up into numerous isolated stratigraphic groups. It was usually not possible to link these together into a convincing site-wide phasing; often there is uncertainty about whether or not a particular group of structural elements should be combined within one phase or separated into several.

A study of the pottery by Jason Monaghan (*AY* 16/8, 1077–85) has shown the very mixed nature of the assemblages from this site, a characteristic attributed to frequent episodes of stratigraphic disturbance. Nevertheless, the Roman pottery recovered in post-Roman levels was consistent with that recovered in Roman levels; there is no evidence within the residual pottery for periods which are not represented among the *in situ* Roman strata (*ibid.*, 1081).

In 1982 during construction for the Coppergate Centre a watching brief, supervised by Nick Pearson, was held over the removal of archaeological deposits not excavated in the main programme of work. This produced a limited amount of information for the Roman period, although it was much more productive for later periods.

What follows is a narrative of the excavated sequence based on a draft by R.A. Hall and D. T. Evans; a much more detailed account by D. T. Evans is available in the YAT archive. Some re-evaluation of that archive has also taken place during the preparation of the narrative to take full account of the work by Jason Monaghan on pottery and the coin dates provided by Richard Brickstock. It has not been deemed appropriate to describe every excavated context, of which there are over 1000. The emphasis has been placed on describing the main phases of topographical development and principal

features within them. The phases are all subsumed under the heading of Period 1 in the overall sequence of activity on the site.

The narrative proceeds on a phase-by-phase basis with the archaeology of the north-western (street frontage) part of the site (where present) preceding that of the south-eastern. Dating evidence for individual contexts is only referred to where it has a direct bearing on interpretation.

The discoveries made during the Coppergate excavation were the direct result of York City Council's far-sighted decision to facilitate archaeological investigation on this site well in advance of proposed redevelopment. In the final stages of the excavation the site's development contractors, Wimpey Property Holdings Ltd and their construction arm Wimpey Construction Ltd, were also extremely sympathetic to archaeological requirements, and continued this policy throughout the archaeological watching brief which accompanied construction work.

The excavation was funded in part from the rescue archaeology budget of the Inspectorate of Ancient Monuments at the Department of the Environment, where successive Inspectors and their superiors responded sympathetically to the project's requirements. Additional funds and resources were donated privately by interested individuals, trust funds and companies, with particularly notable contributions from The British Academy, the Tjaereborg Foundation, Rowntree Macintosh Ltd and C.I. Skipper Esq.

The Coppergate excavation was directed by Dr R.A. Hall and supervised by D.T. Evans (1976–81), I.G. Lawton (1978–81). S.A. Power (1976–8), and

Phase	Archaeology	Date
1	Natural deposits	
2	Features cut into natural and deposits above	Late 1st / early 2nd century
3a	Stone walls and cut features in south-west part of site	Mid-3rd century
3b	Cut features and building-related deposits	Late 3rd–early 4th century
4	Graves and associated features	Mid-4th century
5	Deposits and minor features	?Late 4th century

200

M. Humphreys (1976–8). Excavation was undertaken by many hundreds of student volunteers, by members of York Excavation Group, by staff employed on a succession of job creation schemes, and by small groups of inmates from Her Majesty's Prisons at Thorpe Arch and Askham Grange. A solid core of experience was provided by the team of permanent excavation assistants, among whom John Clark, Sue Duffy, Nick Hindhaugh, Derek Hurst, Lawrence Manley, Liz Neville, Margaret Nieke, Jeff Peters, Nick Price, Julian Richards, Beverley Shaw, Dave Start, Sue Stockwell and Sue Winterbottom made lengthy and dedicated contributions. Site photography was undertaken by Mike Duffy. Post-excavation assistance was provided by Anne Finney and Olwen Beazley. Katie Jones, Kurt Hunter-Mann and Heather Dawson have also made diverse contributions.

The finds and site records are currently stored with York Archaeological Trust under the Trust and Yorkshire Museum accession code 1976–81.7. For the watching brief the relevant code is 1982.22.

The excavation

Throughout the excavated area the natural was a clean, firm, yellowish-brown to brown clay. It sloped down from west to east, from the Nessgate ridge towards the course of the River Foss. At the north-western part of the site natural was encountered at c.9.70m OD whereas in the lowest point, at the south-eastern side, it was at c.6m OD, a drop of nearly 4m in 43m over the length of the site or a gradient of approximately 1 in 11.

Phase 1: south-east

Overlying natural clay in the south-eastern part of the site was a deposit (28858) with a varied description, but typically it was a brown sandy silt and may be weathered natural washed down from the upper part of the slope.

Phase 2: south-east (Fig.130)

In the south-eastern part of the site a number of features, largely shallow post- or stake-holes, in four discrete groups separated by later intrusions were found cutting natural. They include a slot (28824), aligned more or less north–south, traced

over 2.60m, which was 0.25m wide and 0.18m deep. The fill was 28798, a brown very slightly clayey sandy silt. A stake-hole (28826) was set into the base and another (28825) lay immediately to the west. Further to the west of 28824 were small cut features 27253, 27333 and 27379. To the south-east of 28824 were stake-holes 28827–34. South-east of this group was another made up of 28433–5 and 28441. Further south-east were 28614/16/18/20/22/24/26. A post-hole to the south of and in line with 28824 was 28823. All these features may represent the presence of timber structures or fences.

Overlying these features and natural was a group of deposits (19775–6, 19792–3, 26174/7, 26737, 28196, 28442, 28613, 28739, 28748, 28858, 32017, 32869). None of them was extensive, but all but 26737, a brown clay, were either silt or silty clay. Only two produced pottery: 28748 (late 1st–2nd century) and 28739 (2nd century).

Glass-working

An activity that took place near the site, probably during the early 3rd century, was glass-working. The evidence is discussed in detail by Cool *et al.* (1999), but, in summary, it was represented in the archaeological record at Coppergate by, firstly, c.3kg of the sherds of pottery vessels that had been used as receptacles to melt glass; secondly, some blocks of what appeared to be semi-reacted batch materials, suggesting that glass was being made from raw ingredients; and, thirdly, a small quantity of glass fragments of the sort usually associated with glass-blowing. As in the case of a large proportion of the Roman pottery from the site, much of this material was found residually in contexts of the Anglo-Scandinavian era, particularly the period c.850–900, but some came from contexts of Roman date, dated after c.280. The pots themselves are, however, overwhelmingly of Ebor ware, a local type of c.71–250, which had one of its principal production areas some 500m to the north-east of Coppergate (*AY* 16/8, 869–70). Typologically, the pottery suggests that the glass-melting pots were gathered together c.200. Colourless and green soda glass was melted in these pots, and the evidence hints at an episode of glass-melting on a relatively large scale. A small glass-blowing assemblage may represent a separate episode of activity, and it is suggested that the glass-melting was for making window panes. It

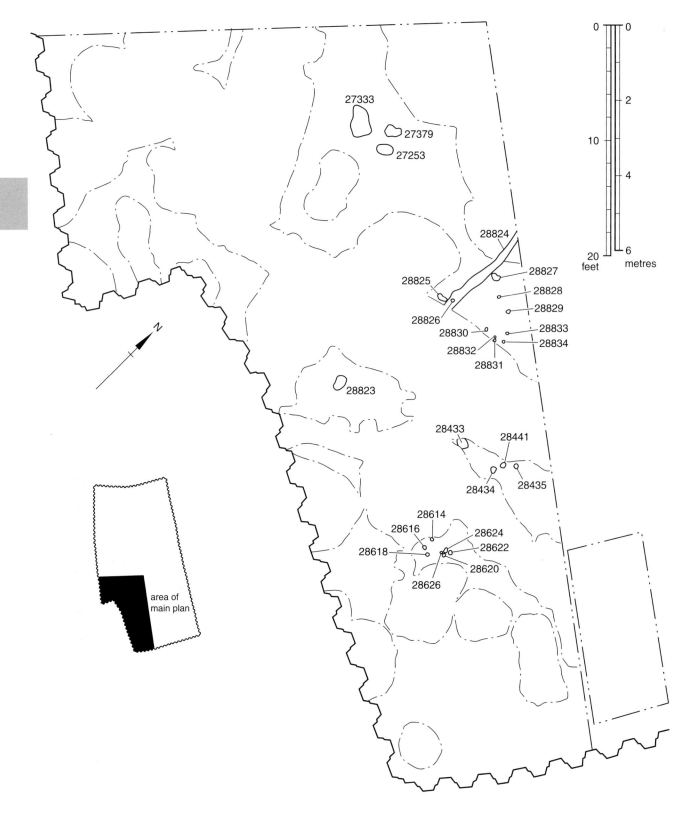

Fig. 130 *16–22 Coppergate: Phase 2, plan of south-eastern part of site showing features cutting natural*

is surmised by Cool *et al.* that glass was made in a military context, perhaps, at the time of the visit of Septimius Severus (208–11), during the presence in York of North African legionary soldiers who are likely to have been familiar with the techniques of glass-making from raw materials.

Phase 3a: north-west *(Figs 131, 134, 147–48)*

Early ditches

Amongst the earliest features cut into natural were fragments of two possible ditches (37033 and 37049) on a roughly north-east/south-west alignment; they were separated by later pit cuts, but may have been the same feature. The north-eastern limit of ditch 37033 is unknown as it lay in an area that was not excavated down to Roman levels. The feature was c.1.40m wide and up to 0.57m deep, and it was filled with a brown clay (37034) below a very dark grey peaty silt (37022). Some 3.6m to the south-west of 37033 were the remains of 37049, very much cut about by later intrusions, which was c.1m wide and 0.40m deep. It was backfilled with 37044, dark grey clay, below 37045, a very dark grey silty clay.

Ditch 36493

North of the two ditch fragments, and cutting 37033, was a ditch (36493), aligned approximately east–west which was recorded in a c.9m length close to the south-western edge of the site. It was c.1m wide and 0.7m deep, and had steeply sloping sides. There were three fill layers: 36538, clean pinkish-grey clay, lay below 36516, black silt with charcoal

Fig.131 *16–22 Coppergate: view south-west (street frontage to the right) of features cutting natural along the street frontage. Trench 31754 (Phase 3b) runs right to left in top left corner with ditch 31954 (Phase 3b) beyond (scale 2m)*

203

and patches of brown clay which in turn was below 36491, dark grey sandy clay with patches of brown sandy clay. The line of 36493 was continued to the east by two other lengths of ditch: 36521 and 37091. 36521 had seven fill layers, all variants on grey-brown silty clay or sandy silt (36520, 36551–6). Ditch 37091 had had six fill layers of grey or brown clay or silty clay (32716–8, 37029, 37036–7). This ditch was probably a boundary and/or drainage feature subdividing the immediate area.

Whereas the latest pottery associated with 36493 was dated to the mid-2nd century, that from several of the layers in 37091 included 3rd- and a few possible 4th-century sherds. This is despite the fact that the feature seemed to be cut at the same stratigraphic horizon all along its recorded length. The correct interpretation of these data remains uncertain; it is not clear whether 36493, 36521 and 37091 are the same feature which is to be dated by the finds in 37091, or whether 36493 is an early feature and 37091 was coincidentally established on a continuation of its line. Alternatively, 37091 may represent a neat and imperceptible recutting of an earlier feature along just a part of its original length.

A brief continuation of 36493 to the west of the later pit 36506 was numbered 31863, of which only a1m length was traced up to the limit of excavation. The feature was at least 0.46m deep and the fill was 31862, a very dark grey sticky clay, with pale brown sand, and a few patches of brown clay, and occasional charcoal flecks. North-west of 31863 was a post-hole (31871), 0.39m deep, which partly lay beyond the trench edge.

North-west of ditch 36493

In the western corner of the site was 34019, a small slot aligned approximately north-west/south-east of which the full extent had been removed by later features. It was up to c.0.34m wide, 0.2m deep and the sides sloped very steeply. The backfill was 31993, dark brown sand with patches of pale brown sand and dark brown silty sand. Cut into the south-east end of 34019, and cut by a later pit, was a small scoop, (34018) which was c.0.15m deep. It was filled with 34017, dark brown silty sand with patches of dark yellowish-brown clay, white sand and yellowish-brown sand.

South-east of 34018–19 and in a narrow strip of natural clay, c.1.20m wide, were cut a group of some 29 post- or stake-holes (34058, 34069–76, 34095–7/9, 34101/3/5/7/9, 34111/3/5/7/9, 34121–2/7/9, 34145/7). The vast majority of these features were no more than 0.10m in diameter and 0.12m deep with the exception of 34058 at the north-west end which was 0.32m in diameter and c.0.20m deep. At the south-east end was a post-hole (36440), roughly rectangular in plan, which measured 0.34m by 0.21m, but the depth was not recorded. The fill was 36439, very dark greyish-brown clayey sand with patches of very pale brown sand. It is possible that 34058 and 36440 represent fence posts with the stake-holes representing wattles between them. The only artefactual material from these features was Flavian samian ware from 34058, and a coin of AD 258–68 (sf12640) from 34100, the fill of 34101. This latter is taken to date the features, although it is possible that they represent several distinct episodes of activity. In any event, it is not possible to interpret their function.

South-east of post-hole 36440 was a cut of unknown function (36477) which had been almost totally destroyed by later features, although the short length of its south-western edge that survived may have belonged to a linear feature more than c.0.50m wide.

At the south-western edge of the site, and cut into natural clay, was the truncated fragment of an irregular feature (31864) which was only 0.20m deep, and varied in width from 0.5m to 0.9m. Insofar as its alignment could be recognised within the short surviving length, it was approximately north-east/south-west. The fill was 31858, very dark grey clay with much pale brown sand and frequent charcoal. Above it was a deposit of clay cut by 31800 and 31863 (see below).

Near to and continuing beyond the south-western trench edge (and cutting through ditch 36493 and feature 31864) was a large pit (36506) at least 3.20m across and 1.50m deep. The earliest fill layer was 36505, a clean, dark brown clay with lenses of dark grey silty clay, succeeded by 36485, a very dark grey slightly sticky clay with frequent small pieces of limestone and sandstone, in turn below 36483, light brown clay with occasional limestone and sandstone pieces.

Slot 31800

Stratigraphically later than the features described above was a slot (31800), aligned almost exactly east–west. It was c.0.46m wide and c.0.38m deep and was traced over a total length of 6.9m, but its eastern and western ends were cut away by later pits. It had steeply sloping sides and a flat base. There was evidence in the form of a soil change, seen only in section, for the original presence of a timber or timbers set in this slot. The soil change had a steep-sided profile some 0.35m deep and 0.21m wide; its clayey fill was barely distinguishable from the remaining backfill in the feature, largely dark grey clay or silty clay (31794/7–8, 31801–3, 36427). A slot numbered 36509 appeared to be a recut of 31800. It was c.0.40m wide with a flattened U-shaped profile. The fill of 36509 was 36504, very dark grey sandy clay with small patches of brown sandy clay.

Deposits

Sealing many of the features described above were thin deposits largely of clayey material which may, in part, be the result of natural accumulation and, in part, of refuse disposal. Details can be found in the archive under Phase 2.

Phase 3a: south-east

Building with stone walls *(Figs 132–38)*

Following the features in Phase 2 came the construction of a building represented by short lengths of stone wall and trenches for robbed walls. Almost all internal deposits had been destroyed by later intrusions.

Description of the building may begin with wall 28944, aligned east-north-east/west-south-west, which continued beyond the south-western limit of the excavation. The foundations were of limestone rubble set in dark brown clay (32938/9, 32801). Above them was a plinth, 0.94m wide, of mortared, roughly squared limestone blocks and above the plinth the wall stood one course high and had a mortared rubble core faced with roughly squared limestone blocks.

At the east end of 28944 another piece of stone wall (28945) returned to the south, but only a very short length of c.1m was recorded due to severe truncation by later pits. This had left only a few disturbed limestone blocks and the foundations of cobbles in clean brown sticky clays (32810). About 1m south of 28945 was a badly disturbed area of limestone set in mortar (32819) overlying a mass of cobbles, possibly representing a very fragmentary continuation of wall 28945.

At its east end wall 28944 appears to have been butted by or, more likely, cut by a wall (28946) at a slight angle. It is suggested that this was later than walls 28944 and 28412 (see below) and had probably been constructed after they had been demolished. It has therefore been assigned to Phase 4 (see below).

South-east of 28944, and probably representing a return at roughly 90°, was wall 28412, although the junction between them had been interrupted by wall 28946 and a short length of robbing trench (37133=37149) of probable post-Roman date. Wall 28412 survived over a length of c.3.1m. The foundations, in a construction trench (37013) c.1.3m wide and 0.9m deep, were of limestone rubble in pale brown mortar (32902 and 37028). The construction trench was backfilled with a number of layers of limestone rubble in dark grey clay (28413/4/7, 32900, 37015/6, 37025). Above the foundations the wall was 0.85m wide, survived to a maximum of two courses high (c.0.18m) and consisted of a mortared limestone rubble core faced with squared limestone blocks up to c.0.3m long. The mortar bonding (37014) was pinkish-white in places and yellowish-brown/red (37020) elsewhere.

At its south end wall 28412 was truncated by a complex of post-Roman pits, but there was no sign of the wall continuing beyond them. However, adjacent to and west of the south end of the wall there was a post-hole (32833), thought to be Roman and immediately north-west a short length of robber trench (37267) of probable post-Roman date. It appeared to be aligned north-east/south-west, 0.95m wide and c.0.5m deep, and had removed a wall in its entirety apart from its lower foundations. These survived as an isolated mass of mortared limestone above layers of cobbles in clay (32799)

Fig. 132 *16–22 Coppergate: view north-west of Roman stone walls 28412 (top), 28944 (lower left) and 28946 (upper left). Scales 2m*

Fig. 133 *16–22 Coppergate: view south of elevation of wall 28944 (scale 0.20m)*

Fig. 135 *16–22 Coppergate: wall 28944 seen from above (north at top) and stub of walling 28945 (right). Scale 0.50m*

which had been cut on all sides by later intrusions and so it was not possible to be certain of its precise relationship with wall 28412.

During the watching brief in 1982 another short length of wall (1982.22, 1331) was observed just outside the limit of the main excavation. It was approximately on the alignment of the robber trench 37267, and it was similar in character to the other walls described above. The wall was a maximum of 1.9m long, and was 0.8m wide; its height was not recorded. Its north-eastern end was irregular, presumably as a result of being truncated by later features, but its south-western end was neatly finished. Beyond the south-west end there was another length of wall running approximately north-westwards at right angles to wall 1331. Only the limestone rubble blocks forming the inner face of this latter wall were recorded, and then only for a length of approximately 1.6m. Nonetheless, it seemed to represent the fourth wall (the others represented by 28944–5 and 1982.22, 1331) of a room measuring c.4.5m north–south by about 5.0–5.5m east–west.

Additional robbing trenches

The building described above extended towards the south-eastern end of the site, its walls defined by robbing trenches. More or less on the same align-

Fig. 136 *16–22 Coppergate: view from above of wall 28412 (north top right corner). Scale 0.50m*

207

Fig. 137 *16–22 Coppergate: section through wall 28412 (view north-west). Scale 0.50m*

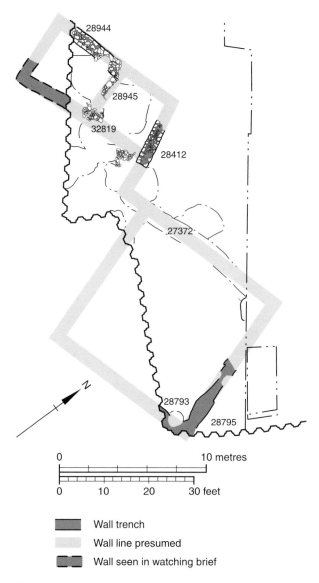

28944

28945

32819

28412

27372

N

28793

28795

0   10 metres

0   10   20   30 feet

▆▆▆ Wall trench

▆▆▆ Wall line presumed

▆▆▆ Wall seen in watching brief

Fig. 138 *16–22 Coppergate: A simplified plan of the Roman building based on surviving Roman walls, and Roman and later robber trenches*

ment as wall 28412 was trench 28795 filled with greyish-brown silty deposits (28333, 28587, 28565). At the north end it was c.0.35m across and 0.18m deep, and near the south end it increased to a width of c.1.1m and a depth of 0.3m. In the south corner of the excavation the trench met, at right angles, part of another linear cut (28793), 0.45m deep, most of which lay beyond the limit of excavation. The fill of 28793 was 28792, grey-brown silty clay. These robbing trenches are thought to be Roman as they were succeeded by 'dark earth' deposits which elsewhere lie between Roman and post-Roman.

At c.90° to 28795 and wall 28412, and running across the site on an east-north-east/west-southwest alignment was another robber trench (27372=28039) c.1.2m wide and 0.5–0.9m deep. Its fill varied to either side of an intrusive postRoman pit (28038). To the south-west of the pit it contained fragments of limestone, micaceous sandstone roofing slabs and roof tile fragments, together with Roman pottery, but also one sherd of AngloScandinavian Torksey-type ware. To the north-east of the intrusion, building debris was absent; in

addition to 65 Roman pot sherds, there was as an amber fragment, not generally found in contexts of Roman date. This robber trench has been dated to the Anglo-Scandinavian period, although the original wall, of which no remains survived, was presumably Roman.

Figure 138 is a simplified plan of the building described above, based on surviving walls and robber trenches; for further discussion see pp.236–7 below.

Other features

Adjacent to the walls and robber trenches described above numerous cut features were identified which were probably broadly contemporary, although an exact relationship with the building could not be established. Once again these features occurred in discrete groups in areas not disturbed by later intrusions.

Near the south-eastern end of the site there was a row of post- and stake-holes on a north-north-east/south-south-west alignment, albeit not parallel to 28795, which may represent an internal partition. South of a post-Roman linear intrusion were 28193, 28262–6, 28290, 28628–9, 28631, 28650 and 28654–8, whilst north of it were 28437–40 (28439 with a post in situ: 28269), 28554 and 28556. Also perhaps representing a partition inside the building was a slot (28788) parallel to 28795, traced for 1.2m. It was 0.4m wide and 0.16–0.27m deep and was filled with 28450, brown clayey sand. Set into the base of the slot was a stake-hole, 28787.

To the west of the features just described was another group of post- and stake-holes which were located inside the building and may also have been functionally related to it: 28779–86, 28749, 26013, 26786. To the north-west was another group of features, probably exterior to, i.e. north-east of, the building including a relatively large feature, oval in plan, 27123, and smaller ones, 27250, 27335, 27370, 27375, 27393, 27430, 28857, 28859–61, 32062–4, 32066–72.

Dug alongside and parallel to wall 28412 was 28564 a feature c.3.5 x 1.2m and 0.88m deep which had six fill layers: the earliest was 32999, very dark grey clay with flecks of pinkish-grey clay, which lay below 32998, dark grey clay with flecks of pinkish-grey clay, and grey clay and flecks of limestone, in turn below 28562, dark grey slightly clayey silt, and then 28561, compact, dark grey silt, followed by 28484, a dark grey very slightly clayey silt and finally 28447, brown sticky clay.

In Trench A, north-east of the main excavation area, there was a short sequence of features which may have been related to the stone building. This began with two short lengths of slot. 19803, aligned north-north-west/south-south-east, i.e. parallel to

the robbing trench, 28795, survived to a length of 0.7m and was 0.5m wide and 0.14–0.25m deep. The fill of 19803 was 19791, brown silty ashy clay with patches of brown clay. Its line was continued to the north by another slot (19795) of which the north end had been removed by 19765 (see below), but the surviving stretch, 1.2m long, was c.0.8–1.0m wide and c.0.5m deep. The fill of 19795 was 19780, brown sandy clay with patches of light yellowish-brown clay and very small patches of yellowish-brown clay, and occasional limestone and tile fragments, then 19794, dark brown clay with a few charcoal flecks. Adjacent to the feature was a small pit 19766, at least 1.1m wide and 0.23m deep, cut by 19765, in turn cut by 19736.

Slot 19803 was cut by another (19802), aligned roughly north-west/south-east with near vertical sides, which was up to c.0.5m wide and c.0.4m deep. The fill of 19802 was 19799, dark grey silty clay with patches of brown clay. 19795 and 19802–3 were covered by a deposit (19754) which was cut by post-hole 19801.

In Exploratory Trench B there were six post-holes (19778–9, 19782, 19784, 19788 and 19790), oval or circular in plan, 0.26–0.56m across and 0.12–0.34m deep, which were probably contemporary with the features in Trench A described above.

Phase 3b: north-west *(Figs 134, 147–48)*

From this point in the sequence some of the deposits contain pottery of Ceramic Period 4a (*AY 16/8*, 866) of the very late 3rd and early 4th centuries (as well as considerable amounts of residual earlier material).

Cut features

Following the deposits and features referred to above there followed an episode in which the probable boundary represented by 36493 described above (Phase 3a, pp.203–9) appears to have been restated on a similar alignment. Pre-dating this, however was a small linear cut (31860), aligned approximately north-east/south-west. It was 0.22m wide and 0.12m deep, and was steep sided and with a flat base. The north-eastern and south-western extents had been destroyed by the later features (31754 and 31778). The fill of 31860 was a very dark greyish-brown silty clay with patches of pinkish-grey clay and occasional cobbles, tile and charcoal (31844).

Two short lengths of linear cut, near the west corner of the site were 31956 and 31990, aligned north-west/south-east. Both had been badly cut about by later features, but had a maximum depth of c.0.2m. The fill of 31956 was a dark greyish-brown silty clay with patches of light brown clay and pinkish-white silty sand and cobbles and charcoal flecks (31933). The fill of 31990 was a dark grey silty clay with patches of brown silty sandy clay and some charcoal flecks (31928).

The restatement of the boundary represented by ditch 36493, which cut both 31956 and 31990, aligned approximately north-west/south-east, was

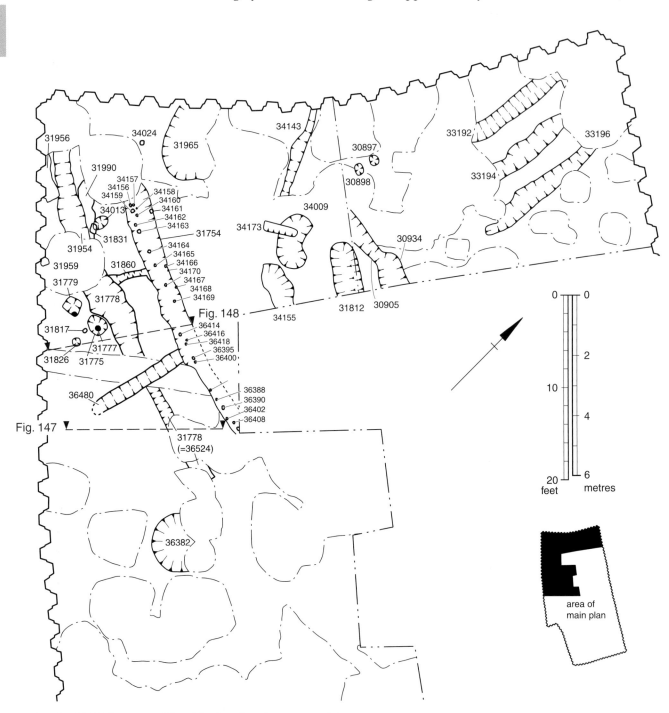

Fig. 139 *16–22 Coppergate: Phase 3b, plan of north-west part of site*

210

found either side of a later pit and numbered 31954 and 31778. As 31954 it was traced for c.3m and was c.0.52–0.88m wide, up to 0.22m deep and had a flattened U-shaped profile. The fill was 31929, a dark greyish-brown silty clay with patches of brown silty clay and brown clay. As 31778 it was traced for c.8m and was c.0.86m wide at the north-west end narrowing to c.0.4m at the south-east end, and it was up to c.0.4m deep with quite steeply sloping sides. The feature had four fill layers: at the base was 36368, dark grey slightly sticky clay with flecks of pinkish-grey clay with occasional charcoal flecks and tile fragments; above this was 31734, a mixture of dark reddish-grey sandy silty clay, very dark grey clayey silt and light reddish-brown clay with charcoal flecks. The next deposit was 31732, very dark grey sandy clay with inclusions of charcoal, mortar and small pebbles, followed by 31731, black silty clay. South-east of another intrusion the feature continued briefly as 36524, of which the fill was 36523, dark grey sandy clay with patches of brown sandy clay and charcoal flecks.

Cutting 31778 at c.90° was 36480, a trench aligned approximately north-east/south-west. It was cut at the north-east end by 31754, but the surviving portion was c.3.6m long. It had vertical sides and a flat base, and was c.0.48m wide and 0.25m deep. The fill was 36369, dark grey sticky silty clay with occasional flecks of pinkish-grey clay and occasional charcoal, limestone and tile.

Parallel to and c.2m north-east of 31954/31778 was 31754 a trench of which both ends were lost to later intrusions, but it was at least 8.40m long. It was 0.9m wide, up to 0.4m deep and had quite steeply sloping sides. The fills were generally of dark grey or black silty clay (31744–5, 31768–9) with the exception of a layer of light olive-brown decayed sandstone mixed with compact iron-pan (31795) at the base. Along the base of the trench was a series of stake-holes (34156–70), mainly subcircular or rectangular in plan, averaging c.0.1m across and 0.1m deep, although one of the largest, 34161, was 0.16m by 0.11m and 0.34m deep. These features suggest the existence of a fence with wattles set in a ground beam for which the feature had been cut. Two coins came from fill layer 31744, one of AD 273+ (sf12130) and the other of AD 271–81 (sf12129).

South-east of 31778 was a large pit (36382) which had cut 36493 (see above), but was otherwise of somewhat uncertain stratigraphic position, although thought to be Roman. It was originally circular in plan but later cut by Anglo-Scandinavian and later intrusions leaving only the southern half intact. What remained was c.2m across and 1m deep. The earliest deposit in the pit was 36563, brown sandy clay with patches of dark grey sandy clay, succeeded by 36502, very dark grey sandy silt, and then unusually for the Roman period two dark brown organic peaty fills (36488–9). The organic material might indicate an Anglo-Scandinavian date, although the fill contained only 4th-century pottery.

Other cuts in the north-west part of the site included three post-holes of varied size and shape (31959, 34013 and 34024). 31959 was roughly circular in plan, c.0.25m in diameter and 0.43m deep. 34013 was a large post-hole, oval in plan, 0.52 x 0.38m and 0.62m deep with a roughly conical profile. 34024 was subrectangular in plan (size not recorded).

South of 31754

Post-hole 31831, immediately north of 31954, was rectangular in plan, measuring 0.26m by 0.17 and 0.15m deep, with near vertical sides and a flat base. Immediately south of 31778 lay four post-holes. They included 31779, roughly square in plan with rounded corners which measured 0.59 x 0.49m and was 0.12m deep. It was filled with a black silty clay deposit and also contained the rather decayed remains of a post of roughly circular section (27482). Approximately 1m to the east was another large post-hole (31775). It was roughly oval in plan, measured 0.7 x 0.52m, and was 0.3m deep with steeply sloping sides and a flat base. It also contained a rather decayed post (31777) of circular section. Just south of 31775 was 31817, very cut about by later features. About 0.50m to the south of 31817 was 31826 (Fig.139), roughly rectangular in plan, c.0.3 x 0.25m and 0.2m deep.

Deposits sealing or stratigraphically later than these cuts included 27474 and 31716 (Fig.148), and 36315 (Fig.119) and 36306, 36383 and 36475 (Fig.147), spreads of limestone rubble and tile which may be the result of demolition.

North of 31754

North of 31754 in the centre of the street frontage strip was a small group of cut features. They included 34143, a slot 0.22–0.42m wide and up to 0.3m deep with U-shaped profile. It ran beyond the site's western edge and being aligned north-west/ south-east, was at a marked angle to the other linear cuts in this phase. It had six fill layers: the earliest was 34152, pinkish-grey sandy clay with patches of very dark grey clay, followed by 34137, very dark grey silty clay mixed with patches of brown sandy clay and light yellowish-brown ash, which in turn was followed by 34085, very pale brown ash, and then 34084, very dark grey slightly sandy clay with flecks of ash and charcoal, and then 34083, brown sandy clay with patches of dark grey, and finally 31590, a mixture of black charcoal and large patches of reddish-brown clay.

Against the north-west edge of the site was pit 31965, large and roughly pear-shaped in plan, at least 2m in length and c.0.6m deep, with sides which sloped steeply down to a flat base. It was filled with 31920, dark grey silty clay, succeeded by 31919, brown clayey sandy silt.

Pit 31812 was oval in plan though its south-east extent was beyond the edge of the excavated area. It was 0.86m across and up to 0.6m deep with a U-shaped profile. There were four fill layers of which the earliest was 31854, very dark grey sandy silty clay, succeeded by 31827, black sandy silty clay with charcoal and occasional limestone flecks, and 31814, brown clay with moderate patches of strong brown sand, and then 31813, very dark grey slightly silty sandy clay with charcoal and tile flecks and some patches of clean brown clay.

South-west of 31812 was 34155, a pit roughly oval in plan which measured c.1.6m by 0.8m and was c.0.3m deep. It was filled with 34150, very dark grey sticky clay with flecks of pinkish-grey clay and occasional charcoal, below 31988, very dark grey sticky clay with patches of pinkish-grey clay and occasional charcoal flecks.

Immediately west of 34155 was a shallow pit (34009), oval in plan. It measured 1.8 x c.1.2m and was c.0.3m deep with steeply sloping sides. It had three fill layers, the earliest being 31984, a mixture of friable, very dark grey and pinkish-grey clay with occasional charcoal flecks. This was followed by 31983, friable very dark grey silty clay with very occasional flecks of pinkish-grey clay and occasional charcoal flecks, and then by 31973, friable very dark grey silty clay with very occasional patches of pinkish-grey clay and occasional flecks of charcoal and tile. Pit 34009 was cut by a very shallow feature (34173), 70mm deep, which had been cut by grave 34089 (see below). It was 1.18m long with vertical sides. The fill of 34173 was a pinkish-grey clay with some very dark grey friable clay and occasional charcoal flecks (34172).

Gully 30905 was 0.50m wide and 0.25m deep with steeply sloping sides. The fill 30904, very dark grey sticky clay with flecks of tile, sandstone and limestone, produced a coin (sf12405) dated AD 270–73. 30905 was cut by another gully on a slightly different alignment (30934), parallel to 31812, c.0.5m wide and 0.5m deep, with steeply sloping sides and a flat base, on an approximately east–west alignment. It was filled with 30901, black clay with flecks of charcoal, tile, sandstone and limestone, and a few fragments of limestone and tile.

Finally, north-west of 30934 were post-holes 30897–8 which were roughly circular, c.0.35m across, and up to 0.3m deep with near vertical sides.

Parallel slots in the north corner *(Fig.140)*

In the north corner of the site were three parallel slots (33192, 33194, 33196) filled with grey-brown sandy clays (33193, 33195 and 33197 respectively) cut into natural clay. These features are difficult to phase and interpret. Originally they were thought to be late 1st century and to represent a timber structure (*AY* 16/8, 1077–8). This dating derived from an assemblage of Flavian pottery, but the fill of 33192 (33193) also contained a coin (sf13928) dated to AD 337, and in the absence of any reason to indicate this was intrusive it must be taken to date the features. Inspection of the archive also indicates that they need not be placed earlier in the stratigraphic sequence.

The slots were aligned north–south and therefore on the same alignment as Trench 36480 to the south (see above), and almost at 90° to the linear features 31754 and 31778/31954. The centre to centre distance between the slots was c.1.5m and each one was c.0.6m wide. The depth varied considerably along each slot from c.0.1m to c.0.3m, but all had a flattened U-shaped profile with gently sloping sides. There was some slight evidence for an eastern return from the north and south ends of the westernmost slot (33192), but later intrusions made it impossible to confirm this. The intrusions also made it impossible to determine the original length of the features, but the maximum surviving lengths were: 33192, c.3.70m; 33194, c.2.90m; and 33196, c.4.40m. The shallowness and irregularity of the slots make it unlikely that they represent a building.

Phase 3b: south-east

Accumulation and minor cuts

The next stage in the stratigraphic sequence in the south-eastern part of the site was characterised by a large number of small clayey and silty deposits, and minor features which probably date to the first half of the 4th century. Details can be found in archive (Phases 8–10). Deposit 33190 contained a coin of AD 341–46 (sf13292).

Phase 4: north-west *(Fig.141)*

The principal development in Phase 4 in the north-western part of the site was the establishment of a small inhumation cemetery represented by six graves containing human skeletons. Apart from 27957 aligned more or less north–south, four graves were aligned north-east/south-west and one (33183) was aligned north-west/south-east. There was also another badly truncated, but approximately grave-shaped and grave-sized shallow cut (33212) which did not, however, contain skeletal remains. Data on the burials are summarised in Table 3. Full details of the human remains will be found in *AY* 5/1 in prep.

Fig. 140 *16–22 Coppergate: view south of parallel trenches 33192, 33194 and 33196 as excavated (scale 0.50m)*

Boundary ditches

Ditch 33162, on a north-west/south-east alignment, was 1.7m long, 0.95m wide and 0.85m deep. It was backfilled with 33161, dark grey clay with patches of very dark grey clay, followed by 33160, dark grey clay with patches of reddish-brown clay and occasional charcoal fragments. The upper fill was 33122, a mixture of grey sandy clay with charcoal flecks and reddish-brown clay. The feature was not traced beyond an intrusion at the south-east end, but it was aligned at 90° to a similar feature, 36353, and together they may have formed two sides of an enclosure, initially perhaps for the cemetery, although 33162 was cut by two of the graves.

South-east of the graves was ditch 36353, aligned north-east/south-west and therefore parallel to the longer axis of four of the graves. It continued beyond the south-west edge of the excavation, and at the north-east end had been truncated by a post-Roman pit (36239), but the 5m stretch recorded was 0.92m wide and 0.38m deep with steeply sloping sides. The fill was 36268, dark grey slightly silty sticky clay with flecks of light brown clay. The fact that this feature cuts the earlier features 31754 and 31778 (see above) is good evidence to show that the earlier pattern of land division had been swept away for the creation of the cemetery. It may also be noted that the ditch and the four graves parallel to it are the best examples of features on the site which are more or less on the same alignment as one of the principal axes of the legionary fortress.

The burials

Grave 27957, aligned north–south, was found in the west corner of the site. Its southern end lay beyond the site edge and the northern end was cut

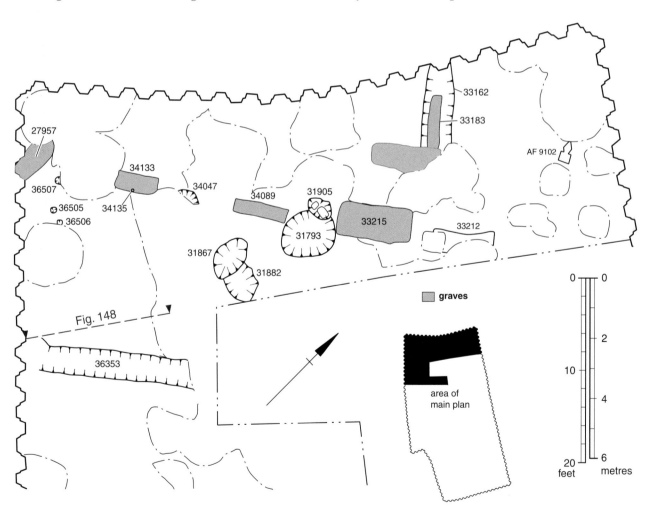

Fig. 141 *16–22 Coppergate: Phase 4, plan of north-west part of site showing cemetery and cemetery-related features*

away by a later pit. The grave was c.1.70m long, 0.80m wide and 0.25m deep, and contained a flexed, articulated skeleton (31006) lying on its left side with the skull (27449) at the north end. An iron nail found along the east edge of the grave suggested that a wooden coffin had originally contained the body. Close to the skull (in context 27402) there was a jet finger ring (sf19800). Below the skeleton was 31007, very dark grey sandy clay with flecks of lighter clay; around the skeleton was 27956, very dark grey clay with flecks of greyish-brown sandy clay, and 27402, very dark grey clay.

North-east of 27957 was grave 34133. The south-west end had been destroyed by an Anglo-Scandinavian pit (27478), but the grave was c.0.58m wide and 0.45m deep with vertical sides and a flat base. In the grave was an extended, supine skeleton (34147A) with its lower arms crossed over the pelvis. The head end was to the south-west and a complete skull (27749), found in pit 27478, almost certainly belonged to the skeleton. Iron nails and a linear stain (34138), c.10mm wide parallel to and following the outline of the cut indicated that the body had been buried in a coffin c.0.45m wide. The material around the skeleton was 34139, brown silty clay and the upper fill of the grave was 34134, brown sticky clay with occasional patches of very dark grey silty clay.

North-east of 34133 was grave 34089 which had been cut by several later intrusions. Only the lowest 0.2m of the cut survived where it measured c.1.84m by 0.48m, and it had near vertical sides. In the base of the cut, lying on its back, was an extended skeleton (34092) with the arms laid along each side. Fragments of the cranium, which originally lay at the south-west end, were found in a cut above the grave. At the north-east end of the grave, beside the feet, were the remains of two pairs of hobnailed boots or sandals (34090), their shape indicated by the position of the nails as no leather had survived. Nails along the edge of the grave showed that the burial had been in a coffin of which there was no other trace. A coin of c.300–10 (sf12639) was recovered from this grave close to the right femur of the skeleton. The backfill layers were 34078–9, clean pinkish-grey clay with occasional patches of friable, very dark grey loam and occasional charcoal flecks, and 34077, friable very dark grey with patches of pinkish-grey clay, patches of light brown sand, and occasional charcoal flecks.

North-east of grave 34089 was grave 33215. It contained an extended supine skeleton (33217) with the arms at each side, head at the south-west end. Once again iron nails and badly decayed wooden planking showed that the body had been buried in a coffin (33216). The grave was rectangular in plan and was c.2.6 x 1.1m and 1m deep. In the base was a secondary cut, c.2m x 0.35m and 0.25m deep, containing the coffin and skeleton. Both cuts had vertical sides. A coin found under the skull was dated to AD 117–38 (sf14088). The backfill was 33208, a crumbly, very dark grey sandy clay with flecks of charcoal, tile fragments, limestone chips and cobbles, followed by 33206, a mixture of dark brown clay and dark greyish-brown sandy clay with occasional charcoal, tile, sandstone, ash, cobbles and limestone fragments.

Cut into 33162 and close to the north-western limit of the site was grave 33183, at least 1.9m long, 0.5m wide and 0.25m deep; this had been cut by

Table 3 Summary of Roman burials from 16–22 Coppergate

Grave No.	Alignment	Age	Sex	Remarks
27957	N–S	20–30	f	Coffin, jet ring by skull
33092	SW–NE	35–45	m	Coffin
33183	NW–SE	17–18	m	Coffin
33215	SW–NE	20–25	m	Coffin, coin under skull
34089	SW–NE	c. 19	m	Coffin, hobnailed boots, coin by right leg
34133	SW–NE	20–30	f	Coffin

grave 33092 which had totally removed the south-east end. The skeleton (33173) was extended and supine with the head at the north-west end. It had been buried in a wooden coffin (33172), the rather decayed but clearly identifiable remains of which could be seen beside and above the inhumation. At least three iron nails were seen against the side of the cut suggesting the coffin that may have been as little as c.0.4m wide. The backfill of the grave was 33185, brown clay with grey clay and charcoal flecks, followed by 33184, brown to dark brown clay with flecks of organic grey clay and occasional charcoal flecks.

North-west of grave 33215 and cutting grave 33183 was grave 33092. It had been partly cut by later intrusions but contained a complete extended and supine skeleton (33104) with the head to the south-west. The left arm lay beside the body while the lower right arm lay bent across the pelvis. The grave was c.2.3m long, 0.8m wide and up to 0.5m deep, with near vertical sides. Nails found close to the edges of the grave suggested that a coffin had contained the body. The fill (33091) was dark grey to dark greenish-brown clay with flecks of charcoal and iron-pan and lumps of brown clay.

North-east of 33215 was a shallow cut (33212), originally rectangular in plan with vertical sides and a flat base. Its form, size (c.2.1m long) and alignment suggest it had possibly been a grave, but it had been extensively truncated by later features and contained no human remains.

Cemetery-related finds

The excavation also revealed three other objects which may relate to this or another nearby cemetery area. Excavation of a medieval pit (36574) south of ditch 36353 exposed a complete mid-3rd-century pottery jar of Knapton type (Form JK2) lodged in its side, with a small slab of micaceous sandstone forming a lid (the reference in *AY* 16/8, p.1080, to this pot, *3813*, as a *JH*2 jar dated 320–60 is incorrect). The jar was lifted intact so that its contents could be micro-excavated under controlled conditions in the conservation laboratory. This failed to reveal traces of anything but soil, and it is therefore assumed that the pot originally held some liquid or organic material, possibly an offering, of which nothing now remains.

Within 3.5m of the north corner of the excavation area, to the north-east of all the excavated graves, a pine cone gritstone finial (AF9102) was found in a layer (30982) attributed to the period c.400–850. The base is a c.0.33m cube and the whole piece is 0.72m high (Fig.142). It is likely to come from a Roman mausoleum which may have been sited close by. In addition, a small fragment of an inscription on what had been a tablet of magnesian limestone (sf13759) found in an 11th- to 12th-century context above the Roman cemetery, probably came from a funerary monument (Fig.143) (Hassall and Tomlin 1979, 346).

Some of the ceramic evidence has been interpreted as indicating the presence of cemetery areas nearby (*AY* 16/8, 1080). A number of sherds of head pots, Romano-Saxon pots and candlesticks dated to

Fig. 142 *16–22 Coppergate: millstone grit finial in the shape of a pine cone, probably from a tomb monument*

Fig. 143 *16–22 Coppergate: fragment of inscribed magnesian limestone tablet probably from a tomb monument*

the mid-3rd–mid-4th century were recovered from the site, although often residual in their contexts. These types often have ritual associations and are sometimes linked with burial rites.

Dating

That the cemetery was in use in or after the early 4th century is clearly indicated by a coin of AD 300–10 in one grave, but pottery and coins from deposits and features stratigraphically earlier indicate a mid-4th-century date, perhaps c.360.

Other features

A number of other features, north-west of the ditch, 36353, appeared to be roughly contemporary with the cemetery. They include four post-holes (36505–7 and 34135 which cut into grave 34133), all roughly circular in plan, 0.1–0.2m across and up to

0.25m deep, but they did not seem to represent an obvious structure.

North-east of grave 34133 was a small pit (34047) which had been largely destroyed but what remained was c.0.60m deep with near vertical sides. The fill was 31961, a mixture of brown sandy silt, brown silty clay, light yellowish-brown sandy silt and dark grey silty clay.

Located between graves 34089 and 33215 was a pit (31793) which was roughly circular in plan, c.1.5m in diameter and 0.85m deep, with an irregular semi-circular profile. It had four fill layers: 31790, greyish-brown clay with a few flecks of very dark grey silty sandy clay and some charcoal flecks; 31782, very dark grey sandy silty clay with a few flecks of clean brown clay and charcoal; 31780, dark to very dark brownish-grey sandy silty clay with flecks of clay and charcoal; and finally 31748, very dark grey slightly sandy silty clay with frequent patches of light brown clay and charcoal flecks. Pit 31793 was cut by a feature roughly oval in plan (31905), c.0.86 x 0.52m and 0.30m deep. It had four fill layers, beginning with 31904, very dark grey clay with occasional charcoal flecks and small patches of light reddish-brown clay. This was succeeded by 31903, light reddish-brown clay with charcoal flecks, and then by 31805, very dark grey sandy clay with a few patches of brown clay and occasional flecks of tile and charcoal. The top layer was 31781, brown clay with some patches of dark grey clay and occasional charcoal flecks.

South-east of the row of graves was 31882, a shallow pit of irregular shape filled by 31885, black sandy silty clay, succeeded by 31763–4, greyish-brown sandy clay. This was cut by 31867, another shallow pit of irregular shape 1 x 1.20m and 0.39m deep, filled by 31866, brown clay, below 31771, dark grey sandy silty clay and 31765 black sandy silty clay.

Phase 4: south-east

Wall 28946 *(Figs 134, 144)*

As noted already, at the north-east end of wall 28944 there was another stretch of stone wall (28946) aligned north-east/south-west, but oblique to 28944. It was not possible to trace 28946 to north-east or south-west as the relevant areas were completely cut away by later intrusions and the junction of 28946 and 28944 was also disturbed. It appears likely, however, that 28946 cut 28944. Its alignment is similar to that of the graves and the cemetery boundary ditch referred to above which suggests that the wall may be contemporary with them. The implication of this interpretation is that the building represented by the other walls and robber trenches described above had gone out of use by this time, i.e. by the mid-4th century.

The construction trench (37083) for wall 28946 was c.1.3m wide and 0.6m deep, and contained a number of foundation deposits (32685, 32824/5, 32983, 37082) consisting of limestone rubble, some pieces laid diagonally, set in yellowish-brown clay. Above the foundations the wall was c.0.75m wide with roughly squared limestone facing blocks, some laid diagonally, and a core of well-mortared limestone rubble and cobbles. It produced pottery of the late 2nd to 4th century.

Phase 5 (late 4th century): north-west

The cemetery described above was succeeded by a certain amount of accumulation interspersed with a number of shallow cut features. Full details can be found in the archive (Phase 14).

Rubble Surface Make up *(Figs 145–146, 148)*

In the west corner of the site, amongst the latest Roman deposits, and distinctly different from what preceded it, was a disturbed surface make up, predominantly composed of limestone rubble (27475). Its northern edge corresponded to the southern side of the earlier (and no longer visible) feature (base of fence line) 31754 (see above, p.211). On this edge the smaller (typically 0.2m square) rubble was replaced by larger blocks measuring up to 0.4 x 0.3m. Such edging could not be recognised anywhere else, due to later intrusions. Another strip of rubble (34497), only 0.2m to the south-east of 27475, may have been part of the same surface.

Fig. 144 *16–22 Coppergate: view south-east of elevation of wall 28946 (scale 0.20m)*

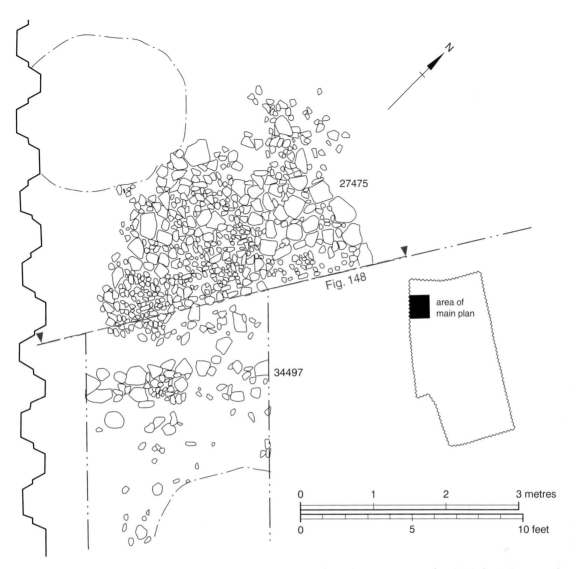

3

Fig. 145   *16–22 Coppergate: Phase 5, plan of north-west part of site showing stone surface 27475/34497*

Fig. 146 *16–22 Coppergate: view south-west of stone surface 27475 (scale 0.50m)*

16–22 Coppergate

NE

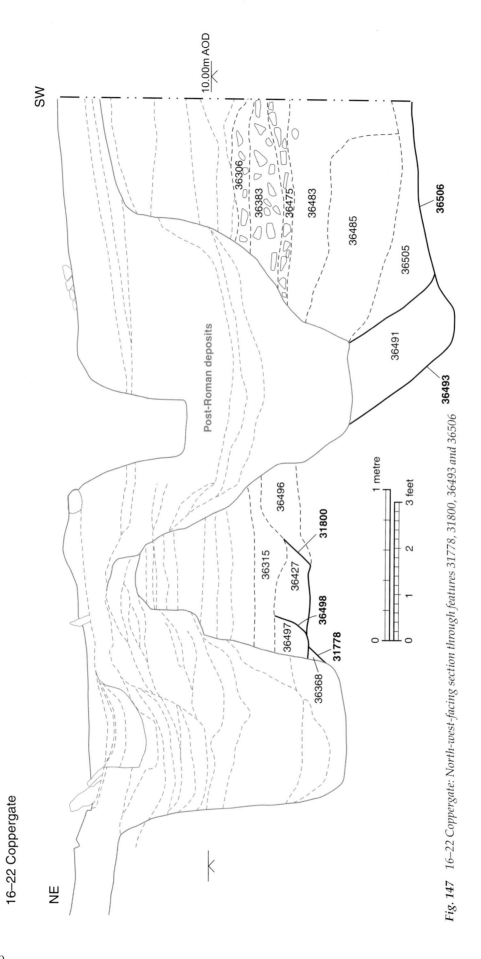

SW

10.00m AOD

36306

36383

36475

36483

36485

36505

36506

36491

36493

Post-Roman deposits

36496

36315

36427

31800

36498

31778

36497

36368

1 metre

3 feet

0   1   2

0   1   2   3

Fig. 147   16–22 Coppergate: North-west-facing section through features 31778, 31800, 36493 and 36506

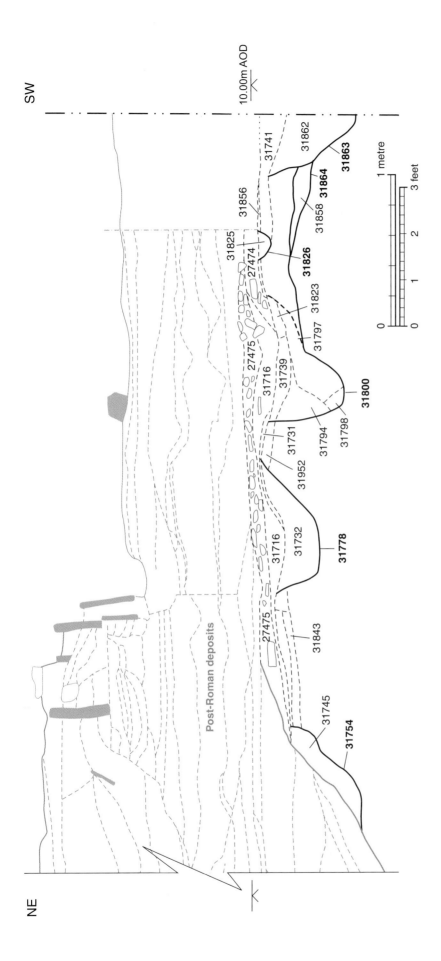

Fig. 148 16–22 Coppergate: North-west-facing section through features 27475, 31754, 31778, 31800 and 31863–4

22 Piccadilly

Introduction

In 1987 York Archaeological Trust undertook an excavation, directed by Nick Pearson, at 22 Piccadilly, the site of the former ABC Cinema (SE60585158; Fig.128, 2; Fig.150). The work was undertaken on behalf of the developers, Wimpey Property Holdings Ltd, who allowed access to the site and generously funded the excavation. It involved four trenches : Trench 1, 3m (east–west) x 6m (north–south), was located in the south-west corner of the site; Trench 2, 3.20 x 3.20m, was in the northern part; Trench 3, 3.20 x 3.20m, was in the centre and Trench 4, 2.80 x 2.60m, was in the south-eastern part.

Finds and site records are currently stored with York Archaeological Trust under the Yorkshire Museum accession code 1987.21.

This report has been developed from an archive report by Rhona Finlayson.

The excavation *(Fig.149)*

The excavation began below the level of the basement slab of the former cinema at a level of c.7–8m OD. This was approximately 4–5m lower than the present day street level of Piccadilly (12.2m OD) which had been built up in the 19th century to minimise periodic flooding from the River Foss. Modern level sloped down towards the south-west and the River Foss. It was not expected that the foundations of the cinema would have destroyed the archaeological deposits to any great degree and in the event only late medieval and early modern deposits had been truncated. Up to 5m of surviving archaeological deposits were encountered on the site, all of which were waterlogged.

Trench 1 *(Fig.149)*

Trenches 1 and 2 were located on what in Roman times was probably the west bank of the River Foss. There was evidence for intermittent activity in the area in the Roman period, although intensive occupation did not begin until the 9th century.

In Trench 1 natural (1087), a yellow sand with occasional patches of brown sand and occasional lenses of light grey clay, was encountered at 4.76m OD. This was overlain by 1086, a deposit excavated only in the western half of the trench, c.0.75m thick, of light grey sandy silty clay with occasional small patches of pink clay, frequent small patches of yellow sand and occasional inclusions of bone, tile, brick and oyster shell. This was cut at a level of c.4.77m OD by a regular, steep-sided, flat-bottomed ditch (1085), probably a drainage channel. It measured 0.50m wide and between 0.40m and 0.50m deep and was aligned east-north-east/west-south-west. The ditch was filled by 1084, dark grey-brown silty clay with frequent inclusions of tile and fragments of oyster shell. The deposit produced coins of Claudius II (AD 268–70; sf483) and Tetricus II (270–3; sf484). Pottery indicates a date after c.280 (*AY* 16/8, 1085). 1084 was very similar in composition to the contexts stratigraphically above it, the first of which was 1068, which was in turn sealed by 1061 and then 1060. These last-named contexts appeared to have been formed by the gradual accumulation of material, much of which could have been deposited as flood debris, sealing the ditch to a total depth of between 0.50m and 0.70m, bringing the level of the ground surface to c.5.30–5.56m OD at which post-Roman activity began. 1068 produced a bone pin (sf408) and 1061 produced coins of Claudius II (268–70; sf456), the Gallic Empire (265–73; sf457) and Tetricus II (270–3; sf458), as well as three bone pins (sfs394, 404, 452), a bone die (sf471) and an amber bead (sf416). 1060 produced a coin of Gratian (367–83; sf436).

Trench 2 *(Fig.149)*

Excavation of natural and Roman deposits took place in an area restricted to 2.10 x 2.10m in the north-eastern corner of the trench. Natural clay (2313) was encountered 5m below the level of the cinema foundations, but excavation was continued for a further 1.50m in order that archaeomagnetic samples could be taken of what were thought to be river sediments. 2313 was overlain by three

222

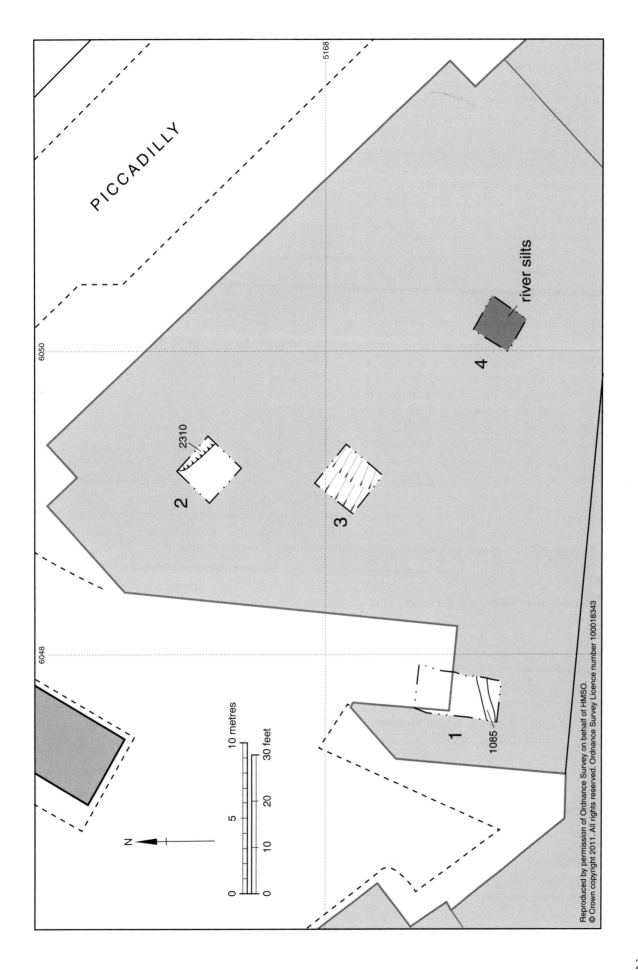

Fig. 149 22 *Piccadilly: Trench location plan with Roman features shown*

223

similar grey silty clay deposits (2309, 2311–12), in total c.0.50m thick, which had probably accumulated through natural deposition of river sediment, although they contained a few inclusions of pot, bone, glass and limestone. The latest of the three, 2309, produced a barbarous radiate coin dated c.270 (sf849), and 2311 produced coins of Marcus Aurelius (170–1; sf802) and Carausius (287–93, sf801). The upper surface of these deposits was at a level of c.4.0–4.19m OD at which 2309 was cut by a shallow feature (2310), subcircular in plan and 0.10m deep, of unknown function, located at the north-eastern edge of the trench and continuing beyond it. It was filled with 2308, a dark brown gritty silt, with occasional inclusions of bone, pot and tile.

2308 was succeeded by 2307, a grey gritty clay, 0.15m thick, with moderate charcoal flecks, and occasional bone and shell fragments. There were also a few sherds of Roman pot and tile. This deposit is thought to have included river sediment which may have resulted from flooding of the area and in this case it indicates that it was within the flood plain of the River Foss in the late Roman period.

Trench 3

Natural clay sloped down from 4.55m OD on the north-western side of the trench to 3.28m OD on the south-east side. This fairly steep slope may have represented the top of the west bank of the River Foss as it was in the Roman period, although no Roman deposits were identified in this trench.

Trench 4

Trench 4 probably lay even closer to the River Foss than Trench 3 in the Roman period. Natural clay lay at c.1.05m OD. The earliest deposits (4008–11) consisted of a c.2.5m depth of clayey silts containing a little organic matter; they were

Fig. 150 *22 Piccadilly: site view north-east towards Piccadilly during mechanical excavation. Trench 1 at the bottom*

apparently deposited largely by the action of water. Context 4010 produced coins of Gallienus (260–8; sf825) and Allectus (293–6; sf824). The level at the top of these deposits was c.4.0–4.08m OD, above which deposition was post-Roman.

38 Piccadilly

Introduction

In March–April 1992 York Archaeological Trust undertook an excavation, supervised by Rhona Finlayson, at 38 Piccadilly (SE60585158; Fig.128, 3). The work was undertaken on behalf of Polar Motor Company (York) Ltd and Wimpey Property Holdings Ltd, and followed a brief issued by the Principal Archaeologist for City of York Council. It involved a trench, 3 x 3m, excavated in Simpson's Yard about half way between the present day River Foss and Piccadilly.

Finds and site records are currently stored with York Archaeological Trust under the Yorkshire Museum accession code 1992.4.

The excavation (Fig.151)

The earliest deposit (1063), probably natural, was encountered at 1.20m OD, 8.70m below modern ground level. 1063 was excavated in a small area in the centre of the trench, but full excavation was not possible because of the flow of ground water into the trench. The deposit, at least 0.20m thick, was a grey silt with small pebbles and occasional fragments of decayed plant matter.

Above 1063 were 1061–2, 0.30m thick deposits of small–medium-sized cobbles and pebbles in clayey sand. They were clearly associated with the succeeding deposit of compact, small and medium-sized cobbles (1060), the make up for a surface found at 1.65m OD. Fragments of animal bone appeared to have been pressed between the cobbles during the use of the surface. Contexts 1060–2 are thought to be Roman as the pottery, all of 3rd-century date, includes many large, unabraded sherds. There is, however, an 8th-century sherd from 1061, thought by the excavator have been intrusive. 1060 produced a quern (sf68) and 1061 produced a bone pin and a bone needle (sfs78–9), while 1062 produced a leather shoe (sf69) and fragment (sf81).

Above the cobbled surface were deposits, 0.30m thick, of sand and sandy silt (1056–9), probably derived from a mix of refuse and riverside flood-deposited layers which dated to the 10th–11th centuries. They were sealed by 2.25m of homo-

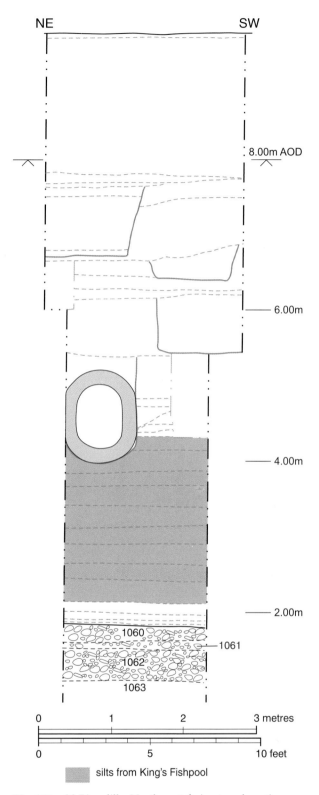

Fig. 151 *38 Piccadilly: North-west-facing trench section*

geneous dark grey silts, excavated in eleven spits (1045–55) thought to be associated with the creation of the King's Fish Pool after the Norman Conquest.

41 Piccadilly

Introduction

In July 1992 York Archaeological Trust undertook an evaluation excavation, supervised by Jane Lilley, at 41 Piccadilly (SE60705140; Fig.128, 4). The work was undertaken on behalf of Jewson Ltd and followed a brief issued by the Principal Archaeologist for City of York Council. The work involved the excavation of six trenches and drilling of eight boreholes (Fig.152). Trenches 1–5 measured 3 x 3m and Trench 6 10 x 1m.

Finds and site records are currently stored with York Archaeological Trust under the Yorkshire Museum accession code 1992.18.

A further excavation of the site by MAP took place in 1998 when Roman burials were found, although there is no reference to them in an interim report (MAP 1998, 12–13).

The boreholes (Fig.153)

A line of eight boreholes was spaced more or less evenly between George Street (east) and Piccadilly (west). They showed that natural sandy clay slopes down from east to west, from 11.45m OD in BH7 to 7.17m OD in BH14, but most of the slope occurs

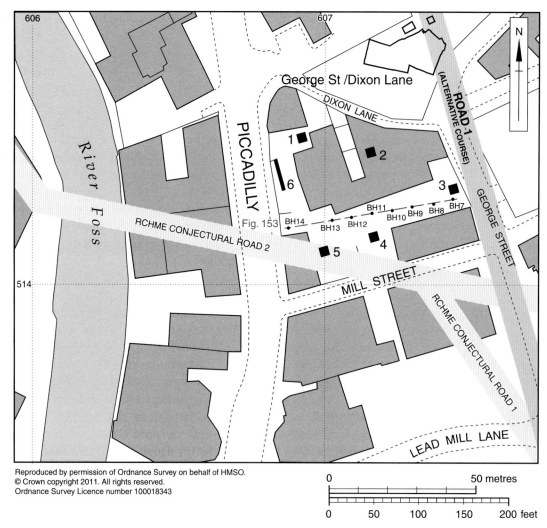

Fig. 152   *41 Piccadilly: Location plan of trenches and boreholes*

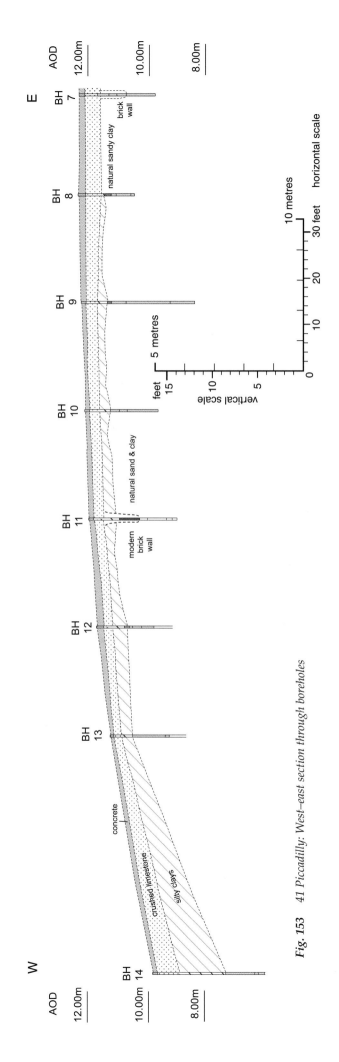

Fig. 153   41 Piccadilly: West–east section through boreholes

between BH13 and BH14. The depth of archaeological deposits in BH8–10 and 12–13 was 0.1–0.4m, considerably less than in BH14 where there was 1.6m of archaeological deposits and in the trenches further down the slope to the north and west. BH7 and BH11 encountered modern brick walls.

The excavation

Trench 1 *(Fig.154)*

The surface of the earliest deposit encountered, a sandy clay silt (1084), possibly natural, lay at 7.41m OD, 2m below modern ground level. It was not fully excavated. 1084 was cut by a stake-hole (1083), filled with sandy silt (1082). 1084 and 1083 were overlain by 1081, a deposit 0.20m thick, of mixed lenses of silt, sand and clay, which was succeeded by 1077 (not illustrated), clayey silt with frequent charcoal and mortar, and in its turn by 1080, a sandy silt. Both 1077 and 1081 contained late 4th-century pottery (*AY* 16/8, 1090).

Above 1080, next to the northern trench edge, were two flat limestone blocks (1078–9) which measured 0.36 x 0.30m and 0.36 x 0.28m. Overlying them was 1068, a deposit of silty clay. This was cut by a stake-hole (1070), 80mm diameter and 60mm deep, backfilled with 1069, clay. In the southern part of the trench there were two further stake-holes (1072, 1074), 100mm diameter and 80mm deep, backfilled with silty clays (1071, 1073). A shallow cut (1076), aligned more or less east–west, 0.50m long and 0.12m deep, was backfilled with silty clay (1075) which contained late 4th-century pottery.

Above these features was a clay and pebble surface make up (1067) which contained late Roman pottery. Above 1067 was a deposit of charcoal (1066) which in turn was succeeded by 1065, a deposit of clay. The date of 1065–6 is uncertain, but deposits above them were 10th–11th century and later.

Trench 2

Natural deposits (2112–14), sand, clayey sand and sand with occasional lenses of gravel, were located at 8.94m OD (south side) and 9.62m OD (north side), 2.96–2.28m below modern ground level. Natural was succeeded by deposits of

Trench 1

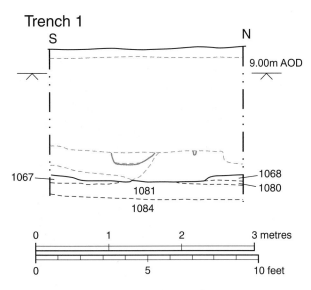

Fig. 154 *41 Piccadilly: Trench 1, east-facing section*

medieval and later date. Residual Roman pottery included a sherd of terra nigra and a few sherds of early Ebor ware (*AY* 16/8, 1090).

Trench 3 *(Figs 155–156)*

Natural (3070, 3072–5) was encountered at 11.63m OD, 0.60m below modern ground level. It was recorded that natural was cut by a number of features. They included fifteen closely spaced stake-holes (3054–68) ranging in diameter from 40mm to 100mm, and in depth from 80mm to 220mm. Three additional stake-holes (3009, 3026 and 3028) and

two post-holes (3011 and 3069) cut into natural are probably contemporary. They ranged in diameter from 80mm to 280mm, and in depth from 50mm to 200mm. The backfill layers (3005, 3025, 3027, 3007 and 3053 respectively) were silty sands. In addition, stake-hole 3067 was cut by a small pit, 3051, which extended beyond the eastern edge of the trench and was backfilled by 3035, silty sand.

These features appeared to be overlain by 3033/3052, a thin deposit of silty sand. This was cut by a shallow gully (3031) on an east–west alignment, 0.50m wide and 40mm deep. It was backfilled with 3019 and 3021, silty sands. These fill layers were cut by further stake-holes (3010, 3020, 3024 and 3030), 80–150mm in diameter and 60–160mm in depth. They were backfilled with silty sand (3006, 3029, 3023 and 3032 respectively).

Although the recorded sequence is as described above, re-examination of the records suggests that it is likely that all the stake-holes belonged to the same phase of activity, but that the cuts of some were missed before excavation of 3033/3052 and in fact cut that deposit. In this case gully 3031, also cutting 3033/3052, becomes the earliest feature as its fill was cut by stake-holes.

Once filled in 3031 was also cut by pit 3014, itself cut away on the west by later features, and extending beyond the southern edge of the trench. It was at least 0.50m deep and the backfill was 3013, a silty sand. 3031 was also cut by pit 3018 of 11th-

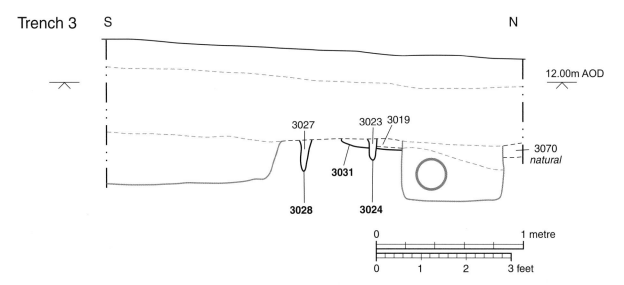

Fig. 155 *41 Piccadilly: Trench 3, east-facing section*

Fig. 156   41 Piccadilly, Trench 3: view east of stake-holes and later features cut into natural

to 12th-century date (fill 3016) and all the rest of archaeology in this trench was medieval and later.

Roman pottery from contexts 3033/3052 and 3035 was late 2nd–early 3rd century.

Trench 4

Natural was found directly below the modern yard surface and there were no archaeological features.

Trench 5

Natural (5003), a sandy clay, was encountered at 10.3m OD, 0.25m below modern ground level. This

was cut by a pit, subrectangular in plan (5002), back-filled with redeposited clay (5001) which contained a few sherds of Roman pottery dated to the late 2nd–3rd century. This feature was overlain by the modern yard surface.

Trench 6

This was machine excavated to a depth of 2.6m (6.9m OD) with a view to locating the medieval churchyard of St Stephen. Neither natural (see also note on BH14) nor Roman deposits were encountered. The churchyard cemetery was found further north in excavations in 2005–6 on the corner of Dixon's Lane and Piccadilly (Fig.128, 18).

229

50 Piccadilly

Introduction

In May–June 1992 York Archaeological Trust undertook an evaluation excavation, supervised by Rhona Finlayson, at 50 Piccadilly (SE60645152; Fig.128, 5). The work was undertaken on behalf of Polar Motor Company (York) Ltd and followed a brief issued by the Principal Archaeologist for City of York Council. The work involved excavation of a trench 3 x 3m located close to the street frontage.

Finds and site records are currently stored with York Archaeological Trust under the Yorkshire Museum accession code 1992.10.

The excavation (Fig.157)

Natural (2136), a grey-blue sandy clay, was located at c.2.60m OD, 7.40m below modern ground level. Above this was 2135, probably natural also; it was a light brown sandy clay with occasional iron-pan and fragments of plant matter, 0.20m thick.

Period 1

Two parallel ditches (2132, 2134), aligned north-west/south-east, were cut into natural. The eastern-most (2132) lay largely beyond the trench edge; only the western edge of it was recorded. It sloped steeply to the base at a depth of at least 0.25m. Ditch 2134 was c.1m wide and 0.35m deep, and the sides sloped down to a rounded base. Both ditches contained dark grey humic, sandy, clay silts (2131 and 2133 respectively). 2131 produced a leather fragment (sf82). Analysis of deposit samples for evaluation purposes produced plants and insects which live in areas of rough grazing or weedy waste ground. Plant remains include those of stinging nettle, dock, hemlock, fat hen, the goosefoots, orache, chickweed and buttercups. In addition there were seeds of fig and opium poppy, and a fragment of box. The samples warrant further examination.

Overlying the ditch fills was 2128, a silty clay, 0.10m thick, succeeded in turn by 2127, mid-brown sandy silty clay, 0.55m thick. 2127 was cut by a post-hole (2130), 0.17m diameter and 0.25m deep which

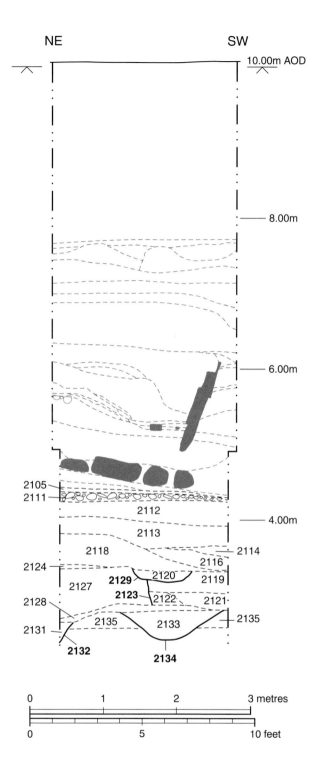

Fig. 157 *50 Piccadilly: North-west-facing section*

contained the remains of a timber post (2125) and clay packing (2126). Stratigraphically later than 2125 was a thin layer (2124) of sandy silt which included concentrations of burnt residues, charcoal and burnt tile. Pottery from the deposits described above suggests a mid–late 2nd-century date (*AY* 16/8, 1090).

Period 2

2124 and 2127 were cut by 2123, a ditch aligned north-west/south-east. Only the eastern edge was recorded and it sloped almost vertically to a flat base at a depth of 0.50m. The primary silt was 2122, an organic clay silt which produced a honestone (sf80). Above 2122 was 2121, sandy silty clay, in turn succeeded by 2119, a silty clay. 2119 was cut by a shallow feature (2129), 0.75m in diameter, filled with clay silt (2120).

Overlying 2120 and 2124 was a series of similar deposits up to 0.90m thick. The first was 2118, a clay silt up to 0.40m thick, the surface of which sloped down from north-east to south-west. It produced a shale bracelet (sf78). On the west side of the trench 2118 was overlain by 2116, clay silt which produced an iron key (sf69) and bone needle (sf77).

2116 was cut by a large post-hole (2117) which extended beyond the north and west edges of the excavation. It contained a clay packing (2115) around the base of the post (2109) of diameter 0.18m which survived to a height of 1.06m. Three stakes (2106–8) to the east of 2109, driven into 2116, formed a north-east/south-west alignment and were probably contemporary with the post. 2109 and 2116 were succeeded by 2114, sandy silt. The next deposit, covering the whole trench, was 2113, sandy clay very similar to the succeeding deposit (2112), the surface of which lay at 4.20m OD. Pottery from Period 2 deposits described above may be dated to the late 2nd–early 3rd century (*AY* 16/8, 1090). 2112 and 2113 each produced a bone pin (sf74 and sf73 respectively).

Above 2112 was a deposit of cobbles (2111), 0.15m thick, which covered the whole trench, probably forming a yard or track. Above the cobbled surface were two deposits (2105, 2110) of humic silt up to 0.10m thick. Pottery from these deposits may be dated to the early–mid-3rd century (*AY* 16/8, 1090), although this only gives them a *terminus post quem*. There was no late Roman pottery from the site. Subsequent deposition was dated to the 11th–12th centuries and later.

York Castle Car Park

In February–March 1995 York Archaeological Trust undertook an excavation, supervised by Amanda Clarke, in York Castle Car Park (SE60555150; Fig.128, 6). The work was undertaken on behalf of City of York Council and followed a brief issued by the Principal Archaeologist. It involved the excavation of two trenches 20 x 1m (Fig.158). Trench 1 on a north-west/south-east line was located to coincide with the western tower of the gatehouse to York Castle. Trench 2 on a north-east/south-west line was positioned in an area thought to coincide with the conjectured line of Roman approach road 2 (RCHMY **1**, 1) and the castle's northern gatehouse passageway and eastern tower. At its south-west end the trench was enlarged into an area 5 x 3m.

Finds and site records are currently stored with York Archaeological Trust under the Yorkshire Museum accession code YORYM : 1995.58.

No Roman deposits were found in Trench 1.

Trench 2 *(Figs 158–9)*

Hand excavation was focused on the area 5 x 3m at the south-west end of the trench where survival of pre-modern archaeological material was greatest. Natural (2023), a light brown sandy clay, was encountered at c.9.10m OD, up to c.2.50m below modern ground level. Overlying natural was

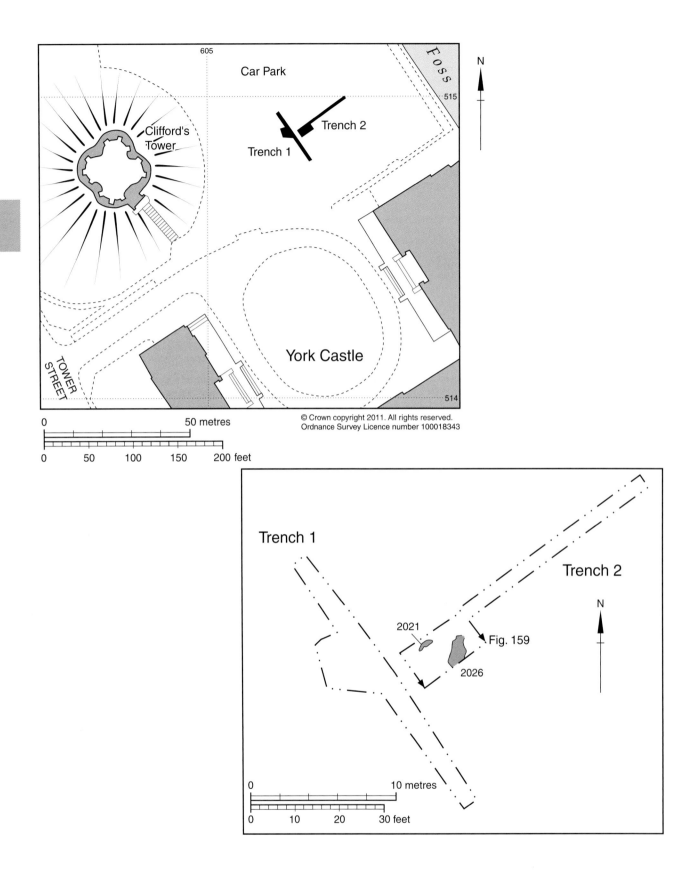

Fig. 158 Castle Car Park: Location plan and plan of trenches

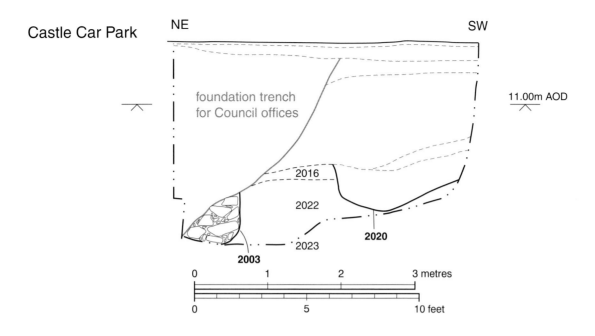

Castle Car Park

NE

SW

foundation trench
for Council offices

11.00m AOD

2016

2022

2020

2023

2003

0   1   2   3 metres

0   5   10 feet

Fig. 159 *Castle Car Park: Trench 2, north-west-facing section*

a deposit (2022) up to 0.85m thick, very similar to natural, being a light brown silty sandy clay with frequent charcoal flecks, occasional limestone fragments and cobbles. This was cut by a shallow feature (2021), cut away on its west and south sides by later pits and to the north by the construction cut for a prison wall. What remained was the fill 2024, a dark grey clay silt with frequent charcoal flecks below a light brown silty sand, 0.20m thick. Pottery from 2021 was dated late 2nd/early 3rd century. Also cut into 2022 was a shallow curving gully (2026), less than 0.25m deep. This was overlain by 2016, grey-brown sandy clay silt with occasional stone fragments and charcoal flecks. Finds included slag, parts of a quern stone (sf55), and a faced limestone block; pottery was late 4th century with some earlier residual material. Roman tile was found in 2016 and 2024. There was also a ceramic vaulting tube (*tubulus*) from 2016, an unusual find of an object often used in the construction of vaults, which had to be kept light in order to span large spaces.

Post-Roman

2016 was cut by a pit, oval in plan (2020) with organic fill (2006, 2019) which was probably Anglo-Scandinavian. Subsequent deposits belonged to the medieval and later periods. There was also a wall footing (2003) on a north-west/south-east alignment which was possibly medieval and part of the gatehouse. Everything below the car park surface was cut through by a foundation trench (2010) for the Council Offices begun in 1937.

Zone 3: Discussion

Natural topography and roads

The excavations in the Foss bank zone described above have, firstly, revealed that the topography in the Roman period was very different from what it is today, and, secondly, suggested that, unlike the banks of the Ouse, those of the Foss were probably marginal land which was not intensively occupied and built up.

On the west side of the Foss at 16–22 Coppergate natural ground level sloped down from 9.2m OD to 6m OD at the south-east end of the site and then sloped again down to c.3.28m OD in Trench 3 at 22 Piccadilly and as low as 1.05m OD in Trench 4. Trenches 3–4 presumably lay on the Roman river bank in an area which was periodically inundated. At times, at least, the Foss must have been wider at this point than it is today and with a flood plain extending further to the north. Further north-east at Garden Place (Fig.128, 13; Fig.160) the base of the proposed early river bed lay at 3.35m OD and on occasions might have been under water at high tide. Perhaps what was found was the top of a beaching point for river craft, given timber shoring to render the bank stable. Natural level in Trench 20 of the 2000 evaluation excavations on the east side of Garden Place was encountered at c.4.15m and so at this point the land probably stood, for most of the time, above the high-water mark. The main channel of the River Foss itself must always, however, have flowed to the south of Carmelite Street. At time of writing (2010) major excavations are taking place in the Hungate area which may clarify the exact location of the Foss in Roman times.

South of Foss Bridge ground level today, on both sides of the river, appears to slope down more gently to the river than it did in Roman times. Over the last 1900 years or so the level has risen considerably in the valley bottom, disguising the natural contours. Modern level in the centre of a site at 17–21 Piccadilly (1991.29; Fig.128, 15) was c.11.6m OD and natural was located in a borehole at c.4.55m OD. To the south-west of this site natural level dropped by c.3.35m to c.1.20m at 50 Piccadilly. Today the drop over the same distance is only c.1.6m (11.6–10m OD). From 17–21 Piccadilly natural level also sloped down to the north-west towards the Foss

and rose to the south-east reaching c.7.40m OD at 41 Piccadilly.

The rise in the level of the river bank since Roman times is partly due to a corresponding rise in the level of the river caused by natural phenomena, but also by the damming of the river to create the King's Fish Pool in the late 11th century and by canalisation in more recent times. Average summer river levels at York today are c.5m OD, but the level of the Ouse and Foss in Roman times when they were tidal is unclear. However, the lowest level at which Roman deposits have been encountered by the Ouse is c.2.5m OD at 23–8 Skeldergate (1989.1; SE60235147) on the south-west bank. At 38 Piccadilly the surface of the earliest Roman deposit, a spread of cobbles, perhaps forming part of a riverside hardstanding, lay at 1.65m OD.

The location of both the Foss banks in Roman times remains uncertain and, in any case, in the absence of any fixed structure on the banks, it would have been continually shifting, in the short term as the tide came in and out and in the long term as river levels rose through the Roman period. On the east side, however, the river's edge can have lain only a short distance to the west of the sites at 38 and 50 Piccadilly and at another site where no Roman deposits were found, at 84 Piccadilly (1991.16; Fig.128, 19), where natural occurred below Anglian deposits at 2.90m OD. One result of this analysis is that the identification as a Roman jetty of the stones at the Inland Revenue Office on the east side of Piccadilly (RCHMY **1**, 64–5) would seem to be ruled out.

On the west side of the Foss opposite 38 and 50 Piccadilly natural level was recorded as c.9.10m OD in Castle Yard on what is still clearly a raised promontory of land between the Ouse and the Foss – the 'Ness' of the Viking Age, preserved in the street name Nessgate. This level suggests a steep slope down to the River Foss in Roman times on the north-east side of what is now the castle precinct. In view of the steep drop on both sides of the Foss adjacent to the castle site, it seems unlikely, if only for this reason, that RCHME's Road 2 crossed the

Foss at the point suggested. In addition, no trace was found in the Castle car park trench on the road's supposed line, although the ground was heavily disturbed here.

Approach road 1 was not seen on its predicted line in the Barbican Leisure Centre area (Fig.161), but may have been completely destroyed by the cattle market (see Zone 4 below, p.261). Had it followed this line then, after crossing what would become the medieval defences into Zone 3, the road would have run briefly along a ridge of high ground above the Foss around St George's church on George Street. Possible Roman road metalling has been observed in George Street (Fig.161,8; p.87, fig.46, *AY*6/1). Assuming that the junction

with Road 2 proposed by RCHME (p.198, Fig.111) is incorrect, then Road 1 might have continued to the north-west. No Roman road was found on the site at the junction of Dixon's Lane and Piccadilly (Fig.128, 18). However, the road may have run a little to the east of it, heading for what is now the site of St Denys church before meeting a revised course for Road 2 which approached York from the east. As discussed under Zone 4 below (pp.261–2), Road 2 approached York along a line close to what is now Lawrence Street and then, after crossing the line of the medieval walls, seems most likely to have taken a line now followed more or less by Walmgate, before crossing the Foss somewhere near Foss Bridge and then heading for the south-east gate of the fortress.

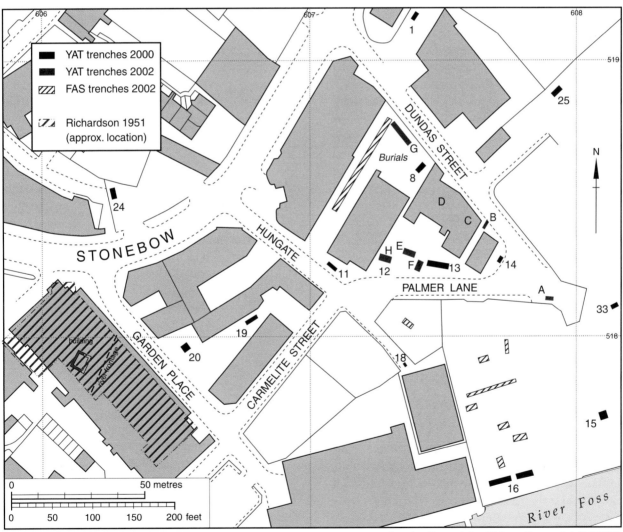

Fig. 160 *Hungate Evaluation Trenches*

An alternative course for Road 1, south-east of the city, is discussed under Zone 4 below, along with the suggestion that another Roman road approached from the south along a line now followed by Fulford Road and Fawcett Street, and then George Street.

Land use in the late 1st–mid-3rd centuries

On the east bank of the Foss Roman activity appears to fall into the pattern established in other extramural areas with a start made in the Antonine period (third quarter of the 2nd century). At 50 Piccadilly the two Roman ditches probably belonged to the early part of that period; they were followed by a sequence which belonged to the late 2nd–early 3rd century. At 41 Piccadilly also activity appears to have begun in the Antonine period, although there is some early pottery residual in later layers.

On the west bank of the Foss there is little evidence from 16–22 Coppergate for occupation until, perhaps, the third quarter of the 3rd century, probably also the date at which the ditch was dug in Trench 1 at 22 Piccadilly. At Coppergate, however, a good deal of earlier pottery was found residual in later and post-Roman layers (AY 16/8, 1078–9) which may have originated in the fortress or in extramural areas nearby of which little is known. In addition, there were the crucibles for melting glass which were dated to the early 3rd century. However, stratified coins and pottery suggest the sequence of structures, ditches and other cut features began in c.260, continuing for perhaps the next 100 years.

Looking at the Coppergate site in more detail, in the north-western half activity probably began in earnest with ditch 36493, on close to an east–west line. It may have served as both a property boundary and a drainage ditch as it followed the natural slope; indeed this latter function may account for its alignment which is somewhat anomalous for Roman York where the main fortress axes were usually followed. The slightly later slot, 31800, north of ditch 36493, was on more or less the same alignment, but whether it was structural or not is unknown. However, further to the north of the ditch there was evidence for timber structures in the form of post-holes and stake-holes, but insufficient

was revealed to make any sense of their character; unfortunately a date of the third quarter of the 3rd century rests on a single coin. South-east of ditch 36493 there was further evidence, in the form of a slot (28824) and post-holes for timber structures and/or enclosures.

Any timber structures were replaced by a stone building probably in the third or last quarter of the 3rd century. Three stretches of stone wall were found in the main excavation and two others in the watching brief, and linked to them were robber trenches which had probably held walls. As noted above, these walls pose difficult problems of interpretation, aggravated by the degree of disturbance by later features. The difference of alignment between walls 28944 and 28946 suggests they should be of different phases; it seems unlikely that they can have been part of the same structure. Although it was not conclusively demonstrated in excavation, 28944, which would have met wall 28412 at more or less a right angle, should probably, along with 28412, be seen as earlier than 28946 (see below).

Taken together walls and associated trenches appear to define a structure at least 21m (east-north-east/west-south-west) x 18m (Fig.138). The function of the structure for which these walls were constructed is uncertain; no floors or other internal features were clearly identified, except for partitions defined by stake-holes. The mode of construction of the building's walls is similar to that of many other Roman buildings in York, especially in the civilian settlements, in respect, firstly, of their rubble foundations and, secondly, their mortared (albeit poor-quality) core and facing stones, existing as thin flat slabs tapered inwards. The original height of the walls is of course unknown, but a width of almost 1m suggests that a single storey built in stone throughout is a good possibility.

Finally, it may be noted that that part of Zone 3, east of the Foss on the north side of Walmgate is largely *terra incognita* as far as the Roman period is concerned. However, evaluation excavations on Speculation Street, adjacent to the walls, by On Site Archaeology in 2002 and 2004 revealed evidence for possible structures represented by rows of stake-holes which were overlain by a sandy deposit containing pottery of late 1st- to 3rd-century date (Bruce 2002; 2004).

Burials

Additions to the isolated burials – all inhumations – recorded by RCHME in the Peasholme Green/Layerthorpe area (RCHMY **1**, 71) include a group of three inhumations and two cremations from evaluation excavations in the Hungate area (Fig.128, 12b; Fig.160) on the west side of Dundas Street (by YAT, Trenches 8 and G, and by FAS). All these burials were dated to the late 2nd–early 3rd century, providing further evidence for the expansion of the cemeteries in this period.

There is no published date for the burials found by MAP at 41 Piccadilly, but the small inhumation cemetery from the north-western part of the 16–22 Coppergate site is mid-4th century (Phase 4). This was probably established following the desertion and at least part-demolition of the stone building. Originally the cemetery may have been confined within a plot defined to the north-east and south-east by ditches (33162 and 36353), before graves cut the north-eastern ditch. Grave 27957 on a north/south alignment may be the earliest, followed by those graves which respected the alignment of the proposed boundary ditches, four aligned north-east/south-west, and one north-west/south-east. The cemetery is the best example of a phase of activity on the Coppergate site in which the alignments of the main axes of the legionary fortress were adopted for land management, this after a period of 100 years or so during which structural and other features had observed a number of different alignments.

The cemetery at Castle Yard (Fig.128, 16) is also thought to be late Roman, although how late is not clear. In terms of land use, what is striking about both the Castle Yard and the Coppergate cemeteries, especially the latter, is that they appear to have been placed in areas hitherto within or close to a settlement of the living. However, they are part of pattern emerging in the 3rd century in which burials encroached on vacant plots of land near to settled areas and in some cases, as at Coppergate, on land formerly used for settlement. It is striking that there is little other evidence for late 4th-century activity at Coppergate (*AY* 16/8, 1081) except for the enigmatic stone surface in the west corner. The site, therefore, fits the pattern of most extramural sites in the mid–late 4th century in which settlement-related activity is largely absent (pp.374–5).

Land use in the late Roman period

At Coppergate at the end of the 3rd century and in the first half of the 4th, the stone building continued to stand and activity around it, involving refuse tipping and the cutting of small features, appears to have been continuous. The evidence presumably reflects the flourishing fortunes of the civilian settlement south-east of the fortress as a whole for which Coppergate was an area of marginal land, used when pressure on space was at its greatest. The building was probably abandoned and in part demolished in the mid-4th century as some of the robbing trenches appeared to be Roman, although the final episode of stone robbing was Anglo-Scandinavian. Whilst its function is uncertain, wall 28946 probably post-dated the demolition of walls 28944 and 28412 and may have been more or less contemporary with the cemetery to the north-west, having much the same alignment as the suggested boundary ditch 36353 and most of the graves. The wall was narrower and slightly different in character from the earlier walls in employing small limestone slabs set at an angle in its foundations and lower courses.

On the other sites in this zone the story of the late Roman period can be quickly told. At 22 Piccadilly 4th-century pottery was found residual in later layers. East of the Foss evidence for activity datable to the 4th century was, unusually, found at 41 Piccadilly, but otherwise the riverside sites produced very little. It may be noted for comparative purposes that at Garden Place, north-west of the Foss, a similar picture emerges with virtually no pottery of the second half of the 4th century (*AY* 16/8, 1077).

In conclusion, the evidence appears to suggest, as noted above, that the Foss banks were marginal land for much of the Roman period and only saw activity when there was pressure on space elsewhere in the late 2nd–3rd century.

3

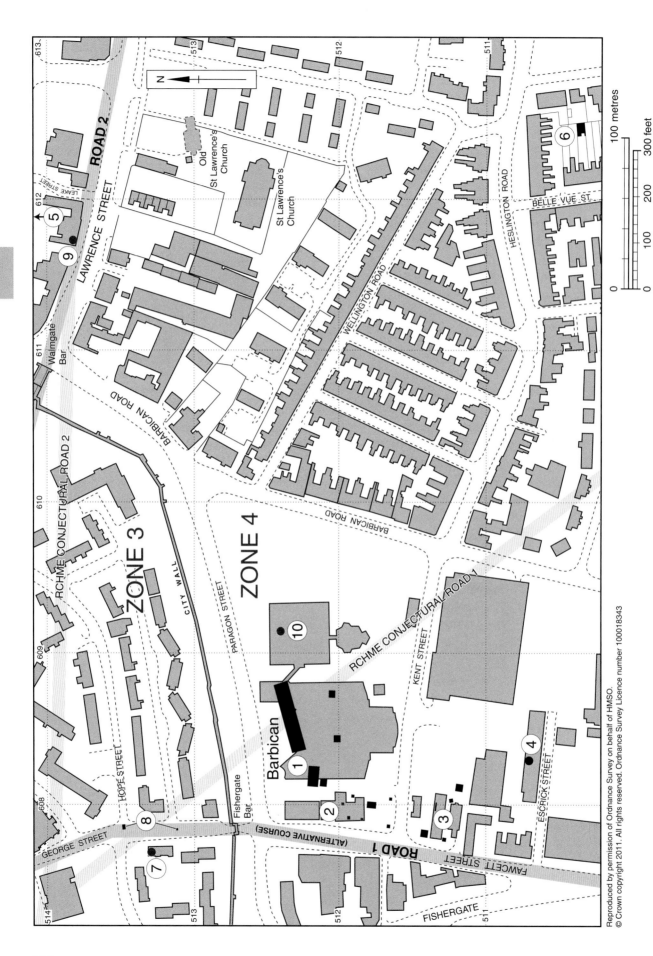

Zone 4: East of the Foss and Ouse (outside the medieval walls)

Introduction *(Figs 54, 161)*

Extramural Zone 4 encompasses an area outside the Walmgate sector of the city walls, east of the River Foss in the Fishergate area and east of the Ouse to the south of this. It also includes the York suburban villages of Fulford, Heslington and Osbaldwick (Fig.54), although the sites described are close to the city centre, except for a Roman burial in a stone coffin found in Fulford, immediately south of the ring road. The discussion below will, however, refer briefly to sites in and around the villages.

Running east–west through the northern side of Zone 4 as far as the ring road is the morainic ridge which rises to c.30m at Heslington Hill (Fig.54, 14) and c.32m OD further east at Kimberlow Hill (Fig.54, 16). As noted in the introduction, this ridge, and its continuation west of the Ouse, was probably part of a route across the Vale of York between the Wolds and the Pennines since the Neolithic (RCHMY 3, xxvii–xxviii; Radley 1974). It has been suggested that the earthwork known as the Green

Dykes, formerly on the boundary between the City of York and Heslington parish, formed a barrier of Iron Age date intended to control this route (Fig.54, 13; Ramm 1966).

Until the archaeological work reported on below, there had been little evidence for the Roman period in this zone apart from two major roads and some burials. The roads are thought to have approached York from the south-east and from the east (Fig.54; RCHMY 1, 1; Road 1 and Road 2). A review and discussion of their lines will be found on p.261 below. As far as burials are concerned, a small cremation cemetery is known in Fishergate and a brick-built tomb was found a little to the south of it in Grange Garth (RCHMY 1, 69). A tile-built tomb was found c.300m to the north of the 17–23 Lawrence Street site (below), and a tomb-stone, since disappeared, but illustrated by Drake (1736, pl.8) was built into the wall of St Lawrence's churchyard, c.200m south-east of that site.

Fig. 161 (facing page) Zone 4: location of sites described in this fascicule (1–6) and other sites (7–10)

1. *Barbican Leisure Centre (1987–8)*
2. *City Arms, Fawcett Street (2001)*
3. *School canteen, Fawcett Street (1998)*
4. *8–9 Escrick Street (1989)*
5. *17–23 Lawrence Street (1989)*
6. *Belle Vue Street (1994)*

7. *Lead Mill Lane (1973) – Zone 3*
8. *George Street: Roman (?) road metalling (1984) – Zone 3*
9. *Lawrence Street: Roman road (1954)*
10. *Paragon Street (1973)*

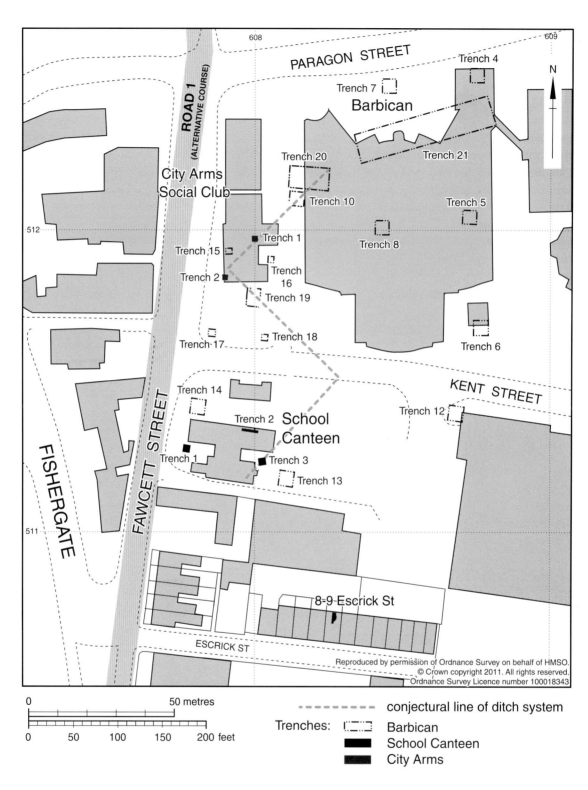

Fig.162 *Barbican Leisure Centre, City Arms, Fawcett Street, and School Canteen, Fawcett Street: plan showing location of trenches, sites and conjectured layout of Roman ditch system*

Barbican Leisure Centre

Introduction

Excavation on a car park site (SE60855120; Fig.161, 1; Fig.162) immediately east of the city walls, bounded by Paragon Street on the north side, Barbican swimming baths to the east, Kent Street to the south and Fawcett Street to the west, took place in 1987–8 in advance of the construction of the Barbican Leisure Centre. Three additional trenches (12–14) were dug on land south of Kent Street. In 1973 excavations to the north-east of the site under discussion, in advance of the construction of the baths (Fig.161, 10; pp.76–8, *AY* 6/1), located two Roman ditches. Prior to its redevelopment as baths and car park the entire area bounded by Paragon Street, Cemetery Road, Kent Street and Fawcett Street had been occupied since 1827 by York cattle market. Its construction had clearly removed a certain amount of earlier archaeological deposits.

In the first phase of work, directed by David Brinklow, in December 1987–January 1988, fifteen 5m square trial trenches (Trenches 1–14 and 19) were excavated and four additional 2m square trenches (Trenches 15–18) were excavated on the presumed site of the church of All Saints, Fishergate, immediately east of what is now Fawcett Street (Trenches 1–3 not illustrated). In the second phase, May–August 1988, two large trenches (20–1) were excavated under the direction of Nick Pearson. It should be noted that two further trenches were excavated adjacent to Trenches 15 and 16 in 1991 as a project in advance of the redevelopment of the site of the City Arms Social Club, Fawcett Street (see below). In 2008 the area south of that new development was excavated in its entirety by On Site Archaeology and the church was located (a monograph on the work is in preparation).

York City Council kindly granted access to the site in 1987–88 and funded the excavations. Particular thanks are due to Brian Lee of the Car Parks Inspectorate, and Graham Stratfold and Paul Chesmore of the Department of Leisure Services for their assistance.

The finds and records are stored at YAT under the Yorkshire Museum accession codes 1987/88.27.

The excavation

Archaeology which can confidently be ascribed to the Roman period was located in five trenches: 10, 13, 19–21, and possibly in Trench 15. Vertical stratification of pre-medieval date was limited in all trenches and artefactual material was scarce. On

Fig. 163 Barbican Leisure Centre, Trench 10: view north-west showing ditch 10047 (left to right). Scale 1m

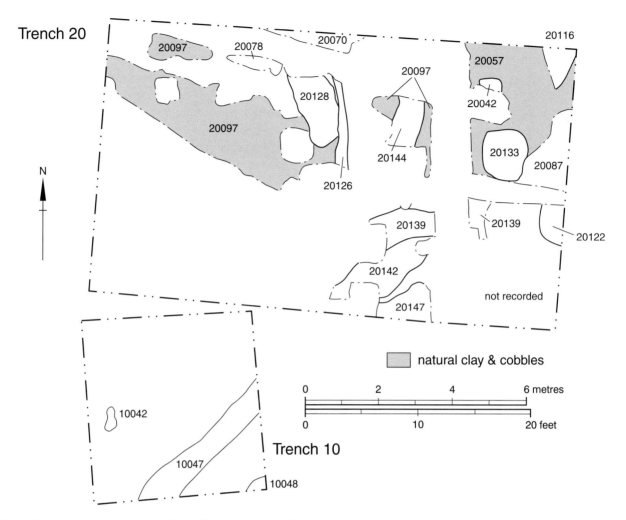

Fig. 164 *Barbican Leisure Centre: Plan of Trenches 10 and 20*

occasions, features and deposits which contained only Roman pottery are thought likely by reason of location and alignment to have been post-Roman. On other occasions features containing no finds have been ascribed to the Roman period for the same reasons.

Trench 10 *(Figs 163–4)*

Natural orange-brown sandy clay with pebbles (10049) was encountered at c.12.15m OD, c.1.35m below modern ground level. The principal feature cutting natural was a ditch (10047) running north-east/south-west across the south-east corner of the trench. It was up to 0.80m wide and up to 0.70m deep. In profile the ditch had a gentler slope on the north-west side than on the south-east which had a slight step immediately above the narrow flat base. The backfill layers were 10046, succeeded by

10044; both were recorded as a mixture of grey and yellow-brown silty clay, but the latter contained more cobbles and pebbles. A continuation of this feature to the north-east was located in Trench 20 (see below).

The natural was cut by two other features which were possibly Roman. A shallow pit (10048) was located in the south-east corner of the trench which largely lay beyond its edges. As recorded it was 0.19m deep and the backfill (10045) was a yellow-grey sandy clay with pebbles. On the west side of the trench there was a small shallow feature (10042), roughly oval in plan measuring 0.60m (north–south) x 0.30m. The backfill was 10041, a brown clay.

In the south-eastern corner of the trench a layer (10043) of orange-brown clay with pebbles was found overlying the ditch, 10047, and pit, 10048. It was succeeded by 10031, a deposit 70mm thick of brown clay with occasional pebbles covering the whole trench. This was cut by post-Roman features.

Trench 13 *(Fig.165)*

Trench 13 was located south of Kent Street. A natural deposit of yellow-white sand (13091) occurred at c.11.85m OD, c.1.70m below modern ground level.

Phase 1

Natural was cut by a number of probable Roman features including a pit (13078) west of the centre of the trench. It was round in plan, 1.05m in diameter, 0.21m deep and backfilled with 13077, grey sandy clay. In addition, there were three shallow cuts, oval in plan, on the west side of the trench (13080, 13082 and13084). 13080, part of which lay beyond the west edge of the trench, measured 0.52m north–south and was filled with 13079, brown silt. 13082, near the south-west corner, measured 0.54 x 0.40m, and was filled with 13081, dark brown silt with occasional charcoal flecks. 13084 measured 0.90m x 0.40m (north–south). It was filled with 13083, grey-brown silty sand with occasional charcoal flecks. On the west side of the trench also were three small post- or stake-holes: 13086, filled by 13085, grey silty clay, and 13088 and 13090, backfilled by 13087 and 13089 respectively, both yellow silty sand.

Phase 2

Much of the centre and west side of the trench was covered by 13076, a light brown sandy clay with occasional charcoal flecks and pebbles which contained some burnt bone.

Phase 3

There were a number of cuts into 13076 including two pits for cremation burials (13055 and 13057) which had both been disturbed by later activity. 13055 existed as a shallow cut, oval in plan, aligned north-east/south-west and measuring 0.38 x 0.30m. It was filled with 13054, brown sandy clay with frequent charcoal flecks which contained burnt bone and a few pot sherds. 13057, immediately north-west of 13055, had a cut subrectangular

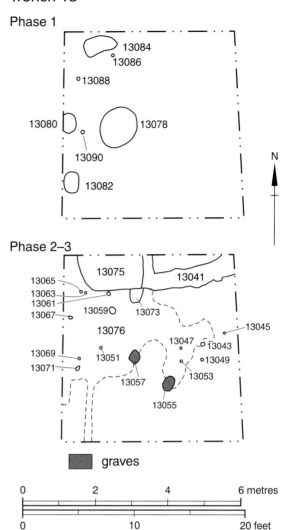

Fig. 165 Barbican Leisure Centre: Plan of Trench 13

in plan, aligned north-east/south-west and measuring 0.30 x 0.28m. It was filled with 13056, brown sandy clay with frequent charcoal flecks which, again, contained burnt bone and a few pot sherds (no date for the pottery from either burial is available).

On the north side of the trench was a small feature (13073), originally oval in plan, cut to the north by 13041 and 13075, and measuring 0.34 x 0.34m. It was filled with 13072, grey-brown silty clay. In the north-west corner of the trench was a shallow pit (13075). About half of it probably lay beyond the northern trench edge; if it had had a regular, rounded plan then its diameter was c.1.50m. The

243

backfill was 13074, dark brown clay with occasional pebbles and charcoal flecks. Although not certain, 13075 appeared to have been cut by 13041, an east–west gully, c.0.10m deep and 0.50m wide. Its west end was not clearly recorded, although it appeared to return to the north. The gully fill was 13040, dark brown clay.

In the centre of the trench there were two clusters of stake-holes cut into 13076, except for 13049 cut into natural, but assumed to be of the same phase. The eastern cluster comprised 13043, 13045, 13047, 13049 and 13053. They were backfilled, respectively, with 13042, 13044 and 13046, all grey silty clay, and 13048 and 13052, both brown clay. The western cluster comprised 13051, filled by 13050 brown clay; 13059, 13069 and 13071, filled, respectively, by 13058, 13068 and 13070, grey silty clay, and 13061, 13063, 13065 and 13067, filled, respectively, by 13060, 13062, 13064 and 13066, yellow sandy clay.

All the features referred to above were sealed under 13039, a deposit up to 0.25m thick of grey silty clay with occasional charcoal flecks and pebbles, which covered the whole trench except where it was cut away by post-Roman features.

Trench 15

Natural orange-brown clay (15017) was encountered at 11.75m OD, c.1.65m below modern ground level. It was overlain by 15016, a deposit 0.15m thick of light brown silty sand; it was undated but was probably Roman. This was cut by three parallel features on an east–west alignment. On the north side of the trench was 15011, a gully or ditch 0.20m deep of which a width of 0.28m was recorded, but of which half lay beyond the north edge of the trench, The fill was a brown silty clay with occasional charcoal flecks and pebbles. In the centre of the trench was a shallow gully (15013), up to 0.50m wide and 0.13m deep, and filled with 15012, a brown silty clay. On the south side of the trench was a ditch (15015), c.0.30m deep, of which a width of 0.45m was recorded, but half of the feature lay beyond the southern trench edge. The fill was 15014, a brown silty clay. All three features were sealed by 15009, a deposit up to 90mm thick, of brown silty clay with occasional charcoal flecks, cobbles and mortar flecks. The few sherds of pottery from these features were Roman, but their align-

ment suggests that these ditches probably related to medieval properties on the Fawcett Street (formerly Fishergate) frontage.

Trench 19 *(Fig.166)*

Trench 19 was located c.15m to the east of Fawcett Street. Natural orange gravelly clay (19056) was encountered at c.12.15m OD, c.1.40m below modern ground level. This deposit was cut by three small features. 19053 in the south-east corner was a shallow, flat-bottomed east–west gully, 0.70m wide and 0.13m deep, of which a length of c.1m was recorded. The backfill (19039) was grey-brown clay. Cut 19054 in the south-west corner of the trench was irregular, measuring up to 0.80m east–west and 1.40m north–south, and up to 0.40m deep; it continued beyond the western trench edge. Its fill was removed with 19051 (see below). 19055 in the north-west corner of the trench was possibly a pit, much of which lay beyond the trench edge; it was 0.17m deep and measured up to 0.70m east–west.

All three features were cut by a large ditch (19052) running north-west/south-east across the centre of the trench. It was up to 2m wide and c.0.75m deep, and its sides sloped down at c.45° to a flat base. The backfill was 19051, brown sandy clay with occasional charcoal flecks, becoming increasingly

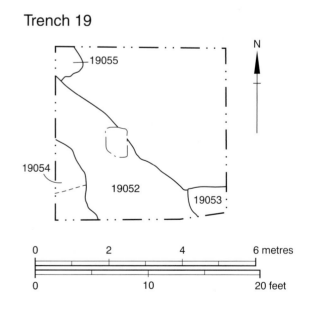

Trench 19

Fig. 166   Barbican Leisure Centre: Plan of Trench 19

pebbly towards the base of the feature. It contained a mid-3rd-century pottery group (*AY* 16/8, 1092).

Subsequent to the infilling of the ditch there may have been some removal of material before the establishment of the graveyard of All Saints since an east–west grave of medieval date was cut into 19051.

Trench 20 *(Figs 164, 167)*

Trench 20 measured 13.6 x 7.4m. Natural clay (20095) was encountered at c.12.35m OD, c.1.15m below modern ground level. It was overlain in much of the northern half of the trench by a clayey deposit (20057, 20081, 20097) containing numerous cobbles and pebbles. There was some doubt during excavation as to whether this constituted a man-made feature, and this seems unlikely. On the northern edge of the deposit an isolated strip (20081) was overlain by deposits 20078 and 20070 which were very similar in character to 20081, but in 20070 a pot sherd of late 1st-/2nd-century date was found.

The deposit just described and the natural were cut by a series of Roman and possible Roman features in the south-eastern half of the trench which had been heavily disturbed by later features.

Ditches or gullies included 20142 on the south side of the trench. It ran north-east/south-west and had a V-shaped profile. The north-west side had a gentler profile than the south-east which had a step immediately above the base. A length of c.1m survived which was 1.20m wide and c.0.45m deep. The deposits contained by 20142 were recorded as 20117, dark grey sandy clay, succeeded by 20134, grey-brown clayey silt; the latter contained pottery dated to the late 1st–mid-2nd century. A continuation of the ditch (20116) was found in the north-east corner of the trench where it was 0.90m wide and 0.54m deep, and the step on south-east side was again recorded. The fill was 20110, dark brown sandy clay with pebbles and charcoal flecks. This ditch in Trench 20 was clearly a north-easterly continuation of the ditch (10047) in Trench 10.

Whilst the ditch described above is certainly Roman, there were a number of features which contained only Roman pottery, but their alignment suggests they are equally likely to be medieval and to relate to properties on Fawcett Street.

Fig. 167   *Barbican Leisure Centre: view north-east of the site under excavation: Trench 21 at top right and Trenches 20 and 10 (latter backfilled) in the foreground*

In the south-eastern part of the trench gully 20137/20147 was recorded running on an east–west alignment for c.4.20m. It was up to 1.10m wide and c.0.39m deep. The backfill (20136/20146) was grey-brown clayey silt with charcoal flecks and pebbles. Immediately to the north was another gully probably running east–west (20139) which cut 20142. A length of 2.80m was recorded. 20139 was 0.95m wide and 0.30m deep, and in profile it had a shallow slot at the base. The fill of 20139 was 20138, dark brown sandy silt with charcoal flecks.

North of 20142, cut into 20097, was 20144, a gully on a north-north-east/south-south-west alignment with a shallow rounded profile of which 1.20m was recorded. It was up to 0.80m wide and 0.35 deep. The backfill was 20143, a brown sandy silt.

About 1m west of 20144 was a shallow scoop (20128) cut into 20097, measuring c.2.20m (north–south) x 1.05m and 0.20m deep. It was filled with 20124, a yellow-grey sandy deposit with pebbles. Cut into 20124 was a narrow, shallow gully (20126), 0.30m wide and 0.20m deep of which 2.40m was recorded. Its alignment was close to north–south and it curved very slightly. The backfill was 20123, a brown clay which produced pottery of late 1st- to 2nd-century date.

In addition to the ditches and gullies, there were a number of other cuts of either Roman or later date. Pit 20133 was located on the east side of the trench, north of 20139 and cutting 20057. It was roughly rounded in plan with a diameter of at least 1.60m and depth of 0.97m. The fill (20125) was brown silty clay with pebbles and charcoal flecks. South-east of 20133 was 20122, of which about half lay beyond the trench edge; it was rounded in plan with a maximum width of 1m and depth of 1.17m. Its fill was 20100, a light brown sandy clay, succeeded by 20120, grey clayey silt. Cutting 20133 and located on the south-east trench edge was 20087, a shallow feature cut away on all sides and continuing beyond the trench edge. It measured 2.20 x 1.20m and was 0.22m deep. The fill 20077/20129 was brown clay with cobbles.

Pit 20133 and feature 20087 may be dated by the latest pottery from pit fill 20100 which was early 3rd century.

North of 21033 a small feature (20042), 0.60 x 0.20m and 0.30m deep, cut into 20057, was itself cut away on its south side by a modern feature. The fill was 20038, brown clay with cobbles.

Trench 21 *(Fig.169)*

Trench 21 initially measured 46.8 x 9.8m, but excavation was only undertaken in the northern half. Natural orange sandy clay (21043) was encountered at c.12.50–12.60m OD, c.1m below modern level. At the eastern end of the trench a shallow linear feature (21081) up to 1.40m wide was found sunk into the surface of the clay and filled with cobbles and pebbles; it is interpreted as being natural. North-east of this a similar cobble-filled feature (21078) was found. At the west end of the trench areas of what were thought to be disturbed natural with numerous cobbles (21041 and 21066) produced a sherd of late 1st- to 2nd-century pot.

Three pits found in the centre of the trench appeared to be Roman. 21014 was oval in plan, measured 1.90m (north–south) x 1.30m and was 1.24m deep. The sides fell away gently before becoming vertical. The backfill was 21011, dark brown silt with charcoal flecks becoming grey and sandy towards the base. Pottery from the deposit was dated late 1st–early 3rd century. About 1.20m to the north-east of 21014 was 21039, roughly oval in plan, measuring c.1.60m (north–south) x 1.25m, and 0.43m deep. The fill (21021) was dark grey silt with occasional charcoal flecks which produced pottery of late 1st- to late 2nd-century date. 21039 was cut

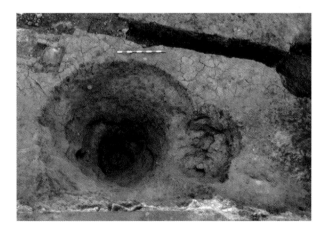

Fig. 168 Barbican Leisure Centre, Trench 21: view south of pit 21010 fully excavated, 21039 to right (scale 1m)

246

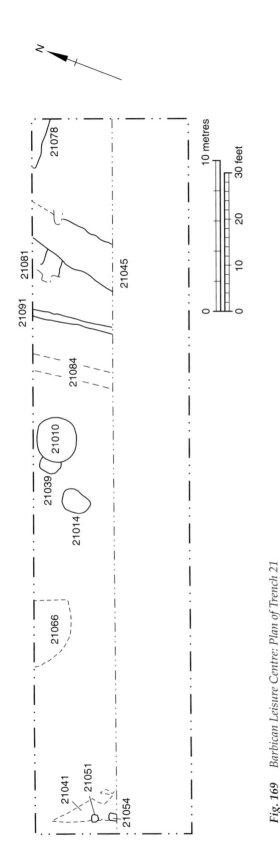

Fig. 169 Barbican Leisure Centre: Plan of Trench 21

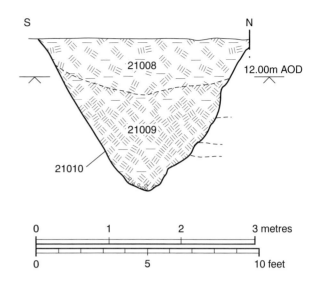

Fig. 170 Barbican Leisure Centre: Trench 21, section of pit 21010

on its north-east side by 21010, a large pit, rounded in plan with a diameter of 3m and depth of 2m; the cut was shaped like an inverted cone (Fig.168; Fig.170). The earliest fill (21009) was a mix of dark brown silt and orange clay which produced pottery of late 1st- to 2nd-century date. It was succeeded by 21008, dark brown clayey silt.

About 4m east of pit 21010 was a ditch (21084) running north–south across the trench. It was up to 1m wide and 0.34m deep with a somewhat irregular profile and a flat bottom. The fill (21076) was dark grey silt mixed with a little orange-brown sand which produced a sherd of samian (undated).

At the west end of the trench two small features produced only Roman pot. 21051, 60mm deep, was probably a post-hole. The fill was 21050, brown sand with cobbles. To the south was 21054, 0.50 x 0.40m and 0.20m deep, which lay largely beyond the south edge of excavation. The fill was 21053, dark brown sand. Both features produced pottery of late 1st- to 2nd-century date.

Subsequent deposits and features in Trench 21 probably belonged to the medieval and later periods and related to properties facing Fawcett Street. They include 21045, a ditch, and 21091, a narrow gully.

City Arms, Fawcett Street

In June 2001 an archaeological evaluation, supervised by Mark Johnson, was undertaken in the car park of the City Arms, Fawcett Street (SE60975118; Fig.161, 2), immediately to the west of the Barbican Leisure Centre. The work was carried out on the instruction of Lawrence Hannah and Partners on behalf of Treatprefer Ltd to a specification prepared by the Principal Archaeologist for City of York Council. This involved the excavation of two trenches 2 x 2m to a maximum depth of 1.80m.

All finds and records are stored in archive under the Yorkshire Museum accession code YORYM : 2001.10748

Trench 1 *(Figs 162 and 171)*

Natural orange-brown sandy clay (1017) was encountered at 12.10m OD, 1.53m below modern ground level. This was cut by a ditch (1014) on a north-east/south-west alignment which unfortunately could not be fully excavated because of restrictions on depth in the specification. It appeared, however, to have been over 2m wide as the upper edges of the cut lay beyond the trench edges. The earliest infill identified (1013) was a pale brown sandy silt with cobbles and pebbles. It produced eight sherds of 2nd- to 3rd-century pottery and a few pieces of Roman tile. 1013 was sealed by 1012, a deposit slightly greyer in colour than 1013. 1012 produced pottery of the Roman period, but also of medieval and post-medieval date thought to have been intrusive. The ditch is probably part of the same ditch system identified in the adjacent Barbican Leisure Centre site.

1012 was cut by a small pit (1011) c.0.30m deep and 0.60m across which continued beyond

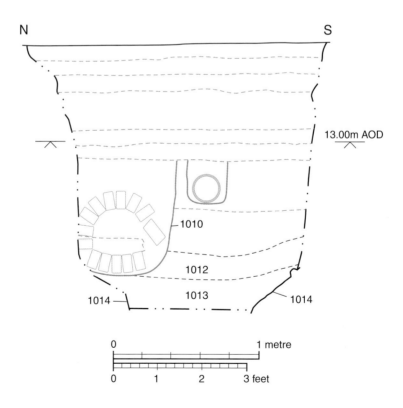

Fig. 171 City Arms, Fawcett Street: Trench 1, west-facing section

the northern trench edge. The infilling (1015) was a grey-brown clayey silt with a few cobbles and pebbles. It contained a single sherd of Roman pottery, a 2nd-century grey ware handle. In addition, a deposit sample produced a small number of well-preserved fish bones including eel and herring. Unfortunately the relationship of this feature with deposits above 1012 was destroyed by a 19th-century culvert (1010). These deposits were up to 0.60m thick. No finds were recovered from them and they are presumably of medieval and later date. Subsequent deposits and features were 19th century or modern.

Trench 2 *(Fig.172)*

Natural (2004) was once again encountered at 12.10m OD. It was overlain by a deposit (2001) of grey-brown clayey silty sand, 0.24m thick, which produced three sherds of 2nd- to 3rd-century date. This was sealed by a deposit (2000), up to 0.50m thick, of dark brown sandy silt. Pottery dated from the medieval and Roman periods. Subsequent deposits and features were 19th century or modern. The further work at the City Arms by On Site Archaeology located a small group of Roman inhumation burials.

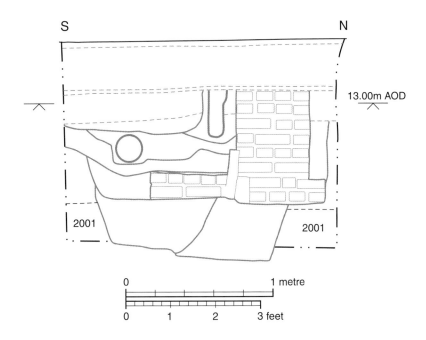

Fig. 172 City Arms, Fawcett Street: Trench 2, east-facing section

School Canteen, Fawcett Street

Introduction

In September 1998 an evaluation excavation, under the direction of Neil Macnab, took place at the former school canteen, Fawcett Street, now Barbican Court (SE60795113; Fig.161, 3) south of the junction with Kent Street. Work took place on behalf of the architects, David Chapman Associates. This report has been adapted from Neil Macnab's Evaluation Report (YAT Field Report 1998/52).

The excavation involved three trenches, two of which (Trenches 1 and 3) measured 3 x 3m and the third (Trench 2) measured 6m (east–west) x 1m.

Finds and site records are stored at York Archaeological Trust under the Yorkshire Museum accession code YORYM : 1998.693.

The excavation

Trench 1 *(Fig.173)*

Trench 1 was located on the western side of the site, c.8m east of Fawcett Street. Natural (1011), a yellowish sandy clay with occasional pockets of cobbles and patches of stiff orange sandy clay, was encountered at 12.08m OD, 1.32m below modern ground level. This was sealed by a deposit, up to c.60mm thick, of grey-brown silty sand (1025) which was undated. In the north side of the trench 1025 had been cut away (1024,1027) before being overlain by a deliberately laid deposit of small to medium-sized cobbles (1001, 1023) in a matrix of grey-brown clayey sand. Five abraded fragments of pottery from the deposit were dated to the 3rd–4th century, although this need not mean it belongs to the Roman period. No strata separated the cobbles from the cut of a north–south gully (1010) of probable Anglo-Scandinavian or medieval date, taking its alignment from Fawcett Street (formerly Fishergate).

Trench 2 *(Figs 174–75)*

Trench 2 lay within the former canteen structure. Natural yellow-brown clayey sand (2012) was encountered at 11.96m OD, 1.44m below modern ground level. This was cut by a shallow gully (2011) on a north–south alignment near the centre of the trench. It was 0.60–0.70m wide and 0.11–0.26m deep with steep, uneven sides and an irregular base. A depression c.0.10m deeper than the base of the gully was located on its east side near the northern edge of the trench. The feature was backfilled with grey-brown sandy silt (2010) which contained two sherds of 2nd- to 3rd-century date. However, in view of its alignment it is likely that the feature is post-Roman. Overlying gully 2011 was a deposit 0.86m thick excavated in four spits (2006–9). The earliest spit contained eight sherds of 2nd- to 3rd-century pottery; later spits contained medieval and later pottery. If gully 2011 were Roman, it is possible, but by no means certain, that the deposit began to accumulate in the Roman period. At the west end of the trench was a cut for a World War II air raid shelter.

Trench 3 *(Figs 176–179)*

Trench 3 was located to the east of the canteen building. Natural light orange-brown clayey sand (3015) was located at 11.81m OD, 1.59m below modern ground level. This was cut by a ditch (3014), on a north-east/south-west alignment, of which the north-west side was fully revealed but

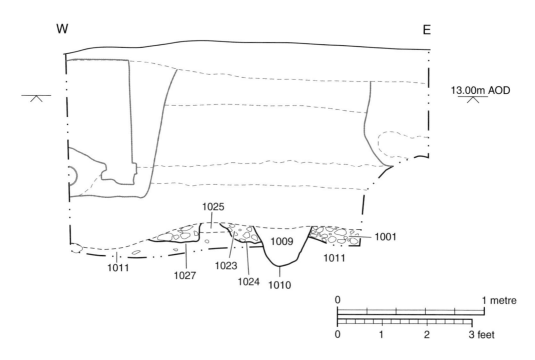

Fig. 173   School Canteen, Fawcett Street: Trench 1, south-facing section

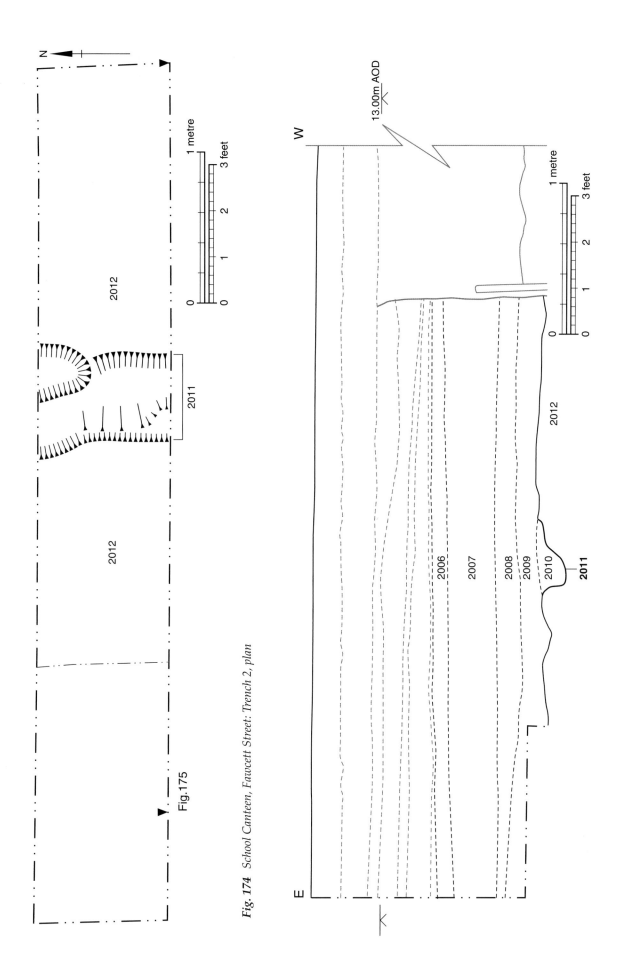

Fig. 174 School Canteen, Fawcett Street: Trench 2, plan

Fig. 175 School Canteen, Fawcett Street: Trench 2, north-facing section

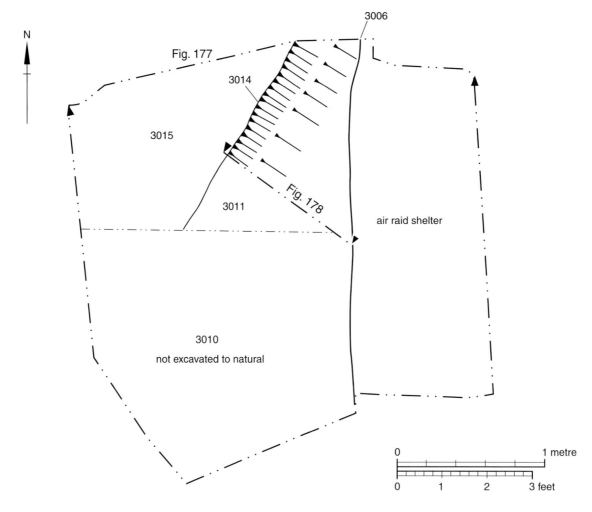

Fig.176 *School Canteen, Fawcett Street: Trench 3, plan*

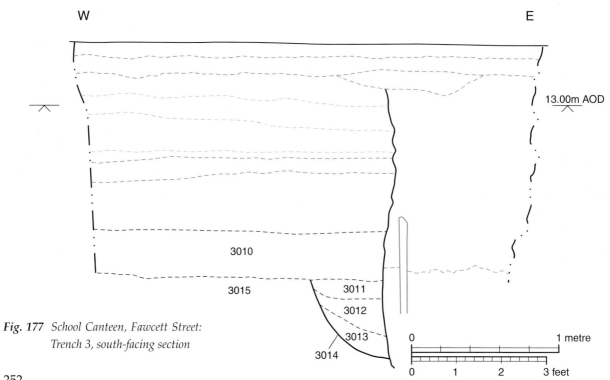

Fig. 177 *School Canteen, Fawcett Street:*
Trench 3, south-facing section

the south-east side was cut away by the air raid shelter. The ditch was recorded as c.1.10m wide and 0.60m deep. In profile the north-west side had a gentle slope but on the steeper south-east side there was some suggestion of a step above the base. The ditch was backfilled with three deposits; the earliest was 3013, light yellowish-brown silty clay, which was succeeded by 3012 and then by 3011, both recorded as grey-brown clay silts. 3012 produced pottery of 2nd- to early 3rd-century date. This feature was overlain by 3010, a deposit producing pottery of 11th- to 13th-century date. Subsequent deposits were medieval and later.

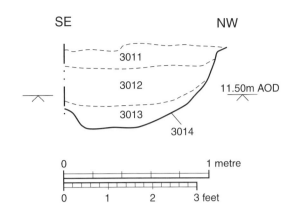

Fig. 178 School Canteen, Fawcett Street: Trench 3, ditch 3014, north-east-facing section

Fig.179 School Canteen, Fawcett Street, Trench 3: south-facing section showing ditch 3014 (bottom centre) and air raid shelter wall (right). Scale 2m

Escrick Street

In July 1989 an evaluation supervised by Niall Oakey took place at the site of a former warehouse at 8–9 Escrick Street (SE60835107; Fig.161, 4). The work, on behalf of Chessingham Estates Ltd, involved a trench c.3.60 (north–south) x 1.60m (east–west).

Natural yellow-brown clay, was encountered at 11.88m OD at a depth of 1.30m below modern level. Natural was overlain by 1006, a light grey-brown deposit, which contained a few sherds of Roman pottery (late 1st–2nd century). 1006 was cut by a medieval ditch running north–south.

The finds and site records are stored at York Archaeological Trust under the Yorkshire Museum accession code 1989.16.

17–23 Lawrence Street

Introduction

In May 1989 an excavation, supervised by Niall Oakey, was undertaken to assess the archaeological potential of an area east of the medieval city walls behind Nos 17–23 Lawrence Street (SE61205143; Fig.161, 5; Fig.180). The work took place in advance of an office development by Kaye Land Developments Ltd, the site owners, who funded the excavation in full. This report has been prepared from Niall Oakey's notes.

The area intended for development covered about 100m², but the excavations were limited to two machine-cut trenches c.2.50–2.75m wide, at 90° to each other. Trench 1, running east–west, was c.32m long and Trench 2, north–south, c.23m long. The trenches were located c.50m north of Lawrence Street which is close to the line of the Roman road approaching York from the east (Road 2; RCHMY **1**, 1, and see below).

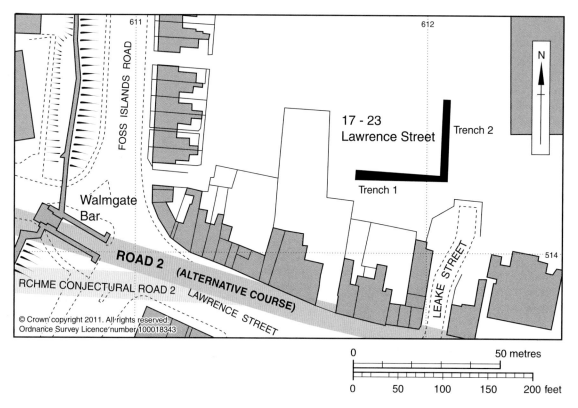

Fig. 180 *17–23 Lawrence Street: Site and trenches location plan*

The records and finds are stored at York Archaeological Trust under the Yorkshire Museum accession code 1989.8.

The excavation (Figs 181–3)

Removal of material derived from modern industrial and domestic activity, together with up to 1m depth of overburden, revealed natural clay at a level of c.11.25m OD, cut by archaeological features predominantly of Roman and Anglo-Scandinavian date. Below the clay which became gradually thicker towards the north of Trench 2 was a glacial sand.

Period 1

In Trench 1 a slot with near vertical sides (1098), c.0.70m wide and 0.60m deep on a north-east/south-west alignment was found. It had been backfilled with redeposited natural, recorded as yellow sand mixed with yellow-orange clay. This slot may have been the base of a timber fence or building wall of which no other trace remained.

Four metres to the east of 1098 a shallow, circular depression (1094) up to 1.20m across and 0.18m deep contained a hearth of burnt clay and charcoal (1093). A second period of burning in the same feature was represented by burnt clay (1092). After going out of use the hearth was sealed by clayey deposit (1087) before the cut for another hearth (1095) was made a little to the west. This cut was of similar shape to 1094, but larger, being up to 1.43m across, and it had a circular depression in the centre giving an overall depth of 0.38m. Cut 1095 was backfilled with burnt material (1086). No material indicative of a specialised use was derived from either of these hearths. Time did not allow the examination of contemporary levels east of hearth 1094.

No finds were recovered from Period 1 contexts, but they are presumed to be Roman.

Period 2

In Trench 1 the Period 1 contexts were sealed by a layer of orange-brown clay mixed with grey-brown silty sand (1085). In the western half of the trench this layer was truncated by post-Roman features; its limit to the east was not established. Deposit 1085 was cut by two stake-holes (1047–8) overlain by a

Fig.181 *17–23 Lawrence Street: view south of Trench 2, features 1050–1 in the centre (scale 1m)*

surface of small cobbles (1042) up to 3.28m wide east–west. Bounding these cobbles to the west was a slot or ditch (1052) which crossed the trench from north-west to south-east. It was c.1m at its wides and 0.47m at its deepest, at the south-east end. Two possible post impressions were seen in the base of 1052, perhaps indicating a structural function and the feature had remained open long enough for the sides to erode and slump to produce an irregular profile. At the base of the feature the fill (1041) was redeposited natural clay and sand while above it was a clayey silt with occasional flecks of charcoal.

In Trench 2 two large, irregular depressions, c.2.50 x c.2m, were cut into the natural clay. The more northerly of the two (1050) had vertical sides, neatly squared off to the north where the cut was more than 0.60m deep, while 1051 to the south was much more irregular in shape and profile, and also shallower. The bottom of both features coincided with the interface of natural clay and glacial sand, except in the south-west corner of 1050 where a hole

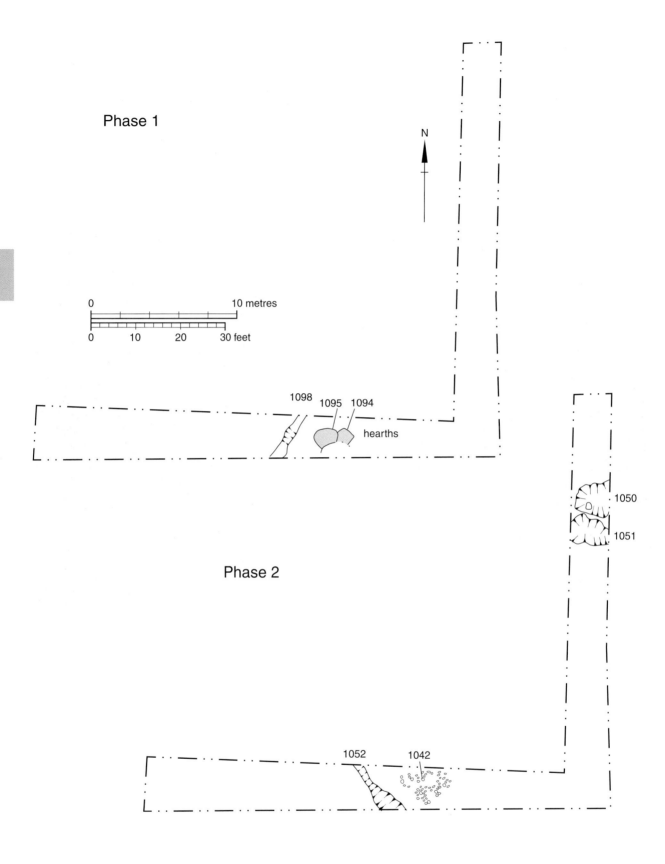

Fig. 182 *17–23 Lawrence Street: Plan of Roman features*

c.0.80m diameter had been dug to a depth of 0.32m below the level of the base of the feature. A stake- or post-hole (1063) had been dug into the clay baulk between the pits and may be associated with them. Features 1050, 1051 and 1063 were all filled with a sandy deposit (1030).

A small amount of pottery was recovered from Phase 2 contexts and dated to the 3rd century (*AY* 16/8, 1092). It included two grey ware sherds from wasters and another six were found residual in later contexts. These waster sherds may indicate that pottery production took place in the area and cuts 1050 and 1051 may have been made to extract clay. Excavation of them had ceased when the bottom of the natural clay was reached; the hole dug down into natural sand in the base of 1050 may have been made to see if more clay occurred below it.

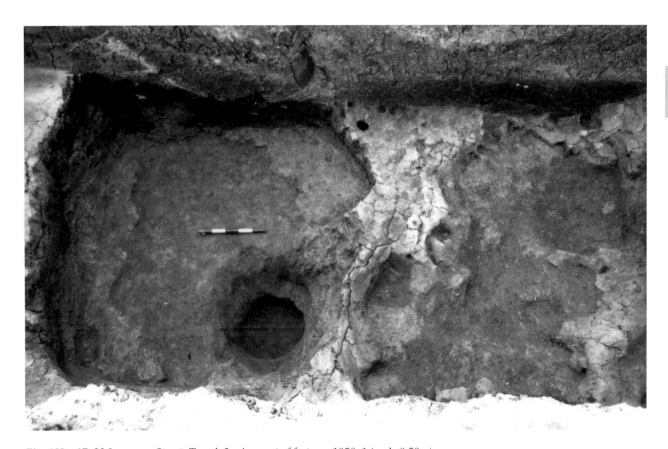

Fig. 183   *17–23 Lawrence Street, Trench 2: view east of features 1050–1 (scale 0.50m)*

Belle Vue Street

Introduction

In May 1994 a watching brief was undertaken by Patrick Ottaway during site clearance for building work at 40 Belle Vue Street, Heslington Road (SE61245105; Fig.161, 6; Fig.185). Work involved a foundation trench c.0.60m wide and 0.75m deep around an area c.6.50 x 5m with a small extension at the north-west corner, 2.50m square. The site was found to have archaeological interest when Roman pottery was recovered near the south-west corner. Further investigation revealed a cobbled layer at a depth of c.0.60m. The western foundation trench was then excavated under archaeological supervision.

All site records are stored at York Archaeological Trust under the Yorkshire Museum accession code YORYM : 1994.0174. The finds were returned to the property owner Mr Colin Bell to whom thanks are due for alerting the Trust to the discovery and allowing access for recording.

Fig. 184 *40 Belle Vue Street: view north of road surface*

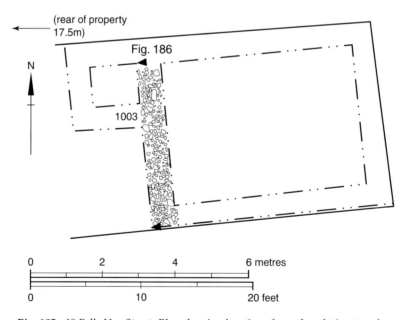

Fig. 185 *40 Belle Vue Street: Plan showing location of new foundation trenches*

The archaeological discoveries

(Figs 184–186)

Natural yellow-brown sand with occasional pebbles was encountered at c.18.15m OD, c.1m below modern ground level. The earliest context was a small pit (1006) in the centre of the trench, circular in plan, 0.85m wide and 0.65m deep. At the base of the pit the natural sand appeared stained, perhaps by burning. On the base was a deliberately laid sandstone slab over which was a smaller magnesian limestone slab. Above these slabs, in matrix of red-brown sandy silt, were a number of large cobbles and fragments of magnesian limestone. At the top of the pit there were a few sandstone slabs laid flat, probably burnt, and a large piece of magnesian limestone c.0.60m long. This pit fill was sealed by 1004, a reddish-brown sandy silt with occasional cobbles and magnesian limestone fragments which covered much of the trench. Overlying 1004 was 1003, medium–large cobbles and occasional magnesian limestone fragments loosely packed in red-brown sandy silt. This deposit was make up for a road or track, c.4m wide, probably running east–west or east-north-east/west-south-west. There were also cobbles in the north side of the southern foundation trench, but elsewhere excavation did not go to a sufficient depth to reveal more of the road. The road surface make up (1003) was overlain by 1002, reddish-brown sandy silt with occasional cobbles, which was in turn below 1001, modern garden soil.

Unstratified pottery and pottery from deposits 1003–4 dated to the late 2nd century.

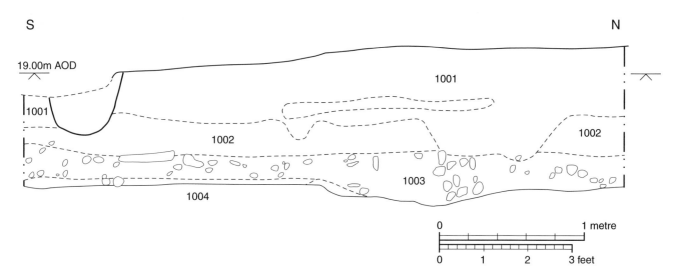

Fig. 186 *40 Belle Vue Street: East-facing section of western foundation trench*

259

A19/A64 Interchange, Fulford

In April 1997 a watching brief was undertaken by Neil Macnab during machine excavation of a drainage trench on the south side of the A19/A64 interchange in Fulford, c.4.5km south of York (Fig.54, 24). A Roman gritstone coffin containing a human skeleton was revealed. The site lay on the west side of the A19 on land which rises slightly towards the south-east and falls towards the Ouse to the west.

Records and finds are stored by YAT under the Yorkshire Museum accession code YORYM : 1997.51.

Unfortunately the burial had been badly disturbed by the machine, but it was possible to see that the coffin with its lid originally measured 2.15 x 0.75 x 0.74m high. The skeletal remains were poorly preserved, although they were probably of a male aged 18–25 years. The body had evidently been covered in gypsum (calcium sulphate). Although this was a custom which probably began in the early 3rd century, use of gypsum is usually taken to indicate a burial of the late 3rd–4th century, a period when it enjoyed a measure of popularity in high-status burials in the York area. Some 35 examples of gypsum burials were recorded in RCHMY **1**. Other burials found in stone coffins at a similar distance from the city as the Fulford burial have been recorded near Heslington church (Fig.54, 15; YPS 1832) and between Middlethorpe and Old Nunthorpe, west of the Ouse (RCHMY **1**, 108)

The context of the Fulford burial is difficult to determine, but it was probably related to a Roman settlement in the immediate area. Roman burials are often adjacent to roads, and although no Roman roads are known in Fulford, it is possible that a road approached York from the south, perhaps originating in Doncaster (*Danum*), passing through what is now Fulford village and heading for a crossing over the River Foss (see discussion below). Roman field systems have been examined at Lingcroft Farm c.1km to the south-west of the burial site (Fig.54, 23; Jones 1988; Jones 1990) and at Germany Beck a similar distance to the north (Fig.54, 22; MAP 1996b). At the latter site the pottery recovered hinted at high-status occupation in the area and a burial in a stone coffin would seem to support this.

4

Zone 4: Discussion

Roads

RCHME's Road 1 (RCHMY **1**, 1) approached York from an as yet uncertain origin point to the south-east. For c.4km from Pool Bridge (c.6.5km south-east of York) to Germany Beck its line is thought to be represented by the parish boundary between Fulford and Heslington and can be seen as a mound (agger) on Fulford golf course. The road itself was observed at Germany Beck in a drainage trench in 1965 (Fig.54, 20; Radley 1966, 559). There is some uncertainty about the course of the road from here to York itself, but if projected in a straight line north-west from Germany Beck, it would run across Low Moor (Walmgate Stray), York Cemetery and then the former cattle market and Barbican Leisure Centre site on Paragon Street. On Fig.161 the line taken from RCHMY **1** is shown passing through Trench 21, although if an exactly straight line from the parish boundary were plotted the road would have run a little to the east of the trench. It is possible that any remains of Road 1 have been removed by the cattle market, although one would, perhaps, have expected to find the roadside ditches. However, until further investigation has been done between Germany Beck and the Barbican site, it has been thought best to continue to show Road 1 more or less on the RCHME line as far as a junction with Road 2 near Foss Bridge (on Figs 54–5 and 57; and see above, Zone 3 discussion, p.235).

Whilst this line for Road 1 may in due course prove correct, it can on topographic grounds be suggested that a road from the south-east would, after leaving Germany Beck, have sought to avoid both the low-lying ground on Low Moor to the north, which is often flooded today, and the steep climb up onto the moraine where York cemetery stands. Instead it might have headed in a more westerly direction across what are now Fulford Road Barracks and then adopted the line of the present Fulford Road, Fishergate and Fawcett Street (Fig.131). In doing so it would have provided an access route to York from the Fishergate Roman cemetery (RCHMY **1**, 69–70). A Roman ditch excavated by FAS in 2001 at the Blue Bridge Lane and Fishergate House site (Fig.54, 11) ran north–south on a line c.10m west of Fishergate and was thought to be a roadside ditch (Spall and Toop 2005a). From Fishergate, the line of Fawcett Street would have taken the

road to the site of Fishergate Bar from where it would have run towards a junction with Road 2 at a Foss crossing (see p.198 above).

The stretch of Fulford Road referred to lies on slightly raised ground above the River Ouse to the west and Low Moor (Walmgate Stray) to the east. The land continues to fall away to the river west of Fishergate. It may also be noted that the presence of a Roman road on the line of Fishergate and Fawcett Street has been envisaged as contributing to the choice of a zone on the east bank of the Foss for the 7th- to 8th-century trading settlement at York (*AY* 7/1, 76–7).

Whether this is an accurate suggestion for a revised line of Road 1 or not, one can still envisage a route of Roman date approaching York from the south along the line of Fulford Road, first of all running along the slight ridge of high ground on which Fulford village now stands (Fig.55) before adopting the line described in the previous paragraph. As already noted, given that Roman burials were often located close to roads, a Roman road through Fulford may account for the burial in a stone coffin, described above, found south of the village. Proximity to a road may also explain, in part, the presence of an unusual dump of coin moulds at St Oswald's School, Fulford (see below).

Road 2 approached York from the east, having branched off Humber Street (heading for Malton) c.10km north of Brough-on-Humber. It is possible that this was the road located at Grimston Bar during construction of the outer ring road in 1975 (Fig.54, 18; p.87, *AY* 6/1), but it is more likely to have been a road approaching from Stamford Bridge to the north-east which was also encountered at Thorntree Hill, Dunnington, in a water pipeline in 1996. The roads from Brough and Stamford Bridge probably met just below (north of) Kimberlow Hill (Fig.54, 16) before running towards the city to Gallows Hole (SE630513, Fig.54, 17) on the old city boundary. From here the road was thought by RCHME to run a little to the north of Hull Road/Lawrence Street before converging on the latter close to Walmgate Bar where, composed of cobbles set in clay, it was seen at a depth of c.2m in a sewer trench in 1954 (SE61175139), and again nearer the Bar in 1915 (Benson 1919, 162). The line mapped by RCHME is probably drawn a little too far to the north as, although the road was recorded close to Lawrence Street at Nos 127 and 131 in 1974 and 1975 (p.89, *AY* 6/1), it was not found by YAT on the RCHME line in the garden of 127 Lawrence Street in 2002 (2002.451) in trenches to the north of that excavated in 1974, or by FAS, c.110m further east, at 1 Hull Road in 2001.

From Walmgate Bar it is likely that the road headed north-west and perhaps ran along a line close to that now occupied by Walmgate itself before, as suggested above, converging on Road 1 at the Foss crossing (see also discussion of Zone 3).

A hitherto unknown minor road came to light in Belle Vue Street. It appeared to run roughly east–west, although it was difficult to determine an exact alignment in a narrow trench. To the west it presumably joined Road 1. Approaching from the east, the road might have formed part of a route into York along the high ground of the moraine east of the city which, as noted above, was probably a route of prehistoric origin. Approaching York from Heslington Hill (Fig.54, 14), such a road would have run through what are now the grounds of The Retreat and the site of an artificial mound known as Lamel Hill where a possible Roman burial has been found (Thurnam 1849; Briden 1984, 164). A Roman road here might explain the location of the Anglian burials at Lamel Hill (*ibid.*) and at nearby Belle Vue House (excavated by YAT, 1983.31) where, in addition, a Roman coffin lid was found. A hoard of 2800 coins dated to 358–9 was found in 1966 at what is now Alcuin College (Carson and Kent 1971) near Heslington Hill.

Land use and settlement in the late 1st–late 3rd century

There is no evidence for Roman structures on the Zone 4 sites described above unless the slots in Trench 1 at 17–23 Lawrence Street were related to a timber building. However, on the periphery of the zone, at Heslington East (Fig.54, 19), immediately south of Kimberlow Hill, a 2nd-century building with a room heated with a hypocaust has come to light which perhaps belonged to a farmstead of which

other remains have now been lost (excavation by YAT 2003–4 and Department of Archaeology, University of York 2008). Otherwise settlement evidence is largely confined to ditches representing, as in other extramural zones, land division in the mid-2nd–early 3rd century.

As far as ditches at Barbican and adjacent sites are concerned, there appear to be two pairs of alignments represented, one, which was undoubtedly Roman, was north-west/south-east or north-east/south-west, and the other was north–south or east–west. In only one place was there any intercutting of features with the two alignments. This was in Trench 20 (see context 20142 above) and it appeared that the feature running east–west cut that running north-east/south-west. Whilst it is possible that some at least of the features running east–west and north–south were Roman, it is most likely, even though they only produced Roman pottery, that they were post-Roman and related to properties of Anglo-Scandinavian or medieval origin on the east side of Fawcett Street, formerly Fishergate, which runs on a more or less north–south alignment, passing through the 12th-century city defences at Fishergate Bar.

Although the evidence is fragmentary, some indication of the existence of an extensive system of Roman land division to the east of Fawcett Street can be deduced from it (Fig.162). A ditch with a distinctive cross-section profile, steeper on the south-east side than on the north-west, and with a step above the base on the steeper side, can be traced running on a north-east/south-west alignment across Trench 20 at Barbican Leisure Centre, continuing into Trench 10 and then probably lining up with the ditch recorded in Trench 1 at City Arms. If continued to the south-west this ditch might have met a continuation to the north-west of the ditch running north-west/south-east recorded in Barbican Trench 19. If this latter continued for some 75m to the south-east of Trench 19 it would have met another ditch running north-east/south-west located in Trench 3 of the School Canteen site. This ditch had a similar profile, with a step on the south-east side, to the ditches in the Barbican.

The ditches recorded on the site of the Barbican swimming baths (pp.76–8, *AY* 6/1) probably formed part of the same system of land division as those already described, although they do not observe quite the same alignment in being roughly east-south-east/west-north-west. At 17–23 Lawrence Street the dominant Roman alignments in much of the York area were again respected in the slot referred to above (north-east/south-west) and a slot or ditch in Trench 1 running north-west/south-east.

As in other zones also, another determinant of ditch alignment was probably the nearest Roman road. For example, in Lawrence Street, at the former D.C. Cook premises (Fig.54, 12), excavated in 2002–3, Roman ditches were found running perpendicular (roughly north–south) to the main approach road (Road 2) from the east (Evans 2004).

Further east in Osbaldwick, Roman ditches, again of late 2nd- to early 3rd-century date were found (by YAT) at a site north-west of the village centre in 2002 (Fig.54, 7; 2002.451). In the southern part of Zone 4, in Fulford, a complex sequence of enclosure ditches was found in evaluation of the site of St Oswald's School in the village centre (Fig.54, 21; MAP 2005b), and all four phases appear to have belonged, as elsewhere, to the late 2nd–early 3rd centuries. In a ditch of the latest phase over 50 fired clay coin moulds were found which must have derived from unofficial minting, probably in the early–mid-3rd century. In what circumstances these unusual objects had ended up in a ditch in what was then a rural area is hard to comprehend, but they would have been contemporary with a smaller group of moulds found near the fortress at 21–33 Aldwark (pp.39–40, *AY* 6/1). More ditches, of much the same date, were found in the evaluation of a large site (76ha) at Germany Beck to the south of Fulford Village (Fig.54, 22; MAP 1996b).

In addition to ditches in Zone 4, there were also Roman pits at Barbican Leisure Centre (Trenches 20–1) and 17–23 Lawrence Street. At Barbican, pits 21014, 21039 and 21010 (and possibly 20133 and 20122 also) all appear to have been dug to respect the prevailing north-east/south-west alignment of the ditches in the area. The function of these pits is difficult to determine, although rubbish tipping appears unlikely in view of their sparse artefactual content. One possibility is that they were dug to recover clay for pottery and tile-making, and then immediately backfilled with whatever came to hand in the vicinity. Another possibility is that they are cess pits, which would account for the lack of artefacts, but this would imply some settlement in

the area for which evidence is at present lacking. At 17–23 Lawrence Street two pits were found in Trench 2 which may have been dug for clay extraction and, as noted above, grey ware wasters were identified in the pottery assemblage suggesting a kiln existed in the area (*AY* 16/8, 1092).

Burials

Roman burials from the Zone 4 sites described above are confined to the inhumation in a stone coffin at Fulford and two undated cremations located in Trench 13 at Barbican Leisure Centre, although a small group of inhumations was found by On Site Archaeology in 2008 at the City Arms site. The discovery of the cremation burials suggests that the 1st – 2nd century cremation cemetery recorded in the Winterscale Street/Melbourne Street area on Fishergate extended further to the north than hitherto known (RCHMY 1, 69). The ditch located in Trench 3 of the School Canteen site may have formed a north-western boundary to the burial plot. It may also be noted that the two graves were themselves on a north-west/south-east line and therefore perpendicular to that ditch. Cremations and an inhumation found in 2001 by FAS west of Fishergate in the grounds of Fishergate House and on the corner of Blue Bridge Lane and Fishergate (Fig.54, 11) allow the western limit of the cemetery to be extended also (Spall and Toop 2005a).

The Fulford burial at present appears to be isolated from any cemetery, but may be seen in the context of Roman settlement evidence in the Fulford area and of other burials in stone coffins, some also covered with gypsum, in York itself and its region (pp.260, 374).

Land use and settlement in the late Roman period

There is very little evidence for late 3rd- to 4th-century activity either at the sites described above or at other sites in Zone 4. As in other extramural zones, the land division defined by ditches appears to have largely gone out of use. Only on the periphery of the zone at Heslington East (Fig.54, 19) does there appear to have been any late Roman restatement of earlier boundaries. In the Germany Beck evaluation (Fig.54, 22) a few sherds of late 4th-century 'Huntcliff-type' pottery were found (Evans 2005). For the most part it appears that much of the zone reverted to being open ground.

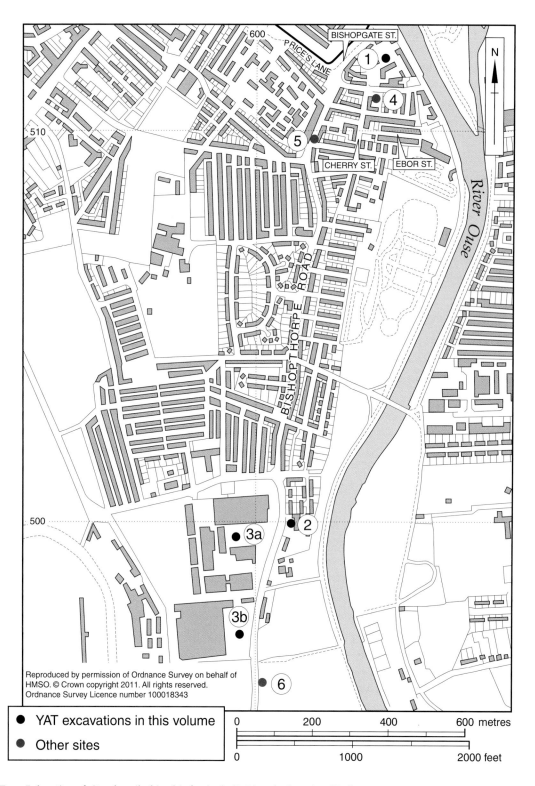

● YAT excavations in this volume

● Other sites

Fig. 187 *Zone 5: location of sites described in this fascicule (1–3) and other sites (4–6)*

1. Terry Avenue/Cherry Hill Lane

2. 292 Bishopthorpe Road (1998) and Old Nunthorpe (1930s)

3a. Terry's Factory (2005), Area B

3b. Terry's Factory (2005), Area D

4. Clementhorpe (1976–7)

5. Bishopthorpe Road – Roman road (1981)

6. Finds made in the 18th century

Zone 5: South-west of the Ouse – the Bishopthorpe Road area

Introduction *(Figs 54, 187)*

Zone 5 encompasses a corridor of land south of the medieval city walls extending from Bishopgate Street and Bishopthorpe Road on the west side to the River Ouse on the east (Fig.54; Fig.187).

Immediately north-west of Zone 5, north-west of Bishopgate Street, the Bishophill/Skeldergate area of the walled city was included in the main Roman settlement south-west of the Ouse, but it was not apparently given buildings and streets until after a major terracing of the slope down to the river in the early 3rd century (Ramm 1976; *AY* 4/1). Further to the south-east, between Falkland Street and Baile Hill, the presence of burials suggests an area initially, at least, outside any Roman settlement (RCHMY **1**, 107–8). Four Roman tombs were lined with tiles bearing Sixth Legion stamps indicating a date after c.120.

Outside the medieval walls a possible approach road to York from the south, not recorded by RCHME, was observed in Bishopthorpe Road, designated Road 12 in *AY* 6/1 (p.101). This may have acted as a focus for a number of burials (RCHMY **1**, 107–8), including inhumations in stone coffins at what are now the junctions of Cherry Street and Ebor Street, and of Bishopgate Street and Price's Lane. The tombstone of Vitellia Procula's child was found on the site of St Clement's nunnery along with 3rd- to 4th-century pots, probably from burials. In addition to burials, on the south side of Clementhorpe evidence for an early 3rd-century riverside terrace was found on which there were the remains of a house which was given an apse and mosaics in the early 4th century (pp.55–83, *AY* 6/1).

Further south evidence for Roman activity was found at Old Nunthorpe in the 1930s (Fig.187, 2; RCHMY **1**, 63) including a skull, probably from a burial, found with a coin of Claudius II (268–70) (Fig.187, 3a; *ibid.*, 108). Further south again on a gravel terrace east of Bishopgate Road, overlooking the Ouse, finds supposedly of Flavian samian, metal objects, oyster shells and numerous cattle bones were made in the 18th century (Fig.187, 6; *ibid.*, 63). In a field near the Ouse between Middlethorpe and Old Nunthorpe four burials in stone coffins were found in the 19th century (*ibid.*, 108).

Terry Avenue/Cherry Hill Lane

In 1986 and 1988 there were watching briefs during construction of housing in an area c.2ha in extent bounded by Bishopgate Street, Terry Avenue and Clementhorpe (Fig.187, 1; Fig.188). They revealed human remains of the Roman period. In 1989 three trenches were excavated archaeologically.

The land in the area slopes down from west to east and Cherry Hill Lane, which connects Bishopgate Street with Clementhorpe, probably runs north–south along the edge of a terrace of Roman origin c.6m above the level of Terry Avenue. This terrace was recorded in the excavation of the Roman house at Clementhorpe (p.56, *AY* 6/1).

The finds and site records are currently stored with York Archaeological Trust under the Yorkshire Museum accession codes 1986.5, 1988.9 and 1989.14.

The 1986 watching brief

In1986 a watching brief by M. Stockwell and A. Davison at SE60275113 (Fig.188) revealed one intact and several disturbed Roman inhumations.

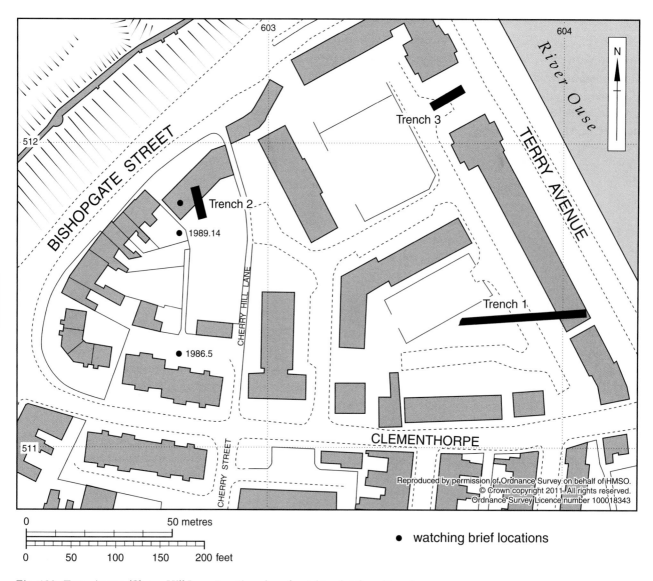

● watching brief locations

Fig. 188 *Terry Avenue/Cherry Hill Lane: Location plan of watching briefs and trenches*

The 1988 watching brief

In 1988 a watching brief by David Brinklow took place at SE60275118 during the cutting of foundation trenches for a new building close to Bishopgate Street.

Work began after the first burial (700) was removed mechanically during building work. The archaeological observations recorded natural reddish-brown clay, at c.0.60m below modern ground level. Six inhumation burials (100, 200, 300, 400, 500, 600) in varying degrees of completeness were found cut into the clay. They were all aligned east-north-east/west-south-west, although the location of the heads is not recorded. One skeleton (300) was found with nails, suggesting it had been coffined. A little pottery, largely 2nd century, was found with the burials (*AY* 16/8, 1137).

The 1989 excavation

The excavation took place under the supervision of Andrew Davison in advance of redevelopment at SE60275117.

Trench 1

Trench 1 was located in a plot on the west side of Terry Avenue near the junction with Clementhorpe. It measured 40 x 3m and was dug on an east–west line. In most of the trench excavation proceeded to a depth of 2m below modern level which at the west end was at c.9.10m OD and at the east 8.50m OD. In addition, six sample areas were machine-dug through the base of the trench at intervals along its length.

A natural orange sand (1004) was encountered at the west end of the trench at between 7.40 and 7.90m OD at a depth of as little as 1.30m below modern ground level. However, the deposit was not recorded elsewhere in the trench and it is assumed to drop away sharply eastwards towards the river. At other points along the trench the earliest deposit (in the machine cuts) was a grey silt (1000–2, 1005), but this deposit was not encountered at the east end of the trench, suggesting that it also slopes down to the river. At the east end the earliest deposit was 1003, a dark grey silty clay, 0.40m thick, which was also found in a machine cut. All these deposits lay below a build up of silty clay (993–4, 997–9) up to 1m deep which was succeeded by recent rubble.

Trench 2 *(Fig.189)*

Trench 2 aligned more or less north–south, 10.5 x 2.90m, was excavated within a warehouse on the corner of Bishopgate Street and Cherry Hill Lane. Natural (2016), a reddish clay, was encountered at between 12.90m OD (south) and 13.15m OD (north) at a depth of 1.30m below modern ground level. This was cut by a shallow grave (2017) in the north-west corner of the trench. It was on an east-north-east/west-south-west alignment and was 0.40m wide and 0.90m long, although the grave continued

beyond the western limit of the site. The head of the skeleton lay at the east end of the grave. The backfill layer was 2013, red clay. There were two iron nails in the cut, but it was not clear if this indicated burial in a coffin. 2017 was overlain by two small patches of mortar (2014–15). These deposits and the grave were overlain by 2007/2012 a dark grey silty clay soil 0.30m thick.

In the northern half of the trench deposit 2007 was overlain by 2011, yellow-brown clay with occasional cobbles and flecks of limestone. This was in turn overlain by 2010, dark orange-brown clay mottled with light red-brown clay containing frequent charcoal flecks. On the surface of 2010, near its southern edge was found a human skull (2009). Although no burial was found in the immediate vicinity, it had, perhaps, been damaged by the cutting of a shallow gully (2008) on a roughly east–west alignment, 0.45m wide and 0.24m deep. This was filled with 2003, a layer of red-brown clay which also covered most of the trench at a thickness of up to c.0.60m. It contained a variety of disturbed human bones including two skulls, a jaw bone, several ribs and a knee cap. Near the middle of the trench on its west side a complete, if fragmented, Dales ware jar (2006) was found.

The pottery from the site suggests activity may have begun in the late 1st–early 2nd century, but the grave and overlying deposits probably date to the early–mid-3rd century (*AY* 16/8, 1137). No pottery datable to later than c.280 was found.

Trench 3

The trench was located on the west side of Terry Avenue. Excavation encountered the rubble-filled cellar of a former fertiliser factory and no earlier archaeological deposits were found.

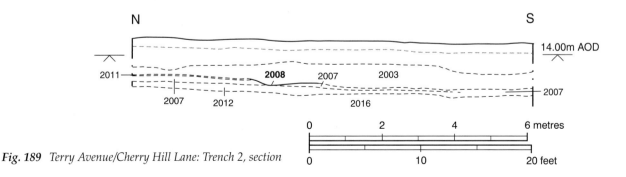

Fig. 189 Terry Avenue/Cherry Hill Lane: Trench 2, section

292 Bishopthorpe Road

Introduction

In July 1998 an evaluation took place, under the supervision of D. T. Evans, on land at 292 Bishopthorpe Road in advance of redevelopment (SE60114997; Fig.187, 2). The evaluation was carried out on behalf of Wimpey Homes Ltd in accordance with a specification drawn up by the Principal Archaeologist for City of York Council. The work involved the excavation of four trenches measuring 4 x 4m (Fig.190). The site lies opposite the Terry's Factory (see below) and more or less where finds were reported at Old Nunthorpe in the 1930s (RCHMY **1**, 63).

The excavation

Only Trenches 1 and 2 produced evidence for Roman activity (Fig.191).

Trench 1

Natural orange-brown sand (1007) was encountered at 12m OD at a depth of 1.4m below modern level. Above 1007 was a deposit of orange-brown silty sand (1006), 0.2m thick. This was in turn overlain by 1005, a 0.5m thick friable orange-brown silty sand with small quantities of cobbles and

Fig. 190 *292 Bishopthorpe Road and Terry's Factory: Location plan of trenches*

268

charcoal, containing fragments of Roman tile and three sherds of late 2nd-century pottery. Subsequent deposits 1000–4 and 1008 contained medieval and later pottery.

Trench 2

Natural, a mix of grey and yellow sand (2011) was encountered at 12.90m OD at a depth of 0.70m below modern ground level. Above 2011 was a deposit of mixed orange clay and gravel (2010), c.0.40m thick. Cut into 2010 was a shallow ditch or gully (2008) with gently sloping sides, aligned east–west. A stretch 1.60m long was recorded in the western half of the trench. The feature had been at least 0.16m deep and 0.85m wide and was filled with mid-brownish-grey silty sand (2007). At its eastern end gully 2008 was cut by a ditch (2006) running north–south of which the eastern side lay beyond the trench edge. The feature had been at least 2.4m wide and 0.27 deep and the western edge sloped down steeply. The fill was mid-brownish-grey silty sand (2005) very similar to 2007 and it contained four abraded sherds of 2nd- to 3rd-century pottery. Both 2006 and 2008 were disturbed and partly cut away by a large late medieval/post-medieval feature (2009) which contained a few more sherds of 2nd- to 3rd-century pottery, and subsequent strata were post-medieval or modern.

No further evidence for Roman activity was found in a watching brief on the site carried out in 1999.

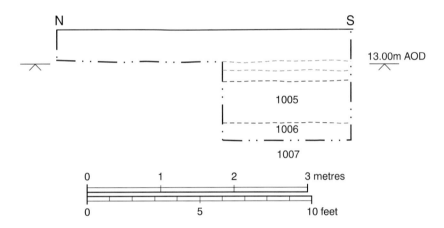

Fig. 191 *292 Bishopthorpe Road: Trench 1, west-facing section*

Terry's Factory

Evaluation excavations were undertaken, supervised by Kurt Hunter-Mann, at the Terry's factory, Bishopthorpe Road (centre at SE 598497; Fig.187, 3a–b), in March–April 2005. The work was sponsored by DTZ Pieda Consulting for Kraft Foods, in accordance with a brief provided by the Principal Archaeologist for City of York Council.

The site lies about 2km south of York city centre, on the west bank of the River Ouse. It is bounded to the east by Bishopthorpe Road, to the south by Knavesmire Stray, to the west by York racecourse and to the north by Campleshon Road. The site is almost 10ha in extent and lies at c.15m OD. It is situated towards the south end of a ridge of slightly undulating high ground that extends along the west bank of the River Ouse from the York moraine. The land slopes down steeply to Knavesmire Stray at the south end of the site, and to the River Ouse beyond Bishopthorpe Road to the east. There is a more gentle slope down to the west towards York racecourse.

Roman archaeology was only identified in two of the twelve trenches (Fig.192), Trenches 10 and 12 in Area D. This report has been compiled from the evaluation report by Kurt Hunter-Mann (YAT Field Report 2005/36).

All records and finds are stored under the Yorkshire Museum accession code YORYM : 2005.505.

269

Trench 10 (Fig.192)

Trench 10, situated towards the north end of Area D, was 29.9m long (east–west) by 2m wide. Natural (1094) was found at c.0.7m below modern ground level. It comprised layers of mid-red-brown silty clay, light orange-grey gravelly sand, orange-brown sand and light orange gravelly clay. The surface of natural sloped down from west to east, from c.15.4m OD to c.15.2m OD.

Cut into natural at the east end of the trench was a shallow ditch or gully (1078), 2m wide by 0.3m deep, aligned more or less east–west, with steep sides and a flat base. It contained a lower fill of dark orange-grey silty clay with occasional to moderate pebbles and cobbles (1099/1100/1104), and an upper fill of mid-brown silty clay (1077/1101/1103/1130). Pottery from the upper fill is dated to the late 2nd–early 3rd century; this included most of an Ebor white ware flagon.

At its west end ditch 1078 came to a T-junction with another, similar feature aligned north–south (1131). This was barely 0.1m deep and contained mid-brown silty clay (1132). Cut into the ditch fills at the junction of 1078 and 1132 was a cut (1117) of uncertain function, rectangular in plan, 2.1 x 0.7m and 0.8m deep. It contained a light brown sandy clay loam (1116) below a mid-orange-brown sandy silt with moderate gravel (1115). Late 2nd-/early 3rd-century pottery was found in 1116.

In the western part of the trench was the south side of a small circular cut (1098). Its mid-brown silty clay fill (1093) included an articulated dog burial. This may have been Roman but there was no dating evidence.

Overlying all of these features and natural was mid-red-brown clay loam (1133), which was c.0.3m thick. This was regarded as plough soil of medieval and later date.

Trench 12 (not illustrated)

Trench 12 measured 24.35m long (north–south) x 2m. Natural (1070) occurred at c.14.85m OD at the north end of the trench, and sloped down steadily to c.14.35m OD at the south end and was on average c.1m below modern ground level. It comprised layers of light yellow-brown sand, light brown clay loam, and mid-brownish-grey silty sand with frequent cobbles. Above 1070 was a light brown clay sand (1121–22) which was c.0.2m thick, but tapered out close to the south end of the trench, probably due to truncation by later ploughing. Roman and medieval pottery recovered from these contexts is thought to have been introduced by plough action or bioturbation.

Deposit 1122 was cut by a shallow but regular east–west cut (1107) with steep sides and a flat base. It contained grey-brown fine sandy loam (1108). Although medieval brick or tile was found in the fill and this feature could therefore have been a medieval plough furrow, it is suspected that it was a Roman ditch of similar late 2nd-/early 3rd-century date as those in Trench 10 and that the brick or tile was intrusive.

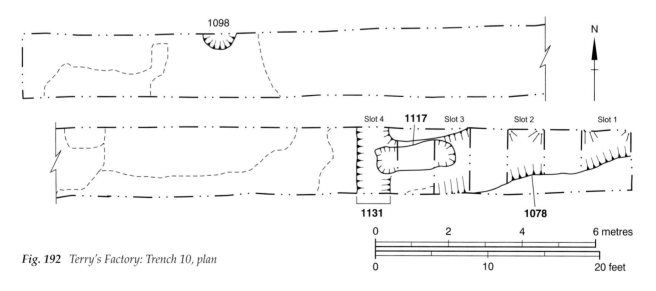

Fig. 192 Terry's Factory: Trench 10, plan

Zone 5: Discussion

The discoveries described above add a little to knowledge of the natural topography of the northern part of this zone. In particular the slope down to the River Ouse in the Terry Avenue area was clearly steeper in the Roman period than it is today which probably accounts for the Roman terrace in the Clementhorpe area (Fig.187, 4; p.56, *AY* 6/1).

Roads

No certain Roman road is known in this zone, although if the cobbles seen in Bishopthorpe Road (Fig.187,5; p.101, *AY* 6/1) do represent a Roman road, it probably approached from the south along the line now taken by the Bishopthorpe Road from Middlethorpe.

Land use in the late 1st–late 3rd century

Apart from the house at Clementhorpe, there is no other evidence for settlement in Zone 5. The field ditches datable to the late 2nd–3rd century at 292 Bishopthorpe Road and Terry's Factory are comparable to numerous other examples in the York area recorded in this publication (for discussion see pp.370–1). Whether aligned east–west or north–south, they may have been dug to respect the line of the suggested road from the south and defined plots along it.

Burials

As far as burials in Zone 5 are concerned, it is now apparent that by the 2nd–3rd centuries the cemetery identified by RCHME on the east side of Bishopthorpe Road extended further north, perhaps as far as the Ouse at Skeldergate Bridge. The burials found within the medieval walls near Baile Hill (RCHMY **1**, 107) may have formed part of the same cemetery at least before the construction of any Roman town defences, assuming that their line followed that of the walls. What is not clear is whether burial in the area remaining outside any defended settlement ceased before the construction of the house at Clementhorpe which would otherwise have been uncomfortably close to cemeteries in active use, in apparent breach of the usual separation imposed in major Roman towns.

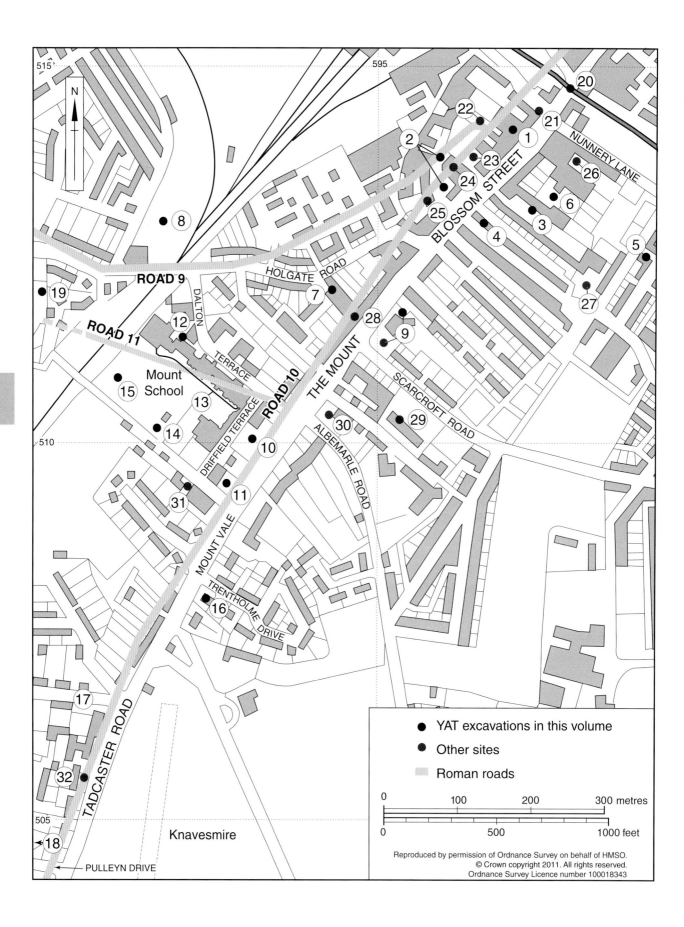

5

Reproduced by permission of Ordnance Survey on behalf of HMSO.
© Crown copyright 2011. All rights reserved.
Ordnance Survey Licence number 100018343

Zone 6: South-west of the Ouse – Blossom Street/The Mount area

Introduction *(Figs 54, 193)*

Extramural Zone 6 encompasses an area within the city ring road west and south-west of the medieval city walls bounded by Zone 5 to the east and the River Ouse to the north-west, but excludes Dringhouses (Zone 7) to the south. However, only three Roman sites are described below, lying west of the East Coast Main Line railway. The morainic ridge, described east of the Ouse under Zone 4 (pp.239–63) continues on the west bank of the Ouse heading westwards towards Acomb (Fig.55), only broken by Holgate Beck. Amongst local high points are the top of The Mount at its junction with Dalton Terrace, Severus Hills, Acomb, and Acomb village.

Two major Roman roads approach York in this zone (Fig.54). The main Roman approach road from the south-west (RCHMY **1**, 3; Road 10), after passing through Dringhouses, corresponds closely if not exactly (see discussion below) to the A64, known successively as Tadcaster Road, Mount Vale, The Mount and Blossom Street. Another major Roman road approached York from Aldborough (*Isurium Brigantum*) to the north-west (RCHMY **1**, 3; Road 9).

It was located on Severus Hills in 1960 (Fig.54, 9) and is then thought to have run to a junction with Road 10 at a site on Blossom Street excavated in 1953–4 (Fig.193, 22; Wenham 1965). Another road joined Road 10 from the west at the junction of what are now The Mount and Dalton Terrace (RCHMY **1**, 3; Road 11).

Hitherto the principal evidence for Roman activity in the zone has taken the form of large cemeteries. One these flanked the approach road from the south-west beginning in the Trentholme Drive area, c.0.9km from the city walls, where there was an excavation in 1951–2 and 1957–9 (Wenham 1968b). Otherwise, until the late 20th century, most information about cemetery derived from chance discoveries made during late 18th- to 19th-century building work (RCHMY **1**). Where Road 10 corresponded to the present line of The Mount a particular concentration of funerary monuments has been discovered, possibly because of the road's location on or close to a natural crest visible at some distance as one approached either from the

Fig.193 (facing page) Zone 6: location of sites described in this fascicule (1–19) and other sites (20–32)

1. 14–20 Blossom Street (1991 and 1994)
2. The Crescent (1981)
3. 35–41 Blossom Street (1990)
4. 47 Blossom Street (1991)
5. 32a Dale Street (1995)
6. All Saints School (1993)
7. 39 Holgate Road (1998)
8. Holgate Cattle Dock (1992)/St Paul's Green (1999)
9. 89 The Mount (1991)
10. 3 Driffield Terrace (2004–5)
11. 6 and 7 Driffield Terrace (2005 and 1981)
12. Mount School: Tregelles (2002–3)
13. Mount School: cable trench (2004)
14. Mount School: science block (1987)
15. Mount School: tennis court/sports hall (1998 and 2000)
16. 147 Mount Vale (1999)
17. St George's Place (1982)
18. Pulleyn Drive: sewer trench (1938) and cable trench (1992)
19. 129 Holgate Road (1980)

20. Micklegate Bar
21. Queen Street/Blossom Street (1826)
22. 18–22 Blossom Street (1953–4)
23. 28–40 Blossom Street (1999) and Blossom Street (2009)
24. Odeon Cinema (1936)
25. 1 The Crescent (1879)
26. Bar Convent (1964)
27. Moss Street, Corporation Depot (2003–4)
28. 112–14 The Mount (1963)
29. All Saints School, Mill Mount (1991)
30. Mill Mount (2005)
31. Elm Bank Hotel (1998)
32. White House

Fig. 194 Location plan of YAT trenches and watching brief areas at 14–20 Blossom Street, 1953–4 trenches and The Crescent watching brief. Site of cremation excavated in 1953–4 and stone coffin found at 18 Blossom Street in 1915

south-west or from the Roman town. The cemetery zone clearly extended as far as what became the medieval defences; an isolated early cremation burial was found at 22 Blossom Street close to the Roman road (Fig.194). A stone coffin was recorded in 1915 at 18 Blossom Street (Fig.194; RCHMY **1**, 94, in which the grid reference is clearly incorrect) and another containing a skeleton with a segmented jet bracelet was found on the site of the former Odeon cinema in1852 (*ibid.*; Fig.193, 24; Fig.197). Burials were also found off Nunnery Lane adjacent to the Bar Convent in 1846 and 1880 (*ibid.*).

The other major cemetery south-west of the Ouse lay north-west of the Roman town, apparently flanking a minor road approaching from the north-west (*ibid.*, 76–91). Large numbers of burials were recovered during construction of the Railway Station and related facilities in the later 19th century, and from time to time others have to come to light in both archaeological excavation and building work.

From the catalogues published in *Eburacum* (RCHMY **1**) it is apparent that these cemeteries were in use for the whole of the Roman period and included examples of a great diversity of burial rites including cremation and inhumation. A variety of containers for the human remains were employed, including stone, lead and wooden coffins, and there is evidence for a great variety of grave goods.

Other types of evidence for activity in the Roman period in Zone 6 have hitherto been sparse, although structures adjacent to the main road from the south-west were recorded at the junction of Queen Street and Blossom Street in 1826 (Fig.193, 21; RCHMY **1**, 53) and at 14–22 Blossom Street in 1953–4 and 1965 (Fig.193, 22; Wenham 1965; Radley 1966, 9). Pits were found at Bar Convent in 1964 (Fig.193, 26; Radley 1966, 565). In the western part of Zone 6 a mosaic pavement is said to have been found in Front Street, Acomb in the 19th century (Fig.54, 8; RCHMY **1**, 63–4).

6

14–20 Blossom Street : excavation and watching brief

Introduction

In May–June 1991 an archaeological excavation, directed by Amanda Clarke, was undertaken at 14–20 Blossom Street (SE596514; Fig.193, 1; Fig.194), No. 20 being the former Forsselius Garage. Queen Street lay to the north-east of the site and Blossom Street to the south-east. The work was undertaken on behalf of Brent Walker Inns and Retail to fulfil a specification prepared by the City Archaeologist and Brian Hobley, the developer's consultant archaeologist. In 1994 a watching brief took place on the site during construction work.

Land at Nos 18–22 Blossom Street had been previously investigated in 1953–4 by L.P. Wenham (Fig.194; Wenham 1965) when it had been designated for redevelopment as York's bus station. Wenham excavated 23 small trenches and found, *inter alia*, a cremation burial, the main approach road to York from the south-west (Road 10) and the junction with another road thought to have originated in Aldborough (Road 9), and part of a Roman stone building immediately north of the junction.

Further excavations in the area took place in 1966–7 directed by D. Stewart (Radley 1967, 9; Radley 1968, 118) in which the main road and south-east roadside ditch were allegedly sectioned and structural material found, but no records survive and the exact location of the trench is unknown. In 1999 re-excavation and slight extension of Wenham's Trench 16 by MAP at Blossom Street relocated the Roman road (MAP 2000, 18–19; Fig.193, 23).

The finds and site records are currently stored with York Archaeological Trust under the Yorkshire Museum accession code 1991.11.

The excavation

The 1991 excavation consisted of five trenches, four (1, 3–5) measuring 3 x 3m and one (2) 4 x 2m (Fig.194). Trench 1 was located within the garage structure and the others lay to the north-west of it. The upper 0.50m in each case was mechanically

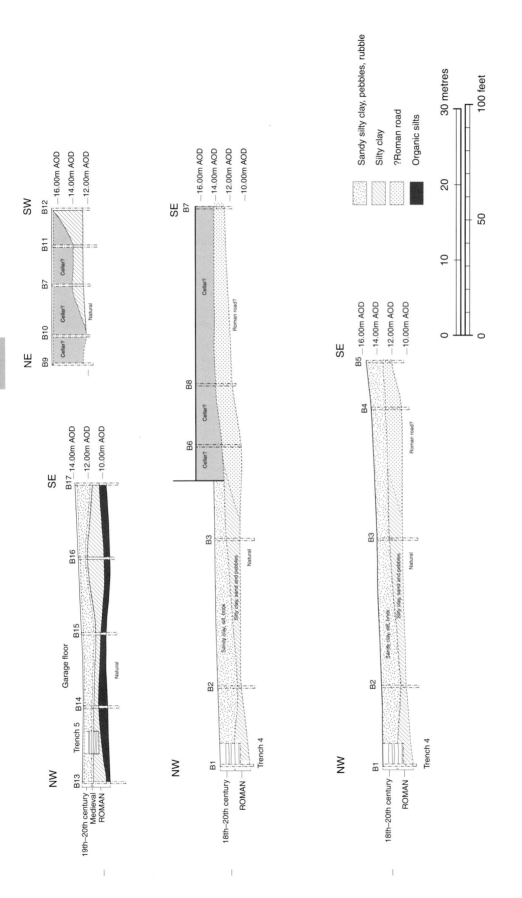

Fig. 195 *14–20 Blossom Street: Site profiles based on boreholes*

excavated. Trench 2 was subsequently extended to the north-west as Trench 8.

It became apparent during the excavation that the arrangement of cellars beneath the garage floor was complex and that more undisturbed archaeological deposits had probably survived than was anticipated. To elucidate the degree of survival two machine-cut trenches (6–7) were dug through the garage floor. That these proved inadequate for evaluation purposes was demonstrated in the watching brief during construction work described on pp.279–87.

Excavation work was supplemented by seventeen boreholes drilled by Sub Soil Surveys Ltd which gave some additional indication of the level of both natural and archaeological deposits across the site (Fig.195).

Trench 1 *(Fig.196)*

Natural was not reached and the earliest deposit (1051), left unexcavated, was encountered at c.14.85m OD, c.1.85m below modern level. Above this was c.1.10m of Roman stratigraphy. Deposit 1051 consisted of spreads of cobbles in clay, perhaps representing a building floor. Immediately overlying it was 1050, ashy silt with small pieces of charcoal and fragments of limestone which may have been accumulation on that floor.

The succeeding 0.50m of deposits was made up of what was thought to be the fill of six intercutting shallow features. The first two (1048–9) were filled with burnt material with fragments of fired clay (1042–3, 1047), probably hearth lining or burnt daub, and the pottery was heat damaged. 1042 also contained large cobbles coated in mortar.

6

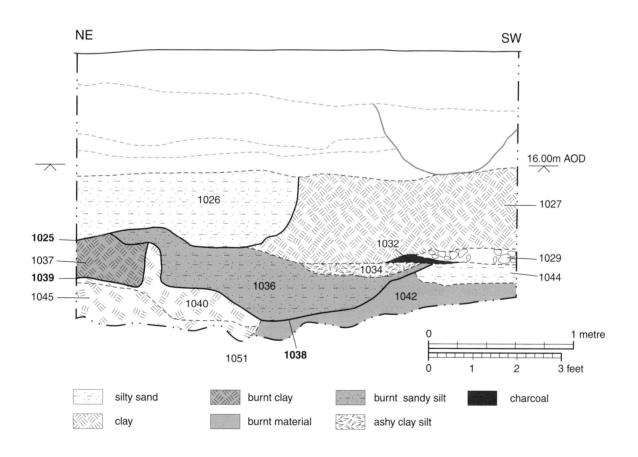

Fig. 196 14–20 Blossom Street: Trench 1, north-west-facing section

The next cut in the sequence (1041) was back-filled with 1045 below 1040, both deposits described as cobbles in clay plus mortar, plaster and limestone fragments. The final three cuts in the sequence, 1039 and 1046, both cut by 1038, were filled with 1037 and 1044. Cut 1038 was filled with 1034 and 1036 respectively. Deposit 1037 was a dark-coloured clay; the other deposits were all composed of crushed burnt residues and small clay mould fragments mixed with charcoal and ashy clay silt.

Next in the sequence was a shallow cut, subcircular in plan (1033), 0.50 x 0.30m. It was filled with 1030, orange-brown clay and cobbles, which suggested the feature was possibly a post-pad. Probably contemporary with 1033 was 1029, a spread of small to medium-sized cobbles in the south-west corner of the trench which was thought to be a floor make up. This was succeeded by 1027, a deposit 0.70m thick of large cobbles, limestone and sandstone blocks in orange-brown clay. This was cut by a large pit (1025) which continued beyond the trench edge, but was at least 1.5m in diameter and 0.45m deep. The fill (1026) was sand in which there were cobbles, sandstone and brick and tile fragments. The deposit produced two bronze coins: sf73 (1st–2nd century) and sf80 (late 3rd century).

Pottery from the contexts described above was largely dated mid-3rd–early 4th century (*AY* 16/8, 1135).

Pit 1025 was succeeded by deposits of 11th- to 12th-century date (1006, 1010–11).

Trench 2

The earliest deposit encountered was 2023–4, the surface of which lay at c.14.20m OD, c.1.50m below modern ground level. It extended for c.2m south-east from the north-west trench edge and consisted of an uneven spread of cobbles and pebbles which also contained mortar, tile, shell and animal bone.

This probably represents the south-east side of the Roman road from the south-west. A slit trench (Trench 8) was mechanically excavated for c.7m north-west of Trench 2 to locate the north-west side of the road. As a result it may be suggested that in its final form the road was c.5m wide. At the north-west end of Trench 8 were deposits of building materials probably associated with the demolition of the building excavated by Wenham in 1953–4 in Trench 7 (Fig.194).

Overlying 2023–4 was 2022, a deposit of grey-brown silty clay. Two human infant bones found in the deposit may indicate the proximity of burials. In the south-east part of the trench was 2017, mottled sandy silt with occasional cobbles and limestone fragments. Pottery from the sequence described above is dated to the late 3rd–early 4th century.

Over 2022 was 2016, 0.16m deep of clayey sandy silt containing pottery of Roman–16th-century date. Above 2016 were deposits of post-medieval–modern date.

Trench 3

Trench 3 was found to be partially located over Wenham's Trench 3 which was shown to have been inaccurately plotted on fig.2 in his 1965 report. Wenham's trench was c.1.8m wide and a 2m length was recorded in Trench 3. Wenham claimed to have encountered natural at c.11.84m O.D, c.1.90m below modern ground level; in 1991 work ceased at c.12.94m OD and no Roman deposits were examined.

Trench 4

The earliest deposit encountered was 4012–13 at 10.94m OD, c.2.30m below modern ground level. 4012–13 was light grey-brown silty clay with charcoal flecks and was left unexcavated. It was succeeded by 4010–11, light brown sandy clay, c.0.50m thick. The pottery from the deposits was dated to the 3rd century. Above 4010–11 were medieval and later deposits.

Trench 5

The earliest deposit encountered, but not excavated, was 5018, a brown silt, at c.11.12m OD, c.1.95m below modern ground level. Overlying this was a homogeneous deposit (5014–17), 0.50m thick, of brownish-grey clay silt with brick and limestone fragments which contained a coin of Claudius II (268–70; sf68). This deposit was overlain by a similar deposit dated to the medieval and later periods.

The boreholes (Fig.195)

Seventeen boreholes formed two north-west/south-east transects and one north-east/south-west transect. There is clearly something of a discrepancy in the level of natural and depth of deposits between what was found on the ground and what was suggested by the boreholes. On the whole the boreholes suggested a depth of archaeology greater by c.1m than was actually found. For what it is worth, however, it may be noted that between Boreholes 13 and 17 there was a gradual rise in the level of what was taken to be natural from c.9.06m to 9.60m. Between Borehole 1 and Borehole 8 natural level appeared to rise from 9.3m to 10.50m in Borehole 3 and 12.80m in Borehole 7. This latter level did not vary greatly in the line between Boreholes 9 and 12. Above natural in Boreholes 1–5 and 13–17 was a band c.3–4m thick of silt deposits thought to be of medieval and Roman date. Above natural in Boreholes 4–8 was c.2m of material described as gritty brown clay with cobbles and pebbles some of which, at least, was probably Roman road make up.

The watching brief (20 Blossom St)

Introduction

In March–April 1994 YAT carried out a watching brief on the site, supervised by Bryan Antoni, during machine excavation of ground beam trenches and excavation of a new cellar prior to the construction of a new café-bar and restaurant. The area involved was in the centre of the former Forsellius Garage building (20 Blossom Street), a part of the site almost entirely beyond the 1991 evaluation trenches 1, 6 and 7 and not evaluated then due to problems of access. It was thought that the area had been extensively cellared and that little archaeology would survive, although a recommendation for further excavation here had been made in the 1991 assessment report. In the event, modern disturbance was minimal and a considerable quantity of archaeological deposits was removed by machine during development without a proper record being made (Fig.197). Archaeological work during the watching brief was, moreover, extremely difficult so relating the sequences and dating individual contexts was nearly impossible.

The area in question was divided into three components (Fig.198). Area 1 had no Roman archaeology; Areas 2–3 will be described in turn and within them the small parcels of stratigraphy to which access was possible, for the most part on the basis of the recorded sections.

The finds and site records are currently stored with York Archaeological Trust under the Yorkshire Museum accession code 1994.1063.

Area 1

No certain Roman strata were identified. At the north-west end there was a build up of featureless

Fig. 197 20 Blossom Street watching brief: view north-west of the site during construction showing the extent of mechanical removal of archaeological deposits in watching brief Areas 2–3

279

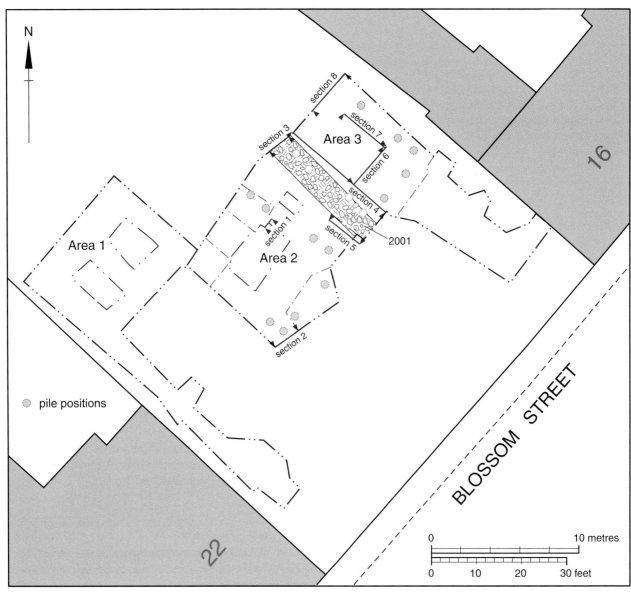

Fig. 198 *20 Blossom Street watching brief: areas investigated showing location of sections and wall footing 2001 for orientation purposes*

dark brown sandy clay silt with occasional brick, tile, cobbles and mortar between 14.60 and 16.30m OD. The lowest part of the deposit may have been late Roman.

Area 2 *(Figs 199–200)*

Section 1 (Fig.201)

A cobbled surface (1) at 12.72m OD was succeeded by a deposit 0.20m thick of cobbles in grey sandy clay silt (2); the top lay at 12.92m OD. Both are interpreted as make-up material for a yard

or floor surfaces. Above layer 2 was a grey-brown, green-tinged clay silt (3) c.0.80m thick with its top level at 13.72m OD. This was cut by a wall foundation trench (35) which had possibly run north-west/south-east. It was 0.70m wide, 0.80m deep and filled with clay and cobbles (36). The feature was succeeded by 37, mid-brown sandy clay silt with frequent cobbles, cut to the north-east by a trench or similar feature (38), possibly for a wall footing. Its earliest fill was 39, small to medium-sized pebbles in matrix of orange-brown sand which was below 40, brown clayey silt with cobbles observed between 39 and the south-west edge of the feature.

280

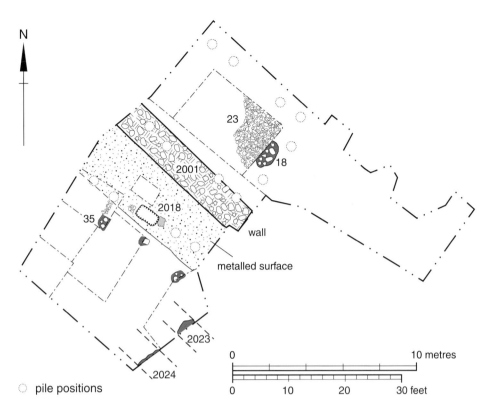

N

23

2001

18

35

2018

wall

metalled surface

2023

2024

○ pile positions

0   10 metres

0   10   20   30 feet

Fig. 199 *20 Blossom Street watching brief: Areas 2 and 3*

Fig. 200 *20 Blossom Street watching brief: Area 2, Section 1 showing (right) foundation trench 35, (left) trench 38 and (base) cobble layer 2 (scale 1m)*

Section 2 (Fig.202)

In the south-eastern part of Area 2 the earliest deposits recorded sloped down from north-east to south-west. The first was a cobbled make up (4) for a surface which lay at c.13.70m OD. This was succeeded by a deposit of dark grey ash and charcoal with occasional slag fragments, succeeded in turn by a light grey-brown clay sand (both numbered 5) and then a thin deposit of charcoal-rich burnt clay (6). Above layer 6 was a deposit made up of laminations of clay, charcoal, grey clay and sand (2020). The area was then levelled off with a deposit of light yellow-brown sandy clay with occasional charcoal flecks (7). This was succeeded by a lens of ash and charcoal in light brown sandy clay (8) which in turn was succeeded by 2025, green-grey gritty clay of which the highest point was at c.14.44m. This was overlain by a thin lens of orange burnt clay (2019). Next in the sequence was 2024, a clay and cobble footing, probably contemporary with 2001 (see below), which probably ran north-west/south-east. Footing 2024 was 0.60m thick and 1.80m wide with its top at 14.75m OD. It was cut to the south-west by feature 41, possibly a pit, filled with 42, grey-brown gritty clay. Everything above 41 and 2024 was removed by machine.

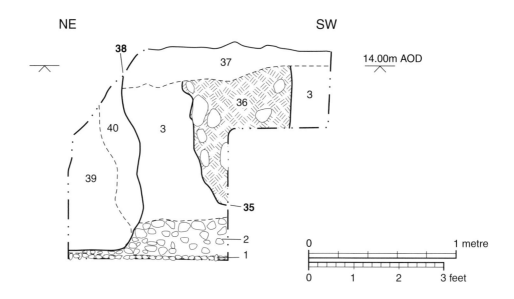

NE   SW

38
37   14.00m AOD
36   3
40   3
39
35
2
1

0   1 metre
0   1   2   3 feet

Fig. 201 *20 Blossom Street watching brief: Area 2, Section 1*

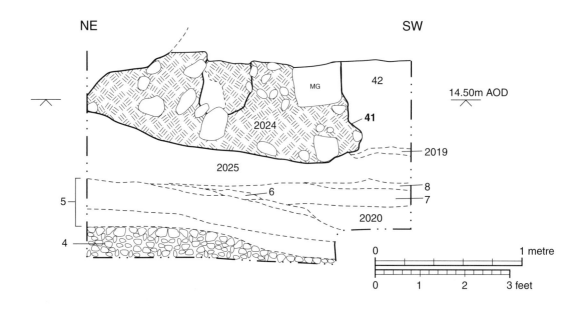

NE   SW

42   14.50m AOD
MG
41
2024
2019
2025
8
6
7
5
2020
4

0   1 metre
0   1   2   3 feet

Fig. 202 *20 Blossom Street watching brief: Area 2, Section 2*

To the north-east of the area just described there was a clay and cobble wall footing (2023), 0.54m deep, with its surface at 14.79m OD (Fig.199). Only a stub was seen so it is not clear what its alignment was, although it may have been part of the same feature as the patch of footing noted 2.5m to the north. In this case the footing would have run north-north-west/south-south-east. It was possibly related also to wall footing 2024 to the south-west. Above 2023 was 2022, a mid-grey-brown sandy

silty clay c.0.15m thick. All deposits above this had been removed by machine.

North-east side of Area 2 (Fig.203)

On the north-east side of Area 2 (at the base of Section 4) was a strip of surviving archaeology with, first of all a tiled hearth (2008), its surface lying at 13.50m OD (Fig.207). It was cut into 2010 to the north-west, a light grey-brown sandy silty clay with

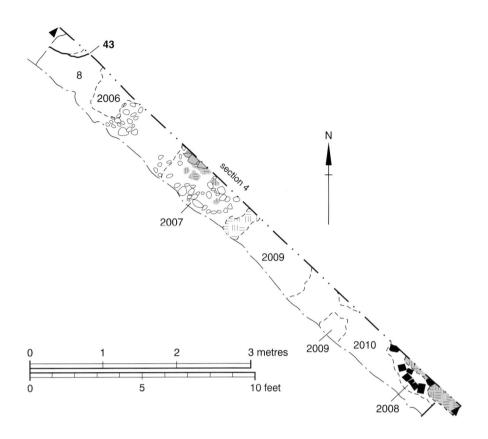

Fig. 203 *20 Blossom Street watching brief: Area 2, plan of the south-east corner*

charcoal and burnt brick which was above 2009, a light grey-brown sandy silty clay. At the north-west end lay a deposit (8), not described, cut by a pit (43), and between 8 and 2009 was a cobble layer (2007), c.1.30m wide.

Section 3 (Fig.204)

On the north-west side of Area 2 deposit 8 was succeeded by 2006, a dark grey-black cinder deposit. Deposits 8, 2007 and 2009 (see above) were cut by 2001, the foundation trench for a wall, c.1.60m wide and 1.20m deep, which was traced for c.10m on a north-west/south-east alignment. The trench was filled with clay and cobble (9) of which the surface lay at 14.20–14.80m OD. Above the clay and cobble were deposits 14 and 15, probably backfilling a robber trench for the wall above the footing.

Section 4: north-east edge of Area 2 (Fig.205)

The base of the recorded section lay at c.13.60m OD. Above deposits 2006–7, 2009 and 2010 (see above and Fig.203) was a deposit (2005) c.1m thick

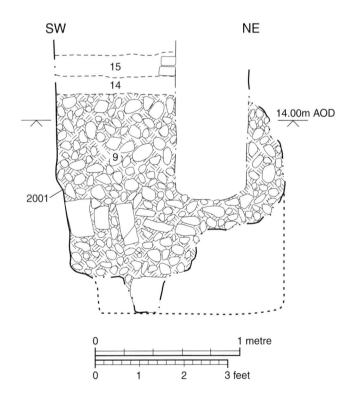

Fig. 204 *20 Blossom Street watching brief: Area 2, Section 3*

283

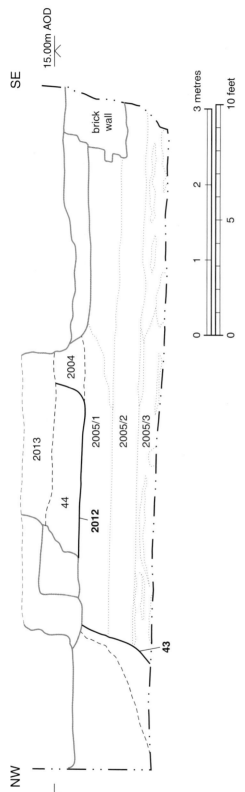

Fig. 205 *20 Blossom Street watching brief: Area 2, Section 4*

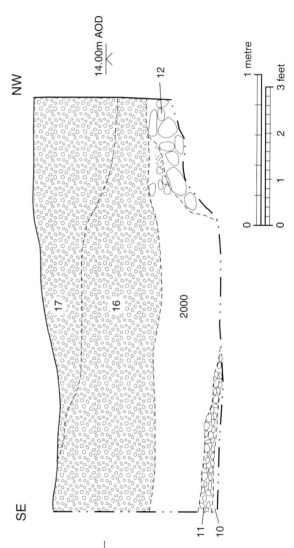

Fig. 206 *20 Blossom Street watching brief: Area 2, Section 5*

Fig.207 *20 Blossom Street watching brief: Area 2, east corner. View from above of hearth 2008. Scale 0.50m*

of yellow-grey clay divided into three spits. The surface of 2005 lay at c.14.60m OD. It was apparently cut by the wall footing 2001 and contained pottery dated late 2nd–early 3rd century. 2005 was also cut by a pit (43) at its north-west end; the cut may have been made from a higher level than shown in the section and it was probably medieval. Above 2005 was 2004, not described, of which the upper surface lay at 15m OD. It was cut to the north-west by a pit (2012), 0.20m deep, filled with grey-brown sandy silt (44). This was overlain by 2013, a mid-grey-brown sandy silt of which the surface lay at 15.37m OD. It was cut by three post-Roman features. All later strata had been removed by machine.

Section 5 (Fig.206)

The base of the recorded section was at c.13.20m OD and the deposits recorded above this had presumably all been cut by the wall footing 2001. Deposit 10 was a mid-grey-brown silt with charcoal which was overlain by cobbles in dark grey clay silt (11) at the south-east end of the section, and by a layer of cobbles (12) at the north-west end. These deposits were succeeded by 2000, a grey sandy clay

with mortar flecking, with its surface at 13.70m OD. Above 2000 were two make-up deposits for a street at least 2.5m wide running north-west/south-east: 16, bands of small–medium pebbles in a matrix of orange-brown gravelly sand or pink clay, overlain by 17, small pebbles in a matrix of compacted green-brown coarse sand with occasional cobbles. The surface of layer 17 lay at 14.45m OD: all subsequent material was removed by machine.

Area 3

Section 6 (Figs 208–209)

In a small area immediately north-east of Area 2, in Section 6, deposits 3006, grey-brown clay silt with charcoal and mortar flecks, and south-west of it, 3009, light brown sand silt, were observed. Over 3006 were deposits 19–21, not described in the site notes.

Deposits 3006 and 3009, and possibly 19–21 (but the relationship was removed by a later robber trench, 3010), were cut by a trench (18) for a cobble footing of which the south-east end and only a short

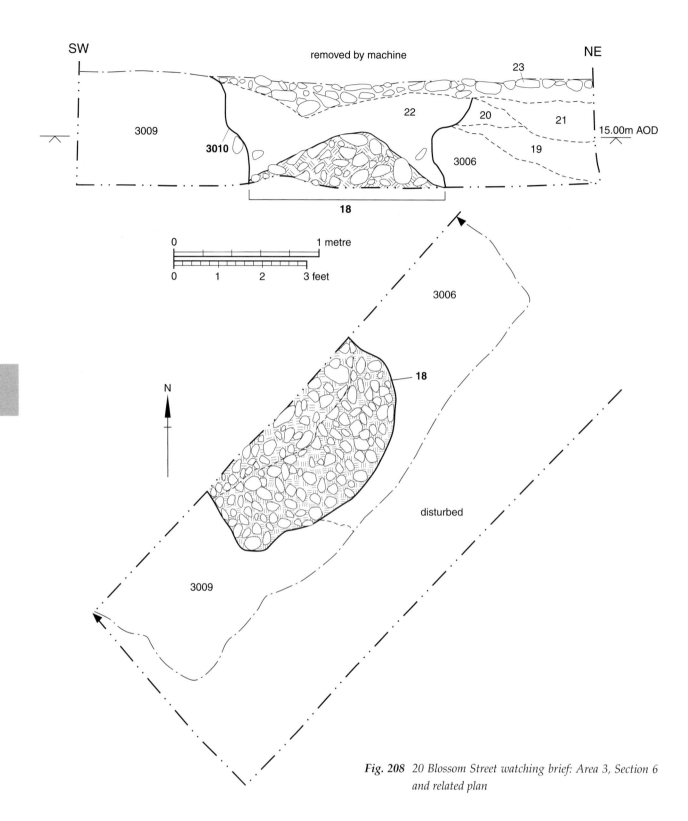

SW

removed by machine

NE

23

22

3009

3010

20

21

15.00m AOD

3006

19

18

0   1 metre

0   1   2   3 feet

3006

N

18

disturbed

3009

Fig. 208 *20 Blossom Street watching brief: Area 3, Section 6 and related plan*

length was recorded. It was c.1.20m wide and its surface lay at 15.03m OD. Its alignment may have been north-west/south-east and it was possibly contemporary with or later than footing 2001. A

robbing trench (3010) from the level of the top of deposits 21 and 3009 was filled with 22, a grey-brown clay silt with occasional cobbles and limestone. Over 22 was make up for a cobble surface

Fig.209 *20 Blossom Street watching brief: Area 3, view south-east of Section 6 showing trench for cobbled footing 18 (scale 0.50m)*

(23) with its top at 15.35m OD. This was thought likely to be medieval.

Section 7 (Fig.210)

At right angles to the north-east end of Section 6 was Section 7, aligned north-west/south-east (facing south-west). The base of the section lay at c.14.75m OD. The earliest layer recorded was 3005 (= 3006, 3009), a pale yellow-brown sandy silt. It was cut by a shallow gully (24) presumably running north-east/south-west, c.0.35m deep and c.1.20m wide. Its fill was 25, a grey-brown sandy silt of which the surface lay at c.15.20m. It was cut on its south-east side by a second gully (26) of which only about a half the width was seen. It was filled with 27, grey-brown clayey silt with charcoal and burnt clay. The make up for the medieval cobbled surface (23) overlay both features.

Section 8: the north-west face of Area 3 (Fig.211)

The deposits recorded in the north-east half of the lower part were probably Roman. The base of the section lay at c.14.56m. The earliest layer (28) was a dark sandy silt. It was penetrated by two post-pipes 29–30 and overlain by 31, dark grey sandy clay, 0.35m thick. This deposit would have probably accumulated around the posts that had formed the two post-pipes. Layer 31 was cut to the north-east by 32, possibly the trench for a wall footing with a sloping side. Its fill (33) was a brown clay of which the surface was at c.15.15m. This feature was overlain by grey clay silt (34) which in turn was overlain by a brown silty clay (35) of which the surface was at 15.40m. At this point in the sequence there was a cut to the south-west for a large pit (3011), thought to be medieval. Layers above 35 and 3011 were also medieval or later.

287

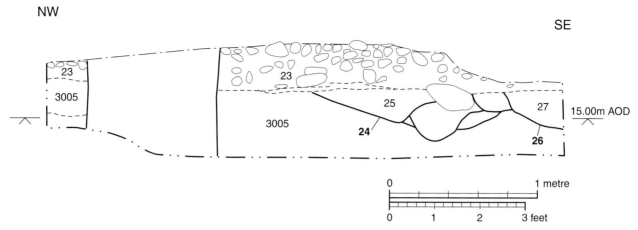

Fig. 210 *20 Blossom Street watching brief: Area 3, Section 7*

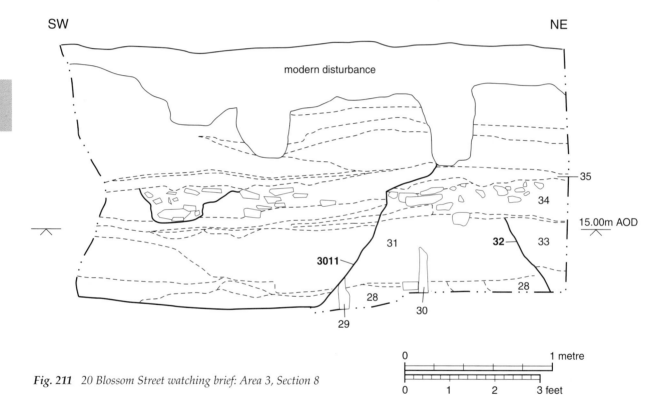

Fig. 211 *20 Blossom Street watching brief: Area 3, Section 8*

Interpretation

Discussion of the discoveries at 14–20 Blossom Street in the context of the zone as a whole will appear below (p.335), but at this point some preliminary interpretation is in order. This is, however, hampered by the incomplete nature of the investigation and, in the case of the watching brief, the unsatisfactory circumstances in which recording had to proceed. The evaluation trenches served to determine the nature of survival in certain parts, but little else. Because they were not excavated to natural one can gain little idea of how what was discovered relates to the history of occupation on the site as a whole. It is not even possible to date the excavated deposits with any degree of accuracy. The inadequacy of the evaluation exercise was demonstrated by the watching brief, which attempted to salvage some information during the mechanical removal of well-preserved archaeological deposits.

In this exercise accurate determination of the character and date of deposits and structures, and their interrelationships, proved more or less impossible. The interpretation which follows below is based as much on a comparison of levels OD as on stratigraphic relationships.

The natural ground level

Although relying solely on borehole evidence for deposit levels can be highly misleading, it is apparent from the survey that the level of natural rises from north-west to south-east. Between Borehole 3 and Borehole 7, for example, it rises by c.2.30m in a distance of c.42.50m. There is a sharp rise between Boreholes 4 and 5, a zone which corresponds to the line of the road running north-east/south-west through the site. If this is an accurate indication of the natural profile, it may indicate the location of a terrace on which the road was constructed. Above natural one can conclude that there is a greater depth of material on some parts of the site than the investigations of 1953–4 had suggested. Below the floor of the Forsellius Garage there was up to c.3.80m as opposed to c.2m recorded in Wenham's trenches, although natural level in the area around the Roman road was recorded as c.12.70m OD in the recent work and by Wenham. It appears therefore that there is a much greater depth of modern overburden on the street frontage than in the rear of the properties.

The Roman road

The latest (4th-century) road surface was partially revealed in Trench 2 where its south-east edge lay on the line recorded by Wenham. The location of the north-west edge found in Trench 8 suggested, however, that the latest surface was c.5m wide. Wenham had recorded a width of 10m which the boreholes suggest was the width before the latest surface was laid down.

Wenham claimed to have found evidence to show that the road was constructed in a shallow trench dug into natural, although this is not shown in the published section (Wenham 1965, fig.3). Unfortunately, it was not possible in the work described above to confirm either the depth of road metalling on the site or the date at which the road was constructed. Further discussion of the road will be found on pp.335–6 below.

The building found in 1953–4 *(Fig.194)*

North-west of the road Wenham (1965) revealed the remains of a structure which he claimed had passed through five phases between the late 1st and the 4th century; a plan of the fifth phase in his figure 2 suggests an alignment oblique to that of the road. The published report is, however, so cursory that it is difficult to ascertain the validity of the proposed sequence or the accuracy of the plan and both should probably be treated with caution. Although no levels OD are quoted in Wenham's report, his earliest context must have occurred at c.12.75m OD, c.2m below modern level. This would be as much as 1m or more above natural as suggested by the boreholes, but they may not be entirely reliable, and the depth of natural in the watching brief compares well with what Wenham recorded. The latest deposits in Wenham's structural sequence probably lay at c.14m OD, which corresponds more or less to the level of the road surface revealed in Trench 2 (14.20m OD). Both may probably be dated to the late 3rd–early 4th century.

The area south-east of the road

The area south-east of the road may be considered under two broad period headings. The first encompasses all deposits and structures pre-dating the massive north-west/south-east wall footing 2001, and the second includes that wall footing and everything after it.

Period 1

In Borehole 7 natural was recorded at c.12.80m OD. This means that the cobbles (1–2) in Section 1 (Fig.201) in the deepest part of the watching brief, which were recorded at 12.72m, are probably sitting on natural and were the earliest deposit recorded. Above this was a second layer of cobbles of which the surface lay at 12.92m OD. These deposits were possibly equivalent to the cobbles (11–12) in Section 5 (Fig.206) further up the slope to the south-east. Together these cobbles may represent a path or track, perhaps c.1.5–2m wide, aligned north-west/south-east. Subsequent to the cobbles there was a build up of silt (3) to a level of 13.72m (Fig.201). This deposit may be material which had washed down the slope and it probably corresponds to material recorded in Fig.203 (8, 2009–10) and Section 5 (2000).

In Section 1 the silt was cut by two features, one probable clay and cobble wall footing (35) running north-west/south-east and another (38) filled with gravel. These features were possibly contemporary with a street located in Section 5 (Fig.206, 16–17), overlying 2000, and with a cobble layer and hearth at c.13.50m OD in Fig.203. The two street metalling layers had a thickness of c.0.75m, the surface of the later lying at 14.45m OD. The street, like the path referred to above, probably ran north-west/south-east, i.e. at 90° to the main approach road from the south-west. To the north-west the ground level may have been deliberately built up to c.14.60m OD (see 2005 in Section 4; Fig.205).

There is no certain dating for this period, but it can probably be accommodated within the late 1st–late 2nd centuries.

Period 2

Probably cutting through the street and layer 2005, although it was not unequivocally demonstrated, was a substantial wall foundation trench (2001) running north-west/south-east and filled with cobbles in clay (Fig.204). The surface of this material lay at c.14.20–14.60m OD. The footing was probably contemporary with two others, also of clay and cobble: 2024 in Section 2 (Fig.202) and 2023 (Fig.199). The surfaces of these footings lay at 14.75m OD and 14.79m OD respectively, but they were located slightly further up the slope to the south-east. 2024 probably ran north-west/south-east, but the alignment of 2023 was unclear. It is not possible to say if footings 2023–4 were part of the same structure as 2001, although it is possible.

Deposit 2004 (Section 4) on the north-east side of the wall footing 2001 probably represents material which post-dates its construction. The surface of 2004 lay at 15m OD. It may be noted that no floor deposit was recorded between layers 2004 and 2005 which could have been associated with 2001; this may suggest that the building of which it was part lay to the south-west. Another footing which was probably contemporary with or a bit later than 2001 was 18, located to the north-east (Section 6); its surface lay at 15.30m OD.

In Section 8 deposit 31 probably corresponded to 2004. Its surface lay at 15.15m OD at which level it was cut by a clay-filled feature (32), possibly a wall footing running north-west/south-east. This was probably contemporary with a gully (24) running north-west/south-east recorded in Section 7 which was cut from the level of 15.20m OD (Fig.208). Over the robbing trench for the wall which had stood on footing 18 and over the fill of layer 24 was a cobble layer (23), thought to be medieval.

In Trench 1 of the evaluation excavation the earliest layers encountered were cobbles at c.14.85m OD, a level roughly equal to the top of deposit 2004 (Section 4), but being a bit higher up the slope they could be contemporary with the wall footing 2001. It is not possible to make much sense of the excavated sequence above the cobbles, but the top of Roman deposits was thought to lie at 15.95m.

The dating of the Period 2 sequence is as problematic as that of Period 1, but wall footing 2001 was probably late 2nd–early 3rd century.

35–41 Blossom Street

Introduction

Between 6 November 1989 and 21 January 1990 an excavation, under the direction of Niall Oakey, was carried out at 35–41 Blossom Street on behalf of Allied Breweries Development Limited (SE59725130; Fig.193, 3; Fig.212). The site was located on the south-east side of the street, c.150m south-west of the medieval city defences, thought to correspond to a boundary of the Roman civilian town.

The site was owned by Allied Breweries Development Limited which proposed to renovate the buildings on the street frontage and build an office complex on the land behind. The plot behind 35–7 Blossom Street contained a yard flanked by garages and workshops which had been occupied most recently by a motorcycle sales and repair company. Constructed predominantly of brick, these buildings included some elements of 18th- or early 19th-century date, but were largely of 20th-century construction. They were demolished in October 1989. The open area behind 39–41 Blossom Street (The Lion and Lamb public house) was covered with tarmac and used as a car park for customers.

Ten small test pits were dug within the development area in June 1988 (YAT archive and accession code 1988.7) and July 1989 (1989.21). Natural sand occurred at c.13.40m OD and was sealed by 1.30–1.70m of a dark brown clayey deposit which contained both Roman and modern pottery. It was overlain by 0.3–0.7m of rubble used to level the area before tarmac or concrete were laid. No human remains or features of archaeological significance were found. Limited archaeological excavation and records of chance discoveries during building work along the south-east side of Blossom Street during the last 200 years did, however, suggest that the area lay within a large Roman cemetery and this consideration prompted an archaeological investigation of those areas likely to be destroyed by redevelopment in 1990.

In 1966 eight trenches 3 x 3m had been excavated in a plot used as allotments immediately south-east of the pub car park (SE59755128) by students of the College of Ripon and York St John under the direction of L.P. Wenham (Radley 1966, 9). Deposits containing Roman pottery were found 0.90m below

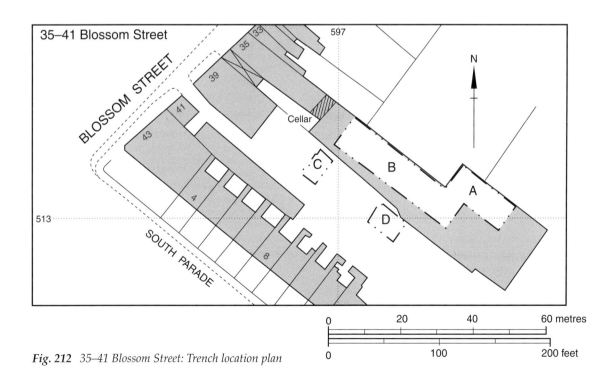

Fig. 212 *35–41 Blossom Street: Trench location plan*

the modern ground surface, together with three 3rd-century coins, a skeleton and a lead *ossuarium*.

The archaeological excavation in 1989–90 reached undisturbed natural over most of the threatened area before the trenches were backfilled with limestone aggregate. The foundations for the development were dug into this backfill, but a watching brief was maintained while service trenches were dug outside the areas of controlled excavation.

The finds and excavation records are held by YAT under the Yorkshire Museum accession codes 1989.21 and 1990.21. This report has been prepared for publication by Patrick Ottaway using a draft written by Niall Oakey in November 1992.

The excavation (Figs 212–213)

Trench A measured 18m (north-west/south-east) x 8m and the contiguous Trench B 34.5m (north-west/south-east) x 8.75m. Modern ground level lay at c.14.80m OD. A mechanical excavator removed c.1m depth of modern foundations and overburden until remains of articulated skeletons and other features became visible. The natural slope of the ground downwards from north-west to south-east and the absence of significant archaeological remains in some areas meant that there was considerable variation in the depth of material removed by mechanical excavation. At the north-western end of Trench B hand excavation began at 14.19m OD, but at the south-eastern end of Trench A the machine removed all deposits down to a depth of 12.8m OD. Five large, rectangular, concrete inspection pits associated with the garage and workshops previously occupying the area were left in Trench A and earlier material was removed from around them.

Surviving stratigraphy was often shallow, being no more than 0.5m thick in parts of Trench B, and it was apparent that the site had undergone a long period of agricultural use in post-Roman times. Plough damage to archaeological deposits was seen at a depth of 13.5m OD (i.e. up to 1.3m below the modern ground surface). Further damage was done by tree roots. Graves and other cuts proved difficult to detect unless the fill contained distinctive material. The depth and intensity of disturbance to

Fig.213   *35–41 Blossom Street: view south-east of excavation in Trench B taking place in December 1989*

archaeological deposits, coupled with the limited amount of time available, forced the adoption of the unsatisfactory excavation technique of removing apparently featureless spits 0.15–0.20m deep with picks and shovels. Inevitably stratigraphic anomalies occurred where later cuts were not detected until their lower fills were recognised.

No hand excavation took place in a strip on the south-west side of Trench B at its north-west end because of the disturbance caused by a 19th-century brick-lined well. Most archaeological deposits above natural were recorded and removed in the south-eastern two-thirds of Trench B, but in the north-western third time only allowed a sample of the archaeological deposits to be examined.

Two small trenches (Trench C, 8.3 x 5m, and Trench D, 9 x 6.75m) were mechanically excavated to the south-west of Trench B (in land belonging to 39–41 Blossom Street) under archaeological supervision. No skeletons were seen.

Period summary

The excavated deposits and features have been divided into the following period groups, dated for the most part by pottery (*AY* 16/8, 1130–5).

1. Early–late 2nd century
2. Late 2nd–early 3rd century
3. 3rd–early 4th century
   - 3ai, c.200–25
   - 3aii, c.225–50
   - 3aiii, c.250–300
   - 3a (undivided), c.200–300
   - 3b, c.300–25
4. c.325–400
5. c.400 +

Period 1 *(Fig.214)*

The natural, a greyish-white sand, was encountered at 13.7m OD at the north-west end of the site and at 12.69m OD at the south-east end. It was overlain by deposits of dark brown-black silty sandy clay (1017–18, 1025, 1030, 1068, 2075, 2207, 2391) containing predominantly late 1st-/early 2nd-century pottery.

Cut into these deposits were a number of ditches and other features. Later activity had usually destroyed the horizons from which these features were cut and it is doubtful if all of them were contemporary. However, the stratigraphic evidence, the date of the pottery recovered from them and their distinctive character, which differed from any archaeological remains found in later periods, combine to suggest that these features may all be assigned to this period.

Ditches in Trench B

Three parallel ditches (2400–1, 2406) aligned north-east/south-west were found in the centre of Trench B. All of them had been truncated by later activity. Ditch 2400, 1.42m wide, was the deepest at 0.47m and had a rounded terminal at its north-east end. The ditch sides were near vertical and the base concave. The fill was 2381, a dark grey-brown clayey silt. Ditch 2406 was 2.5m south-east of 2400 (measured centre to centre). It was U-shaped in cross-section, and was c.2.6m wide and 0.27m deep. The backfill deposit (2393) was a light brown silty

sand. Ditch 2401, a further 4.5m to the south-east (centre to centre), was 0.49m wide and 0.09m deep. Its backfill was 2398, a dark brown sandy silt.

A gap c.4m wide separated the terminal of 2400 from the tip of another possible ditch (2390), also cut on a north-east/south-west alignment, which continued beyond the north-east edge of Trench B. 2390 was 0.24m wide and 0.14m deep and its fill (2387) was a mid-brown silty clay. The rounded end of 2314, also probably a ditch, was found c.4m to the south-east of 2390; it was in line with 2406 (see above) to the south-west. The fill of 2314 was 2306, a grey-brown clayey silt.

At right angles to the ditches described above were two parallel rows of cut features on a north-west/south-east alignment. They probably began life as two ditches which had been disturbed by later activity. In excavation the south-westernmost alignment appeared to include three cuts. Cut 2408 at its north-west end was U-shaped in cross-section, 1.34m wide and 0.32m deep with a backfill (2403) of slightly clayey silty sand. South-east of 2408 was 2248 an irregular cut, 0.69m long, 0.53m wide and 0.13m deep, of which the backfill was 2245, a dark brown deposit with frequent pebbles. To the south-east again was 2247 an irregular shallow cut 2.12m long, 0.84m wide and 0.12m deep of which the fill was 2229, an ashy dark grey-brown deposit with frequent charcoal flecks.

The second alignment c.3m to the north-east included two components. Over most of its length it was represented by 2364 up to 0.95m wide and 0.28m deep, but very shallow indeed at its north-west end. The fill layers were 2372, light brown sandy silty clay, succeeded by 2344, a very dark brown-black deposit with frequent pebbles. A deposit (2376) of yellow-brown silty sand may have been all that remained to show the feature existed north-west of 2364. At the south-east end of the alignment was 2385 of which the fill was 2380, a light brown sandy clay silt.

There were two additional truncated shallow cuts, possibly ditch cuts, to the east of this latter alignment. 2311 was not fully recorded, but in the stretch excavated was 0.15m deep, up to 1m wide and filled with 2307, a light to mid-brown sandy clay. 2267 was 1.63m long, 0.66m wide and 0.13m deep, and the backfill was 2266, a mid-brown-grey silty clay.

Ditches in Trench A and the south-eastern part of Trench B

To the south-east of the features described above was a series of cut features which had probably existed as two ditches, separated by a gap, on a slightly different north-east/south-west alignment from the ditches 2400–1, 2406 described above.

On the north-east side of the gap a ditch recorded as cuts 1038/1053 ran across Trench A and was 2.21m wide and 0.7m deep with sloping sides and a steep-sided, flat-bottomed slot at the base. At its south-west end the ditch had a vertically sided terminal.

Two stake-holes (1069 and 1070) were found cut into the base of the ditch; a third (1074) was found on its south-eastern slope and a fourth (1076) was found immediately to the north-west of the ditch. The fill of these features (1063–4, 1073, 1075 respectively) was a dark brown silty sand.

At its north-east end the ditch was badly disturbed and the only fill layer identified was 1028, a dark brown sand. Preservation was much better in the south-western part and the sequence was as follows. The earliest fill was 1055/2096, a dark brown-grey silty sand, succeeded by 1052, a brownish-grey-green sandy silt with frequent charcoal flecks, succeeded in turn by 1050/2084, a light brown-yellow silty sand with frequent cobbles, sealed by 1048/2083, a yellow-brown silty sand. These deposits probably derived from both erosion of the ditch sides and the accumulation of refuse. The ditch was then recut (1082) over a distance of 3.6m from the south-west terminal (to the north-east tree roots had disturbed the feature) with a maximum width of 1.6m. The recut was U-shaped in cross-section and rows of iron nails found along its sides suggest that it was plank-lined. The backfill was 1046/2072, a yellow-brown sandy silt with frequent charcoal flecks and pebbles.

In the gap c.2m wide between the north-eastern and south-western ditches a large irregular depression (2089) was found which may have resulted from frequent passage through it. The fill (2088/2198) was a black to brown silty sandy clay.

South-west of the gap was a short length of ditch (2199), 3.3m long, 2.6m wide and 0.97m deep. With steep sides and a steep-sided slot at the base, it was similar in character to the north-eastern ditch. The earliest infill layer was 2237, a blue-grey sandy clay. This was cut by a large post-hole or small pit (2236) which penetrated the base of 2199 at its northern end. The fill of 2236 was 2238, a red-brown sand, succeeded by 2235, a dark brown-black silty deposit. Subsequent ditch fills were 2232, a mixed white and brown sandy deposit, probably weathering from the sides, and then further weathering deposits: 2223, lenses of grey clay, sand and black silt, succeeded by 2220–1 and 2209, silty sands, and then 2213, black silt mixed with sand. The latest deposits were 2162, light grey-brown silt; 2164, dark brown silt; 2168, light brown silty clay; 2169, pale pink clay; 2173, grey-green silty sand; 2181, grey-brown silty sand; and 2194, dark grey-black silty clay.

Pottery indicates that the recut ditch 1082 and ditch 2199 were filling up after c.150.

On the south-west side of Trench B context 2260, not excavated but recorded in plan and seen in section after the removal of a modern intrusion, appeared to be the fill of a continuation of the ditch alignment of which a length of 5.5m was exposed with its north-east end lying immediately to the south-west of 2199.

Pit

In the north-eastern corner of Trench A the cut of either a rubbish pit or a well (1071), near circular in plan, 1.9 x 1.5m, was excavated to a depth of c.1m, but could not be bottomed because of ingress of water. It was filled with 1037/1054, a dark grey-brown deposit with lenses of sand, succeeded by 1034 and then 1022, mixed grey-brown sandy deposits. Near this feature was a grey sandy deposit (1027) which contained animal bones and was probably the base of a truncated rubbish pit.

Period 2 *(Fig.215)*

After initially silting up naturally, the ditches of Period 1 were finally filled in by deposits (recorded under 48 separate context numbers) largely of brown-grey and brown clayey silty sand, in total at

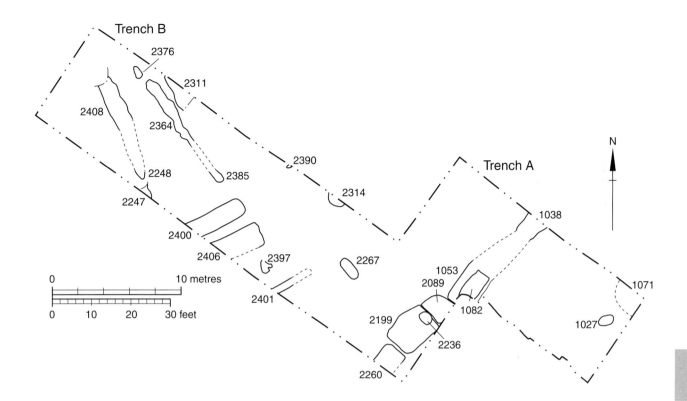

Fig. 214 *35–41 Blossom Street: Period 1 plan*

least 0.3m thick which accumulated over the whole site.

A marked difference could be seen between the accumulation at the north-western end of Trench B, where small discrete deposits could be identified, and the majority of the site where there was a single homogeneous layer (removed as a number of spits). This probably reflects the medieval and post-medieval distinction in land use between gardens or yards at the north-western end of the site and agricultural land to the south-east where ploughing had caused great damage. An island of discrete layers occurred in the small area enclosed by the later mausoleum (Period 3) where structural remains may have protected them from plough damage.

These deposits contained an appreciable quantity of pottery (*AY* 16/8, 1130–1), animal bone, and numerous other artefacts including household articles, personal equipment and dress accessories, but, apart from a few fragments of tile, little building material.

Contemporary with the accumulation of the deposits referred to above, or occurring very soon after, were a number of small pits. In the south-eastern part of the site the cuts were shallow, all of them being less than 0.3m deep, probably as a result of truncation. They included in Trench A, 1045, an irregular cut 1 x 0.52m, filled with 1044, a light brown silty clay with frequent charcoal.

At the north-west end of Trench B was 2295, roughly rectangular in plan, 1.05 x 0.4m and 0.23m deep, filled with 2285, grey-green sandy silt. Immediately to the south-east was 2407, irregular in plan, 1.6 x 0.5m, and cut by 2334; both were unexcavated. They were cut by 2329, irregular in plan, 0.6 x 0.4m and 0.34m deep, filled by 2318, grey-green sandy silt. It was cut by 2309, another irregular cut of similar size, filled by 2286, grey-brown sandy silt.

South-east of these features was 2324, a cut irregular in plan, 1.04 x 0.86m and 0.4m deep, filled with 2315, brown clayey sand. South-west of it was 2399, which had been roughly circular in plan, but was cut away to the north-west; what remained was 2m in diameter and 1.4m deep. The fill was 2383, a brown silty sandy clay which contained a human left femoral shaft. Next to 2399 was a possible posthole (2368), 0.18 x 0.14m and 70mm deep, filled by 2367, silver-grey sandy clay.

South-west of 2399 was 2389, badly disturbed by later features. Originally it was probably circular in plan and it was 0.46m deep. The fill was 2384, grey sandy silt. 2389 was cut by 2375, also disturbed by later activity, but which had been circular in plan, 1.2m in diameter and 0.83m deep. It was backfilled by 2357, grey-brown sandy clayey silt, below 2355, reddish-brown clay, below 2354, mid-brown silty sandy clay with frequent charcoal flecks. Immediately north-east was 2341, a feature rectangular in plan, 0.8m wide, c.1.4m long and 0.5m deep. It was filled by 2340, 2339 and 2335, brown silty sandy clays, which were succeeded by 2332, grey clayey sandy silt with patches of charcoal and fragments of burnt clay. 2332 was below 2328, yellow-brown

sandy clay with charcoal and many burnt clay fragments, in turn below 2327 grey-brown silty clay.

In the centre of the trench was 2330, subrectangular in plan (not fully recorded), 1.4 x 1m, filled with 2321, light brown sandy clay silt with patches of ash and charcoal. Close together at the south-east end of Trench B were two cuts subcircular in plan: 2187, 0.92 x 0.74m, filled with 2186, a dark grey-brown silt, and 2190, 0.85 x 0.64m, filled with 2189, brown silty sandy clay.

Most of the features described above were probably dug to deposit domestic refuse, but pits 2341 and 2375 appear to have contained burnt residues, possibly derived from some form of manufacturing process.

Although the level from which they were cut is uncertain, two other features probably belonging to Period 2 were 2216 and 2259 (not illustrated). 2216 was located at the north-western edge of Trench B

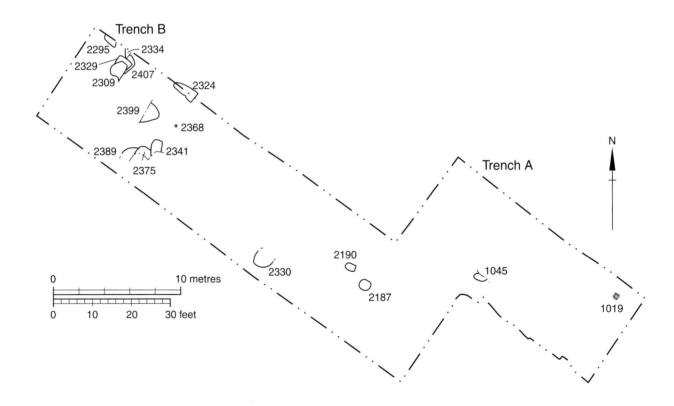

Fig. 215 *35–41 Blossom Street: Period 2 plan*

and it was a 0.7 x 0.7m deposit of black silt which may have been the lowest fill of a pit. Two metres to the south-east was 2259, a trench 3.2m long, 0.74m wide and 0.28m deep, which was filled with 2218, a dark brown sandy silt which contained a little slag.

Dating of Period 2 to the late 2nd–early 3rd century derives largely from the large quantity of pottery recovered (*AY* 16/8, 1131). The mixed nature of material suggested to Monaghan (*ibid.*) that it derived from 'levelled-out rubbish heaps of several periods'. Coins from the accumulation deposits of this period include examples of Domitian (sf484) from 2193, of Trajan (sf933) from 2157, and three of Hadrian (sfs453, 458, 946) from 2157, 2156 and 2239 respectively.

Finally, a feature which was difficult to phase accurately was a square setting (1019) at the east end of Trench A formed by three slabs of sandstone set on their edges placed on a horizontal slab of the same material. The dark brown deposit (1021) within

the setting contained mid-2nd-century pottery and flecks of burnt bone, while nearby was found the circular, lead-alloy base of an ossuary (sf15). This was probably a disturbed cremation burial.

Period 3 *(Figs 216–223)*

In Period 3 there was a change in land use with the establishment of a cemetery. Period 3 is divided into two, 3a and 3b (see above), and Period 3a itself is divided into three subphases. Period 3a began with the inhumation of two individuals (Period 3ai, c.200–25). Subsequently a stone mausoleum was erected around these burials in which up to four further burials took place (Period 3aii, c.225–50). A further phase of activity included more possible burials (Period 3aiii, c.250–300). During the lifetime of the mausoleum two inhumations were made immediately outside it. These could not be assigned to any particular subphase and are assigned simply to Period 3a. Finally the building was systematically demolished to its foundations (Period 3b, c.300–25).

6

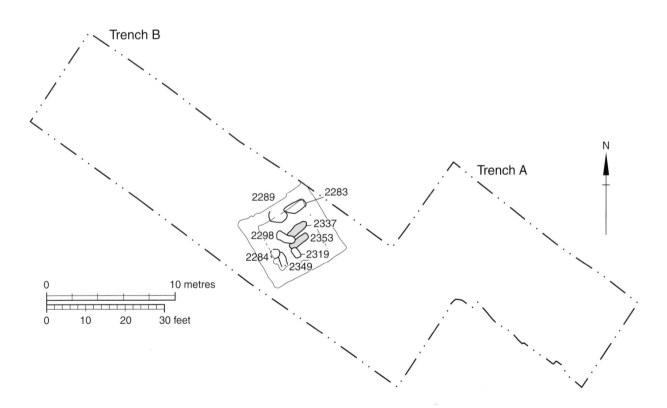

Fig. 216 *35–41 Blossom Street: Period 3ai plan*

For the pottery from Period 3 see *AY* 16/8, pp.1131–2; note that the mausoleum is referred to there as the 'second mausoleum' as at time of writing it was thought there was an earlier structure (see below Period 3ai for discussion).

A detailed study of the graves from this site will be found in *AY* 5/1, but a summary of grave alignment, the age and sex of the skeletons, and any grave goods will be found in Table 4. The size of grave cuts and of cuts which may have been graves will be found in Table 5.

Period 3ai *(Fig.216)*

Burials

Cut into the Period 2 deposits in the south-eastern half of Trench B were two graves (2337 and 2353) aligned north-east/south-west. The skeleton in grave 2353 had been buried in a coffin, indicated, in this case as in others, by the survival of iron nails, with a pair of shoes or boots placed next to the right leg surviving as iron hobnails (Fig.217). The fill of this grave was cut at its south-east corner by a shallow pit (2319), rectangular in plan, 0.78 x 0.5m. It was backfilled with 2312, a brown sandy silt which contained pieces of coal and frequent charcoal fragments, and also the broken base of a glass bottle (sfs944, 956, 986) and an antler toggle (sf989), placed upon a bed of oyster shells. These items may represent an offering of ritual significance.

Associated features

Contemporary with the graves and feature just described were four truncated, shallow cuts (2283–4, 2289 and 2349) all roughly rounded in plan. Cut 2283, 1.5 x 1.2m and 0.25m deep, was filled with 2280, a dark grey-brown silty sand. Cut 2349, 1.2 x 1.1m and 80mm deep, was filled by 2346, a grey-brown sandy clay. Cut 2289, 1.2 x 1m and 0.26 deep, was filled with 2287, a grey-brown sandy clay, while 2284, which cut 2349, was 0.7 x 0.42m and 0.17m deep, and filled with 2282, a grey clayey silt. The significance of these features is not apparent, although they may have housed posts and thus indicate the presence of a timber structure of a form which is no longer apparent.

Contemporary also were two further shallow cuts, both rectangular in plan (2278 and 2310; not illustrated). 2310, which cut feature 2319 and grave 2353 (above) was 1.34 x 1.16m and 0.15m deep and was filled with 2301, a light grey-brown sandy silt. It was cut by 2278, 1.32 x 1.2m and 0.15m deep, which was filled with 2272, a grey-brown sandy silt. Immediately south-west was a shallow scoop (2298) which cut graves 2337 and 2353. It measured 1.46 x 0.66m and was filled with 2290, large cobbles and fragments of limestone, mortar, brick and tile. 2298 was cut by a shallow scoop, oval in plan (2279; not

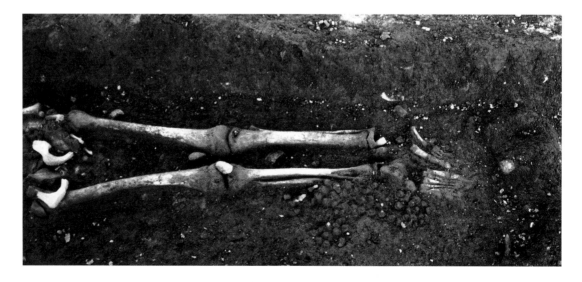

Fig. 217   *35–41 Blossom Street, Trench B: view north of burial 2353 (Period 3a i) in the mausoleum, showing hobnails from footwear by the lower legs*

illustrated), 2 x 1m and 0.2m deep, which was filled by 2271, a light brown silty sand.

Scoop 2279 and the other features described above were overlain by 2257, a light brown clayey sandy silt. The inclusion of 30 pieces of slag in this deposit suggests that it was composed of material which had been brought from elsewhere to act as levelling. 2257 also contained a coin of Antoninus Pius (138–61; sf661).

Period 3aii *(Fig.218)*

The mausoleum *(Figs 219–221)*

Deposit 2257 was cut into by the construction trenches for a small mausoleum, 6m (c.20 Roman feet) square, aligned with one axis north-east/ south-west and the other at 90° to this. It survived largely as four flat-bottomed foundation trenches (2256), each 0.88m deep and 0.92–1.20m wide at the top. Only the east and west corners of the foundation trench were fully excavated and at the base there were large pieces of limestone rubble below a deposit, 0.40m deep, of cobbles set in clay (2154). Away from the corners redeposited natural sand took the place of the limestone rubble. Little of the superstructure of the building survived except at the north corner where there were traces of outer and inner faces of coursed limestone rubble which bounded a core of mortared limestone fragments (2170 and 2172).

The systematic demolition of the stone-built mausoleum in Period 3b had removed almost all remains of its superstructure, but the scale of the foundations indicated a substantial structure. The extra effort taken with the demolition of the north-western wall (see below) suggests that this side was visually the most impressive, as might be expected since it faced towards the main road from the south-west, and probably contained the entrance.

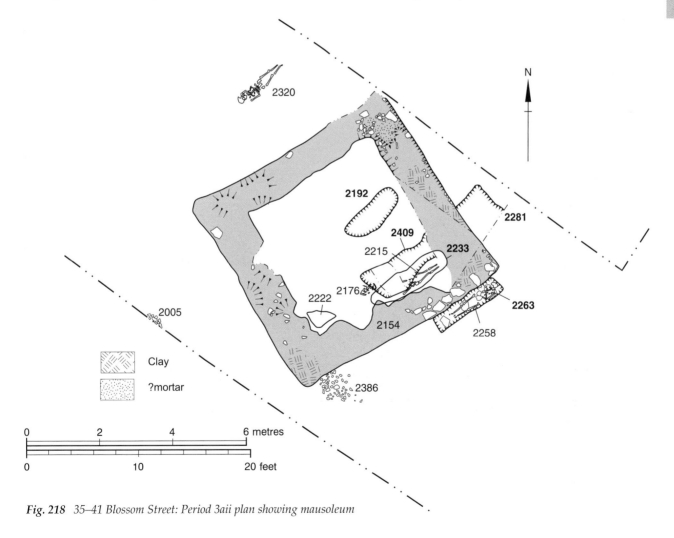

Fig. 218 *35–41 Blossom Street: Period 3aii plan showing mausoleum*

Small quantities of *opus signinum* and plaster found in the backfill of cuts inside the mausoleum may derive from its internal decoration and the numerous pieces of tile found in the robber trenches for the walls (2155) probably came from the roof.

The structure appears to have been built such that graves 2337 and 2353 (Period 3ai; see above) were located in the centre. Further burials were made within and in the immediate vicinity of the mausoleum during the span of its life.

Table 4 Summary of Roman burials at 35–41 Blossom Street

Grave	Skeleton	Alignment (location of head given first)	Age	Sex	Grave goods
Period 3					
No cut	2176	SW/NE	18–25	f	
2233	2215	SW/NE	15–20	–	
2263	2258	SW/NE	25–35	f	Pot containing chicken bones
No cut	2325	SW/NE	adult	–	
2337	2333	SW/NE	40–50	m	
2353	2348	SW/NE	11–15	–	Shoes with hobnails
Period 4					
1040	1036	NW/SE	adult	f	Iron knife (sfs209–10)
1049	1042	NW/SE	1–2	–	
2041	2035	NW/SE	35	m	
2068	2042	NW/SE	30–40	m	Copper-alloy brooch (sf71)
No cut	2045	NW/SE	adult	–	
2064	2062	NW/SE	40+	f	
2071	2066	NW/SE	30–40	f	
2078	2074	NW/SE	30–40	f	
2110	2094	NW/SE	40–50	m	
2135	2125	NW/SE	12–16	–	
2127	2126	NW/SE	30–40	m	
No cut	2133	NW/SE	adult	f?	
No cut	2136	NW/SE	3–5	–	
2148	2139	NW/SE	20–25	f	
2180	2177	NW/SE	adult	–	
No cut	2200	NW/SE	3–5	–	Pot
2226	2224	NW/SE	35+	f	
No cut	2227	NW/SE	2–3	–	Glass beads (sf553), 2 shale bracelets (sfs555–6)
2244	2243	NW/SE	30–40	f	
No cut	2246	NW/SE	adult	m	
2144	2251	NW/SE	3–5	–	
2264	2261	NW/SE	35–45	m	
2270	2269	NW/SE	5–7	–	
No cut	2313	SE/NW	13–17	–	
2369	2366	NW/SE	50+	m	

Table 5 35–41 Blossom Street: Dimensions (in metres) of cuts for graves (bold) and grave-like features

Context	L	W	D
Period 3			
2085	1.54	0.76	0.46
2109	1.24	0.50	0.26
2115	0.70	0.40	0.20
2129	0.80	0.50	0.22
2192	1.76	0.66	0.42
2233	2.36	0.66	0.24
2263	2.00	0.40	
2337	1.80	0.70	0.28
2353	1.62	0.54	0.26
2409	2.10	0.94	0.11
Period 4			
1039	1.32	0.48	0.58
1040	0.80	0.55	0.35
1049	0.80	0.55	0.35
2041	1.46	0.90	0.13
2056	1.97	0.59	–
2065	0.60	0.50	0.10
2068	1.30	0.30	0.33
2071	2.12	0.65	0.39
2077	1.85	0.60	0.23
2078	2.04	0.80	0.19
2098	1.40	0.40	0.02
2110	2.00	0.90	0.26
2113	1.28	0.32	0.15
2120	n/a		
2127	1.80	1.20	0.31
2135	1.60	0.47	0.31
2144	1.04	0.46	0.13
2148	1.25	0.70	0.14
2161	1.40	0.56	0.31
2180	1.70	0.50	0.19
2210	1.92	0.69	0.11
2211	1.60	0.58	0.14
2226	2.09	0.76	0.71
2244	2.00	0.92	0.50
2252	1.48	0.73	0.13
2264	2.20	0.79	0.20
2270	0.85	0.60	0.15
2274	1.12	0.71	–
2369	1.93	0.54	0.05

Graves and other features in the mausoleum

Grave 2233, in the east corner of the structure, appeared to have been partly cut into the foundations. Its cut was irregular in plan, aligned south-west/north-east. The fill was 2204, a dark grey-brown clay silt in which there was the truncated, supine skeleton of an unsexed teenager (2215). Immediately to the south-west the upper half of a female skeleton (2176) was found lying on its right side on a similar alignment, but no grave cut was detected.

There were two other probable disturbed graves (2192 and 2409) in the mausoleum on the same alignment as those just described. Cut 2192, oval in plan, was in the centre of its north-east side. It was filled by 2185, a dark yellow-brown, sandy silt with fragments of limestone and mortar which contained, in the north-eastern half of the cut, the disarticulated bones of two males, one 8–12 years of age and the other c.18–25 years. Finds included four iron nails (sfs1365, 1367–8, 1375), a piece of glass (sf1371) and a bone pin (sf1372). Cut 2409, irregular in plan, postdated grave 2233 in the east corner of the structure. It also contained a limited amount of disarticulated human bone in the fill (2196), a mid-yellow-brown sandy silt with fragments of limestone, mortar and *opus signinum*.

A shallow deposit of mixed white and grey-brown sand (2222) was located in the south corner of the building, and all deposits of this period were sealed by a deposit (2163), 0.20m thick, of orange-brown sand which contained fragments of limestone, mortar and *opus signinum*.

Period 3aiii *(Fig.222)*

Possible graves in the mausoleum

Continued use of the mausoleum is indicated by four cut features which were located in its north-eastern half. All were rectangular in plan, aligned north-east/south-west and resembled graves. Cut 2109 was filled with 2108, a brown sandy silt. It was cut by 2085 which was filled with 2082, grey-brown sandy silt in which were found a copper-alloy ring (sf161) and stud (sf181), and ten iron nails suggesting that the feature had contained a coffin or some other form of container. South-east of 2085

Fig. 219 *35–41 Blossom Street, Trench B: view north-west of the mausoleum. Scale 2m*

Fig. 220 *35–41 Blossom Street, Trench B: view north-east of the north corner of the mausoleum showing facing stones and wall core. Scale 0.50m*

Fig. 221 *35–41 Blossom Street, Trench B: section through mausoleum wall footing 2154 (south-east side). Scale 0.20m*

was 2129 filled with 2116, a yellow-brown deposit. Further to the south-east was 2115 which was filled with 2112, light brown sandy silt. All of these features were too small to have contained adult inhumations and no human bone was recovered from them, but they were large enough for burials of infants or children, whose bones are less likely to survive than those of adults.

Period 3a

Two further graves were dug in the vicinity of the mausoleum during its period of use which could not, however, be assigned to a particular subphase but have been shown on Fig.218. Grave 2263 was dug against the south-eastern wall. The cut, rectangular in plan, contained an adult female (2258), originally in a wooden coffin which rested on four pieces of limestone (2262) laid on the floor of the cut. Another limestone fragment found on the pelvis of the skeleton may formerly have rested upon the top of the coffin. In the backfill of the grave (2241) a Dales ware pot containing the complete skeleton of a chicken – presumably a votive offering – was found. Two metres to the north-west of the mausoleum was adult skeleton 2320. No clear cut was detected, but in the material around the skeleton (2325), a silty deposit with flecks of mortar and plaster, there were nails which showed it was buried in a coffin.

A shallow cut (2281), rectangular in plan, 1.5 x 1m, immediately to the north-east of the mausoleum may represent the truncated base of another grave. It was filled with 2277, a light grey-brown sandy silt with frequent clay patches and charcoal flecks in which three iron nails and an iron ring (sf1535) were found.

Also not easy to phase exactly was a patch of densely packed cobbles (2386) at the south corner of the mausoleum which may have been the remnant of a path running along its south-east side. At the south-western edge of Trench B a small area of cobbles in clay (2005) was very similar to the foundation material (2154) of the mausoleum. However, no trace of any structure was found in Trial Trench D to the south-west and a watching brief showed that most of the archaeological deposits between Trenches B and D had been destroyed by a large 19th-century drain.

Period 3b: c.300–25 *(Fig.223)*

The mausoleum probably went out of use in the later 3rd or early 4th century. Following the demolition of the superstructure, a trench (2155) of surviving depth 0.12–0.25m had been dug to remove the lower parts of the walls on all sides. It was filled with 2057, an orange-buff sandy mortar containing patches of a dark brown deposit and large fragments

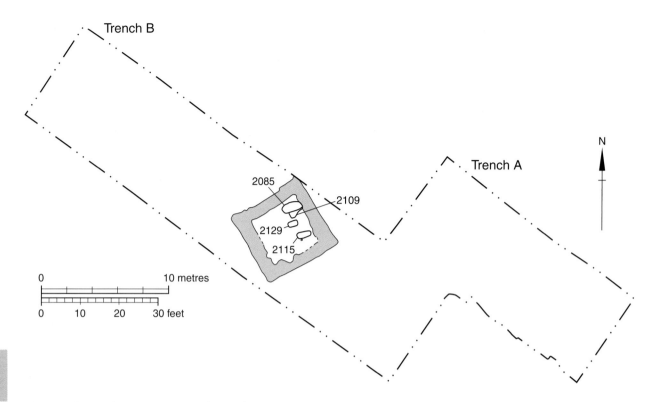

Fig. 222 *35–41 Blossom Street: Period 3aiii plan*

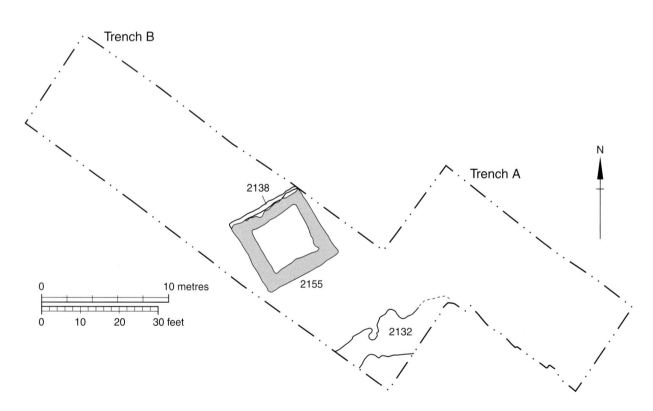

Fig. 223 *35–41 Blossom Street: Period 3b plan*

of sandstone, limestone, tile and mortar. It also produced a coin of Elagabalus (218–22; sf342) and some fragments of human bone. On the north-west side of the mausoleum the trench was made deeper (2138), 0.68m wide and 0.41m deep. It was backfilled with a brown sandy silt with limestone fragments and off-white mortar (2121) which produced a coin of Tetricus I (271–3; sf329).

To the south-east of the mausoleum, deposits 2019 (not illustrated), an orange-brown sandy deposit, and 2132, a mottled yellow-brown sandy deposit, may have represented further backfilling of subsidence caused by the settling of the Period 1 ditches. The finds from these deposits included six pottery counters (sfs373, 378, 388, 391, 404, 417), a bone counter (sf594), four bone pins (sf440, 595, 631–2) and a bone needle (sf621).

Period 4: c.325–400 *(Fig.224)*

The archaeology of this period encompasses a second phase of use of the site as a cemetery, but it had been badly truncated by post-Roman ploughing. While some graves were seen to cut through deposits of the 4th century and earlier, others were not detected until the natural sand was reached. However, they were assigned to this period on the basis of associated pottery and a common north-west/south-east alignment, at c.90° to that of the Period 3 graves.

Material (2044) described as a grey-green silty deposit with limestone fragments was excavated in the area of the Period 1 ditches in Trench A and the south-eastern part of Trench B. It resembled 2019 and 2132 (Period 3b) in containing large quantities of finds, but in addition to residual 2nd- and 3rd-century pottery it contained early 4th-century sherds. A number of similar deposits (2091, 2149, 2165, 2171, 2175, 2205) were found on other parts of Trench B. One of these deposits (2205), a brown silty sand with frequent mortar fragments, which filled a depression (2212), contained thirteen pieces of painted plaster. Subsequent to these deposits the site became a cemetery once again.

The cemetery

Twenty-five burials were recorded, together with eleven probable graves in which no skeletal material survived. Alignment, age and sex of the skeletons, and grave goods, are summarised in Table 4. The size of the cuts for graves and grave-like features is given in Table 5.

If the skeleton found immediately to the south-east of the site in 1966 (Radley 1967, 9) is part of the same group then the cemetery zone measured at least 50m north-west/south-east by 20m north-east/south-west. No burials were located in Trial Trenches C and D to the south-west. The location of grave 2246 at the north-west end of Trench B, at some remove from its nearest neighbours, suggests that others on the relatively high ground in this area may have fallen victim to later ploughing or other activity.

A truncated ditch cut (2228), aligned north-west/south-east, found in the north-western part of Trench B, may represent a boundary ditch on the south-west side of the cemetery area. It was recorded over a length of c.2.34m but continued to the north-west into an unexcavated area. It was up to 1.86m wide and 0.19m deep. It was filled with 2197, a brown sandy deposit.

The graves

Except in cases where they had been made shallow through truncation, most grave cuts were sub-rectangular in plan and up to 2.50m long. No grave cuts were detected for infant skeletons 2200 and 2227 and five other burials.

As noted, the majority of the graves and probable graves shared a common north-west/south-east alignment. All the skeletons had their heads at the north-west end of the grave, except for 2313 which was at the south-east end (no grave cut). Three of the grave-like cuts without human remains (1039, 2056, 2113) were aligned north-east/south-west. Cut 2056, cut by grave 2127, contained a coin of Magnentius (350–1; sf160).

The conformity of the majority of the graves to a common alignment and some indication of the use of rows suggest that the cemetery was well organised and that care was usually taken not to disturb earlier burials. The only examples of intercutting were provided by grave 2110 which clipped grave 2148, and grave-like Cut 2098 which clipped grave

6

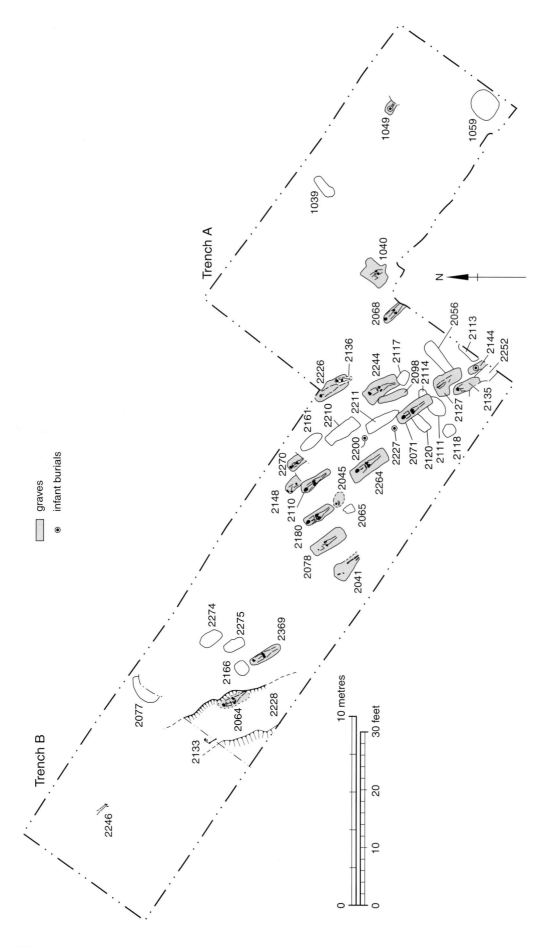

graves

● infant burials

Trench A

Trench B

N

1049

1059

1039

1040

2068

2056

2113

2144

2252

2226

2136

2244

2117

2098

2114

2135

2127

2118

2071

2120

2111

2161

2210

2211

2200

2227

2270

2264

2148

2110

2045

2180

2065

2078

2041

2274

2275

2369

2166

2077

2064

2133

2228

2246

10 metres

30 feet

0

0

10

20

Fig. 224 35–41 Blossom Street: Period 4 plan of cemetery

Fig. 226 *35–41 Blossom Street, Trench A: view north-west of burial 1049 (Period 4) with skeleton of an infant also showing the surviving traces of a coffin with iron fittings (scale 0.50m)*

Fig. 225 *35–41 Blossom Street, Trench B: view north-west of burial 2244 (Period 4) showing prone skeleton 2243 and stone lining of grave cut (scale 0.50m)*

2244. In addition, it should be noted that the infant burial 2136 was found in the backfill of grave 2226 containing an adult ?female skeleton (2224). This was probably the deliberate burial of a mother and child. The lack of intercutting may mean that the cemetery was not used over a long period, unlike, for example, Trentholme Drive where nearly 150 years of use had resulted in frequent intercutting and multiple alignments (Wenham 1968b). It may also mean that the graves were marked by mounds or posts of some kind. No clear evidence for this survived, but two cuts (2114 and 2117), subcircular in plan, may have held markers. Cut 2114, cut by grave 2071, which measured 0.42 x 0.47m and 60mm deep, may have been the site of a post for grave 2127. It contained

2103, a dark brown silty deposit with much charcoal. 2117, cut into the south-east end of grave 2244, was a shallow depression 0.80 x 0.60m, filled by 2105, a dark brown silty sand.

The skeletons in all the surviving burials were extended and supine, except for the female in grave 2244 who was prone (Fig.225), although the position of the arms varied. In the most common position (eight cases) the arms were folded across the stomach region.

Nine adult graves contained evidence of coffins held together with iron nails. The fill of a grave-like feature 2077 (2067) contained eleven iron nails and the initial deposit (2131) within the medieval feature which truncated it contained fourteen nails. When plotted, their positions confirmed the existence of a coffin. Any evidence from another eight graves had been lost through disturbance and a number of others contained only one or two nails in the fill. Coffins not utilising iron nails would not have been detectable because the soil conditions on this site did not allow survival of organic material, although, exceptionally, in grave 1049 (Fig.226) the skeleton (1042) lay on the stain of a coffin base (1047). There were also iron nails in this grave's backfill layer (1031), a dark brown deposit which contained a few wood fragments. Graves 2071 and 2244 were lined with limestone and cobble packing which may have held boards lining the grave.

In a few of the graves there were objects which may have been deliberately deposited as grave goods; see Table 4 for a summary.

Other features

Other features belonging to Period 4 included at the extreme south-east end of Trench A, away from the surviving burials, a substantial post-pit (1059), 1.5m across, roughly rounded in plan and 0.4m deep. It was filled with 1058, mid-grey sandy silt, which surrounded a decayed post position (1057), 0.85 x 0.58m and 0.23m deep. This was filled with 1056, dark grey-brown sandy silt and then 1013

dark grey clayey silt. A shallow cut 2111, cut by grave 2071, was oval in plan, 1 x 0.50m, and was filled with 2097, a dark brown-black sandy deposit with frequent charcoal flecks and lumps of burnt clay in which many iron objects were found.

At the south-east end of Trench B were 2118, a small shallow feature filled with dark brown silty clay (2104) and 2166 (not illustrated), a cut rounded in plan, 0.84 x 0.72 and 0.19m deep, filled with 2152, dark brown sandy silt with frequent charcoal fragments.

Period 5: c.400–c.1100 *(Fig.227)*

This period included features which cut the Period 4 cemetery and were sealed by later medieval plough soil. They include at the south-east end of Trench B a vertically sided pit 2049, rectangular in plan, 1.33 x 0.90 and 0.55m deep, which was filled with 2033, a dark grey-brown clay deposit in which some human bone was found. East of it was a pit (2070), oval in plan, 1 x 0.48m and 0.66m deep. The features were succeeded by deposits 2006 and 2018 which contained Roman pottery. Above them deposits apparently derived from ploughing were dated to the later medieval period.

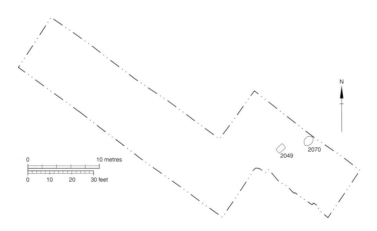

Fig. 227 *35–41 Blossom Street: Period 5a plan*

The Crescent

In 1981 two gas pipe trenches were observed by David Brinklow in The Crescent (SE59585135; Fig.193, 2). In Trench 1 at the rear of The Odeon Cinema there was a cobbled surface at a depth of c.2m. This was thought to be Roman and a continuation of RCHME's approach road 9 believed to originate in Aldborough and found nearby in Wenham's excavations at 18–20 Blossom Street. In Trench 2 near the junction of The Crescent and Blossom Street no archaeology was observed, although this is near to No. 1 The Crescent where the main Roman road from the south-west (Road 10) was observed in 1879. The road was also seen during construction of the Odeon itself in 1936.

The site records have the Yorkshire Museum accession code 1981.10.

All Saints School, Nunnery Lane

In October 1993 an evaluation excavation, supervised by D. T. Evans, was undertaken at All Saints School, Nunnery Lane (SE59735133; Fig.193, 6; Fig.228), to a brief by the City Archaeologist in advance of an extension to the school buildings. The principal trench (1) measured 5 x 2m; two other small trenches (2–3) were excavated, but did not reach Roman deposits.

The finds and site records have the Yorkshire Museum accession code 1993.15.

Trench 1 *(Fig. 229)*

Natural, a coarse off-white sand (1017) was reached at c.12.10m OD, 2.70m below modern ground level. This was overlain by a mid-brown

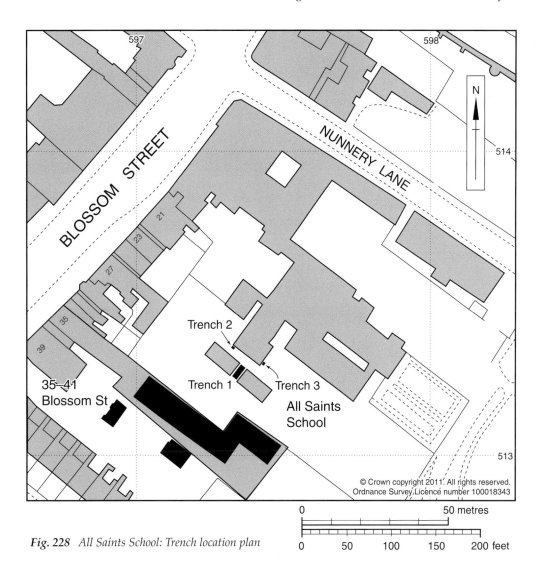

Fig. 228 *All Saints School: Trench location plan*

309

silty deposit (1016), up to 0.30m thick which was not excavated. Cut into 1016 were two parallel shallow ditches (1014–15) of U-shaped cross-section, on a north-east/south-west alignment. They were both c.0.70m wide and up to 0.30m deep. The fill of 1014 was a dark grey slightly sandy deposit (1012) and the fill of 1015 was dark greyish-brown sandy deposit (1013). A small quantity of pottery from these ditch fills was late 1st–3rd century.

Overlying the ditches was a build up, 0.20m thick, of a dark grey-brown slightly sandy deposit (1011) containing pottery of the 11th century. Above this were deposits and features of the medieval and post-medieval periods including a well (1003) which cut down through the Roman ditches.

A human skeleton observed in the south-east trench side was undated but probably Roman, representing an extension to the south-west of the cemetery zone adjacent to the Bar Convent.

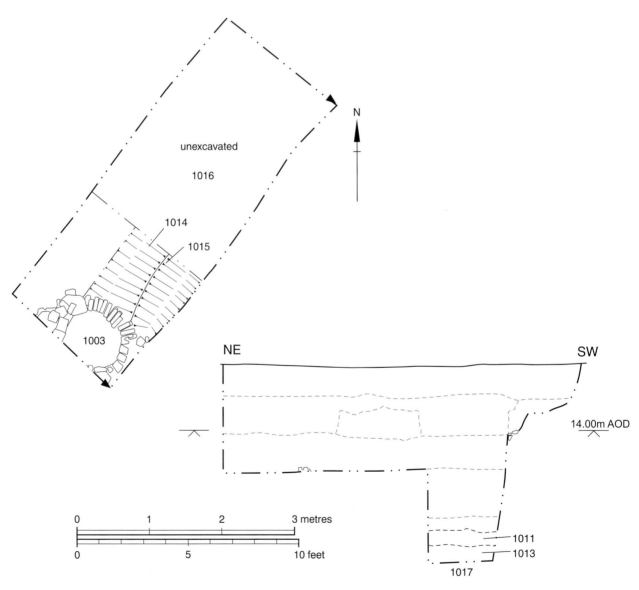

Fig. 229 All Saints School: Trench 1 plan and north-west facing section

32a Dale Street

A watching brief was undertaken by D. T. Evans at 32a Dale Street (SE59865124; Fig.193, 5; Figs 230–1) on 8 June 1995.

The records and finds are stored by York Archaeological Trust under the accession code YORYM : 1995.0354.

A builder's trench (Trench 1) was being dug as part of work to underpin and extend the property when human remains were found. The trench was completed under archaeological supervision; it was 7m long, 0.60m wide and 0.70m deep and at the base cut down through c.0.15m of natural, grey mottled orange clay (1005). This can be seen in the section recorded below the south-east corner of No. 32a (Fig.231). Natural was overlain by a mid-brown sandy deposit (1002) which was cut by a grave (1004) filled with brown silty clay (1003). A human skull survived in the section. The grave had probably been aligned north-west/south-east with the head to the north-west. Several fragments of human bone and a few sherds of 3rd- to mid-4th-century Roman pottery were found in the region of the skull during digging; other bones found during unsupervised digging had also come from this area. As in the case of the burial from All Saints School (above), this was probably part of the cemetery zone previously recorded to the north-west, adjacent to the Bar Convent.

6

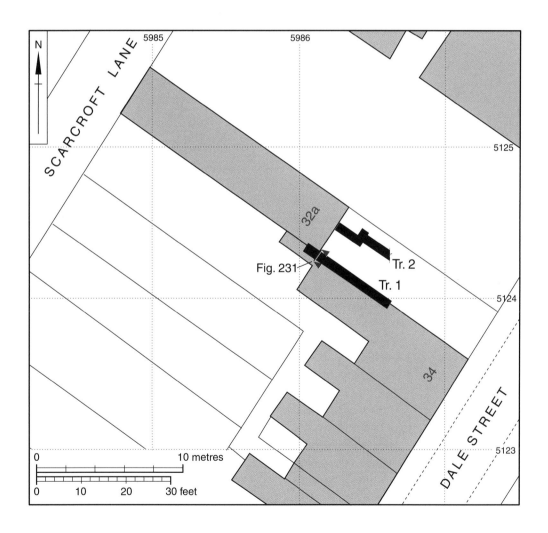

Fig. 230 *32a Dale Street: Site and trench location plan*

In the area of the building the grave was succeeded by a deposit of brick rubble (1001). A second trench (2) was dug c.2m to the north-east of the first in an area where modern ground level was 0.60m higher. Although this meant there had been less disturbance of archaeological deposits, no datable Roman features or deposits were found.

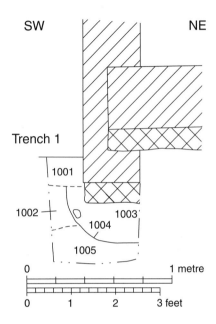

Fig. 231   *32a Dale Street: Trench 1, south-east-facing section*

39 Holgate Road

In August 1998 an evaluation excavation supervised by Mark Johnson was undertaken at Holgate Motors, 39 Holgate Road (SE59455119; Fig.193, 7; Fig.233), to a brief from the Principal Archaeologist for City of York Council, in advance of a housing development by K.W. Linfoot Plc. Two trenches were excavated. Trench 1 (3 x 3m) was located close to the junction of Holgate Road and St Catherine's Place, and Trench 2 (6.20 x 1m) in the south-east corner of the property. In addition four boreholes were drilled on the site: A and B (during the archaeological excavation), and 1 (in the centre of Trench 1) and 2 (south of Borehole B) before the excavation.

All records and finds are stored by York Archaeological Trust under the Yorkshire Museum accession code 1998.332.

Fig. 232   *39 Holgate Road, Trench 2: view north-west with ditches 2005 (foreground) and 2007. Scales 0.50m (bottom) and 1m*

Trench 1

The trench was located at the base of a steep slope running down from south-east to north-west. Although excavated to a depth of 1.60m, neither natural nor Roman archaeology were located.

Trench 2 *(Figs 232, 234)*

Natural orange-brown clayey sand (2011) was encountered at between 14.84m (north-west) and 15.28m (south-east) at a depth of 1.07–1.20m below

0   50 metres

0   50   100   150   200 feet

▨▨▨ Line of Roman road

– – – Line of ditches

Fig.233   *39 Holgate Road: Trench location plan*

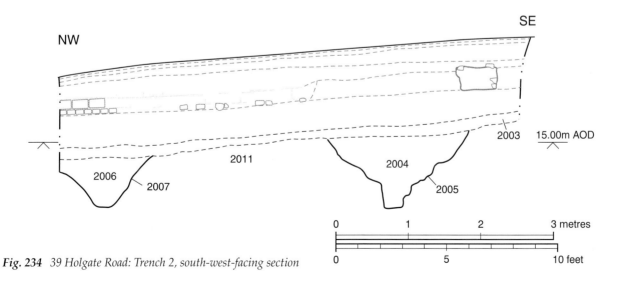

Fig. 234   *39 Holgate Road: Trench 2, south-west-facing section*

modern ground level. Natural was cut by two ditches, both aligned north-east/south-west, of which the largest was 2005. It was c.1.92m wide and 0.96m deep, and had slightly uneven sides sloping at c.45° and a pronounced slot with near vertical sides at the base. The fill (2004) was a light brown sandy deposit which contained over 60 sherds of pottery, the latest belonging to the second half of the 4th century, a certain amount of Roman tile and animal bone, much of it butchered, with c.50 pieces of chopped and split cattle limb shafts (cf. *AY* 15/2, 82). In addition, there were two bone hairpins (sfs13–14) and a coin (sf17) of Victorinus or Tetricus I (c.268–73).

At the north-west end of the trench, 2.40m north-west of 2005, was the second ditch (2007). It was at least 1.30m wide, the north-west edge lying beyond the trench edge, and 0.68m deep. The sides sloped down at c.45° to a rounded base. The fill (2006) was a pale brown sandy silt. It contained pottery, in which, again, the latest sherds belonged to the second half of the 4th century, as well as tile

and the humerus of a human infant. At the extreme south-east end of the trench was a probable post-hole (2009), subcircular in plan, 0.35m diameter and 0.15m deep. The fill (2008) was a brown sandy deposit with cobbles, originally perhaps packing, which produced two sherds of 2nd- to 3rd-century date. A shallow amorphous feature (2002) in the centre of the trench and continuing beyond its south-west edge contained pale grey-brown sandy silt. The features described above were sealed by 2003, a layer of pale yellowish-brown sandy silt up to 0.14m thick in which there were a few sherds of pottery, all Roman. This was overlain by a series of deposits of medieval and post-medieval date.

Boreholes

The four boreholes showed that the natural level slopes down from south-east to north-west at a steeper angle than the modern ground level and that there were c.2.5m of deposits above natural at the north-west end of the site and c.2.2m at the south-east end.

47 Blossom Street

In December 1991 an excavation, supervised by Bryan Antoni, was undertaken at 47 Blossom Street (SE59635130; Fig.193, 4; Fig.235). The work was undertaken on behalf of Chicken Cabins Ltd and followed a specification issued by the Principal Archaeologist for City of York Council. It involved a trench 4m (north-west/south-east) x 1m at the rear of a property which stands on the corner of Blossom Street and South Parade.

Finds and site records are stored with York Archaeological Trust under the Yorkshire Museum accession code 1991.22.

The excavation *(Figs 235–6)*

Any pre-modern archaeological deposits had been substantially destroyed by modern drain

trenches (1006 and 1008) and a 19th-century well (1003), leaving only a few islands of earlier strata.

The earliest deposit excavated (1025) was found in the north-east corner of the trench at 14.64–14.84m OD, 1.12–1.32m below modern level. It was thicker (300mm) at the north-west end than at the south-east (80mm) and consisted of a dark grey-brown clay silt containing cobbles, limestone, sandstone, brick and tile fragments. A feature (1024) containing cobbles in orange-brown sandy clay (1023) of which no record survives, is said to have cut 1025. The pottery from contexts 1023 and 1025 is dated to the 3rd century (*AY* 16/8, 1135).

Succeeding deposits and features were medieval or later in date.

6

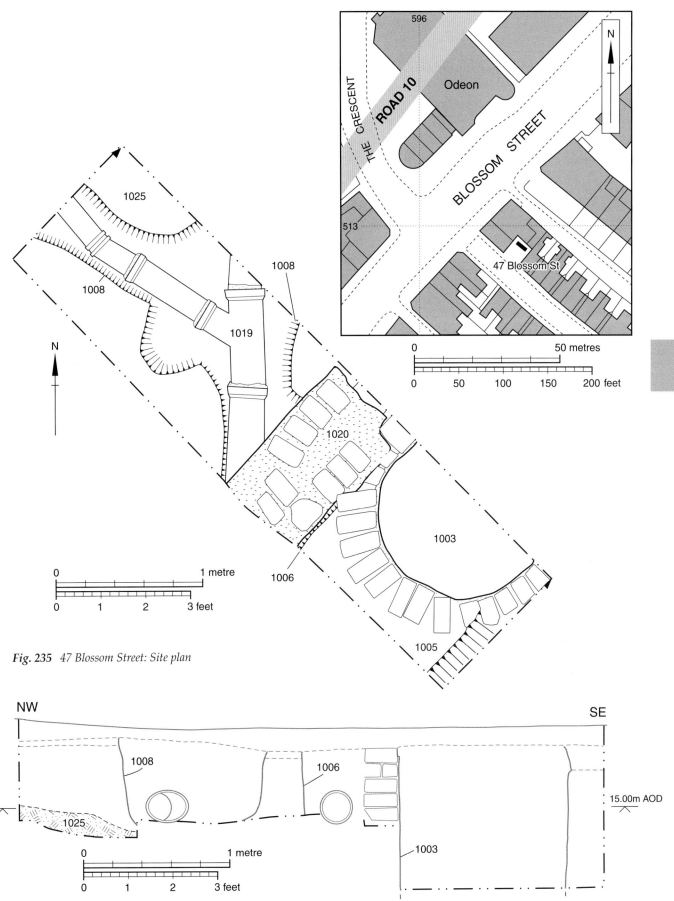

Fig. 235 *47 Blossom Street: Site plan*

Fig. 236 *47 Blossom Street: South-west-facing section*

315

3 Driffield Terrace

Between 31 August 2004 and 31 January 2005 a site measuring c.24 x 14.5m was excavated at 3 Driffield Terrace (SE59324510; Fig.193, 10; Fig.237). The work was directed by Bryan Antoni and Mark Johnson, assisted by Eliza Gore. The site had been evaluated in 2003 by FAS who found evidence for Roman burials and post-medieval structures. The excavation was undertaken in advance of redevelopment by Moorside Developments to a brief prepared by the Principal Archaeologist for City of York Council. This report covers the archaeology of the site before its use as a cemetery, details of which will be published in detail elsewhere, although a brief summary of the burials will be found below.

All artefacts and site records are stored at YAT under the Yorkshire Museum accession code YORYM : 2004.354.

The site lies between Driffield Terrace and The Mount, near a high point on the moraine (see pp.113–115). The main Roman approach road to York from the south-west (Road 10) lies no more than c.18m to the south-east of the site and numerous Roman burials have been found in the vicinity before the excavations described here. Eight urns, a lamp and a fibula, which may well have come from graves, were found in 1807 in the formal gardens behind Mount House (no longer extant), which fronted The Mount in the late 18th century (RCHMY **1**, 97).

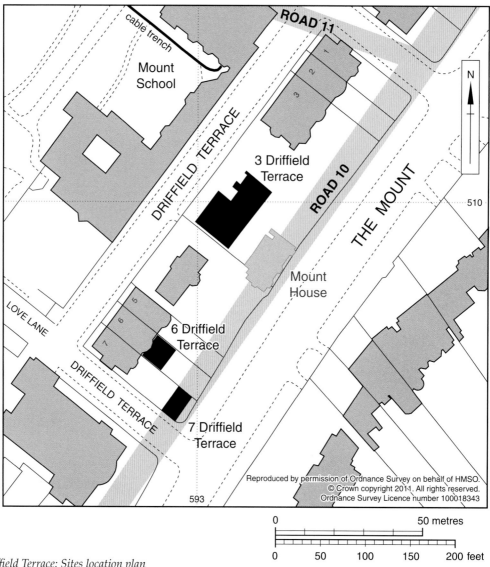

Fig. 237 *Driffield Terrace: Sites location plan*

Natural gravel and clay lies at c.19.80m OD, c.1.5–1.8m (south corner) below modern level but falls away to the south-west.

Ditch 4056 *(Fig.238)*

Cutting into natural (4060) and best defined in the south-western half of the site, was a shallow ditch (4056). It appeared to run more or less north-east/south-west across the site, but was not parallel to the line of the main approach road from the south-west. The ditch was typically 1.0–1.2m wide and 0.3m deep, with a flat or rounded base. It was backfilled with dark greyish-brown silty sand with occasional patches of dark pink clay and moderate charcoal flecks (4051). The fill layers contained a small amount of 2nd-century pottery.

Pit 4488 *(Figs 238–9)*

Cut into natural (4060) on the south-eastern edge of the site was a large pit (4488), probably circular in plan, with vertical sides, of which probably about half lay within the trench. It was c.5m in diameter and was excavated to a depth of c.3m, but the bottom was not reached.

The earliest recorded fill level in the pit was 4518, a firm mid-grey-brown clay. It was overlain by 4517, soft grey clay silt with occasional charcoal flecks and frequent cobbles. An unusual find in this deposit was a withy tie (sf396), perhaps for a barrel. 4517 was overlain by 4516, soft grey silt with patches of yellow sand, frequent cobbles and moderate charcoal. This contained a short wooden

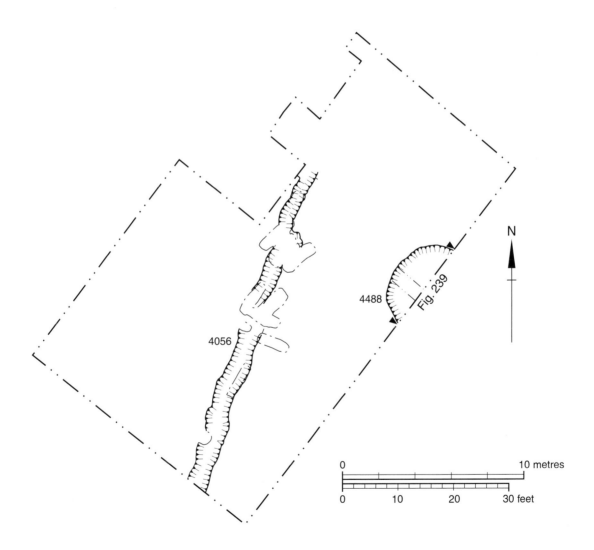

Fig. 238 3 Driffield Terrace: Plan of earliest Roman features

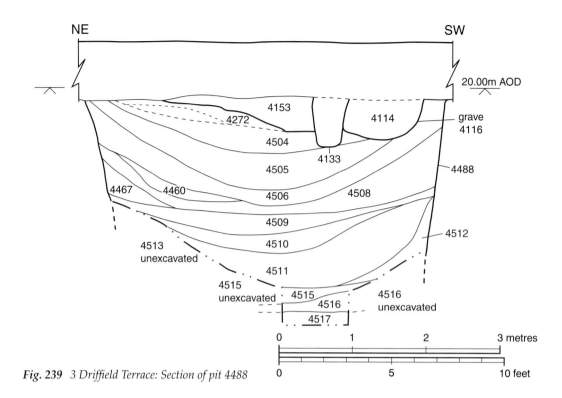

Fig. 239 *3 Driffield Terrace: Section of pit 4488*

plank (sf397). Above 4516 was 4515, a grey-pink clay, with occasional charcoal flecks and moderate cobbles. Above this was 4514, brown-orange silty clay, with occasional grey sand and frequent charcoal flecks. 4514 was succeeded by what appeared to be deposits of redeposited natural down the side of the pit: mixed orangey-brown and grey clay with moderate cobbles (4512–13).

Above the redeposited natural was 4511, dark brown-grey sandy silt with patches of grey-brown and pink clay, and occasional cobbles. It was succeeded by 4510, pink-brown clay with patches of grey sand and moderate cobbles. Above 4510 was 4509, dark brown-grey silty clay with occasional charcoal flecks.

Found in the top of deposit 4509 were the legs of a human skeleton (4469). They lay below deposit 4467, compact, mid-grey-brown silt sand with occasional charcoal flecks and lenses of mid-orange sand. In turn 4467 lay below 4508, firm mid-brown-grey silty clay with occasional pebbles and limestone fragments. This deposit was succeeded by 4460, friable, dark grey silty sand with frequent charcoal and burnt clay which was below 4507, mixed brown-grey sandy silt with mottled orange-brown sandy silt and patches of pale brown-grey clay with frequent cobbles and pebbles, and occasional limestone

fragments. In turn 4507 was below 4506, friable, brown-grey sandy silt mottled with small patches of orangey-yellow sand and occasional charcoal flecks. This was below 4505, mid-brown-pink clay silt mottled with orange sandy patches and patches of grey pink clay, and flecks of charcoal. 4505 was below 4504, soft, mid-pinkish-brown sandy silty clay with frequent charcoal flecks which in turn was below 4272, dark brown-grey sandy silty clay with occasional pebbles and charcoal flecks.

4272 was succeeded by 4153, the earliest of a series of clayey deposits which built up on the site during its use as a cemetery. 4153 was cut by Grave 4116, aligned north-east / south-west, itself cut by a small pit (4133). The cemetery included 56 inhumations and twelve cremations dated to the late 2nd – early 3rd centuries. The inhumations were remarkable for being, with the exception of three infants, exclusively of adult male individuals, some 30 of whom had been decapitated, probably by execution ante mortem. Another part of the same execution cemetery, in which some of the graves were later 3rd – 4th century, was excavated c.80m to the south-west at 6 Driffield Terrace in 2005 (Fig.136; Hunter-Mann 2006). More decapitated skeletons were found on the site of The Mount School, Science Building (Fig.103.14 and see below).

7 Driffield Terrace

In 1981 an observation by David Brinklow at the rear (south-east) of the property occupied by The Albert Hotel, 7 Driffield Terrace (SE59295093; Fig.193, 11; Fig.237), revealed a cobbled surface at a depth of c.1m below the then ground level. This was the main Roman road to York from the south-west (RCHMY 1, 3; Road 10) near to its north-western edge, although the edge itself was not apparently seen.

The site records have the Yorkshire Museum accession code 1981.1031.

The Mount School

Introduction

During the period 1980–2004 a number of small-scale excavations and observations have taken place in the property of The Mount School, Dalton Terrace (Fig.240). This lies in an area crossed by RCHME's Road 11 and Roman burials have come to light here on a number of occasions (RCHMY 1, 100–1). Still to be seen in the school is the tombstone of Lucius Baebius Crescens found in 1911 during construction of the gymnasium (*ibid.*, 121).

Stone coffin

In 1980 a coffin first uncovered at The Mount School in 1932 (Dickinson and Wenham 1957, 291–3) was re-excavated by the school archaeological society under the supervision of York Archaeological Trust (Yorkshire Museum site code 1980.1034). The coffin was located close to Love Lane (Fig.240) and was aligned north–south with the head of the skeleton at the north end. The lid was found at a depth of 0.50m below modern ground level. The coffin was of mill-stone grit with a slightly coped lid now broken in two (as a result of being lifted by a crane in 1932). It contained the skeleton of a robust female aged c.40. The head and feet had been encased in gypsum; originally the remainder had rested in a bed of gravel and both gypsum and gravel had been covered with sand. A clay and cobble ramp, noted in 1932, and thought to be for manoeuvring the coffin into its pit, was also observed.

The science building

In 1987 a watching brief was undertaken by David Brinklow during the construction of a new science building (Fig.193, 14; Fig.240). Although the site lay within a known area of Roman cemetery, it was, unfortunately, only possible to record one of the foundation trenches; other trenches were excavated mechanically without any archaeological record.

The site records have the Yorkshire Museum accession code 1987.15.

Natural lay c.0.50m below modern ground level and the graves were cut from c.0.30m below modern level. Graves containing the complete or partial remains of 19–20 individuals were recovered, along with a cremation. The inhumations appear to have been aligned north-west/south-east, i.e. at 90° to the main Roman road from the south-west which lay c.35m to the south-east. The remains of up to fourteen adults and six juveniles were recovered. Of the adults six were male and three female, but the remainder could not be sexed. Of particular interest were the skeletons of four adult males who had clearly been decapitated, suggesting this was part of the same cemetery zone as that excavated nearby at Nos 3 and 6 Driffield Terrace (above). The cremation was contained in a local grey ware pot, probably 3rd-century in date, and associated with it was a broken white flagon and other sherds (*AY* 16/8, 982, 1135, fig.385, *3789*).

The sports hall: 1

In May 1998 an archaeological evaluation was undertaken by Mark Johnson of an area on the western side of The Mount School property close to the point where Love Lane crosses the East Coast Main Line railway (SE59135108; Fig.193, 15; Figs 240–1). This was occupied by tennis courts which were to be replaced by a sports hall. Three trenches 5 x 2m were excavated. The stone coffin re-examined in 1980 lay to the south-east of Trench 1.

The site records have the York Archaeological Trust and Yorkshire Museum accession code 1998.41.

319

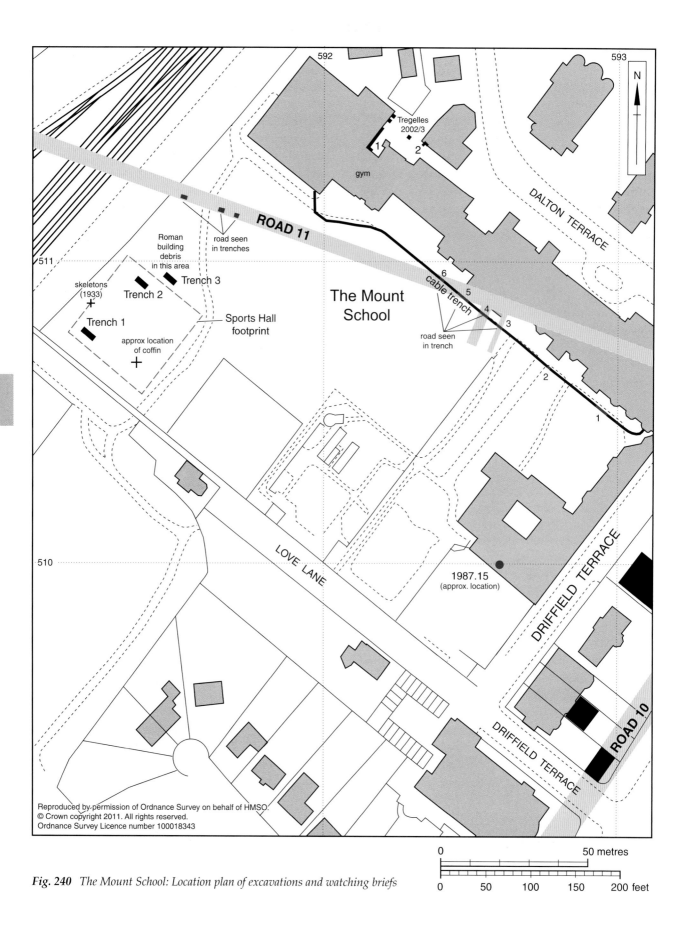

Fig. 240 *The Mount School: Location plan of excavations and watching briefs*

Although a few sherds of Roman pottery were found, there were no deposits or features of the period. This was partly due to a recent gravel pit found in Trenches 2–3, previously recorded by Dickinson (Dickinson and Wenham 1957). However, the presence of natural immediately below the tennis court in an area where Dickinson had found human remains, including the coffin noted above, suggests reduction of ground level at the time the courts were laid in 1985.

The sports hall: 2

In April and June 2000 a watching brief was conducted by D. T. Evans on foundation trenches dug for the construction of the new sports hall (Fig.240). Five sections were recorded (Figs 241–2).

The site records have the Yorkshire Museum accession code YORYM : 2000.501.

No archaeological deposits or features of certain Roman date were identified. In Sections 2–4 natural was encountered at c.17m OD, c.0.25–0.30m below the modern ground surface. A feature at least 1.6m wide and 2m deep cut into natural observed in Section 4 may, however, have been Roman (or another more recent gravel pit). Its main fill was coarse gravel mixed with brown sand. In Section 1 natural occurred at c.16.0–16.45m OD and was overlain by c.1m of deposits of uncertain date but probably, in part, pre-modern. In Section 5 (Fig.242) the top of natural (5004–5) lay at c.16.70m OD. It was cut by a possible feature (5003) at the north-west end, 0.50m deep, and was overlain by c.0.30m of deposits of uncertain date but again probably, in part, pre-modern (5001–2). In the south corner of the area clearance during construction produced some human bone, possibly from a disturbed burial.

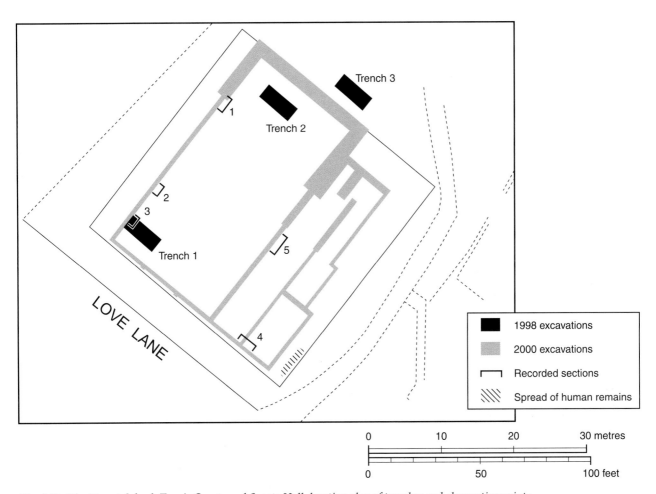

Fig. 241 The Mount School: Tennis Courts and Sports Hall, location plan of trenches and observation points

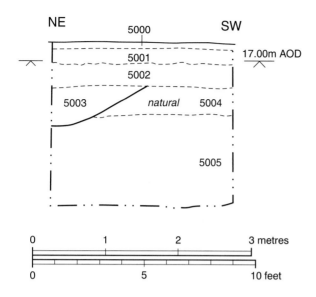

NE   5000   SW

17.00m AOD

5001

5002

5003   *natural*   5004

5005

0   1   2   3 metres

0   5   10 feet

Fig. 242 *The Mount School: Sports hall 2000, Section 5*

Tregelles School

From October 2002–March 2003 an archaeological watching brief was undertaken at Tregelles Junior School, Dalton Terrace (SE59225125), during groundwork in advance of a new building (Figs 240, 243). The watching brief was carried out on behalf of Nicholas Associates, and followed a brief issued by the Principal Archaeologist for City of York Council.

All finds and site records are currently stored by York Archaeological Trust under the Yorkshire Museum accession code YORYM : 2003.1. This report is based on a site report by Isabel Mason (YAT 2003/32).

Three engineer's test pits dug to examine existing foundations revealed nothing of interest, but significant archaeology was encountered during excavation for new foundations. Trench 1 was 6 x 1.3m and ran north-east/south-west with a return 3m long to the south-east against the wall of an existing building. Trench 2, L-shaped with each arm 1.4m long, lay 15m to the south-east.

Trench 1 *(Fig. 243)*

Natural (1001) was encountered at c.0.65m below modern ground level. It was overlain by a deposit (1008) of mid-brown silty clay with occasional flecks of both limestone and ceramic building material, 0.36m thick. This was cut by a pit (1013) the base of which was not reached as it lay below the limit of the excavation. The earliest fill recorded was 1005, a, blue-grey silty clay, mottled with occasional dark grey patches. This was overlain by 1006, orange-brown silty clay with small rounded pebbles and occasional ceramic building material, 0.30m thick. Pit 1013 was cut by a much larger feature, probably a ditch (1012), on a north-west/south-east alignment, which measured in excess of 3.5m in width. The earliest fill recorded, against the south-west edge, was 1002, 0.7m thick, a dark brown clayey silt with patches of dark yellow sand, and occasional charcoal flecks. This was overlain by 1003–4, orange-brown silty clay with occasional limestone fragments and pebbles. Eight sherds from 1002 and 1004 were dated to the late 2nd century.

These features were overlain by modern debris and cut through by concrete bases.

Trench 2

Natural (1001) was found at a depth of 1.7m below modern ground level and was cut through by a pit (1011) 1m in diameter and 1.1m deep. The earliest fill (1010), 0.30m thick, was a ginger-brown gritty sandy silt, with frequent flecks of charcoal and ash, occasional flecks of burnt clay, sandstone fragments and pebbles. Fragments of ceramic building material, slag (sf3) and fired clay (sf4), which was possibly furnace lining, were found. The upper fill (1009), 0.80m thick, was very similar as it was a plastic, ginger-brown gritty sandy silt with occasional flecks of burnt clay and charcoal, fragments of tile, slag, sandstone fragments and pebbles. Pottery from pit 1011 was dated to the late 2nd century.

The pit was overlain by modern material.

The cable trench

An archaeological watching brief on the mechanical cutting of new electricity cable trenches was undertaken between 3 and 10 August 2004. The

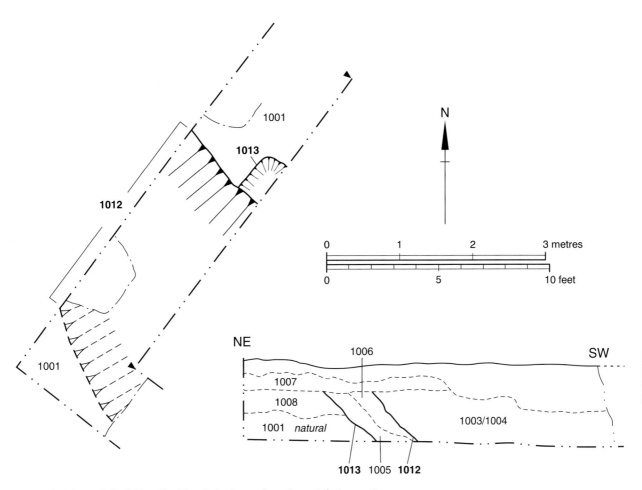

Fig.243 *The Mount School: Tregelles Trench 1, plan and north-west-facing section*

trench, c.135m long, 0.60–0.70m wide and 0.80m deep, lay immediately south-west of the main school block (Fig.240). Limited hand excavation was carried out in places where archaeologically significant deposits were encountered.

The work was carried out on the instructions of the Dossor Group acting on behalf of The Mount School.

All site records and finds are currently stored by York Archaeological Trust under the Yorkshire Museum accession code YORYM : 2003.290. What follows is based on the field report by Brian Milner and Mark Johnson (YAT 2004/67).

Six stretches of the north-east side of the trench were recorded in section, and they are described beginning with Section 1 at the south-east end (Fig.244).

Section 1

Natural clayey sand with cobbles (3014) occurred at 0.80m below modern level and sloped down gradually to the north-west. Natural was cut by a pit (3011), 0.50m wide and 0.20m deep, filled with 3010, greyish-brown clayey sand. In this deposit there were a number of human bones which appeared to be disarticulated and so the feature was not a conventional grave. It was dated by three sherds of 2nd-century pottery. Also over natural was 3009, a grey-brown clayey sand with occasional cobbles. This would presumably indicate that Roman archaeology lies very near the surface here. 3011 could have been part of a larger Roman feature filled with 3008, a grey-brown clayey sand with occasional cobbles which produced one sherd of Roman grey ware. Later deposits and features appeared to be modern.

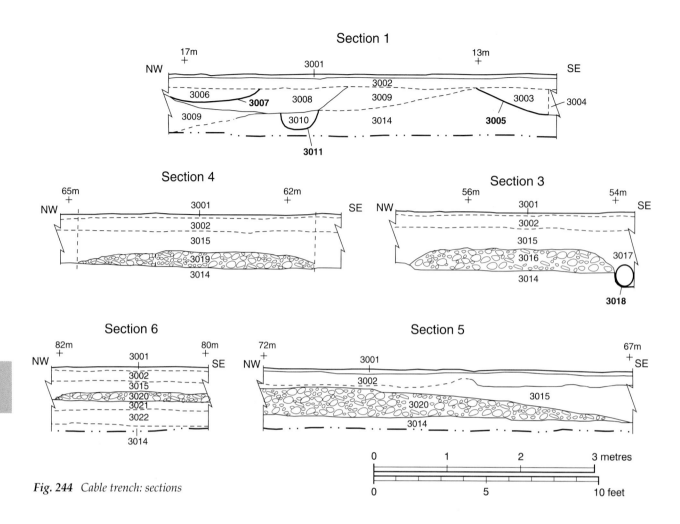

Fig. 244 *Cable trench: sections*

Section 2 (*not illustrated*)

Natural was overlain by 3015, grey-brown clayey sand with occasional cobbles, 0.54m thick, probably a largely modern deposit. A fragment of human skull and a fragment of pelvis were found at the base of the deposit.

Section 3

Natural was overlain by 3016, a deposit of cobbles 2.30–2.70m wide and up to 0.30m thick, which is thought to have been metalling for a track or narrow road running north-east/south-west with a slight camber on each side. On the south-east side 3016 was cut by a feature (3018) at least 0.20m deep. In the fill (3017) were three fragments of millstone grit laid on the same alignment as the cobbles. Above 3016 and 3017 was 3015 (described under Section 2) succeeded by other modern deposits.

Section 4

Above natural was 3019, a deposit of cobbles, at least 2.20m wide and 0.20m thick, which is thought to have been metalling for another track running north-east/south-west with a camber on each side. The cobbles produced ten sherds of late 2nd- to early 3rd-century pottery, including two joining sherds from each of two samian cups, and a coin of Trajan. Above 3019 were 3015 and modern deposits.

Sections 5–6

In Section 6 natural (3014) was overlain by 3022, reddish mid-brown clayey sand which was in turn overlain by 3021, probably redeposited natural. In Section 6 3021 and in Section 5 natural (3014) were succeeded by 3020, a layer of cobbles up to 0.35m thick making up the metalling for a road more substantial than those in Sections 3–4.

This was probably RCHME's Road 11, also previously recorded in what is now The Mount School's property to the north-west. Deposits 3021–2 formed the sort of low linear mound characteristic of Roman roads which allow the road to have a camber on each side. In what was probably the centre, in Section 6, the road's overall thickness was c.0.46m. When joined up with the road as recorded to the north-west and in Dalton Terrace to the south-east, it is clear that the road ran north-west/south-east with a width of c.5m (Fig.240). Deposit 3020 produced nine sherds of 2nd-century Roman pottery and nine fragments of Roman tile. Above deposit 3020 were 3015 and modern deposits.

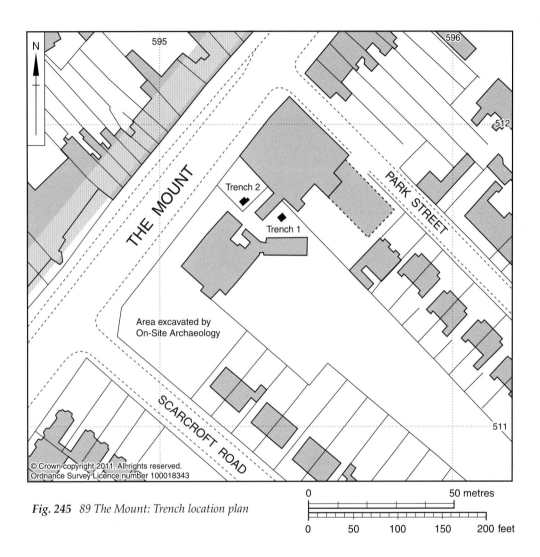

Fig. 245 *89 The Mount: Trench location plan*

89 The Mount

In February 1991 an evaluation excavation, supervised by Rhona Finlayson, took place at 89 The Mount (SE59535118; Fig.193,9; Figs 245, 248) in advance of development by Shepherd Retirement Homes Ltd. Initially two trenches 2 x 2m were excavated north-east of a building – now the Hotel du Vin – on the street frontage. However, because of extensive modern disturbance in Trench 2, it was extended by an area 1 x 1m to the north-east in an attempt to locate pre-modern archaeological deposits.

The finds and site records are stored under the Yorkshire Museum accession code 1991.4.

Trench 1 (*Fig.246*)

Natural orange clay with occasional lenses of coarse sand was found at c.16.10m OD, c.0.80m below modern ground level. This was cut by a ditch (1019) aligned north-west/south-east, 1.25m wide and c.0.45m deep with a V-shaped profile. It was backfilled with sandy clay (1018) which pottery suggests dates to the early–mid-2nd century. This was cut by another ditch (1017) of similar profile, c.0.80m wide and 0.70m deep, aligned north-west/south-east. It was backfilled with 1016, brown sandy silt. Above this was a thin layer (1014) of brown sandy silty clay succeeded by another thin layer (1012). Pottery suggests these backfilling layers are late 2nd–early 3rd century. Later deposits and features were post-Roman.

Trench 2 (*Fig.247*)

Natural clay was again located at c.16.10m OD. It was cut by a substantial post-hole (2019), 0.45m in diameter and 0.43m deep. Above it was a shallow cut (2015) containing tightly packed cobbles (2014), possibly a post-pad replacing the earlier post-hole. Stratigraphically later was a ditch (unnumbered), aligned north-west/south-east (parallel to ditch 1017 in Trench 1), 0.80m wide and 0.50m deep. It was filled with 2011, a sandy clay. Above the ditch was a deposit c.0.15m thick of sandy silt with patches of clay (2008–10) which was undated. Subsequent deposits and features were post-Roman. Pottery from the sequence was dated, as in Trench 1, to the late 2nd–early 3rd century.

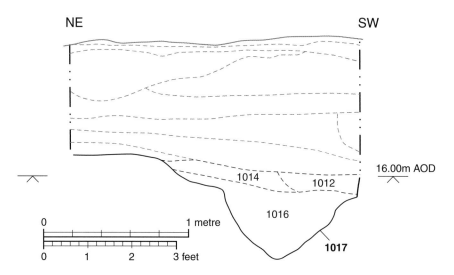

Fig. 246 *89 The Mount: Trench 1, north-west-facing section*

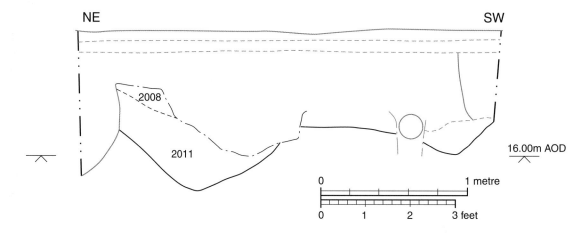

Fig. 247 *89 The Mount: Trench 2, north-west-facing section*

Fig. 248 *89 The Mount, Trench 1: view south-east showing ditch 1017 (scale 1m)*

In 2005–6 extensive excavations by On Site Archaeology took place to the south-west and south-east of the hotel in advance of redevelopment, revealing a number of burials including one in a stone coffin.

147 Mount Vale

A human burial was recorded in a watching brief under the garage at the rear of 147 Mount Vale (Fig.193, 16). It had been heavily disturbed by digging a trench for a new water pipe.

The bones lay at a depth of c.0.85m below modern ground level. No grave cut was perceived, but the skeleton appeared to be aligned south-west/ north-east. A fragment of grey ware pottery associated with the skeleton was dated to the 3rd century.

The burial belonged to the same cemetery zone as that excavated on Trentholme Drive in 1951–6 (Wenham 1968b). Two inhumation burials were found in the front garden in 1967 (Radley 1968, 117)

Finds and records are stored under the Yorkshire Museum accession code 1999.961.

St George's Place, Tadcaster Road

In 1982 a watching brief was conducted by David Brinklow in St George's Place, on the north-west side of The Mount (SE59025066; Fig.193, 17; Fig.249), during the excavation of a sewer trench.

The site records have the York Archaeological Trust and Yorkshire Museum accession code 1982.1004.

Natural, encountered at a depth of c.0.70m, was a red-brown clay interleaved with sand. Between No. 2 on the north side of the street and the boundary of Nos 7–9 on the south side, i.e. a distance of c.30m, three layers of large cobbles (up to 0.20–0.50m diameter) were observed in the trench side which were thought likely to be Roman. At the base the cobbles had been rammed down into the natural clay. Above the cobbles there was c.0.50m of modern road make up.

The road observed at this site is unlikely to be the main Roman road to York from the south-west (Road 10; RCHMY **1**, 3) which is thought to lie to the south-east. However, a recorded width of 30m suggests that the sewer trench is likely to

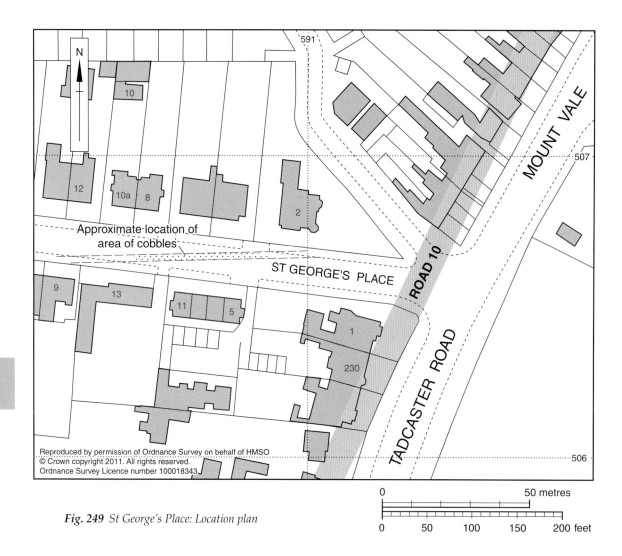

0   50 metres

0   50   100   150   200 feet

Fig. 249 *St George's Place: Location plan*

have cut along the line of or obliquely through a minor road approaching the main road from the north-west, or, perhaps a yard surface.

Pulleyn Drive cable trench

In a cable trench on the corner of Pulleyn Drive and Tadcaster Road an inhumation burial was found (Fig.193, 18). This is presumably an outlier from the main cemetery zone which flanks the Roman approach road from the south-west, being 375m from Trentholme Drive, hitherto thought to lie at the south-western limit of that zone.

Finds and records are stored under the Yorkshire Museum accession code 1992.1015

Holgate Cattle Dock and St Paul's Green

Described under this heading are two archaeological investigations on a site bounded to the east by the East Coast Main Line railway, to the west by Watson Street and Railway Terrace, and to the south by St Paul's church (SE59215130; Fig.193, 8; Fig.250). The first, an excavation supervised by Kurt Hunter-Mann in July 1992, took place at what was then known as Holgate Cattle Dock, on behalf of British Rail. The second, in April–June 1999, was a watching brief supervised by Bryan Antoni, at what was then known as St Paul's Green, Holgate, on behalf of Barratt Homes. Both investigations were based on briefs from the Principal Archaeologist for City of York Council.

Holgate Cattle Dock

Two trenches, 2m wide, were excavated mechanically to a point close to the surface of natural. A section of each was recorded, along with deposits in the base of Trench 1.

All records and finds are stored by York Archaeological Trust under the Yorkshire Museum accession code 1992.19.

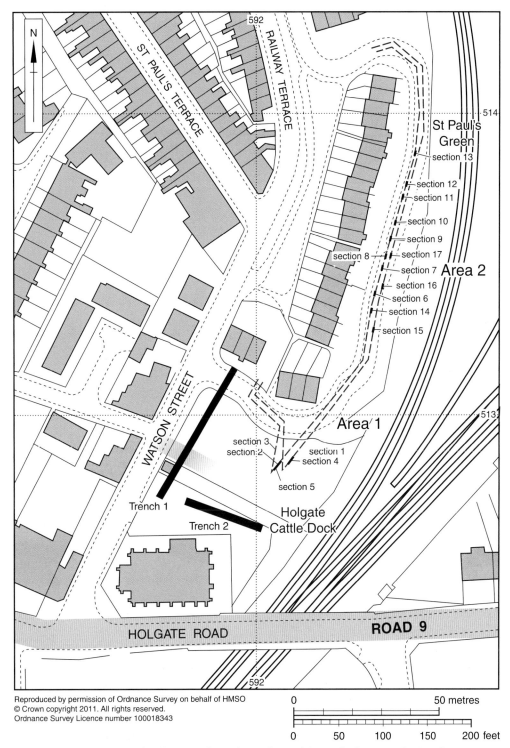

Fig. 250 *Location plan of Holgate Cattle Dock trenches and St Paul's Green service trench*

329

Trench 1 *(Fig.251)*

Trench 1 measured 51m (north-east/south-west). Natural light grey sand (1005) was encountered at c.12.60m OD, 1.9m below modern ground level. Examination of the deposit by the Environmental Archaeology Unit at York University suggested it was waterlain; it included abundant oospores of aquatic green algae in the family *Characeae* (stoneworts), indicating deposition in a static or slow-flowing body of water. Overlying natural at about 13.50m OD near the south-western end of the trench was a yellow sandy silt (1010). It was overlain by silty clay (1004) which may have been levelling for an overlying deposit of cobbles set in silty clay (1001). It formed the make up for a surface 4.1m wide and up to 0.50m thick which was aligned roughly west-north-west/east-south-east. The cobbles produced a sherd of pottery dated to the late 2nd–early 3rd century on the basis of which the surface is thought to have been Roman. It probably represented a minor road or track in which case deposit 1004 might be seen as the low mound below it, as seen in other Roman roads, for example, in The Mount School cable trench (pp.319–325). Evidence from the St Paul's Green trench (see below) suggests that, locally at least, the land to the north of the road sloped down sharply, perhaps by as much as c.1m, to the Roman level at the southern end of that trench because of an underlying geological feature.

Overlying the cobbles and natural elsewhere in the trench was a series of sandy silty deposits of unknown date, the earliest being 1005–7, up to 1.30m thick (at the northern end of the trench). They were succeeded by modern features and deposits.

Trench 2 *(Fig.252)*

Trench 2, south-east of Trench 1, measured 27.20m (east–west). Natural was encountered at c.12.50m OD, c.2.4m below modern ground level, at the western end of the trench, and rose towards to c.13.10m OD at the east end. Overlying natural was a series of sandy, silty and clayey deposits up to 0.7m thick, but only 0.2m thick at the western end of the trench. These deposits are thought to have been largely naturally formed. Eight metres from the east end of the trench was a shallow pit (unnumbered), 4.40m in diameter and 0.80m deep. The backfill of the pit (2003) was a sandy clay which produced one sherd dated to the 2nd–3rd century. Overlying 2003 and the natural were deposits of silty clay c.0.30m thick at the east end of the trench, but at least 1m thick at the west; they were probably largely of medieval and later origin.

St Paul's Green, Holgate

Introduction

The watching brief monitored a mechanically excavated trench for mains services. As a result of unexpected discoveries of the prehistoric period a borehole survey of the site was also undertaken in August 1999.

All records and finds are stored by York Archaeological Trust under the Yorkshire Museum accession code 1999.251.

The service trench *(Fig.250)*

The first part of the service trench extended for c.155m on a roughly north–south line and a second stretch ran back to the north from the southernmost point of the first to a connection with the existing sewer. The trench was 2m wide, 1.6m deep at the north end and 3m deep at the south end. The trench sides were selectively drawn at intervals where archaeological deposits of particular interest were encountered (Figs 253–6).

Area 1: south end of the site *(Figs 253–4)*

Five sections were recorded in this area. In Section 4 the earliest deposit recorded was a light grey-white fine sand with occasional gravel lenses (209). Above this was a similar deposit incorporating frequent lenses of brown peaty silt (208). Taken together, all five sections (1–5) showed that the surface of deposits 208–9 sloped down from north-east to south-west, over a distance of 3.5m, from c.11.07m OD to c.10.4m OD.

Overlying 208–9 was a layer of peat which contained large tree fragments (207). It was c.0.10m thick at the north-east end of Section 4 and c.0.8m thick at the south-west end. The peat was also observed in Sections 1–3 and 5 (context 242) and its surface appears to have sloped down from north-east to south-west from c.11.76m OD (north-east end of Section 4) to 10.8m OD (in the region Section 5). During work on Section 3 a Neolithic stone axe was found in the peat. Overlying 207 in Section 4 was a brown peaty clay silt (204), c.0.25m thick. This included numerous burnt pebbles, probably used as pot boilers, and pottery of the Late Neolithic/

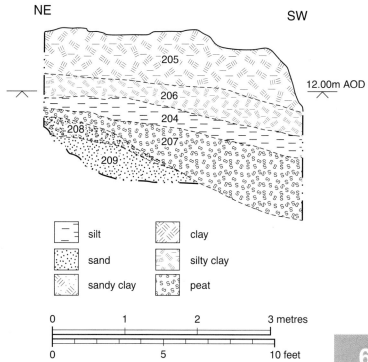

Fig. 253 *St Paul's Green: Area 1, Section 4*

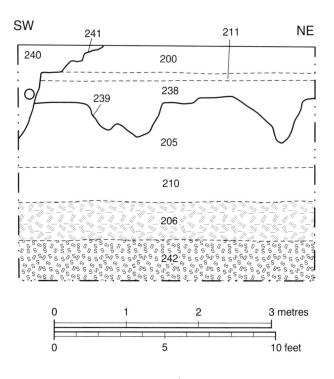

Fig. 254 *St Paul's Green: Area 1, Section 5*

331

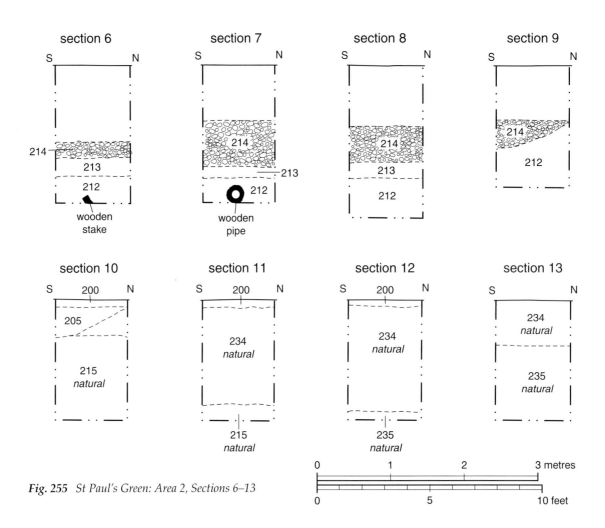

Fig. 255 *St Paul's Green: Area 2, Sections 6–13*

Early Bronze Age. This sequence is interpreted as the gradual infilling of a naturally created pond, or 'kettle hole', formed during glacial melting. The borehole survey showed that it was c.30m in diameter and 5.5m deep.

Above 204 (Section 4) and above the peat in Sections 1–3 and 5 was a deposit of blue-grey silty clay (206), 0.40–0.60m thick, which sloped down from north-east to south-west from 12.2m OD to 11.30m OD. It is not clear how this was deposited, but it was probably natural waterlain accumulation in what would still have been a sunken area. A samian sherd and some Roman tile were found in the upper part of this deposit suggesting that at least some of it accumulated in the Roman period.

In Sections 1 and 5 deposit 206 was overlain by 210, a light grey sandy silt, 0.42m thick. Above 210 in Sections 1 and 5 and above 206 in Sections 2–4

was 205, orange-brown sandy clay with occasional pebbles, stone fragments and charcoal flecks. 205 and 210 were probably levelling deposits and the finds of pot and tile suggest a medieval date. They were succeeded by medieval and modern features.

Area 2: centre of the site *(Figs 255–6)*

In Sections 10–12 the deposits observed were largely natural (215, 234–5) which rose from south to north where it was recorded at 12.85m OD, but had probably been truncated by modern levelling. In Sections 6–9, 14–15 and 17 natural deposits were overlain by deposit 212, recorded over a distance of c.32m. It consisted of light grey silts and sands with black mottling in which there were wood fragments. It was thought to be largely waterlain. The base of the deposit was not reached at the north end of the trench (Sections 6–9) but in Section 15 was seen to be 1.1m thick (Fig.256). The surface of 212 was at

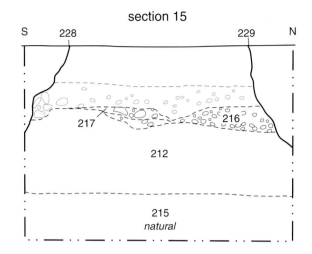

section 15

S 228   229 N

217   216

212

215
natural

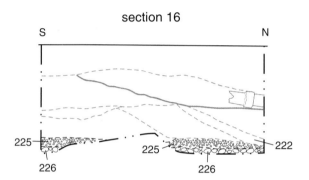

section 16

S   N

225   222
226   225
           226

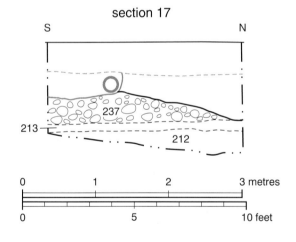

section 17

S   N

237
213
212

0   1   2   3 metres

0   5   10 feet

Fig. 256 *St Paul's Green: Area 2, Sections 15–17*

12.2m OD at its north end (Section 9) and south end (Section 15), but dipped to c.11.25m OD in the area of Sections 6–8 and 17. This betrayed the existence of a second kettle hole which was subsequently plotted by boreholes. Deposit 212 produced some fragments of Roman tile, a wooden peg or offcut (sf4), but, most remarkably, two joining pieces of a wooden water pipe (sfs5–6; Section 7). No cut for a trench to take the pipe was recorded, but presumably one had been dug into 212. The pipe appeared to have been laid roughly east–west. It is made of elm and cylindrical and although only about two-thirds of its circumference survived, it clearly had a central bore of 110mm.

Above deposit 212 in Sections 6–8, 14 and 17 was deposit 213, recorded over a distance of c.20m. It was a 0.10–0.20m thick, grey-brown humic silt which contained decayed plant fibres and occasional charcoal flecks. Above 213 was 214 (Sections 6–9 and 14), equivalent to 216–17 (Section 15), 226 (Section 16) and 237 (Section 17), existing as cobbles in brown sandy silt with occasional limestone and mortar fragments. It was recorded over a distance of c.32m and was up to 0.60m thick in the centre (Section 7). In Section 16 deposit 226 was overlain by 225, gravel in dark brown sandy silt. Fifteen Roman sherds of 2nd- to 3rd-century date, as well as Roman tile, came from this deposit, but there was also a sherd of 11th- to 12th-century date and fragments of medieval and later tile. These post-Roman finds may have been intrusive, in which case the trench may have cut through a Roman street, perhaps running roughly north–south, or a surface make-up deposit with some other function. Deposits above the cobbles were of medieval date based on the brick and tile found in them and they were succeeded by modern deposits and features.

6

129 Holgate Road

In 1980 building work at the rear of the Kilima Hotel, 129 Holgate Road (SE59045121; Fig.193, 19), revealed a Roman inhumation burial which probably represents a western outlier of the cemetery zone found during railway construction around Holgate Bridge in 1837–9 (Fig.57; Fig.257; RCHMY **1**, 100–1). No grave cut was detected, but the skeleton was well preserved. It was aligned north-east/south-west and appeared to lie on its left side. The knees were both slightly bent, the right more than the left. The skeleton was that of a male aged c.35 years and he was buried with footwear, of which the iron hobnails survived, and a silver ring worn on his left hand. The deposit around the bones contained 2nd- to 3rd-century pottery.

The finds and records are stored under the Yorkshire Museum accession code 1980.31.

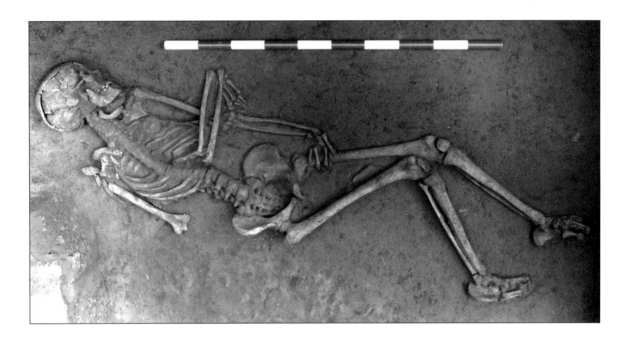

Fig. 257 *129 Holgate Road: view of burial (scale 1m)*

Zone 6: Discussion

Approach road 10 from the south-west

(Figs 193–4)

In 1910 road metalling with a 'central gritstone channel' was recorded at a depth of c.1m immediately inside Micklegate Bar (Fig.193, 20; Benson 1911, 18; RCHMY **1**, 51). This was thought to be Roman, and Benson's *Archaeological Plan of York*, published in 1926, projected the course of the main Roman road from the south-west running from the Bar to a location in Tanner Row, close to the River Ouse, where metalling, again thought to be Roman, was recorded on the 1853 OS map (RCHMY **1**, 3). After crossing the Ouse, the road line was continued to the *porta praetoria* of the fortress at St Helen's Square (RCHMY **1**, 13). Doubt was cast on Benson's line by L.P. Wenham's discoveries outside Micklegate Bar in Blossom Street (Fig.193, 22) in 1953–4 (RCHMY **1**, 3, 63, fig.51; Wenham 1965). Some 40m to the north-west of a continuation of Benson's line projected south-west from Micklegate Bar, a major road running north-east/south-west was found. It was 10m wide with the metalling, up to 1m thick. The excavations, already referred to, by D. Stewart in 1966–7, apparently sectioned the road again, although the grid reference given in the brief notes in *Yorkshire Archaeological Journal* (*YAJ*) is clearly inaccurate (Radley 1967, 9; 1968, 118) and no records of Stewart's work survive. The 1968 note in *YAJ* did, however, report that a ditch running along the south-east side of the road was excavated and found to be 1.83m (6 feet) wide and 1.52m (5 feet) deep, although the grid reference given suggests it was the on the north-west side of the road.

As has been described above, the road was investigated again by YAT in the evaluation of 1991. This confirmed a width of c.10m. In 1999 in an evaluation by MAP at 28 Blossom Street, re-excavation of Wenham's Trenches 14 and 16 revealed the road once more (MAP 2000). To the south-west of Wenham's site there are records of the road being found at the Odeon Cinema in 1936 (Fig.193, 24; Fig.201), at 1 The Crescent in 1879 (Fig.1, 24), and at 112–14 The Mount (then Lister and Edmond's Garage) in 1963 (*YAJ* 1964, 176; Fig.193, 28). The course of the road was further refined (Fig.193, 23;

Fig.194) in 2009 when excavation by YAT behind the street frontage buildings of 28–40 Blossom Street failed to locate the road, suggesting it lay a little further to the north-west than previously thought.

The road appeared again at 7 Driffield Terrace (Fig.193, 11), presumably close to its north-western edge although no edge was seen. It then appears to have run a little to the north-west of the Tadcaster Road but the road metalling recorded in St George's Place (see above) is unlikely to represent the road further to the west than mapped by RCHME. About 100m to the south-west of St George's Place the road was located at The White House, Tadcaster Road (RCHMY **1**, 3; Fig.193, 32). In 1938 it was observed by A. Raine during sewer works in Pulleyn Drive a little further to the south-west (Fig.193, 18). The next sighting to the south-west was on the north edge of the Hob Moor allotments (Wenham 1957; RCHMY **1**, 3) and south-west again the Roman road was excavated at 230 Tadcaster Road, The Voltigeur Hotel, by the York Excavation Group in 1985 (*YAJ* 1986, 201). The York Excavation Group also recorded the road at 304 Tadcaster Road in 1984, near the historic boundary between York and Dringhouses (see below p.341, Zone 7, for its continuation).

If projected on a straight line to the north-east from 14–20 Blossom Street the road would cross the line of the medieval city walls c.30m west of Micklegate Bar. If assumptions about the line of Roman defences being on the same line are correct (see p.119), then there was presumably a gate at this point. Continuing on a straight line the road would reach the river crossing at the probable site of the Roman bridge over the Ouse at the north-east end of Tanner Row. The road was recorded more or less on the predicted line at 27 Tanner Row in 1971 and then at Wellington Row in 1987–90 where a c.4m depth of road make up, 10m wide, was located close to the bridgehead (Ottaway 2004, 50–1). North-east of the Ouse the road continued as the fortress *via praetoria* as far as the headquarters building located where York Minster now stands.

Other roads

The second road which was found joining Road 10 by Wenham in 1953–4 has been taken to be the approach road from the north-west, with its origin in the Roman town at Aldborough (RCHMY **1**, 3; Road 9). This is probably what was also found in The Crescent watching brief (Fig.193, 2), immediately to the south-west of the Odeon Cinema. It is thought to have then taken the line now followed by Holgate Road in the vicinity of Holgate Bridge (over the railway) before running north-westwards to Severus Hills where it was recorded in 1960 (Fig.54, 9).

Another road identified by RCHME (RCHMY **1**, 3; Road 11; Fig.193) was thought to join the main road from the south-west close to the point where Dalton Terrace joins The Mount today. The line was based on the records of a road found in Dalton Terrace in 1955 and in what are now the grounds of The Mount School (Fig.240). A line between the two would correspond more or less with the principal road found in The Mount School cable trench (Fig.244, Sections 5–6). The width of the road was probably c.5m. In more or less all cases Roman roads outside the city centre have suffered from post-Roman degradation by ploughing etc and so only width, not the thickness and character of metalling, can usually be used to determine their status. Although at 5m this road is about half the width of Road 10 as recorded in Blossom Street, there is, none the less, a good case for it being an alternative road from Aldborough approaching in a straight line from Severus Hills, sticking to high ground as much as possible, to join the road from the south-west at the top of The Mount (Fig.54). The two other roads or tracks cut by the cable trench were thought to have run north-east/south-west and perhaps gave access from the main road into the cemetery zone to the south-west (Fig.240).

Minor roads recorded in the excavations described above include one observed in the watching brief at 14–20 Blossom Street where there was metalling 0.75m thick and at least 2.5m wide on a north-west/south-east alignment. This was not a primary feature of the site, but it may have been part of a street system developing in the area in the 2nd century on the south-east side of the main road from the south-west. The street's life probably came to an end with the construction of the building represented by the wall footing 2001 (see below).

Another cobbled street (c.4m wide) was found in Trench 1 at Holgate Cattle Dock on a roughly west-north-west/east-south-east alignment. It appears to have been laid down in the late 2nd–early 3rd century and so would have formed another element in the expansion of the street system of Roman York into an area not previously settled. A second possible Roman street was found in the watching brief trench to the north.

Land use and settlement in the late 1st–mid-3rd century

The excavations described above and others in Zone 6 suggest a complex picture of settlement and land use which is far from clearly understood. The only evidence for structures, however, comes from around Road 10 as it approaches the principal Roman settled area south-west of the Ouse. On the north-west side of the road Wenham found two short lengths of wall meeting at the west corner of a small stone building close to the junction of Roads 9 and 10. Wenham claimed there were five phases dating from the late 1st to the 4th century, but the published report is so brief as to make this impossible to verify. The brief notes of his work in 1966–7 in *YAJ* claims that Stewart found part of a 2nd-century building in the area, perhaps also on the north-west side of the road, allegedly destroyed by fire. Some hint of architectural grandeur also suggested by the walls found in the watching brief at 14–20 Blossom Street was provided by his apparent discovery of a gritstone column base.

The evidence for a structural sequence south-east of Road 10 at 14–20 Blossom Street could not be fully elucidated or dated. It seems likely, however, that buildings accompanying the side street noted above existed from early in the 2nd century. In this case they were more or less contemporary with those recorded c.250m to the north-east in the area of the Old Station, inside what is presumed to have later become the defended urban settlement.

Initially, however, both sites should probably be seen as early components of a settlement developing along the route to York from the south-west.

Early structures at Blossom Street were clearly swept away for what must have been a very substantial stone wall aligned north-west/south-east, and a number of other walls which may all have been part of the same building (Figs 198–9, 165). The footings (2001) for the principal wall were unusually large, c.1.60m wide and 1.20m deep, comparable in dimensions to those of the legionary fortress wall, and exceeded in York only by those of the legionary *principia* basilica and the bath house found at 1–9 Micklegate in the town south-west of the Ouse. The walls in the watching brief are thought to date to the late 2nd–early 3rd century and so there is further evidence here for the construction at this time of monumental buildings in the civilian settlements in Roman York after a period of rapid expansion (p.370). In the case of the building at Blossom Street it must have dominated the approach to the town, but its function is, of course, unknown. Another part of the same building complex may be represented by structural remains apparently found in 1826 on the corner of Blossom Street and Queen Street to the north-east of No. 14 (Fig.193, 21; RCHMY **1**, 53).

Elsewhere in Zone 6 settlement evidence largely takes the form of land division by means of ditches, and of refuse tipping and burials. At 35–41 Blossom Street a series of early–mid-2nd-century ditches, possibly dug in more than one phase, lay on alignments clearly respecting that of the main road from the south-west. They may have defined plots of land along the line of the main road initially used for agricultural purposes before being taken over for burial.

Other sites south-east of the main road have also produced ditches respecting its alignment, although probably a little later than those at 35–41 Blossom Street in being late 2nd–early 3rd century and so comparable in date to many other ditches recorded in extramural areas (see pp.370–1). At All Saints School (Fig.193, 6), 25m north-east of 35–41 Blossom Street, and 60m south of Bar Convent, there were two ditches on a north-east/south-west line. At the Moss Street depot (Fig.193, 27) an L-shaped ditch with arms aligned north-east/south-west and north-west/south-east was found (Toop 2008). They were superseded by two parallel ditches

with a space 2m wide between them, thought to be mid-3rd century. They were aligned north-east/south-west although not quite on the same alignment as Road 10 from the south-west.

At 89 The Mount (Fig.193, 9), c.220m south-west of 35–41 Blossom Street, there were ditches which respected the alignment of Road 10. At All Saints School, Mill Mount (Fig.193, 29), an evaluation trench in 1991 produced a gully and a ditch, both probably respecting the line of Road 10 and dated after c.175; they were followed by the use of the area for burials (MAP 1991). Nearer the main Roman road at Mill Mount (Fig.193, 30; Spall and Toop 2005b) the earliest phase (1A) consisted of post-holes and ditches, aligned north-east/south-west or north-west/south-east, probably of late 2nd- to early 3rd-century date, again probably defining land units facing the main road which were subsequently used for burial. Opposite Mill Mount, north-west of The Mount, a shallow ditch was found at 3 Driffield Terrace (Fig.193, 10; Fig.238) which, unusually, did not exactly follow the Roman road's alignment, although it was close to it. This was also apparently the case of a ditch of mid–late 2nd-century date located in 1998 at the Elm Bank Hotel (Fig.193, 31; Hopkinson and Ferguson 1998) which was nearer to being north–south than north-east/south-west.

Finally, as regards ditches, note may be made again of what may have been a very substantial ditch encountered at Tregelles School (Fig.193, 12; Figs 242–3); its alignment appeared to be north-west/south-east and so it was more or less parallel to Road 11, c.40m to the south-west. It was too far away to have been a roadside ditch, but being c.3.5m wide is unlikely to have been a simple field boundary; what function it had must, however, remain unknown.

The ditches at 35–41 Blossom Street were followed in the later 2nd century by extensive deposits apparently containing occupation refuse which may derive from buildings in the immediate area or from core areas of the Roman town to the north-east. One can envisage refuse being carried along the main roads and, legitimately or otherwise, being deposited on open ground on the roadside. Deposition of refuse was also suggested by Monaghan's analysis of the pottery assemblage from the roadside at 112–14 The Mount (Fig.193, 28; *YAJ* 1964; *AY* 16/8, 1135). Pits probably for refuse were found in L.P. Wenham's unpublished excavation at the Bar Convent, Blossom Street (Fig.193, 26; *YAJ* 1966, 565). Although some earlier and later pottery was found in the site assemblage, the dating of the majority was confirmed as 2nd–3rd century (*AY* 16/8, 1130). Another apparent refuse pit was found at Tregelles School, but that which was half-sectioned at 3 Driffield Terrace seems to have been a feature of a different order. With a diameter of c.5m and depth of at least 3m it may perhaps have been a well; adjacent to the main approach roads from the south-west and another road from the north-west, it could conveniently have been used by both travellers and local residents. Alternatively, the pit may have been dug to gain materials for road building or maintenance. In any event, the character of the deposits in the feature, in which there were very few finds, suggests it was filled in deliberately before the area was turned over to cemetery use.

Burials

The extent and character of the Roman cemeteries outside the civilian town south-west of the Ouse has been exhaustively described by RCHME (RCHMY **1**, 76–107). Since that publication in 1962 there have been important pieces of fieldwork where it has been possible for the first time to study not only the burials themselves in a formal excavation but also to place them in the context of developing land use. Little new has been found in the cemetery on Nunnery Lane near the city walls except for those skeletons reported above from Dale Street and All Saints School (Fig.193, 5–6). However, the burials at the sites of 3 and 6 Driffield Terrace (Fig.193, 10–11) and also those at The Mount School (Fig.240) make important contributions to knowledge of the large cemetery lining the main road from the south-west (RCHMY **1**, 98–100). This can now be expanded to take in new areas south-east of the road at, firstly, 35–41 Blossom Street which produced 25 3rd- to 4th-century inhumation burials. Also close to the main road burials have been found at 89 The Mount (Fig.193, 9) by On Site Archaeology and at Mill Mount by FAS (Fig.193, 30; Spall and Toop 2005b). At this latter site thirteen inhumations of 3rd-century date were found including one in a stone coffin in which the body was covered in gypsum. Four more inhumations of

late 2nd- to early 3rd-century date were found in an evaluation trench at All Saints School, Mill Mount (Fig.193, 29; MAP 1991). The cemetery zone can also be extended to the south-east to take in late Roman burials at Moss Street depot (Fig.193, 27; Toop 2008). Further to the south-west the burial at 147 Mount Vale (Fig.193, 16) was part of the Trentholme Drive cemetery zone. The Pulleyn Drive burial (Fig.193, 18) indicates that occasional burials were made in roadside locations even further to the south-west. The inhumation at 129 Holgate Road is an outlier of the cemetery around the Holgate railway cutting (RCHMY **1**, 60).

As far as the chronological development of the cemeteries south-west of the Ouse is concerned, the evidence is of such variable quality and so diverse that it is difficult to establish patterns (Jones 1984). However, enough is known to show that the cemeteries did not expand in a linear manner along the sides of the main road from the south-west with the earliest nearest the settled areas. By the mid-2nd century burials were being made up to 1.5km south-west of Micklegate Bar (at Trentholme Drive) while there were still unused areas available nearer to settlement in the late 2nd–early 3rd centuries many of which were now taken in, probably as a result of population pressure. A particular preference appears to have been expressed for the land around the top of the morainic ridge where The Mount now meets Dalton Terrace and Albemarle Road. However, the 35–41 Blossom Street and Moss Street depot sites may be telling us that from the late 3rd to the early 4th century there was a preference, also seen elsewhere in the city, for making burials as close to the settled areas as possible.

Further discussion of the York cemeteries appears on pp.367–375 below.

Land use and settlement in the late Roman period

There is little substantial evidence for a continuation of any activity in Zone 6 in the late 3rd–4th centuries except for burial. In Monaghan's survey of pottery assemblages from York only two of Ceramic Period 4a (280–360) were identified outside the Roman town south-west of the Ouse (*AY* 16/8, fig.314). One of these was the Railway Station cemetery and the other 35–41 Blossom Street where the latest inhumations probably belong to the mid-4th century. There were no assemblages of Ceramic Period 4b (360–410) except at Clementhorpe (see Zone 5). To this picture, however, may be added the site at 39 Holgate Road (Fig.193, 7), north-west of Blossom Street (excavated after the completion of *AY* 16/8), where pottery from the latest ditch fills appears to date to the second half of the 4th century.

As far as the roads are concerned, the 4th century may, from evidence of 14–20 Blossom Street, have witnessed the narrowing of the main road from the south-west, although it was impossible to determine when it went out of use. The narrowing and disuse of roads and streets in the late Roman period has been recorded elsewhere in York at, for example, Wellington Row where the main road from the south-west was again involved (Ottaway 2004, 148).

6

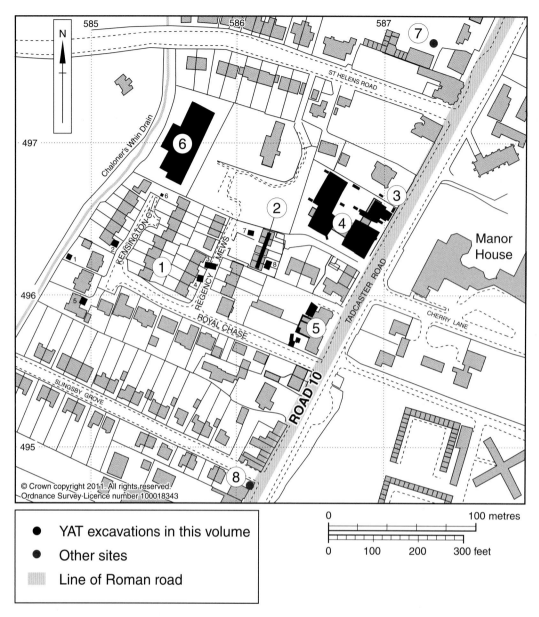

● YAT excavations in this volume

● Other sites

▓ Line of Roman road

0   100 metres

0   100   200   300 feet

Fig. 258 *Zone 7: location of sites described in this fascicule (1–6) and other sites (7–8)*

1. 52–62 Tadcaster Road (Royal Chase) (1995)

2. 26–30 Regency Mews (1997)

3. Starting Gate Evaluation (1996)

4. Starting Gate Excavation (2003)

5. The Fox (1997)

6. 27 St Helen's Road (1994)

7. 28 Tadcaster Road

8. Methodist Chapel

Zone 7: Dringhouses

Introduction *(Figs 54, 258)*

Extramural Zone 7 encompasses Dringhouses, now a suburb of York, but formerly a discrete village, which lies c.3.25km south-west of the centre of York. Dringhouses is approached from York by the A64/Tadcaster Road, the line of which corresponds closely to that of the main Roman road to York from the south-west (Fig.54; Fig.258; RCHMY **1**, 3; Road 10; see also p.361). As noted above, the road has been recorded at 304 Tadcaster Road, a little to the north-east of Dringhouses. The historic boundary between York and Dringhouses on the west side of the Tadcaster Road corresponds to Mayfield Grove; south of here the Roman road was sighted in Dringhouses itself in St Helen's Road in 1902. The course of the road appears to stick closely to a narrow finger of the York moraine running south-west from the city centre which continues to Copmanthorpe, a further 3.25km to the south-west (Fig.55). Natural ground level falls away on either side in Dringhouses. For example, in the 160–200m between the Tadcaster Road and Chaloner's Whin drain to the west, excavations at 52–62 Tadcaster Road recorded a drop of c.2.50m.

Hitherto, other Roman discoveries in the Dringhouses area have taken the form of burials (RCHMY **1**, 107). In addition, a carved stone relief of a smith, probably an altar dedicated to Vulcan rather than a tombstone, was found in the grounds of the Manor House on the opposite side of the Tadcaster Road to St Helen's Road in 1860 (RCHMY **1**, 107, 128). In 1995–7 Dringhouses was the scene of archaeological excavations described below which took place in advance of housing development. The main objective was to evaluate the extent of survival of archaeological deposits and to get an impression of the history and character of settlement in the Roman period. In 2003 a major excavation took place on the site of the former Starting Gate public house (Fig.54, 10; Fig.258, 3; McComish 2006). A report is available on-line at www.yorkarchaeology.co.uk but this is summarised below and the discoveries discussed on pp.361–3.

52–62 Tadcaster Road and 26–30 Regency Mews

Two pieces of excavation work at 52–62 Tadcaster Road, subsequently known as Royal Chase and Regency Mews, are described below, the first being an evaluation, the second further excavation based on the results of that evaluation (Fig.258, 1–2). Both were undertaken following briefs from the Principal Archaeologist for City of York Council.

52–62 Tadcaster Road

In June 1995 an archaeological evaluation, supervised by Rhona Finlayson, took place on land to the rear of 52–62 Tadcaster Road (centre at SE58504960). This involved excavation of eight trenches covering a total of c.180m², although only three (3–4 and 8), on the eastern side of the site, yielded archaeological material of Roman date. The natural in all areas was a yellow-brown clay which sloped down slightly from north-east to south-west over the site.

All records and finds are stored by York Archaeological Trust under the accession code YORYM : 1995.55.

Trench 3 *(Fig.259)*

Trench 3 measured c.8m (east–west) x 4m. Natural clay (3005) was encountered at 13.70m OD, c.0.60–0.70m below modern ground level. In the south-east corner of the trench, cutting the clay, there was a probable ditch (3003), aligned north-east/south-west, at least 1.20m wide, of which only the north-western side was found; it sloped down steeply to a flat base at a depth of 0.27m. The backfill (3002) was brown silty sand and contained a sherd of late 1st- to 3rd-century pottery. Above 3003 were post-medieval and modern deposits.

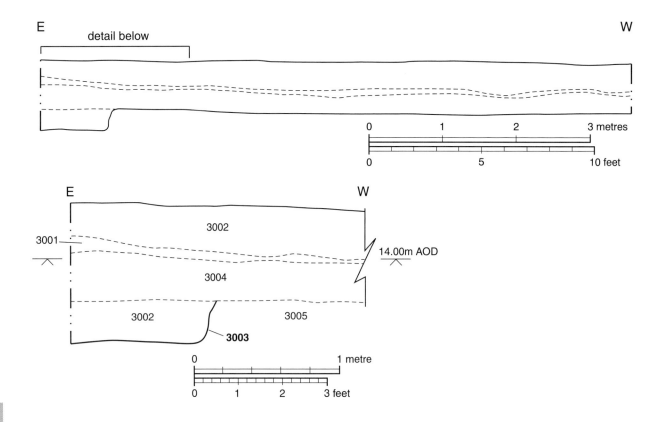

E   detail below   W

0   1   2   3 metres

0   5   10 feet

E   W

3001

3002

14.00m AOD

3004

3002   3005

3003

0   1 metre

0   1   2   3 feet

7

Fig. 259 *52–62 Tadcaster Road: Trench 3, north-facing section*

Trench 4 *(not illustrated)*

Trench 4 measured 4 x 4m. Natural clay was, as in Trench 3, at 13.70m OD. The clay was cut by a ditch (4004) on a north-east/south-west alignment which may have been a continuation to the south-west of the feature in Trench 3. The south-east side sloped down at c.45° from the horizontal while the north-west side sloped down more steeply. The backfill (4003), silty sand, contained a 2nd- to 3rd-century sherd and a fragment of Roman imbrex tile.

Trench 8 *(Fig.260)*

Trench 8 measured 6m (north-east/south-west) x 4m. Natural clay was encountered at c.14.35m OD, 0.40m below modern ground level. This was cut by a feature (8008), probably a ditch, 2.1m wide, which curved as it ran across the southern end of the trench. The western side of the feature sloped more gently than the eastern down to a flat base. The backfill (8005) was a silty clay sand with occa-

sional charcoal flecks. It contained abraded pottery of late 1st- to 3rd-century date and some Roman tile.

In the south-east corner of the trench deposit 8005 was cut into by a pit (8006) which continued beyond the trench sides, but was seen to be subrectangular in plan. It had near vertical sides, a flat base, and was 0.40m deep. The backfill (8007) was a mid-grey-brown silty clay with frequent charcoal flecks. It contained no artefacts and was therefore undated.

In the northern part of the trench was a cut (8004), 0.20m deep, which continued beyond the northern edge of trench. The fill (8002) was largely cobble packing, suggesting a structural feature, possibly a post-hole. It contained abraded sherds of late 1st- to 3rd-century date and Roman tile. Above the features described were deposits of modern material including 8003.

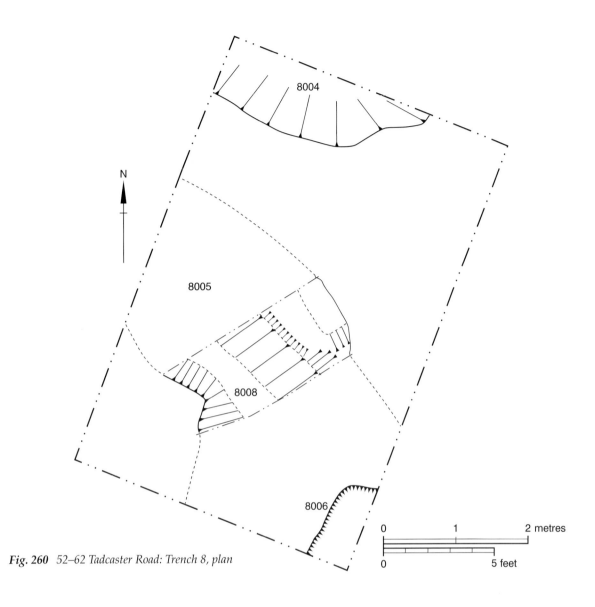

Fig. 260 *52–62 Tadcaster Road: Trench 8, plan*

26–30 Regency Mews

In December 1997 an excavation, supervised by Mark Johnson, was carried out in advance of house building at 26–30 Regency Mews (part of the Royal Chase development),Tadcaster Road (SE58624963). The excavation consisted of a single trench measuring some 23.10m north-east/south-west by 2m, located immediately (c.6m) west of Trench 8 in the evaluation excavation. The work was undertaken in advance of a housing development by K.W. Linfoot plc.

All records and finds are stored by York Archaeological Trust under accession code YORYM : 1997.186.

The natural clay was recorded in the southern half of the trench at c.14.30m OD, c.0.50m below modern ground level. It was overlain by 1002, a yellowish-brown sand containing small amounts of silt which is thought to be a relict soil layer. During machining it proved necessary to cut into 1002, typically by a depth of some 0.10m, in order to reach material that was free from modern disturbance in the form of pockets of silt, brick, concrete and oil contamination.

A number of features of Roman and later date cut deposit 1002. It is thought that a feature (1007)

343

in the centre of the east side of the trench was of Roman date, but it seems clear that only a part of it was found, the remainder continuing beyond the trench edge. It measured 2.40m, north–south, x 0.5m, had steep sides and was 0.41m deep. The fill was a pale grey, slightly silty sand (1006). It produced two sherds of 3rd-century pottery and a small amount of brick and tile fragments. It seems likely that feature 1007 formed a terminal to the probable ditch (8008), recorded in Trench 8 of the evaluation.

Other features on the site, all of medieval date, included an east–west ditch at the southern end of the trench, probably a property boundary, and a quarry pit in the northern half of the trench. A few 2nd- to 3rd-century Roman pot sherds were found residual in these features.

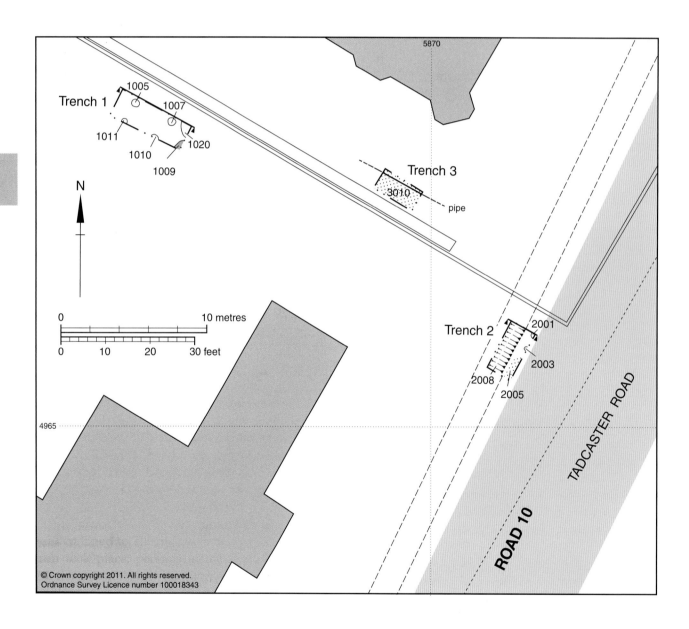

Fig. 261 *Starting Gate Evaluation: Plan showing location of trenches*

The Starting Gate Evaluation

In July 1996 an archaeological evaluation, supervised by Kurt Hunter-Mann, took place in advance of an extension to The Starting Gate Restaurant, Tadcaster Road (SE58694966; Fig.258, 3; Fig.261). Work was undertaken on behalf of Whitbread plc, to a brief from the Principal Archaeologist for City of York Council. Three small trenches were excavated: Trenches 1–2 in The Starting Gate property and Trench 3 in the grounds of the Willow Bank Hotel immediately north-east of its boundary with The Starting Gate.

All records and finds are stored by York Archaeological Trust under accession code YORYM : 1996.170.

Trench 1 (Fig.263)

Trench 1 was 5m (west–east) x 1.8m. Natural was clay (1025) below mottled light orange–mid-brown sandy silt (1023) which was encountered at c.16m OD, c.0.49m below modern ground level.

Cut into natural in the north-east corner of the trench was a pit (1020) of which three-quarters lay beyond the trench edges. The sides sloped down at a slight angle to a depth of 0.40m. The pit was backfilled with 1008, a grey sand, overlain by 1030, a brown sand. A few abraded sherds of pottery from 1008 are Roman, but of no exact date.

Natural was cut by two large post-holes (1005 and 1007) on a west–east line (Fig.262). They may have been cut from a higher level and were therefore contemporary with two other post-holes (see below), but were in an area truncated by mechanical excavation. The two post-holes were roughly circular in plan and 0.70m in diameter. In the centre of each was a dark brown silty deposit 1012 (in cut 1005) and 1013 (in 1007) which probably marked the location of wooden posts c.0.20m square. Post-hole 1005 was otherwise filled with a grey-brown silty deposit (1001) and packing material (1002) including a quern fragment and tile. Post-hole 1007 was filled with a brown sandy deposit (1006) and stone packing (1018).

Fig. 262 *The Starting Gate, Trench 1: view west with cut features; the figure is excavating post-hole 1005, and post-hole 1007 is in the centre*

Except in an area 1.2m wide at the east end of the trench, natural was overlain by 1022, a gravel deposit, 30–100mm thick. Cut into the gravel on the south-west side of the trench and extending beyond it were two more post-holes on a west–east line (1014–15), probably contemporary with the two described above. They were c.0.40m in diameter and filled with stone packing in a brown silt deposit (1010–11).

In the south-east corner of the trench was a deposit of slag (1009), probably derived from iron smelting (Fig.265). Overlying 1009 and the gravel 1022 was 1028, a brown silty clay, and overlying pit 1020 at the east end of the trench was 1029, a brown sandy silt. Over 1028–9 was a thin deposit of pebbles and stone fragments (1021).

In the absence of much in the way of pottery or other diagnostic finds it is difficult to date the sequence described above, although pit 1020 appears to be Roman and the gravel surface make up, post-holes and slag deposit are probably Roman also. Deposits 1021 and 1028–9 may have accumulated during the later Roman–medieval periods.

7

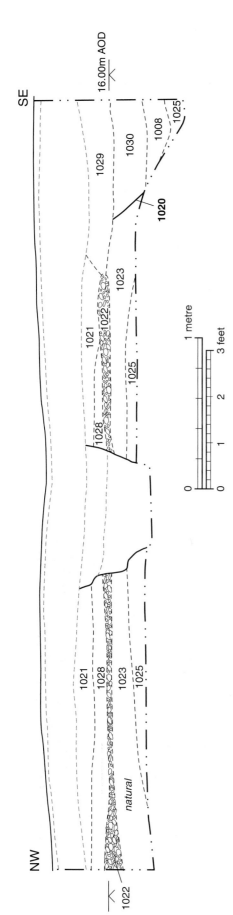

Fig. 263 *Starting Gate Evaluation: Trench 1, south-facing section*

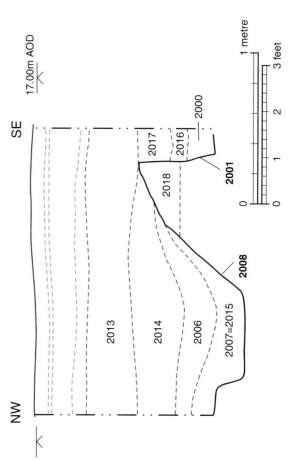

Fig. 264 *Starting Gate Evaluation: Trench 2, south-facing section*

Fig. 265 The Starting Gate, Trench 1: view south of the south-east corner showing slag deposit 1009. Larger scale 1m

Trench 2 *(Fig.264)*

Trench 2 was 3.2m (north-east/south-west) x 1.8m. Natural (2018), a mottled sandy deposit, was encountered at c.16.30m OD, 0.73m below modern ground level. Cut into natural was a ditch (2008), aligned north-east/south-west (Fig.266) which probably ran along the north-west side of an early phase of the main Roman road to York from the south-west when it was either narrower than it became in the mid-2nd century, as revealed in the main Starting Gate excavation (see below), or when it lay a little to the south-east of the later line. The north-west side of the ditch lay beyond the trench edge, but it was at least 1.65m wide and 0.75m deep. The ditch fill was 2007/2015, a dark brown silty sand, overlain by 2006, a similar deposit with frequent cobbles; above this was 2014, a grey-brown sandy silt. Fill layer 2006 produced late 1st- to 2nd-century pottery, and a sherd of 11th- to 12th-century gritty ware, which was thought to be intrusive, as well as Roman tile.

Cut into natural also, on the south-east side of the trench, near its north-east end, were two post-holes (2001 and 2003). Post-hole 2001 lay largely

Fig. 266 The Starting Gate, Trench 2: view north-west of the north-east end of the trench showing ditch 2008 (scale 1m)

347

beyond the north-east and south-east sides of the trench, but was at least 0.22m diameter and 0.50m deep. The fill layers were 2000/4, a grey sandy deposit which was below 2016, a grey-brown sandy deposit, in turn below 2017, a grey silty deposit. One half of post-hole 2003 lay beyond the south-east side of the trench, but as seen it was 0.35m diameter and 150mm deep. The fill was 2002, a stony, sandy deposit. Above natural in the south-east corner of the trench was a spread of cobbles (2005). Overlying all the features described was a sandy silt (2013), c.0.30m thick.

Once again, the lack of finds makes dating the sequence described difficult, but the ditch, post-holes and cobbles were probably Roman and deposit 2013 had probably accumulated during the late Roman–medieval periods.

Trench 3

Trench 3 was 3m (north-west/south-east) x 1.5m. Natural (3005), a mixed silt and sand deposit, occurred at c.15.95m OD, c.0.55m below modern level. Overlying natural was 3004, a dark silt 150mm thick. This was overlain by a layer of cobbles, loosely set in a silty deposit (3002), which appeared to slope down to the north-east so that it was 0.25m thick on south-west side of the trench but less than 100mm thick on the north-east side (Fig.267). This slope was caused by a modern cut for a pipe running north-west/south-east along the north-east side of the trench. The cobbles were overlain in the centre of the trench by a silty deposit (3003) up to 0.20m thick, in turn overlain by 3001, a dark brown silty deposit. 3002 is probably Roman, but 3001 and 3003 contained medieval and post-medieval pottery.

Fig. 267 *The Starting Gate, Trench 3: view west with cobble deposit 3002*

7

The Starting Gate Excavation

Following on from the evaluation in 1996, in September–October 2003 an excavation, directed by Jane McComish, took place at the site of the former Starting Gate public house at 42–50 Tadcaster Road (SE 58694966; Fig.258,4; Fig.270). The excavation was undertaken on behalf of Hearthstead Homes to a brief from the Principal Archaeologist for City of York Council. What follows is a summary of the report by Jane McComish (2006) which can be found online at www.yorkarchaeology.co.uk.

The site records are currently stored by YAT under the Yorkshire Museum accession code YORYM : 2003.303.

Introduction

The excavation consisted of two principal trenches. Trench 1 (40 x 20m) was located adjacent to the Tadcaster Road street frontage. A strip 20 x 6m was left unexcavated as modern services had destroyed the underlying archaeological deposits.

Trench 2 (39 x 20m) was located to the north-west of Trench 1.

In both trenches the natural was sand of various colours. In Trench 1 the surface lay at c.16.06–16.18m OD except in the extreme south-western corner where the level dropped to 15.60m OD. In Trench 2 natural sloped down from c.15.4m OD along the south-eastern side of the trench to 15m OD along the north-western side.

Period 1 *(Figs 268–9)*

The earliest features in Trench 1 were for the most part examined in three roughly 2m wide slots. They included a ditch, 1160, recut as 1085/1168, aligned north-east/south-west, up to c.3m wide and 1.2m deep. A complex series of backfills produced pottery of the mid-2nd century. It may be noted that this was in line with a ditch (1024) of similar dimensions thought to be the earliest feature in the evaluation at The Fox (see below). To the south-east of ditch 1168 was a more or less contemporary ditch

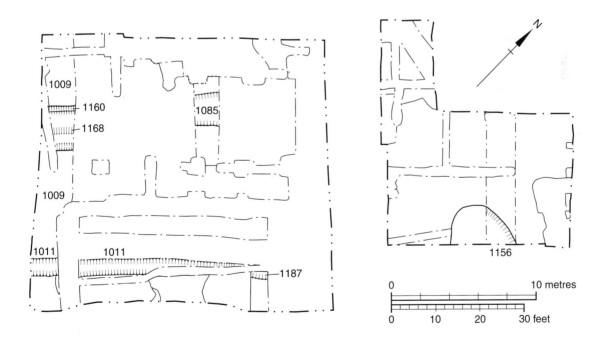

Fig. 268 *Starting Gate Excavation: Trench 1, earliest Roman features (Period 1)*

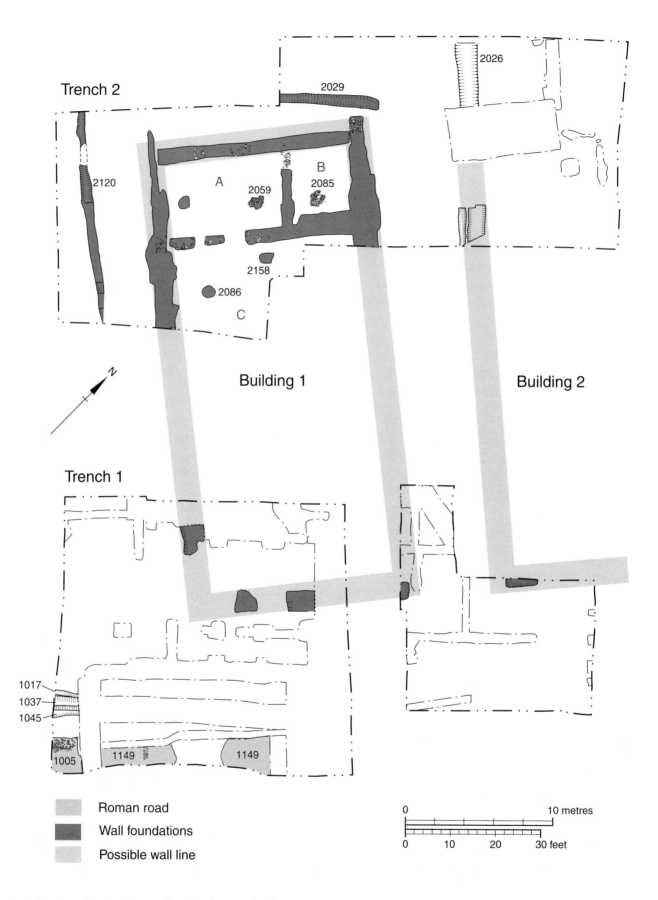

Trench 2

2029

2026

2120

A

2059

B

2085

2158

2086

C

N

Building 1

Building 2

Trench 1

1017

1037

1045

1005

1149

1149

Roman road

Wall foundations

Possible wall line

0   10 metres

0   10   20   30 feet

Fig. 269 *Starting Gate Excavation: Trenches 1 and 2, features related to Roman road and Buildings 1–2 (Periods 1–2)*

(1011/1187) c.1.20 wide and 0.80m deep. It may have defined the north-west side of the zone occupied by the main road from the south-west which did not impinge on the site at this time. In the north-eastern part of Trench 1, partly beyond the south-east edge of the trench, there was a large pit (1156) which was c.4.5m wide; it was excavated to a depth of c.1.2m.

Immediately to the north-west of and later than ditch 1011 was a shallow gully (1017) on a north-east/south-west line. It was recut as a ditch (1045), c.1m wide and 0.70m deep which was later itself recut as a slightly smaller ditch (1037). These ditches were probably dug to run alongside the Roman road, some cobbled layers (1005 and 1149) of which appeared to have lain immediately to the south-east. Presumably they were not, however, part of a primary road surface as pot sherds in them were mid-2nd century. It may be noted that ditches 1011 and 1045 were probably on an alignment a little to the north-west of that of the suggested

roadside ditch in Evaluation Trench 2, which may have belonged to an earlier date when the road was either narrower or lay further to the south-east.

In Trench 2 the earliest feature may have been a grave (2154) in which there was an adult skeleton laid south-east/north-west, crouched on its right side. The crouched position was commonly used for pre-Roman Iron Age inhumations in Yorkshire, as in the case of the Arras Culture burials on the Wolds (Stead 1991, 35) or burials found west of York, and nearer to the city, at Micklefield (Brown et al. 2007, 99-103) and Ledston (Sumpter and Marriott 2005, 5-12). However, the crouched position is also known in the region after the Roman conquest (Philpott 1991, 56). In the south-western part of the trench there was a group of three short lengths of ditch (2132, 2138, 2162) aligned north-east/south-west, containing pottery of the mid-2nd century, presumably broadly contemporary with ditch 1168 in Trench 1.

7

Fig. 270 *The Starting Gate: site view of the main excavation*

A group of two linear slots and four post-holes aligned north-west/south-east at the south-west end of Trench 2 may represent part of a timber structure, the majority of which lay to the south-west. Feature 2069 was cut by a grave (2127) aligned north-east/south-west, containing an infant skeleton which, like that in grave 2154, was laid flexed on its right side. It was buried with a sheep's jaw.

Period 2 *(Fig.269)*

In both trenches there now followed an episode of building construction. This was represented by a series of foundation trenches for exterior walls 0.75–1m wide and 0.6–1.1m deep filled with clay and cobbles. These dimensions suggest construction at least in part in stone. The remains can probably be interpreted as forming parts of two strip buildings of typical Roman character, arranged end-on to the main Roman road. Building 1, of which much more of the plan was recovered, measured c.31m north-west/south-east by c.15.65m, a ratio of length to width of about 2:1. Building 1 was subdivided at its north-west end where there were two rooms of unequal size (A and B). Patches of clay and cobbles (2059, 2085–6 and 2158) may, perhaps, represent pads for posts forming part of the structure.

To the south-west of Building 1 a space, perhaps an access alley, c.3m wide separated it from a linear gully (2120) packed with cobbles which may have supported a timber partition separating one property from the next. North-west of the building was a ditch (2029) of unknown function, 0.80m wide and 0.50m deep. To the north-east of Building 1 another space, c.6.4m wide, separated it from Building 2 of which only short stretches of the south-west and south-east walls were recorded. North-west of Building 2 was a ditch (2026) continuing the line of its south-west wall.

These two buildings were probably constructed in the late 2nd century but their life appears to have been brief, probably no more than 50 years.

Period 3 *(Fig.271)*

After demolition of the buildings a reorganisation of the site took place. In Trench 1 there was a spread of cobbles up to 9m wide, aligned north-east/south-west, of which, perhaps, the cobbled layer in Evaluation Trench 3 was also a part. At the north-east end of Trench 1 there was a north-west/south-east line of probable post-pads (1073–4, 1081) suggesting a timber structure. On the south-east

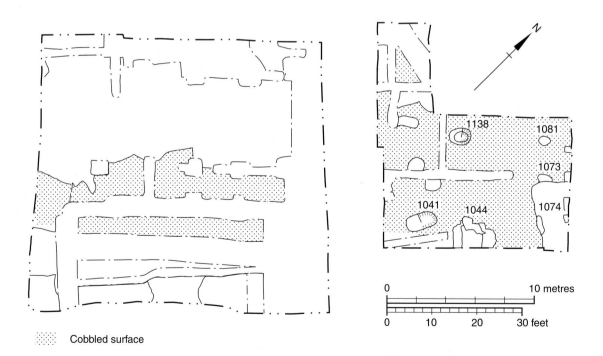

⠿ Cobbled surface

Fig. 271 *Starting Gate Excavation: Trench 1, Roman features of Period 3*

side of the north-eastern part of the trench were a number of fragments of limestone (1044) which may have lined a hearth. Two small pits of roughly oval plan (1041 and 1138) also cut the cobbles.

In Trench 2 a substantial ditch (2077/2095), recut on three occasions, was aligned north-west/south-east on the line of the alley south-west of Building 1. It did not, however, continue south-east into Trench 1. The pottery from the ditch fills dates to the early 3rd century. South-west of the ditches lay a hearth (2070) filled with charcoal and ash. On the north-west side of Trench 2 there was another burial (2087), an adult inhumation aligned north-east/ south-west and laid out in typical Roman fashion, extended and supine.

Neither trench produced evidence for late Roman activity, although there may have been considerable truncation of strata by modern development.

The Fox Public House

In July–August 1997 York Archaeological Trust carried out an archaeological investigation and a watching brief at The Fox public house, Tadcaster Road (SE5865 4958; Fig.258, 5; Fig.272) supervised by Neil Macnab. The work was carried out on behalf of Bass Taverns Ltd to a brief from the Principal Archaeologist for City of York Council in advance of the renovation of the pub, and the emplacement of foundations for a new extension and access road to the rear of the property. The proposed development involved an area of c.1800m²; the area under investigation lay just to the west of a standing building at 60 Tadcaster Road and the public house on its north-east side. As a result of the excavation the pub is now known as The Fox and Roman.

The initial phase of work involved the excavation of a single trench (Trench 1), 3 x 3m, directly to the rear of 60 Tadcaster Road. The results were such that excavation of a further three trenches was specified in areas where ground disturbance was proposed. The first (Trench 2), measured 3 x 2m, and was excavated on the line of the foundation trenches for the new extension. Trenches 3 and 4, measuring 4 x 3.8m and 5 x 2.2m respectively, were aligned on the access road. In total an area of 41.2m² was excavated to varying depths, depending on the depth of proposed groundworks. The overall investigation formed a 2% sample of the development area.

Following the excavation a watching brief was carried out during the machine digging of the foundation trenches for the new kitchen extension at the rear of the buildings. Due to the depth of these excavations, over 2m in some trenches, only a limited record of the deposits seen was possible, as trench collapse was a danger.

All records and finds are stored by York Archaeological Trust under accession code YORYM : 1997.70.

This report is based on an evaluation report by Neil Macnab.

Trench 1 (Fig.273)

Trench 1 was mechanically excavated to a depth of c.0.40m to remove overburden. Natural orange-brown silty sand, with occasional charcoal flecks (1021) was encountered at 15.18m OD, c.1.20m below modern level. This was cut by a ditch (1024) and gully (1023), both Roman. The ditch was only partially excavated and its alignment could not be accurately determined, although its probable continuation (ditch 5 on Fig.272) in Foundation Trenches A–C (see below) suggest it was north-east/south-west and approximately parallel to the main Roman road from the south-west, lying c.12m away. Ditch 1024 was filled with 1025, a grey silty sandy clay with orange and brown mottling, moderate charcoal flecking and cobbles at the base of the deposit.

Ditch 1024 was cut by gully (1023), aligned east-north-east/west-south-west. It was 0.20m wide and 0.14m deep, with steep, near-vertical sides and a flat base. The fill (1022) was a dark grey silty clay with frequent charcoal flecks and occasional gravel inclusions. It produced a sherd of samian pottery dateable to the 1st or 2nd century.

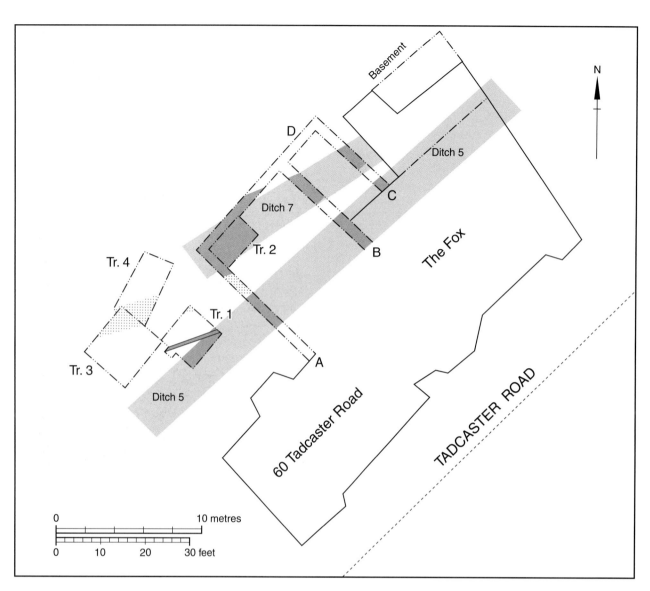

Fig. 272 The Fox: Location plan of trenches

In the north corner of Trench 1 natural was overlain by a deposit (1017) of small to medium-sized rounded cobbles, cut away to the south-west by a modern pipe trench. The cobbles formed part of a path, also recorded in Trenches 3 and 4. Two sherds of 2nd- to 3rd-century pottery were found amongst the cobbles. The path probably had the same alignment as gully 1023, which suggests that they were contemporary.

Directly overlying the cobbled surface and the other features described above was a deposit (1018), 0.22m thick, of mottled mid-orange-brown silty sand which contained a little gravel. It also contained four sherds of Roman pottery dateable to the 2nd century.

Cut into 1018 was a shallow grave cut, rectangular in plan (1020) and on the same north-east/ south-west alignment as gully 1023 below. The grave measured c.1.38m long, 0.58m wide and 0.10m deep. Within it was part of a male human skeleton (1014) laid out with the head at the north-east end and the legs flexed (Fig.274). A modern pipe trench had destroyed the north-eastern end of the grave, removing the skull, upper rib cage, spine and left arm. On the index finger of the right hand was a copper-alloy ring (sf100) (Fig.275). At the foot of the skeleton there was an almost complete, but broken, black burnished ware jar, of mid–late 3rd-century date. The grave cut was backfilled with dark grey silty clay with moderate amounts of charcoal flecking (1019).

354

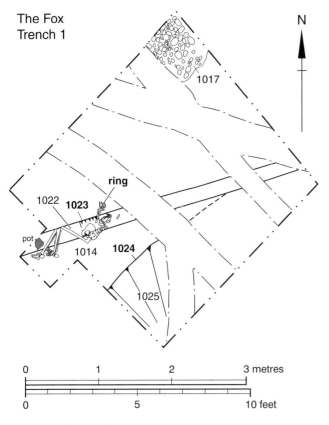

The Fox
Trench 1

0   1   2   3 metres

0   5   10 feet

Fig. 273   The Fox: Trench 1

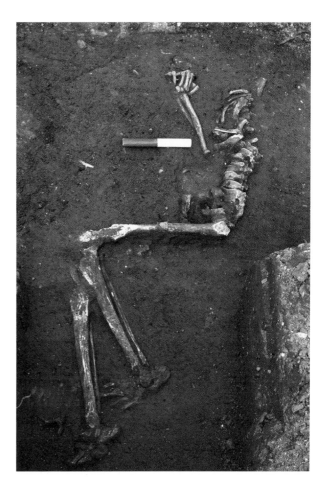

Fig. 274   The Fox Public House, Trench 1: burial 1020 (scale 0.20m)

In the north corner of the trench, in an area c.0.70m long and 0.30m wide, 1018 was overlain by a thin layer (1016), up to 50mm thick, containing metalworking slag. Its relationship with the grave was not established. Deposits 1016, 1018 and the grave were all overlain by a mid- to dark grey-brown sandy silt with occasional charcoal flecks and gravel (1015), up to 0.38m thick. It contained 23 sherds of Roman pottery including some of late 3rd-/early 4th-century date, a sherd of 9th-century York ware, two sherds of 11th- to 12th-century gritty ware and one sherd of 13th-/14th-century date. This deposit was cut into by several phases of modern service trenches.

Trench 2 *(Not illustrated)*

In Trench 2 a limit of 1.5m below a modern level of 16.37m OD was placed on the depth of archaeological excavation by the depth of foundations for the new extension. Natural was not encountered and the trench was thought to have been wholly

Fig. 275   The Fox Public House, Trench 1: detail of burial 1020 showing hand with ring on the index finger (scale 50mm)

355

within a ditch (unnumbered), probably on a north-east/south-west alignment which was also recorded as ditch 7 in Foundation Trenches A–D (see below). The ditch was not bottomed and the earliest deposit excavated, at least 0.20m thick, was a mid-grey clay silt (2009) containing frequent flecks of charcoal. This was sealed by a grey-brown silty sandy clay deposit (2008) again containing frequent charcoal which contained nine sherds of Roman pottery, four of which were of calcite-gritted ware, dateable to the late 3rd/early 4th century.

Cut into deposit 2008 was a shallow subrectangular pit (2007) with gently sloping sides, aligned north-east/south-west, and 1.20m long, 0.51m wide and 0.10m deep. The backfill (2006) was a dark grey silty clay with occasional pebbles. This was sealed by 2005, a dark grey-brown clay silt with occasional cobbles, 0.26m thick. Deposit 2005 was dated to the mid–late 4th century by a sherd of Crambeck grey ware. In the south-west corner of the trench it was cut by an 18th- or 19th-century well or cistern (2004). Subsequently,

a dark grey silty clay (2000) accumulated over the whole trench which probably represented a medieval and post-medieval garden or plough soil.

Trench 3 *(Not illustrated)*

Natural (3017) was encountered at 15.73m OD. Cutting into this on the south-east side of the trench was a heavily disturbed feature (3016), coming to a rounded north-west end and cut away on its south-west side by a later pit. The surviving north-east side of 3016 had an irregular stepped appearance. The feature was excavated to a depth of 0.43m, but not bottomed. The backfill (3015) was a mid-brown silty clay with orange-brown mottling and frequent charcoal flecking. It produced two sherds of Roman and one sherd of Iron Age or native-style Romano-British pottery.

Overlying 3015 was a layer of brown silty clay with orange-brown mottling (3014) which contained five sherds of Roman and eleven sherds

Fig. 276 *The Fox Public House, Trench 3: view north of cobbled path (Trench 4 beyond). Nearer scale 0.20m*

of Iron Age or native-style Romano-British pottery. Deposit 3014 was, in turn, overlain by a deposit of small to medium-sized cobbles (3010), similar to 1017 (above) and 4004 (see below), which together made up a path or track c.1.8m wide (Fig.276).

South of the cobbles (3010), and parallel to them, were two gullies (3011–12). Gully 3011, truncated at both ends by later features, was steep-sided with a flat base, and 2.30m long, 0.43–0.60m wide (increasing in width towards the south-west) and 0.13m deep. It was filled with a mid-greyish-brown silty clay with orange-brown mottling, a moderate amount of charcoal flecking and occasional cobbles (3009). To the north-west of 3011, 3012, truncated at its south-west end, was 3.94m long, 0.52–0.98m wide (again increasing in width towards the south-west) and 0.17m deep. It had sides of varying degrees of steepness and a flat base. The fill (3008) was a dark grey silty clay containing moderate amounts of charcoal flecking and occasional small pebbles. Neither gully produced any finds.

A large pit (3013) on the south-west side of the trench was probably next in the sequence. It was difficult to ascertain its relationship with the two gullies described above as this had been destroyed by a post-medieval pit, but it is likely that pit 3013 was later than both the cobbled path (3010) and the gullies. The pit, probably rectangular in plan, continued beyond the south-west and south-east trench sides, but, as found, was 2.82m long and 1.30m wide, and had steeply sloping sides. It was not fully excavated as it continued below the depth limit imposed by construction. The fill was a dark grey clay silt with yellowish mottling, frequent charcoal flecks and occasional cobbles (3006). There were no finds, but the pit may have been Roman.

A layer, up to 0.11m thick, of grey sandy clayey silt containing frequent charcoal flecks and occasional cobbles (3005), sealed the contexts described above and covered the majority of the trench. This was overlain by a dark grey silty clay (3002), 0.10m thick, which contained moderate amounts of charcoal, occasional small limestone fragments and mortar. Deposit 3002 was cut by the post-medieval pit (3007) which was succeeded by post-medieval deposits and modern features.

Trench 4 *(Not illustrated)*

Natural was encountered on the south-western side of the trench. This was overlain by a well-preserved cobbled deposit (4004), taken to be part of the same path feature as 1017 and 3010. Pottery recovered from this deposit suggests that the path was laid in the early 3rd century.

Sealing the cobbled surface was a deposit of mid-brown sandy silt with moderate amounts of charcoal inclusions (4001), up to 0.20m thick. The pottery recovered from 4001 was late 3rd or early 4th century, although a denarius of Vitellius (AD 69; sf101) was also found. Deposit 4001 was probably cut along its north-east side by a feature which was not fully excavated, but whose uppermost infill layer was a dark grey-brown silty deposit (4000). This feature cannot have been the ditch encountered in Trench 2 or Foundation Trenches A–D which must have come to an end or returned somewhere between Trenches 2 and 4. Deposits 4000–1 were succeeded by modern features and deposits.

The watching brief

This was carried out on the foundation trenches for the new extension to the kitchen and helped to define further the alignments of the cobbled path and the two ditches crossing the site.

Foundation trench A

The natural was cut by the two Roman ditches. A complete cross-section was recorded of the ditch (5 = 1024 in Trench 1) in the centre of the trench. It was 2.8m wide and 0.85m deep, with steep sides and a rounded bottom. It was backfilled with dark orange-grey sandy clay, containing frequent cobbles at the base of the feature. To the north-west of this ditch was the cobbled trackway, measuring 1.80m wide, already described in Trenches 1, 3 and 4. Unfortunately the relationship of ditch 5 and the path could not be determined. Part of the second ditch (7), seen in Trench 2, was recorded at the north-west end of this foundation trench. It was 0.70m deep and had a steep south-eastern side and a flat base. It was backfilled with greenish-grey silty clay with frequent charcoal inclusions. Overlying this was a series of Roman to post-medieval garden and plough soils to a depth of between 0.60m and 1.05m.

Foundation trench B

Natural clay was again cut by the two Roman ditches (5) and (7). Another complete cross-section through ditch 5 was recorded at the south-east end of the trench and seen to be 2.85m wide and 0.5m deep, with moderately steep sides and a rounded base. The fill was again recorded as a greyish dark brown clay silt. At the north-west end of the trench a complete cross-section through the second ditch (7) showed it to be 2.15m wide and 1.20m deep. It appeared to contain two fills. The primary fill was a light grey silty clay and contained frequent cobbles. This was overlain by a dark greyish-brown clay silt. A possible cobbled surface was revealed overlying ditch 7 but this was of uncertain date and extent and may relate to a former yard of the medieval or post-medieval period. The ditches were sealed by

medieval and post-medieval garden soils to a depth of 0.82m and the upper portion of the fill of ditch 5 was disturbed by a modern concrete footing.

Foundation trench C

The north-west edge of ditch 5 was seen to a depth of 0.5m and it contained a dark grey-brown clay silt with frequent charcoal inclusions. A cross-section through the second ditch (7) showed it to be 1.8m wide and 0.70m deep. It was backfilled with a mid-grey silty clay. Overlying these ditches was a thick layer of post-medieval and medieval garden soil up to 0.70 m deep.

Foundation trench D

This trench (north-east/south-west and joining the north-west ends of A-C) only revealed part of ditch 7 at its south-western end, measuring 0.70 m deep. No other features or structures were revealed within the trench, in which there was a series of garden soils up to 0.75 m in depth.

27 St Helen's Road

In 1994 a small-scale evaluation excavation was undertaken along with a geophysical survey at 27 St Helen's Road (SE58574971; Fig.258, 6, Fig.277) by Geoquest Ltd. This revealed a shallow gully aligned north-east/south-west of Roman date (Noel 1994). As a result, in November–December 1997 an archaeological watching brief was carried out by Neil Macnab during site stripping of an area of 900m² in preparation for the concrete raft foundation for a residential care home. The work was carried out on behalf of York Housing Association, as agents for Abbeyfield York Society Ltd, to fulfil a planning condition imposed by City of York Council.

The area investigated lay immediately to the west of the standing building at 27 St Helen's Road,

at the bottom of a steep slope. On the western side of the site there is a small stream, Chaloner's Whin Drain; to the north lie properties on St Helen's Road and, to the south, the Royal Chase development.

All records and finds are stored by York Archaeological Trust under accession code YORYM : 1997.194.

Natural was recorded 0.46–0.70m below modern ground level. At the north end of the site four linear features (1010, 1012, 1014 and 1016), aligned north-west/south-east were found, and all but 1012 ran the whole width of the site. 1010 was c.3m wide, 1014, c.1.3m wide, 1016, c.1.5m wide, and 1012 was 0.95m wide. 1012 was partially excavated and revealed as a

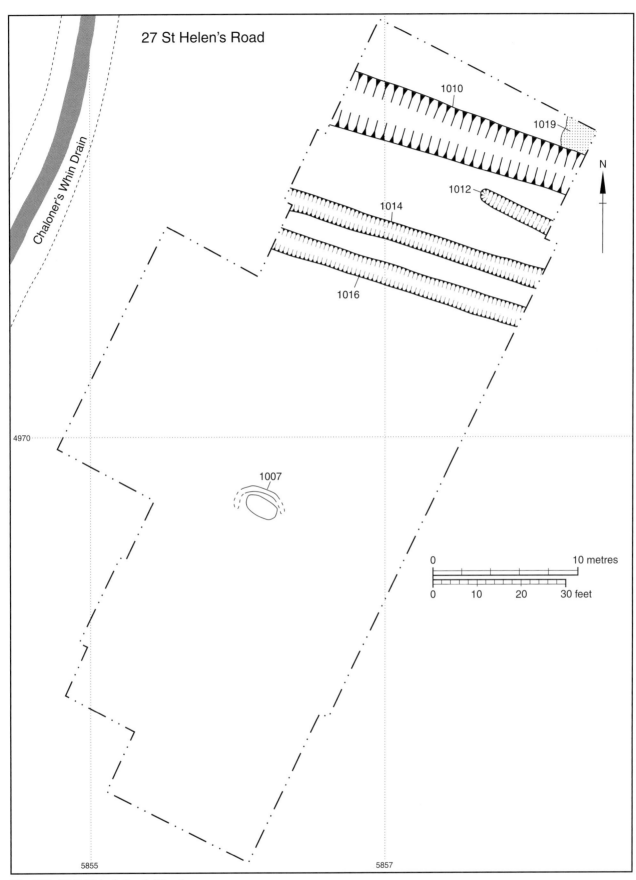

Fig. 277 *27 St Helen's Road: Site plan*

shallow feature, 0.12m deep. The fill (1011) was, like 1009 (fill of 1010; cleaned not excavated), an orange-brown silty clay. Fill layer 1011 also contained charcoal and burnt bone. The fills of 1014 and 1016 (1013 and 1017 respectively; also cleaned but not excavated) were bluish-brown silty clay. Fill layers 1011, 1013 and 1017 produced nine abraded Roman sherds between them. All these features are probably Roman ditches or gullies and may represent rein-statement of a boundary over a period of years.

In the north-east corner of the trench a disturbed spread of cobbles (1019), cut by 1010, was found. Its significance is unknown, but it produced a small ceramic flask or unguent pot of a type often found in burials.

In the centre of the site there was a small cut (1007), oval in plan, 1.0 x 0.60m; it was unexca-vated, but cleaned. The fill was dark grey-brown silty clay (1006) which produced an abraded Roman sherd. To the south another cut (2.2 x 1.35m) was probably a tree hole.

Above the features described above were deposits of sandy and silty clay which were cut by modern land drains overlain by modern over-burden.

7

Zone 7: Discussion

The Roman road from the south-west

It is likely that the route for the main Roman road to York from the south-west (RCHMY **1**, 3; Road 10) was established soon after the Roman conquest in c.71, even if construction came a little later. At Wellington Row, c.3km to the north-east, where the road reached the River Ouse, excavations indicated a late 1st- to early 2nd-century date for the first layer of surface make up (*AY* 16/8, 1108). However, no such clear evidence exists for any other site where the road has been recorded. As far as the course of the road is concerned, the Blossom Street/Mount Vale/Tadcaster Road area in York itself is discussed elsewhere (p.335) and the following refers solely to Dringhouses. As noted above, the Roman road was recorded at 304 Tadcaster Road a little north-west of the modern road line, and in Dringhouses itself the road was seen in 1902 in St Helen's Road, presumably close to the junction with Tadcaster Road. Excavations at The Starting Gate show that here the Roman road lay largely under the modern road; only a roadside ditch and a little possible metalling occurred within the site. RCHME must therefore be correct in suggesting that from the Methodist Chapel (SE586495) on the corner of Slingsby Grove and Tadcaster Road, a little to the south-west of The Fox, the Roman road is coincident with the Tadcaster Road as it continues further to the south-west (Fig.258).

As far as the date of the road is concerned, the early ditch (1011) at The Starting Gate, which probably defined the road corridor, even though it was not, perhaps, large enough to be a drainage ditch of usual type, is dated to the mid-2nd century. The later ditch immediately to the north-west (1045) and the road metalling appear to have been more or less the same date, but neither need be associated with either the layout of the route or with the first phase of road construction. The ditch located in Evaluation Trench 2 was not apparently picked up again in the watching brief subsequent to the main Starting Gate excavation, but may run under the pavement alongside the Tadcaster Road; the Roman pottery in it was late 1st–2nd century. If this is indeed an early Roman feature, and the medieval sherd was intrusive, it has a better claim to be a roadside drainage ditch, being a fairly substantial 1.65m wide and 0.75m deep.

Land use and settlement in the late 1st– mid-3rd century

No evidence for pre-Roman activity was found on any of the sites described above, although several sherds of possible Iron Age pottery from The Fox may indicate a human presence in the area before the Roman conquest. In addition, the flexed inhumation from The Starting Gate in the native tradition may be pre-Roman, although its alignment north-west/ south-east could be interpreted as respecting the main Roman road from the south-west.

In areas to the west of the main road from the south-west a number of ditches or gullies were found which presumably represent a Roman land division exercise (Fig.278). Their alignment in most cases respected that of the road. Early in the sequence at The Starting Gate (Trench 1) was a ditch (1160) more or less parallel to the Roman road and c.12m north-west of it. Although it did not appear in the eastern part of Trench 1, it seems quite likely that this is the same ditch that was found to the south-west at The Fox (ditch 1024 in Trench 1 and ditch 5 in the foundation trenches). This probably formed part of a major piece of landscape organisation of the mid-2nd century. Other, minor ditches on the same alignment and of the same date were found in Trench 2 at The Starting Gate. In the evaluation at 52–62 Tadcaster Road two ditches on a north-east/south-west line were found. At 27 St Helen's Road four shallow ditches, probably 2nd century, were found running north-west/south-east, i.e. at 90° to the road. Two shallow ditches appearing to respect the road line, and one which did not, were also found at 28 Tadcaster Road, immediately north of St Helen's Road (MAP 2004). An unusual aspect of the sequence at The Fox is the apparently new alignment, east-north-east/west-south-west, introduced probably in the late 2nd–early 3rd century, after the disuse of the earlier ditch, by the gully in Trench 1 and adjacent path in Trenches 1, 3–4 and Foundation Trench A.

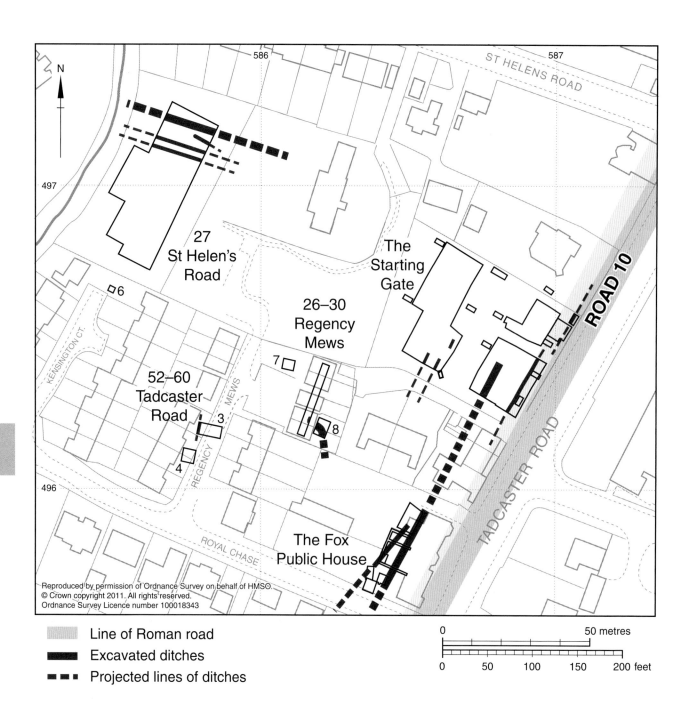

Line of Roman road
Excavated ditches
Projected lines of ditches

0   50 metres

0   50   100   150   200 feet

Fig. 278 Alignment of Roman ditches and gullies in excavated areas

Structural evidence from the Dringhouses sites was confined to The Starting Gate where construction took place, perhaps in the late 2nd century. McComish (2006) has interpreted the remains as those of a single building, perhaps a roadside *mansio,* based in part on the large group of associated pottery with a high proportion of amphorae and vessels for serving food and drink. However, it is more likely that they represent two strip buildings (Fig.269) of characteristic Roman type set end-on to the Roman road within properties probably defined by fenced or ditched boundaries. The location of these boundaries was probably determined by the earlier layout in that the south-east walls of Buildings 1 and 2 lie along the line of an earlier ditch. These buildings may well be representative of a larger roadside settlement at Dringhouses of a type well known in Roman Britain. Locally there are examples at Shiptonthorpe on the York– Brough-on-Humber road (Millett 2006), and at Stamford Bridge at the crossing of the Derwent on the road from York to the east coast (Lawton 1994; NAA 2005).

The creation of a roadside settlement at Dringhouses in the late 2nd century is of a piece with the expansion of Roman York itself at this time, indicating economic growth in the region. In addition, some reorganisation of the settlement pattern took place as population was attracted to roadside sites by the opportunities they presented. What is perhaps surprising about Dringhouses is that, based on the evidence from The Starting Gate, the settlement did not apparently survive into the late Roman period. By the mid-3rd century the buildings had been demolished. A reorganisation of the site involved a major ditch restating the boundary between Building 1's plot and that to the south-west in Trench 2, and the creation of the wide cobbled surface in Trench 1 running parallel to the main road. This has no obvious function, although it may have formed the base for timber structures of which no remains survived except, perhaps, for the post-pads at the north-east end of Trench 1 and the four substantial post-holes in two pairs in Evaluation Trench 1.

Evidence for the character of activity in the Roman period at Dringhouses is sparse, although the ditches probably divided up and drained the land for agricultural purposes. The only evidence for crafts was the iron-smelting slag in Evaluation Trench 1 at The Starting Gate, which gives some context to the relief of Vulcan found in the grounds of the Manor House. The Starting Gate buildings presumably served some commercial as well as residential function which, as noted, may have involved the sale of food and drink to passers-by.

Burials

Four inhumation burials found on the sites described here add to previous evidence from Dringhouses (RCHMY **1**, 107): three at The Starting Gate and one at The Fox. Their presence suggests the sort of *ad hoc* burial in vacant land towards the rear of roadside plots which can be seen in other roadside settlements. The earliest burial (2154) from The Starting Gate was crouched on its right side, as was the infant (2127). In this respect both are in the local Iron Age tradition (Philpott 1991, 56) and the former could be pre-Roman, although the latter is clearly 2nd century. The other two burials conform to Roman practice in being extended and supine.

Land use and settlement in the late Roman period

Evidence for activity after the early–mid-3rd century at Dringhouses is sparse. At The Fox the ditch encountered in Trench 2 and in the Foundation Trenches, which appears to introduce a new alignment to that site, was filling in the 4th century. At The Starting Gate truncation may have removed later Roman stratigraphy, but one would have expected cut features of any size to have survived and none appears to have done so. On the basis of the evidence from Dringhouses presented above there was a roadside settlement here with its surrounding field systems which enjoyed a brief existence in the mid-2nd–mid-3rd century.

7

363

Concluding Discussion

In this section an attempt is made to pull together some of the themes which have emerged in the previous description and discussion sections, and relate them, within a chronological framework, to the study of Roman York as a whole.

Late 1st–early 2nd century

Late Iron Age settlement

As noted in the Introduction, evidence for the Late Iron Age in the immediate York area is limited. None of the sites described above produced further evidence for activity in the period, although a few sherds of hand-made pottery in the native tradition came from The Fox, Dringhouses, and from the Germany Beck evaluation (Zone 4; Evans 2005).

The approach roads to York

In addition to the establishment of the legionary fortress at York and forts in the region as a whole, an important component of the Roman conquest of the north was the laying out of the principal land-based communication routes and, subsequently, their formal establishment as major roads. In many cases this was probably a two-stage process, with the army allowing a period of time to ensure that the most favourable route had been found. In the Yorkshire region construction of Roman roads with layers of metalling and flanking ditches usually appears to have taken place in the early–mid-2nd century rather than the late 1st. This has, for example, been demonstrated in the excavation of a section through the York–Brough-on-Humber road at Shiptonthorpe, c.30km south-east of York (Millett 2006, 45), and in excavations on Dere Street at Catterick (Wilson 2002, 126, 217).

The road network around Roman York (Fig.54) is well known in broad outline as a result of RCHME's survey published in *Eburacum*, and work published in *AY* 6/1; a few amendments have also been suggested in this fascicule in respect of Road 1 on its approach to York (see Zones 3 and 4, pp.235–6, 261); Road 2 from Brough-on-Humber as it approached

the fortress (Zones 3 and 4), and Roads 3 and 4 from Malton and Stamford Bridge (see Zone 2, p.192). The course of Road 10 from the south-west has been amended slightly in the Blossom Street area and Dringhouses (Zone 6, p.335; Zone 7, p.361).

The main approach roads are likely to be early in origin as they linked York to other military sites of the late 1st century including Brough-on-Humber (Road 2), Catterick (Roads 6–7), Malton (Roads 4A and 4B) and Aldborough (Road 9), although a fort is only suspected at the last named and the original military site may lie at Roecliffe, a little to the west (Bishop 2005). Road 1, whose place of origin is uncertain, may also be early if it did link the Fishergate cemetery, with its early cremation burials, to the centre of York (p.261). These presumptions aside, there is still archaeological evidence for the date of construction of only two of the approach roads to York within the city ring road. Road 3, which approached York from the north-east, was sectioned at Apple Tree Farm c.3km distant (Fig.54, 6) and the second phase of metalling was dated to the early 2nd century (Wenham 1968a, 56). The earliest surface of the road from the south-west (Road 10) was dated to the early 2nd century in excavations at Wellington Row (*AY* 16/8, 1109) and 18–20 Blossom Street (*AY* 16/8, 1135; Wenham 1965, 529). Further to the south-west at The Starting Gate, Dringhouses, a roadside ditch and road metalling were dated to the mid-2nd century, but may not have been primary features, the majority of the road lying under the present Tadcaster Road. To the major roads of this early period one may add one minor road or street, described above (Zone 6), probably of the early 2nd century, which was recorded at 14–20 Blossom Street where it joined Road 10.

Settlement

The use of the term *canabae* ('booths') by RCHME to describe early settlements outside the fortress and their relationship to a legionary *territorium* has been discussed in the Introduction. Our knowledge of early settlement outside the fortress remains sparse, because of a lack of opportunities for excavation, but the sites described above and other recent excavations and research, notably on pottery, allow some broad outlines of development to be proposed.

Based on the survey of York's Roman pottery in *AY* 16/8 (see especially fig.309 which maps the occurrence of CP1 assemblages), activity in the pre-Hadrianic period appears to have occurred on sites close to the fortress and on the principal Roman approach roads. Percentages of samian pottery from the principal sources of supply at selected sites in the York area are shown in Table 6 and add to the general picture of the shifting foci of activity in the Roman period as a whole. Of particular interest, perhaps, is the occurrence of South Gaulish samian, imported in quantity to Britain until c.110 (Dickinson and Hartley 1971). The samian from Les Martres-de-Veyre dates to the first half of the 2nd century, the Central Gaulish ware dates largely c.150–200 and East Gaulish to the late 2nd–early 3rd century.

The north-east bank of the Ouse, if not the south-west, was probably in use from the late 1st century onwards for the movement in and out of troops and supplies. At 39–41 Coney Street the first phase of a timber granary was dated to the late 1st century and the second to the early 2nd century (pp.7–11, *AY* 6/1; *AY* 16/8, 1085). In addition, there was a timber structure, probably early, found nearby at Spurri-

ergate, sealed by a later street (RCHMY **1**, 59). At 16–22 Coppergate (Zone 3), in the absence of structures, the early pottery (*AY* 16/8, 1078–9) must have originated in refuse, perhaps brought either from the fortress or adjacent extramural settlement. East of the fortress (Zone 2) were legionary kilns which produced tiles and the pottery known as Ebor ware (*AY* 16/8, 869–70). The first episode of production identified by Swan and McBride (2002, 193) dates to the late 1st century.

North-west of the fortress a potentially early timber structure, aligned on the fortress, was found at St Mary's Abbey (RCHMY **1**, 47; Fig.58, 16). In addition, some early pottery and glass came from Wilmott's excavations there (Simpson 1995; Cool 1998; *AY* 16/8, 1096–7). This is clearly an area which would repay further investigation. Traces of another early timber building were found at 31–7 Gillygate (pp.49–53, *AY* 6/1; Fig.58, 17). Other sites north-west of the fortress to produce appreciable quantities of CP1 pottery are 45–57 Gillygate (above, pp.125–31; Fig.58, 2), and 52 Bootham (Fig.58, 13; Keen 1965; *AY* 16/8, 1097).

South-west of the Ouse, as already noted, the term extramural should strictly refer to all settlement until the Roman defensive circuit, thought to correspond to the medieval walled circuit, was established, perhaps as late as the early 3rd century

Table 6 Percentage of samian types from selected York sites (% EVEs) in descending percentage order of South Gaulish

Site	SGS	LMDV	CGS	EGS
Swinegate	91.5	8.5	0	0
Interval Tower NE6	86.0	0	14.0	0
39–41 Coney St	64.0	0	36.0	0
Bedern South-West	61.5	0	25.5	13.0
16–22 Coppergate	45.0	6.0	34.0	15.0
35–41 Blossom St	14.0	7.0	73.5	5.5
21–33 Aldwark	6.5	1.5	72.0	20.0
Peasholme Green	0	0	90.0	10.0
Wellington Row	1.0	1.5	81.5	16.0
1–9 Micklegate	0	0.5	83.5	16.0

(Source: *AY* 16/8)

Key: italics = fortress sites; bold = extramural sites north-east of the Ouse; other = sites south-west of the Ouse;
SGS = South Gaulish; LMDV = Les Martres de Veyre; CGS = central Gaulish; EGS = east Gaulish

(p.119). However, the discussion in this section of the evidence for buildings and activity in extramural areas largely excludes that relating to the main area of urban settlement south-west of the Ouse, which will be dealt with in detail in Volume 4 of the *Archaeology of York*. The question should, none the less, be posed here as to whether an early nucleus of settlement anywhere on the south-west bank of the Ouse can be identified from which the later urban settlement would, in due course, develop.

Very little evidence for early activity has been found in river front areas. Reference again to fig.309 in *AY* 16/8 may direct our attention, first of all, to Wellington Row where there was a little late 1st- to early 2nd-century pottery associated with Road 10 as it approached the river crossing (*AY* 16/8, 1109–10), but where there was otherwise little evidence for early activity. Major sites at Tanner Row and 1–9 Micklegate produced virtually no South Gaulish samian (Table 6) or other early pottery. However, part of a bath house taken to belong to the years before c.120 was discovered in 1852 at Fetter Lane, south-east of the main road from the south-west. This included a room with a floor made of stamped tiles of the Ninth Legion (RCHMY **1**, 52); the building was probably the predecessor of a very substantial bath house of the late 2nd century partly excavated at 1–9 Micklegate. Further to the south-west lies the Air Raid Control Centre site close to the city walls which was excavated, somewhat hastily, in 1939 (RCHMY **1**, 54–6). Precursor to a very substantial stone structure was a timber building associated with 'military pottery' and 'exotic' sherds of early type (*AY* 16/8, 1124–5). A survey of the pottery from the site by Perrin (1975) noted that 19 out of the 71 (27%) samian vessels, of which fragments were found, were of South Gaulish origin.

To the south-west of what would become the main urban settlement there are a few sites with appreciable amounts of CP1 pottery on the line of the main road from the south-west including Bar Convent, Blossom Street (*AY* 16/8, 1135), and 14–20 Blossom Street (this fascicule) where a road or street and other features may belong to this early period (pp.289–90). In addition, there are the sites at 89 The Mount (*ibid.*, 1135) and 35–41 Blossom Street, both in this fascicule; at the latter South Gaulish made up 14% of the total samian from the site (Table 6), a low figure when compared with Coppergate and

Coney Street, north-east of the Ouse, but significantly higher than that recorded at Wellington Row and 1–9 Micklegate near the river bank.

Although the evidence remains sparse, a model for the early development of settlement south-west of the Ouse which fits the facts, such as they are, is that it developed along the line of the main approach road from the south-west with a nucleus lying between what is now Blossom Street and the higher ground to the north, now within the city walls. Settlement did not, however, extend onto the lower slopes of the valley of the Ouse, to areas around the bridgehead or on the river bank until the mid-2nd century.

Burials

An important question for the study of land use in Roman York is the location of the cemeteries (Fig.57). The interlocking use of space for the living and space for the dead is a complex subject and the two parts cannot be treated separately (although for more details of cemeteries and burial practice see *AY* 5). Unfortunately, as York's Roman cemeteries were extensively investigated in the 18th–early 20th centuries when recording was haphazard, it is difficult to get a clear picture of cemetery development, although a model in which they simply expanded outwards from settled areas cannot be sustained, either north-east or south-west of the Ouse (Jones 1984, 37).

Cremation was introduced to York and its region for the disposal of the adult dead by the Romans, but there are very few cremation burials of the pre-Hadrianic period which can be associated with either the fortress or early settlement. A small group of early cremations was found c.0.72km north-west of the fortress, adjacent to Road 7, at the junction of Clifton and Burton Stone Lane (RCHMY **1**, 73; *AY* 16/8, 1098). Another small group was found on the east side of Fishergate in 1876–7, c.1km south-east of the fortress (RCHMY **1**, 69). Excavation in 2000–2 on the west side of Fishergate, in the grounds of Fishergate House (Fig.54, 11), recovered four more (Spall and Toop 2005a). Two cremation burials from Trench 13 at the Barbican extend this cemetery northwards, but are undated. Other early isolated cremation burials come from Exhibition Square, only c.60m from the fortress north-west gate, and south-west of the Ouse from the south-east side of Road 10 at Blossom Street (Fig.194; *AY* 16/8, 1135; Wenham 1965, 531). South-west of the Ouse also, the early 2nd-century tombstone of the Ninth Legion soldier Lucius Duccius Rufinus was found, albeit *ex situ*, close to the main road from the south-west, within the medieval walls, at Holy Trinity Micklegate (RCHMY **1**, 122); the monument may, none the less, indicate the presence of an early cemetery in that area. A tomb monument for a second Ninth Legion soldier was found further to the south-west, close to the main approach road, in the Driffield Terrace area where extensive cemeteries would develop (RCHMY **1**, 126). Further afield, there is the flexed inhumation from The Starting Gate, Dringhouses, in the local Late Iron Age tradition, although it may be early Roman. Otherwise the local population may have continued to use a method of disposal of the dead which did not involve formal burial.

The mid-2nd century (c.120–60)

The Ninth Legion left York sometime before 120 and was replaced with the Sixth *Victrix* by the Emperor Hadrian (117–38). Quite what this entailed in terms of the number of soldiers based in York itself in the period under discussion in this section is uncertain, but it is clear from epigraphy that the Sixth Legion was engaged in construction work on Hadrian's Wall in the 120s and 130s, and subsequently on the Antonine Wall in the 140s. The legion's presence on the northern frontier is taken to be the context for what, on the basis of pottery, has been called a 'dearth of good evidence for activity in 120–40, not just in the fortress but in the extramural areas also' (*AY* 16/8, 839). However, during the years 120–60, corresponding to Monaghan's Ceramic Period 2a (*AY* 16/8, 863–4), the new garrison in York clearly felt the need to make its own pottery, and a Hadrianic phase of manufacture has been identified in the material from the kiln zone east of the fortress (Swan and McBride 2002, 193). By c.140 the legionary kilns had once more ceased to operate, although pottery production in the Ebor ware tradition continued in the immediate York area at Apple Tree Farm, Heworth (Fig.54, 6; *AY* 16/8, 870–1; Lawton 1992–3).

Roads

Although Road 10 from the south-west must have earlier origins, what may have been a new roadside ditch of this period further north-west than that located in Evaluation Trench 1 was found, along with the edge of the metalled road itself, in The Starting Gate excavation.

Settlement

The mid-2nd century (early Antonine period) saw the first indications of activity south-west of the Ouse in the bridgehead and riverside areas. Dated to this period was, for example, a street recorded at Wellington Row on a north-west/south-east alignment which joined the main road from the south-west (*AY* 16/8, 1108–10). Nearby, at 5 Rougier Street, a substantial stone wall and part of a structure employing large stone pillar bases, probably a granary, was found (*AY* 16/4, 247). In the extramural areas one can identify early examples of the ditches (discussed in more detail below) which served to divide up the land in many parts of the environs of Roman York. The sites in question include 50 Piccadilly (Zone 3), 35–41 Blossom Street (Zone 6) and The Starting Gate (Zone 7).

Burials and cemeteries

Cremation remained the principal if not exclusive means of disposal for the adult dead in York and its region in the early Antonine period, and burials are much more common than hitherto. In addition, what would become large cemeteries were beginning to develop around the settlement fringes at York (Fig.57). Using the data in *Eburacum* for the most part, Jones (1984) plotted the location of cremation cemeteries, showing, first, that they were close to the main approach roads and, second, that they were often at some considerable distance from the fortress. In addition to Fishergate and Burton Stone Lane referred to above, other cemeteries with cremations are known at Clifton Fields c.0.74km north-west of the fortress and adjacent to Road 6, and at two sites in Heworth c.0.85km to the north-east of the fortress, close to the Roads 3 and 4A. South-west of the Ouse cremation burials of c.140 onwards have been found as much as c.2km from the river crossing at Trentholme Drive (Wenham 1968b; *AY* 16/8, 1135).

The late 2nd–3rd century (c.160–280)

The level of activity in Roman York as a whole, as indicated, for example, by the deposition of artefacts, construction of buildings and infrastructure, and expansion of cemeteries, appears to have increased markedly in the third quarter of the 2nd century and continued to increase into the first quarter of the 3rd (Ceramic Periods 2b–3a, *AY* 16/8). Initially the historical context for this was probably, at least in part, the return of the Sixth Legion from the northern frontier and the prevailing peaceful conditions in Britain as a whole. On its return the legion set about reconstructing many of the fortress buildings in stone and completed the reconstruction of the defences with a stone wall, gates and interval towers, the work probably being completed by the time of the Emperor Septimius Severus's arrival to campaign in the north in AD 208 (*AY* 3/3, 210–15, 292–4).

Roads

There is little to be said about the major approach roads to York in the period under discussion except in the cases of Roads 10 and 11. At Wellington Row, where Road 10 approached the Ouse, a sequence of gravel layers was interrupted by what is interpreted as a deliberate attempt to raise the level, possibly for a bridge (see p.115; Fig.55; Ottaway 2004, 93–4). The watching brief in the cable trench at The Mount School, described above (pp.322–5), appears to have confirmed the course and dimensions of Road 11 which joined Road 10 from the north-west where The Mount meets Dalton Terrace today. As discussed above, the origin of Road 11 could be Aldborough, although the metalling found in the cable trench appears to be dated by associated pottery to the late 2nd century, suggesting that this was not the earliest road from Aldborough, which would remain Road 9. Also recorded in the cable trench, approaching Road 11 from the southwest, there appear to have been two minor cobbled tracks which are undated, but probably contemporary with it.

Elsewhere within the settled areas a number of other new roads or streets are known from excavation to belong to the late 2nd–early 3rd century. An addition to the network east of the Foss, described above, was the minor road found in Belle Vue Street which probably approached York from the high ground of the moraine to the east. No new streets have been found north-east of the Ouse, but it may be recalled that the two stretches of a riverside street found south-west of the fortress at Spurriergate (RCHMY 1, 59) and 39–41 Coney Street (p.14, *AY* 6/1) are now thought unlikely to have been connected to approach road 2 (see discussion of Zone 3, p.235). In both cases they have been dated to c.225 (*AY* 16/8, 1085). At its south-east end this street may have terminated in the area of what is now York castle, where there was a late Roman cemetery, whilst its north-west end made for the south-western fortress gateway (*porta praetoria*). A continuation to the north-west as Road 5 (RCHMY 1, 2) may be of the same date. South-east of the fortress, another street perpendicular to the riverside street was also found at the Spurriergate site. Further north-east two minor roads were discovered at 21–33 Aldwark (Fig.94, 9; pp.36–40, *AY* 6/1).

South-west of the Ouse the street network was developing within what was now emerging as a settlement of urban character with riverside streets at Wellington Row and Skeldergate (*AY* 4/1, 5–14), and others in Bishophill. In the extramural areas described above a hitherto unrecorded Roman road or track, probably of the late 2nd–early 3rd century, was found at Holgate Cattle Dock, and another possible example was recorded to the north of that site at St Paul's Green. The metalling of both of these was, like that at Belle Vue Street, fairly insubstantial and did not seem to have been repaired, so presumably their life was short, although they may have survived as unmade tracks into the late Roman period.

Settlement

North-east of the Ouse (see also discussion for Zones 1–4) the evidence suggests that, except on its north-east side, the extramural areas around the fortress became fairly well built up in the late 2nd century, although many of the structural remains are difficult to date exactly. However, it seems that 16–22 Coppergate remained peripheral to the main settled area around the fortress until the mid–late 3rd century, and thus continued to be a suitable place for refuse tipping. Somewhere in the immediate area, but not on the site itself, there appears to have been glass-making in the early 3rd century (Cool *et al.* 1999). The establishment by means of a ditch (36493) of a boundary on a roughly east–west line appears, on the basis of pottery and coin evidence, to belong to the third quarter of the 3rd century. At more or less the same time a large stone building with at least four rooms was erected. Although little can be said about it because of its almost complete obliteration in the late and post-Roman periods, the existence of the building on low-lying ground near the Foss may indicate continuing pressure on space in a well-populated area.

In the area east of the fortress, where pottery and tile kilns were sited, there was a third episode of production, accompanied by kiln waste disposal, in the Severan period (Swan and McBride 2002, 193, 195–6). The waste was spread over a wide area, being found not only in the Peasholme Green trench excavated by MAP, but also reaching the Peasholme Green site dug by YAT south-east of the street (*AY* 16/8, 1075; see above Zone 2), and 21–33 Aldwark, where two episodes of disposal were identified (pp.36–40, *AY* 6/1; *AY* 16/8, 1068–70). These sites were, however, clearly peripheral to the main settlement nucleus around the fortress. Although the two roads at 21–33 Aldwark had been laid out in the late 2nd century, the site was still otherwise open ground and deemed suitably remote from settlement for a human burial (p.36, *AY* 6/1).

North-west of the fortress there are hints of an important area of settlement in what is now the St Mary's Abbey precinct, with what may have been substantial stone buildings (see Zone 2 above). There is little to add from the work described in this fascicule, except for a possible timber structure at 45–57 Gillygate. Further away from the fortress to the north-west there was some hint in work reported above of roadside settlement at St Peter's School to add to what has been found previously (RCHMY **1**, 65).

South-west of the Ouse, following the first signs of development in the mid-2nd century referred to above, the late 2nd–early 3rd centuries was when settlement grew rapidly around the bridgehead and along the river front as recorded in excavations since 1981 at sites such as Tanner Row (*AY* 16/4, 244, 250–4) – two timber buildings on an artificial terrace; 1–9 Micklegate (*AY* 16/8, 1099) – bath house; and

Wellington Row (*AY* 16/8, 1110–13) – stone buildings. Within the same time frame but beginning slightly later, perhaps, settlement expanded into the Bishophill area to the south-east where a great riverside terrace was constructed for housing (*AY* 4/1, 30–7). Another terrace was found south-east of the medieval walls (and suggested Roman defences) at Clementhorpe, where evidence for the expansion of settlement in the early 3rd century took the form of a large house with several rooms (pp.56–9, *AY* 6/1). As far as the extramural sites south-west of the Ouse described in this fascicule are concerned, the late 2nd–early 3rd century are also the period in which most of the activity appears to have taken place. Of particular importance was the sequence recovered from 14–20 Blossom Street, suggesting the existence of a monumental building flanking the approach road from the south-west, of a similar character to some of those found in other parts of the Roman town. Further along the main road from the south-west, at Dringhouses, the development and life of part of a small roadside settlement with its strip buildings also appears to belong to the late 2nd–mid-3rd century.

Ditches

A review of the settlement and land use evidence in the extramural zones would not be complete without reference to the ditches which commonly appear on sites in all the extramural zones. Dating of these ditches is often difficult, firstly, because they produce little pottery or other dateable material and, secondly, because pottery from the fill of a ditch does not strictly date its cutting. However, if it is assumed that the ditches under discussion usually filled up soon after they were cut, it is striking that a great deal of ditch digging appears to have taken place in the late 2nd–early 3rd century. In some cases, for example, at County Hospital Foss Bank, ditches were recut, either on the same or on a very similar line, but this is unusual and the fill descriptions given in the site records seem to imply that they silted up naturally after a fairly brief episode of use.

Another striking feature of these ditches is that, for the most part, their alignments followed that of the nearest main approach road. For example, those south-west of the Ouse almost exclusively adopted the north-east/south-west alignment of the main road from the south-west, or lay perpendicular to it. The distinct impression is thus created of a process of land management in the York area driven by some controlling agency, presumably of official status.

Ditches had been a feature of the Roman landscape in York since the arrival of the army, and at first were primarily dug either for defence of the fortress or for roadside drainage. However, beginning in the mid-2nd century, it seems that an enclosed landscape began to emerge in the environs of Roman York, a landscape divided up by ditches and also, perhaps, accompanying banks which do not survive. Similar enclosed landscapes had existed since the Late Iron Age in many parts of the region, for example on the magnesian limestone belt to the west of York (Burgess 2001, 264–8), on the chalk wolds to the east (Stoertz 1997, 65–7) and the northern edge of the Humberhead Levels to the south (Horne 2003). However, only on the sand and gravel of the moraine at Heslington East (Fig.54, 19) and on the sand at Naburn (Fig.54, 23) is there good evidence for enclosed landscapes of pre-Roman origin in the immediate York area.

Why this mid–late 2nd-century land division around York was undertaken is not clear. However, it may to some extent, at least, be related to an intensification of agriculture in order to use the land in the environs more efficiently to provide a better food supply for a growing population at a time when there was both a large, permanent garrison in the fortress and an expanding civilian settlement. The creation of well-drained fields may perhaps have been required to increase arable production at the expense of pasture, with the ditches also serving to keep browsing and grazing animals away from crops. In other circumstances, as at The Starting Gate, Dringhouses, ditches seem to have been dug either to define and prepare land for building, or in others again to create burial plots.

In terms of their size the ditches were quite varied (summarised in Table 7), although the recorded dimensions were, in some cases at least, clearly affected considerably by later truncations and disturbance. The table lists examples which appeared to be relatively well preserved and for which reasonably reliable data on dimensions could be gained. A normal ratio of width to depth might be considered to lie between c.1.5:1.0–3:1; any figure

greater betrays a ditch which is very shallow in relation to its width and probably indicates truncation. Both width and depth may vary over the length of a ditch (where this occurred the figures in Table 7 are a rough average), but width was typically in the range 0.50–2.0m and depth 0.25–1.0m. These ditches were, therefore, considerably less substantial than the defensive ditches around the fortress, originally c.4.4–5.1m wide and 1.4–1.5m deep (AY 3/3, 191). The only ditch in Table 7 which does stand out in terms of its unusual size (3.2 x 0.85m) is that found at Water Lane for reasons which are not readily apparent (see Zone 1 discussion). In addition, what appears to have been a very substantial ditch, in excess of 3.5m wide, was recorded, but could not be fully excavated to determine its depth, at the Tregelles School site on The Mount.

Cross-section profile is another aspect of these ditches which can be difficult to determine because of erosion, disturbance and other factors, but although they usually appear to have simple U- or V-shaped profiles modified by flattish bases, there are examples of ditches in which the profile has a distinct step down on one or both sides to a slot at the base. Good examples published in this fascicule are in the ditches at Water Lane (recut 7019), Barbican Leisure Centre, School Canteen, Fawcett Street, and 35–41 Blossom Street, and in the later Roman ditches at 39 Holgate Road. The stepped profile has also been recorded in ditches at the former D.C. Cook Garage, Lawrence Street (Fig.54, 12; Evans 2004). The slot at the base is thought to have aided the ditch-cleaning process as it allowed a spade to be run along it easily. Because these slots are often found in Roman fortifications, where they are sometimes referred to as 'ankle-breakers', they are sometimes thought to indicate that a ditch was military work. There is, however, no indication that this was the case for the examples quoted above.

Finally, another unusual feature recorded in two ditches, one at 2 St Maurice's Road (1024) and the other at 35–41 Blossom Street (1082), was the presence of lines of iron nails suggesting a wooden lining. A late Roman example recorded in a channel cut into main Roman road from the south-west at Wellington Row probably indicated that it had been used for the town water supply (Ottaway 2004,148), but for the ditches cited here drainage is a more likely reason for a lining.

Table 7 Dimensions (in metres) of selected ditches

Site	No.	Width	Depth	Width:Depth
Zone 1				
45 Gillygate	1078	0.82	0.55	1.49
45 Gillygate	1093	1.4	0.8	1.75
Water Lane	7021	3.2	0.85	3.76
Zone 2				
2 St Maurice's Road	1020	0.7	0.25	2.8
2 St Maurice's Road	1024	0.6	0.25	2.4
2 St Maurice's Road	2009	1.2	0.4	3
2 St Maurice's Road	2015	1.8	0.44	4.09
County Hospital Foss Bank	20	1	0.52	1.92
County Hospital Foss Bank	55	1.8	0.6	3
County Hospital Foss Bank	57	0.6	0.3	2
County Hospital Foss Bank	90	0.65	0.3	2.17
County Hospital Foss Bank	92	0.45	0.25	1.8
County Hospital Foss Bank	97	1.8	1.35	1.33
County Hospital Foss Bank	106	0.8	0.35	2.29
County Hospital Foss Bank	110	2.4	0.9	2.67
County Hospital Foss Bank	115	1	0.25	4
County Hospital Foss Bank	134	1.6	0.6	2.67
County Hospital Foss Bank	148	1	0.9	1.11
County Hospital Foss Bank	1005	1.4	0.55	2.55
County Hospital Foss Bank	1013	0.4	0.2	2
County Hospital Foss Bank	1021	0.2	0.15	1.33
County Hospital Foss Bank	1027	0.45	0.37	1.22
County Hospital Foss Bank	1033	1.8	1	1.8
County Hospital Foss Bank	1042	1.2	0.3	4
County Hospital Monkgate	481	0.4	0.27	1.48
40–8 Monkgate	3019	0.75	0.5	1.5
40–8 Monkgate	3006	0.6	0.25	2.4
Zone 3				
50 Piccadilly	2134	1	0.35	2.86
Zone 4				
Barbican	10047	0.8	0.7	1.14
Barbican	19052	0.8	0.75	1.07
Barbican	19653	0.7	0.13	5.38
Barbican	20142	1.2	0.45	2.67
School Canteen Fawcett St	3014	1.1	0.60	1.83
17–23 Lawrence Street	1052	1	0.47	2.13

Table 7 *(contd)*

Zone 6				
39 Holgate Road	2005	1.92	0.96	2.00
89 The Mount	1016	0.8	0.7	1.14
All Saints School	1014	0.7	0.3	2.33
All Saints School	1015	0.7	0.3	2.33
35–41 Blossom Street	1038	2.21	0.7	3.16
35–41 Blossom Street	2199	2.6	0.97	2.68
35–41 Blossom Street	2390	0.24	0.14	1.71
35–41 Blossom Street	2400	1.42	0.47	3.02
35–41 Blossom Street	2401	0.49	0.09	5.44
35–41 Blossom Street	2408	1.34	0.32	4.19
3 Driffield Terrace	4056	1.2	0.3	4.00
Zone 7				
Fox and Roman	7	2.15	1.2	1.79
Fox and Roman	1023	0.2	0.14	1.43
Fox and Roman	1024	2.8	0.85	3.29
St Helen's Road	1012	0.95	0.12	7.92

Burial and cemeteries

As settlement expanded, due to a rise in population on both sides of the Ouse at York, so it would seem did the Roman cemeteries which came to occupy large areas, especially north-west of the fortress, and west and south-west of the town south-west of the Ouse. In addition, vacant plots almost anywhere, it seems, were used for individual graves or small groups of burials. North-east of the Ouse, in Zone 2, County Hospital Monkgate and County Hospital Foss Bank produced groups which can be dated to the late 2nd–3rd century. These sites were at no great distance from the fortress and it may be that whereas originally cemeteries were sited at some distance from the fortress and other settled areas, by the late 2nd century it was accepted that they could be moved closer in if space was available. The two earliest burials (Phase 3ai) made at 35–41 Blossom Street may also be seen as part of this process, being much closer to settled areas south-west of the Ouse than, for example, the Trentholme Drive cemetery founded in the mid-2nd century.

Other important new information for the organisation of the cemetery flanking the road from the south-west and its expansion in the period under discussion has come from recent excavations by YAT and others. The sites at 3 and 6 Driffield Terrace (excavated by YAT) and Mill Mount excavated by FAS (2005), for example, provide further evidence that the high ground on top of The Mount, close to the point where Road 10 met Road 11, was a preferred location for burial. Previous discoveries in the area show that it often accommodated people of high social status, although it is not clear whether the unusually large number of decapitated burials at 3 and 6 Driffield Terrace were of high or low status individuals. The south-western cemetery was presumably sufficiently large to accommodate a wide range of burials. However, whether the cemetery was zoned or otherwise organised on the basis of factors such as status remains uncertain.

On the south-east side of the settled area, more information has also come to light for the previously known cemetery around Bishopgate Street with the discovery of the burials on the Terry Avenue/Cherry Hill Lane site (Zone 5) providing yet another example of the way cemeteries were moving closer to a settled area in this period.

Further afield, away from the main cemeteries of York itself, evidence for burial remains sparse. Two inhumations, buried in the usual Roman manner, supine and extended, were found at Dringhouses, apparently in suitable vacant land near the main road. As noted in the discussion of Zone 7, this is known in other roadside settlements in the region. Although one of these burials (at The Fox) was accompanied by a pot and wore a bronze ring, these were probably people of no great social standing. However, there are examples of burials in rural areas in Yorkshire employing stone coffins, sometimes inscribed, of persons who presumably belonged to the local elite. Burial in a stone coffin is well known in York itself, but described above is an example from Fulford, c.3km south of the city, which can be set alongside two from Apple Tree Farm which also produced evidence for a lead coffin, (Zone 3; Fig.54, 6; Wenham 1968a, 50–2), and two from Heslington (Zone 4; Fig.54, 15; YPS 1832). All of these burials are difficult to date, but may well belong to the period under discussion rather than the late Roman period. The Fulford burial, like many others in stone coffins, was covered with gypsum, a local custom which as noted (p.260) probably has its origins in the 3rd century.

The late Roman period (c.280–410)

A convenient break in this discussion of Roman York is provided by the change from from Mona-ghan's CP3b to CP4a. In discussing the introduction of calcite-gritted ware, one of the most common types of late Roman pottery in York, he suggests that the date at which Ceramic Period 3b gave way to 4a was c.280 (AY 16/8, 866, 908). He also comments that no site shows a smooth transition from CP3b to CP4a, claiming that the change in the character of pottery assemblages was quite sudden, perhaps due to a new approach to official procure-ment policy for the army. Ceramic Period 4 is itself subdivided by Monaghan into 4a and 4b with the division occurring in c.360 when painted Crambeck ware was introduced. In addition, Monaghan

notes that as the 4th century progressed, the ratio of calcite-gritted ware to Crambeck ware in site assemblages increases steadily – sites which were occupied until the end of the 4th century or early 5th would therefore have a high ratio between the two types.

Roads

Information on the fate of the principal approach roads in the late Roman period is rather limited; outside the centre of York ploughing and other agencies have probably removed or disturbed the latest surfaces such that it is impossible to say whether the roads survived until the end of the 4th century or beyond. North-east of the Ouse at 108–10 Bootham, for example, an undated late surface of Road 6 was succeeded by plough soil, and yet later surfaces may have been lost altogether. However, as they were protected by later strata, and not subjected to ploughing, it was possible to see that the minor roads at 21–33 Aldwark seem to have survived into the 4th century, but at some stage, probably before its end (Period 4, p.42, AY 6/1) were covered by layers of roofing slabs and other debris.

South-west of the Ouse Road 10 in its final phase at 14–20 Blossom Street (Trench 8) appears to have been narrowed to c.5m, about half its original width. An episode of narrowing was also recorded near the bridgehead at Wellington Row (Ottaway 2004, 148).

Settlement

Whilst the civilian settlements north-east and south-west of the Ouse appear to have flourished in the late 3rd–mid-4th century, there is relatively little evidence for activity or settlement in the extramural areas except for burial. Other than burial, extramural sites with CP4a pottery noted in AY 16/8 (fig.314), all north-east of the Ouse (and fairly close to the fortress), are limited to 26–8 Marygate, St Maurice's Road, 22 Piccadilly, Garden Place, and 16–22 Coppergate where refuse tipping and the cutting and recutting of ditches and gullies took place (see above). The only new structure appears to have been that at 21–33 Aldwark, north-east of the Ouse, with a mosaic pavement dated to the early 4th century (pp.40–2, AY 6/1). South-west of the Ouse, the house at Clementhorpe acquired a new apse and mosaics at much the same time (ibid., pp.57–63).

Very few ditches, such a prominent feature of many extramural sites in the 2nd–early 3rd century, can be dated to the late 3rd–4th century. The only examples described above are from 2 St Maurice's Road (Zone 2), 22 Piccadilly (Zone 3) and 39 Holgate Road (Zone 6). It is not clear whether land boundaries were now marked in ways which do not survive in the archaeology (perhaps with hedges) or whether the agricultural regime in the later Roman period no longer required distinct land parcels.

From the mid-4th century onwards it appears, on the basis of ceramic evidence, that an even more marked divergence developed in the character and level of activity between, on the one hand, the fortress and town south-west of the Ouse, and, on the other, the extramural areas. Only 22 Piccadilly and 41 Piccadilly (in both cases unconnected with any features), north-east of the Ouse, and Clementhorpe, south-west of the river, produced pottery groups of CP4b (*AY* 16/8, fig.315). At 16–22 Coppergate it seems unlikely that the stone building survived beyond c.350. Building walls 28412 and 28944 (pp.205–7) were probably demolished before being cut through by wall 28946. On the basis of its alignment it is suggested that this latter may have been contemporary with the small cemetery on the west side of the site, although the wall's function is uncertain (see Zone 6 discussion). The ratio of calcite-gritted ware to Crambeck ware was low at Coppergate, suggesting an early end to activity, and no coin was recovered from a Roman context dateable after AD 364. Nearby at 22 Piccadilly the ratio of calcite-gritted ware to Crambeck ware in stratified Roman deposits at this site was also low. In contrast there is a high calcite-gritted ware to Crambeck ware ratio at Clementhorpe suggesting this site, close to the town south-west of the Ouse, was occupied to the end of the century, although the latest coin was of Gratian (378–83). None of the sites described in this publication produced coinage of Valentinian II (375–92) or later emperors.

Burials

Burial at one of Roman York's more distant cemetery areas at Trentholme Drive ceased in c.280 (*AY* 16/8, 1135) and late Roman burials are usually found closer to the settled areas. On the basis of the type of grave goods, re-use of earlier sarcophagi and gypsum burials (although this may be a custom with its origins in the 3rd century), it is apparent that 4th-century burials occur in many of Roman York's principal cemetery areas including Castle Yard, and St Mary's/Bootham Terrace, north-east of the Ouse (Jones 1984). One can now add the burials at 26–8 Marygate, dated to the late 3rd century, and those at 16–22 Coppergate of the mid-4th century. This is also likely to be the date of the burials at Wentworth House (The Avenue), although the evidence is a single coin found in a grave fill layer. South-west of the Ouse late burials have been found in the Railway Station cemetery, to which those in Period 4 at 35–41 Blossom Street can be added. Other late 3rd- to mid-4th-century Roman burials south-west of the Ouse from recent work include at least some of those excavated at 6 Driffield Terrace (Hunter-Mann 2006) and a group of four from Moss Street (Toop 2008, 26–7). However, in spite of all the new evidence for cemeteries it has, as yet, not been possible to identify with any certainty burials belonging to the final decades of the 4th century or to the early 5th.

Intramural and extramural at Roman York: a summing up

The review of Roman archaeology in the environs of York presented in this fascicule, set in the context of what is known of the history and topography of Roman York as a whole, has allowed a more rounded picture of those two topics to emerge than has been available hitherto.

In brief, the story of Roman York probably began with some preliminary military activity north-east of the Ouse in the late Neronian period which was followed by the establishment of the fortress in c.71 and by the laying out and construction of most, if not all, of the main approach roads in the late 1st–early 2nd century. Activity outside the fortress was probably confined initially to the north-east bank of the Ouse and to areas close to the main approach roads on the north-east and south-west banks, and east of the Foss.

In the mid-2nd century the pace of settlement growth quickened to take in areas on all sides of the fortress, except, perhaps, the north-eastern, and on the south-west side of the Ouse it took in areas close to the bridgehead and the river bank. The expansion of what became a civilian settlement of urban character was accompanied by the erection of some monumental public buildings on both sides of the river. They may have included an example immediately outside the presumed town defences south-west of the Ouse (at 14–20 Blossom Street). Promotion of the civilian settlement to provincial capital and *colonia* status, probably during the reign of Caracalla (211–13), is one plausible context in which construction of defences around the main settled area south-west of the Ouse took place, thereby also creating a true extramural area on this bank of the river. From the mid-2nd century onwards the cemeteries expanded considerably within all extramural areas, along the approach roads to the fortress and settled areas. Otherwise, much of the land in the environs of Roman York was divided up by ditches in the mid-2nd–early 3rd century. These ditches may have served both to define ownership and to promote drainage as part of a change in the agricultural regime. The newly enclosed landscape extended as far to the south-west as Dringhouses where a small settlement appears to have developed, presumably to take advantage of the commercial opportunities presented by one of the main approach roads to York itself.

In the late 3rd and early 4th centuries the legionary fortress remained an important army base for the north of England and the civilian settlements on both sides of the Ouse continued to flourish. However, except in the cemeteries, most extramural areas produce relatively little evidence for activity of any description. This includes the Dringhouses settlement which, according to present evidence, was abandoned. In addition, the enclosed landscape created 100 years or so previously appears to have disappeared.

After the mid-4th century both the garrison in the fortress and the population in civilian settlements probably declined in size. In addition, the distinction between the fortress and town south-west of the Ouse, on the one hand, and the extramural areas, on the other, in terms of evidence for settlement and activity, becomes very marked. No certain burials of the last decades of the 4th century or early 5th have yet been identified.

The fortress and *colonia*, twin elements which had made York unique in later Roman Britain, may have survived as occupied sites until the early 5th century, but evidence for any human settlement thereafter in either is largely absent until the 7th–8th centuries (*AY* 7/2). After about 350 years the process of rise to become one the principal economic, political and social centres of the Roman empire had been followed by a fall which was probably complete before 450.

Résumé

Ce fascicule constitue une mise au point des données fournies par l'archéologie sur les environs de York dans le cadre de nos connaissances de l'histoire et de la topographie cette ville à l'époque romaine. Ce travail nous permet de présenter ces deux thèmes de manière plus exhaustive qu'il n'a été possible jusqu'à présent.

En bref, une zone d'activité militaire au nord-est de la rivière Ouse datant de l'époque Néronienne marqua probablement le début de la phase romaine dans l'histoire de York. Une forteresse y fut établie autour de 71 apr. J.-C. et la majorité des axes de communication principaux furent construits vers la fin du 1er ou au début du 2nd siècle apr. J.-C. La zone d'activité en dehors de la forteresse était probablement limitée à la rive nord-est de la rivière Ouse ainsi qu'aux abords immédiats des voies d'accès de part et d'autre de l'Ouse et à l'est de la rivière Foss.

Vers le milieu du 2nd siècle apr. J.-C., la croissance de la zone d'habitat s'accéléra nettement, englobant tous les alentours de la forteresse, à part, peut-être, le flanc nord-est; au sud-ouest de la rivière Ouse les quartiers d'habitation s'élevaient le long des berges près de la tête du pont. La croissance de cette agglomération, qui devint un habitat civil à caractère urbain, vit en même temps la construction de bâtiments publics monumentaux des deux côtés de la rivière, comme par exemple un bâtiment à l'extérieur de l'enceinte présumée des remparts, au sud-ouest de l'Ouse (au no. 14–20, Blossom Street). La ville acquit le statut de capitale provinciale et de *colonia* probablement pendant le règne de Caracalla (211–213 apr. J.-C.). Cet évènement fournit un contexte plausible pour la construction d'un complexe défensif autour de la zone d'habitat principale au sud-ouest de l'Ouse, créant ainsi un quartier *extra muros* sur cette rive. A partir du milieu du 2nd siècle l'implantation des cimetières s'accrut considérablement dans toutes les zones extra-murales, le long des voies d'accès menant vers la forteresse et les secteurs d'habitat. Aux alentours de York, une grande partie de la campagne fut divisée par des fossés entre le milieu du 2nd siècle apr. J.-C. et le début du 3ème. Ces fossés auraient pu servir tout aussi bien pour définir des parcelles que pour améliorer le drainage dans le cadre d'une restructuration du système agricole. Cette nouvelle campagne découpée en parcelles s'étendit jusqu'à Dringhouses au sud-ouest, où un petit établissement se développa, sans doute établi pour profiter des possibilités de commerce le long de l'une des principales route menant à York.

Vers la fin du 3ème et le début du 4ème siècle, la forteresse légionnaire demeura une base importante pour le Nord de l'Angleterre et l'établissement civil des deux côtés de l'Ouse continua à prospérer. Cependant, en dehors des cimetières, il existe peu d'indices d'activité dans la plupart des zones *extra muros*, y compris l'habitat de Dringhouses, qui fut apparemment abandonné. De plus, les parcelles créées un siècle auparavant semblent également avoir disparu.

Il est probable qu'après le milieu du 4ème siècle la population déclina, tant dans les effectifs de la garnison de la forteresse que dans la population civile. De plus, les différences entre la forteresse et la ville au sud-ouest de l'Ouse d'une part, et les quartiers *extra muros* d'autre part s'accentuèrent. Quant aux sépultures, aucune tombe datant des dernières décennies du 4ème siècle ou du début du 5ème siècle n'a été identifiée.

La forteresse et la *colonia,* ces deux éléments jumeaux qui firent de York une ville unique dans l'Antiquité tardive de la Grande-Bretagne, survécurent peut-être comme lieux d'habitat pendant les premières décennies du 5ème siècle; ensuite, les données qui pourraient documenter une occupation manquent largement jusqu'au 7eme–8ème siècle apr. J.-C. (*AY* 7/2). Ainsi, au bout de 350 ans, le processus de croissance qui permit à York de devenir un centre économique, politique et social prééminent dans l'empire romain se termina par un déclin qui s'acheva probablement avant 450 apr. J.-C.

Zusammenfassung

Die Bericht über römische Archäologie Yorks und seiner Umgebung, der in diesem Band dargestellt wird, hat noch nie dagewesene Erkenntnisse über die Geschichte und Topografie des römischen Yorks hervorgebracht.

In aller Kürze dargestellt hat die Geschichte des römischen Yorks wahrscheinlich mit militärischer Aktivität nordöstlich des Flusses Ouse während der späten neronischen Ära begonnen. Dem folgte circa 71 n.Chr. der Bau der Festung und im späten 1. und frühen 2. Jahrhundert die Planung sowie der Bau der meisten (wenn nicht sogar aller) Zugangsstraßen. Aktivitäten außerhalb der Festung haben sich anfangs wahrscheinlich auf das nordöstliche Ufer der Ouse, auf das Gebiet in der Nähe der Zugangsstraßen und auf beiden Ufer des Flusses Foss sowie seine auf das Gebiet östlich des Flusses Foss beschränkt.

Mitte des 2. Jahrhunderts hat sich der Besiedlungsprozess beschleunigt und sich auf Gebiete zu allen Seiten der Festung ausgebreitet, vielleicht jedoch mit Ausnahme des Nord-Ostens. Auf der südwestlichen Seite der Ouse wurden Gebiete in der Nähe des Brückenkopf und des Ufers besiedelt. Diese Erweiterung, deren zivile Besiedlung einen städtischen Charakter annahm, wurde von der Errichtung einiger imposanter öffenticher Gebäude auf beiden Seiten des Flusses begleitet. Wahrscheinlich beinhaltete das auch ein Objekt unmittelbar außerhalb der mutmaßlichen Wehranlagen der Stadt, südwestlich der Ouse (14–20 Blossom Street). Die Ernennung der zivilen Siedlung zur Hauptstadt der Provinz und die Verleihung des „Colonia"-Status, wahrscheinlich während der Herrschaft von Caracalla (211–213), ist wahrscheinlich der Grund für die Errichtung von Abwehranlagen um das am dichtesten besiedelte Gebiet südwestlich der Ouse. Hierdurch wurde auch ein klar abgegrenztes Gebiet außerhalb der Stadtmauern diesseits des Flusses geschaffen. Ab dem mittleren 2. Jahrhundert breiteten sich die außerstädtischen Friedhöfe entlang der Zugangsstraßen zur Festung und außerhalb besiedelter Gebieten beträchtlich aus. Außerdem wurde ab dem mittleren 2. bis zum frühen 3. Jahrhundert viel Land in der Umgebung des römischen Yorks mit Hilfe von Gräben aufgeteilt. Diese Gräben könnten der Abgrenzung von Eigentum sowie der Drainage, als Teil einer Umstrukturierung in der Landwirtschaft, gedient haben. Die neu erschlossene Landschaft dehnte sich im Südwesten bis nach Dringhouses aus. Hier entstand wahrscheinlich eine kleine Siedlung, vermutlich um von kommerziellen Vorteilen zu profitieren, welche die Lage an einer der Hauptstraßen nach York mit sich brachte.

Während des späten 3. und frühen 4. Jahrhunderts blieb die römische Festung ein wichtiger Militärstützpunkt für den Norden Englands und auch die zivilen Siedlungen auf beiden Seiten der Ouse prosperierten weiterhin. Jedoch zeigen die meisten außerstädtischen Gebiete, mit Ausnahme der Friedhöfe, zu dieser Zeit relativ wenige Anzeichen irgendwelcher Entwicklung. Das gilt auch für die Dringhouse Siedlung, die nach momentanen Kenntnisstand aufgegeben wurde. Zusätzlich scheint die etwa 100 Jahre zuvor erschlossene Landschaft verschwunden zu sein.

Ab Mitte des 4. Jahrhundert ist die Besatzung der Festung, wie auch die Zivilbevölkerung vermutlich zurückgegangen. Zusätzlich wurde die Abgrenzung zwischen Festung und Stadt südwestlich der Ouse auf der einen und den außerstädtichen Gebieten auf der anderen Seite, sehr deutlich. Bis jetzt konnten keine eindeutigen Begräbnisstätten der letzten Jahrzehnte des 4. oder des frühen 5. Jahrhundert identifiziert werden.

Die Festung und die „Colonia", die zwei Merkmale, die York im späten römischen Britannien einzigartig machten, könnten bis ins frühe 5. Jahrhundert als bewohnte Gebiete überlebt haben. Jedoch sind Beweise für eine menschliche Besiedlung danach und bis zum 7. – 8. Jahrhundert weitgehend nicht vorhanden. Nach einer etwa 350 jährigen Entwicklung zu einem der wichtigsten wirtschaftlichen, politischen und sozialen Zentren des Römischen Reichs folgte der Niedergang des römischen Yorks der wahrscheinlich bereits 450 n. Chr abgeschlossen war.

Abbreviations

AY	*Archaeology of York*
CP	Ceramic period (as in *AY* 16/8)
FAS	Field Archaeology Specialists
MAP	MAP Archaeological Consultancy
RCHME	Royal Commission on Historical Monuments for England
RIB	Roman Inscriptions of Britain
YAJ	*Yorkshire Archaeological Journal*
YAT	York Archaeological Trust

Bibliography

Addyman, P.V. and Black, V.E. (eds), 1984. *Archaeological Papers from York presented to M.W. Barley* (York)

AY. Addyman, P.V. (ed.). *The Archaeology of York* (London and York)

3 *The Legionary Fortress*:

1 J.B. Whitwell, 1976. *The Church Street Sewer and an Adjacent Building*

2 A.B. Sumpter and S. Coll, 1977. *Interval Tower SW5 and the South-West Defences: Excavations 1972–75*

3 P.J. Ottaway, 1996. *Excavations and Observations on the Defences and Adjacent Sites, 1971–90*

4 R.A. Hall, 1997. *Excavations in the* Praetentura: *9 Blake Street*

4 *The Colonia*:

1 M.O.H. Carver, S. Donaghey and A.B. Sumpter, 1978. *Riverside Structures and a Well in Skeldergate and Buildings in Bishophill*

6 *Roman Extramural Settlements and Roads*:

1 D. Brinklow, R.A. Hall, J.R. Magilton and S. Donaghey, 1986. *Coney Street, Aldwark and Clementhorpe, Minor Sites and Roman Roads*

7 *Anglian York*:

1 R.L. Kemp, 1996. *Anglian Settlement at 46–54 Fishergate*

2 D. Tweddle, J.Moulden and E. Logan, 1999. *Anglian York: A Survey of the Evidence*

8 *Anglo-Scandinavian York*:

4 R.A. Hall, D.W. Rollason, M. Blackburn, D.N. Parsons, G. Fellows-Jensen, A.R. Hall, H.K. Kenward, T.P. O'Connor, D. Tweddle, A.J. Mainman and N.S.H. Rogers, 2004. *Aspects of Anglo-Scandinavian York*

10 *The Medieval Walled City north-east of the Ouse*:

6 R.A. Hall and K. Hunter-Mann, 2002. *Medieval Urbanism in Coppergate: Refining a Townscape*

11 *The Medieval Defences and Suburbs*:

1 J.D. Richards, C. Heighway and S. Donaghey, 1989. *Union Terrace: Excavations in the Horsefair*

12 *The Medieval Cemeteries*:

2 G. Stroud and R.L. Kemp, 1993. *Cemeteries of St Andrew, Fishergate*

14 *The Past Environment of York*:

6 A.R. Hall and H.K. Kenward, 1990. *Environmental Evidence from the* Colonia

15 *The Animal Bones*:

2 T.P. O'Connor, 1988. *Bones from the General Accident Site, Tanner Row*

16 *The Pottery*:

4 J.R. Perrin, 1990. *Roman Pottery from the* Colonia 2: *General Accident and Rougier Street*

8 J. Monaghan, 1997. *Roman Pottery from York*

Benson, G., 1911. *An Account of the City and County of the City of York, Vol.1* (reprinted 1968)

Benson, G., 1919. *Later Medieval York: the city and county of the City of York from 1100 to 1603, Vol.2*

Bishop, M.C., 2005. 'A new Flavian military site at Roecliffe, North Yorkshire', *Britannia* **36**, 135–223

Briden, C., 1984. 'John Thurnam, 1810–1873', in Addyman and Black 1984, 163–5

British Geological Survey, 1983. *York*, Sheet 63 (scale 1:50,000)

Brown, F., Howard-Davis, C and Brennand, M., 2007. 'Iron Age and Romano-British landscapes', in F. Brown, C. Howard-Davis, M. Brennand, A. Boyle, T. Evans, S. O'Connor, A. Spence, R. Heawood and A. Lupton, *The Archaeology of the A1 (M) Darrington to Dishforth DBFO Road Scheme*, Lancaster Imprints **12**

Bruce, G., 2002. *The Working Men's Club, Speculation Street, York, Report on an Archaeological Evaluation,* On Site Archaeology Report OSA02EV10

Bruce, G., 2004. *Speculation Street, York, Report on an Archaeological Evaluation,* On Site Archaeology Report OSA04EX01

Burgess, A., 2001. 'The Iron Age', in I. Roberts, A. Burgess, and D. Berg (eds) *A New Link to the Past: the Archaeological Landscape of the M1–A1 Link Road*, Yorkshire Archaeol. **7**, 260–9

Carson, R. and Kent, J., 1971. 'A hoard of Roman 4th century bronze coins from Heslington, Yorks', *Numismatic Chron.* **11**, 207–25

Cool, H.E.M., 1998. 'Early occupation at St Mary's Abbey, York: the evidence of the glass', in J. Bird (ed.), *Form and Fabric: Studies in Rome's Material Past in Honour of B.R. Hartley*, Oxbow Monogr. **80**, 301–5

Cool, H.E.M., Jackson, C.M. and Monaghan. J., 1999. 'Glass-making and the Sixth Legion at York', *Britannia* **30**, 147–62

Dickinson, B.M. and Hartley, K.F., 1971. 'The evidence of potters' stamps on samian ware and on mortaria for the trading connections of Roman York', in R.M. Butler (ed.) *Soldier and Civilian in Roman Yorkshire* (Leicester), 127–42

Dickinson, C. and Wenham, L.P., 1957. 'Discoveries in the Roman cemetery on The Mount, York', *Yorkshire Archaeol. J.* **39**, 283–323

Drake, F., 1736. *Eboracum: or, the History and Antiquities of the City of York, from its original to the present time. Together with the history of the Cathedral Church and the lives of the Archbishops, etc* (London)

Evans, D.T., 2004. *Beyond the Walls of York: the Road to Hull,* Archaeology of York Web Series **2**, www.iadb.co.uk/dccook/intro.htm

Evans, J., 2005. 'Pottery' in MAP 1996b

Gentil, P., 1988. *G.F. Wilmot's Excavation at St Mary's Abbey, York,* unpublished B.A. dissertation, Dept of Archaeology, York University

Gustavsen, L., 2004. *Heworth Croft, Heworth, York, Archaeological Evaluation,* FAS Report

Hargrove, W., 1818. *History and Description of the Ancient City of York* (York)

Hassall, M.W. and Tomlin, R.S.O., 1979. 'Roman Britain in 1978: II Inscriptions', *Britannia* **10**, 339–56

Hopkinson, G. and Ferguson, M-C., 1998. *Elm Bank Hotel, The Mount, York, An Archaeological Evaluation,* On Site Archaeology Report OSA98EV02

Horne, P. D., 2003. Rural settlement in Roman North Yorkshire, an aerial view, in R.A. Butlin (ed.), *Historical Atlas of North Yorkshire*, 58–61

Hunter-Mann, K. 2006. *An Unusual Cemetery at The Mount, York,* Archaeology of York Web Publication **6**, www.iadb.co.uk/driffield6/index.php

Johnson, M., 2005. *A Roman Camp and Prehistoric Site at Monk's Cross, York,* Archaeology of York Web Publication **4**, www.iadb.co.uk/mcross/index.htm

Jones, B. and Mattingly, D., 1990. *Atlas of Roman Britain* (Oxford)

Jones, R.F.J., 1984. 'The cemeteries of Roman York', in Addyman and Black 1984, 34–42

Jones, R.F.J., 1988. 'The hinterland of Roman York', in J. Price, P.R. Wilson and C.S. Briggs (eds), *Recent Research in Roman Yorkshire, Studies in Honour of Mary Kitson Clark,* Brit. Archaeol. Rep. Brit. Ser. **193** (Oxford), 161–70

Jones, R.F.J., 1990. 'Natives and the Roman army: three model relationships', in H. Vetters and M. Kandler, *Akten des 14 Internationalen Limeskongress 1986 in Carnuntum* (Vienna), 99–110

Keen, L., 1965. 'Excavation at 52 Bootham, York, 1964', *Yorkshire Archaeol. J.* **41**, 360–3

King, E. 1975. 'Roman kiln material from the Borthwick Institute, Peasholme Green: a report for the York Excavation Group', in P.V. Addyman, 'Excavations in York 1972–3, First Interim Report', *Antiq. J.* **54**, 213–17

Lawton, I.G., 1992–3. 'Apple Tree Farm 1987–1992: an Ebor ware kiln site', *Yorkshire Archaeol. Soc. Roman Antiq. Sect. Bull.* **10**, 4–8

Lawton, I.G., 1994. '*Derventio*: a Roman settlement at North Farm, Stamford Bridge', *Forum* (Annual Newsletter of CBA Yorkshire) 1994, 8–13

Lawton, I.G., 1997. 'The Roman roads around Stamford Bridge', *Forum* (Annual Newsletter of CBA Yorkshire) 1997, 23–9

MAP (MAP Archaeological Consultancy), 1991. *An Archaeological Evaluation at All Saints School, Mill Mount, York*

MAP, 1995. *Archaeological Evaluation at 52 Monkgate, York*

MAP, 1996a. 'Recent Work by MAP Archaeological Consultancy Ltd', *Forum* (Annual Newsletter of CBA Yorkshire) 1996, 13–21

MAP, 1996b. *Germany Beck – Fulford. Archaeological Sample Excavations: Interim Report*

MAP, 1998. 'Projects in 1998: MAP Archaeological Consultancy Ltd', *Forum* (Annual Newsletter of CBA Yorkshire) 1998, 12–21

MAP, 2000. 'Recent work by MAP Archaeological Consultancy Ltd', *Forum* (Annual Newsletter of CBA Yorkshire) 2000, 18–20

MAP, 2004. *Land to the Rear of 28 Tadcaster Road, Dringhouses, York, Proposed Residential Development, Archaeological Evaluation*

MAP, 2005a. *7–15 Spurriergate, York, Archaeological Assessment Report*

MAP, 2005b. *St Oswald's School, Fulford, York, North Yorkshire, Archaeological Assessment Report*

McComish, J., 2006. *Roman occupation at the site of the former Starting Gate Public House, 42–50 Tadcaster Road, Dringhouses, York, UK*, Archaeology of York Web Publication **8**, www.iadb.co.uk/i2/i2_pub.php?PP=39

Millett, M. (ed.), 2006. *Shiptonthorpe, East Yorkshire: Archaeological Studies of a Romano-British Roadside Settlement*, Yorkshire Archaeol. Rep. **5**

NAA (Northern Archaeological Associates), 2005. *Stamford Bridge, Water Pipeline*, Archaeological Watching Brief and Excavation. Post-Excavation Assessment Report, NAA05/05

Noel, M., 1994. *Geophysical Survey of Land at 27 St Helen's Road, York*, unpublished report by Geoquest

Ottaway, P., 2004. *Roman York* (Stroud, 2nd edition)

Perrin, J.R., 1975. *A Study of the Roman Pottery from an Excavation of the Roman Civil Baths, York in 1939, Air Raid Control Centre Site*, unpublished M.Litt. dissertation, University of Newcastle

Philpott, R., 1991. *Burial Practices in Roman Britain: A Survey of Grave Treatment and Furnishing AD43–410*, Brit. Archaeol. Rep. Brit. Ser. **219** (Oxford)

Phillips, D. and Heywood, B., 1995. *Excavations at York Minster, 1: From Roman Fortress to Norman Cathedral* (London, HMSO)

Radley, J., 1966. 'Yorkshire archaeological register', *Yorkshire Archaeol. J.* **41**, 555–65

Radley, J. (ed.), 1967. 'Yorkshire archaeological register', *Yorkshire Archaeol. J.* **42**, 1–9

Radley, J. (ed.), 1968. 'Yorkshire archaeological register', *Yorkshire Archaeol. J.* **42**, 110–18

Radley, J. and Simms, C., 1970. *Yorkshire Flooding – Some Effects on Man and Nature* (York)

Radley, J., 1974. 'The Prehistory of the Vale of York', *Yorkshire Archaeol. J.* **46**, 10–22

Ramm, H.G., 1958. 'Roman burials from Castle Yard, York', *Yorkshire Archaeol. J.* **39**, 400–18

Ramm, H.G., 1966. 'The Green Dykes, a forgotten Yorkshire earthwork', *Yorkshire Archaeol. J.* **41**, 587–90

Ramm, H.G., 1976. 'The Church of St Mary Bishophill Senior, York: Excavations, 1964', *Yorkshire Archaeol. J.* **48**, 35–68

RCHMY. Royal Commission on Historical Monuments for England: *An Inventory of the Historic Monuments in the City of York*. **1**: *Eburacum, Roman York* (1962); **3**: *South-West of the Ouse* (1972) (HMSO, London)

RIB: Collingwood, R.G. and Wright, R.P., 1965. *Roman Inscriptions of Britain* **1** (Oxford)

Richardson, K.M., 1959. 'Excavations in Hungate, York', *Archaeol. J.* **116**, 51–114

Simpson, G., 1995. 'The samian pottery', in Phillips and Heywood 1995, 272–90.

Spall, C.A. and Toop, N.J., 2005a. *Blue Bridge House and Fishergate House, York. Report on Excavations: July 2000–July 2002*, published on-line at http://www.archaeo-logicalplanningconsultancy.co.uk/mono/001/index.html

Spall, C.A. and Toop, N.J., 2005b. *Post-excavation Assessment, Mill Mount, York*, FAS Report

Stead, I.M., 1991. Iron Age Cemeteries in East Yorkshire, English Heritage Archaeol. Rep. 22

Stephens, M.R. and Ware, P., 1995. 'Recent work by MAP Consultancy', *Yorkshire Archaeol. Soc. Roman Antiq. Sect. Bull.* **12**, 12–15

Stoertz, C., 1997. *Ancient Landscapes of the Yorkshire Wolds*, RCHME

Sumpter, A.B. and Marriott, J.J., 2005. 'The 1976 excavation', in I. Roberts (ed.) *The Iron Age Settlement at Ledston: A Report on the Excavations of 1976 and 1996*, ASWYAS Publ. 7

Swan, V.G. and McBride, R.M., 2002. 'A Rhineland potter at the legionary fortress of York', in M. Aldhouse-Green and P. Webster, *Artefacts and Archaeology: Aspects of the Celtic and Roman World* (Cardiff), 190–234

Thomas, C., 1981. *Christianity in Roman Britain* (London)

Thurnam, J., 1849. 'Description of an ancient tumular cemetery, probably of the Anglo-Saxon period at the Lamel Hill, near York', *Archaeol. J.* **6**, 27–39 and 123–36

Toop, N., 2008. 'Excavations at Moss Street Depot, Moss Street, York', *Yorkshire Archaeol. J.,* **80**, 21–42

Welfare, H. and Swan, V., 1995. *Roman Camps in England: The Field Archaeology*, RCHME

Wenham, L.P., 1957. 'Two discoveries of the Roman road between York and Tadcaster', *Yorkshire Archaeol. J.* **39**, 276–82

Wenham, L.P., 1965. 'Blossom Street excavations, 1953–5', *Yorkshire Archaeol. J.* **41**, 524–90

Wenham, L.P., 1968a. 'Two excavations', *Yorkshire Phil. Soc., Ann. Rep. Trans for the Year 1967*, 41–60

Wenham, L.P., 1968b. *The Romano-British Cemetery at Trentholme Drive York*, Ministry of Public Buildings and Works Archaeol. Rep. **5** (HMSO, London)

Wilmott, G.F., 1952–3. 'St Mary's Abbey, York', *Yorkshire Architect. Yorkshire Archaeol. Soc. Ann. Rep. and Summary of Proceedings 1952–3*, **8**

Wilmott, G.F., 1953–4. 'Excavations at St Mary's Abbey', *Yorkshire Architect. Yorkshire Archaeol. Soc. Ann. Rep. and Summary of Proceedings 1953–4*, 12–13

Wilson, P.R., 2002. Cataractonium: *Roman Catterick and its Hinterland. Excavations and Research 1958–1997*, part 1, Counc. Brit. Archaeol. Res. Rep. **128**

Wilson, P.R., 2009. 'The Roman expansion into Yorkshire reconsidered', in A. Morillo, N. Hanel and E. Martín, *XX International Congress of Roman Frontier Studies*, Anejos de Gladius, **13**, 103-12

YAJ, 1964. 'The Yorkshire Archaeological Register for 1963', *Yorkshire Archaeol J.* **41**, 160–77

YAJ, 1966. 'The Yorkshire Archaeological Register for 1965', *Yorkshire Archaeol J.* **42**, 160–77

YAJ, 1986. 'The Yorkshire Archaeological Register for 1985', *Yorkshire Archaeol. J.* **58**, 199–205

YEG (York Excavation Group), 1967. 'Archaeology in York', *Yorkshire Phil. Soc. Ann. Rep. 1967*, 17–18

YEG (York Excavation Group), 1968. 'Archaeology in York', *Yorkshire Phil. Soc. Ann. Rep. 1968*, 20–1

YPS, 1832. *Yorkshire Phil. Soc. Ann. Rep. 1832*

Acknowledgements

Acknowledgements to persons and parties involved with the 16–22 Coppergate excavation are to be found on pp.200–201. York Archaeological Trust gratefully acknowledges a grant from English Heritage towards the publication of the excavations at 16–22 Coppergate.

For the other sites thanks are due to the site owners, individually named in the reports, for access and in many cases financial support.

Paula Ware kindly made reports of the excavation by MAP at St Oswald's School Fulford available to the author for reference. Unpublished reports by organisations other than YAT were consulted with the permission of John Oxley, Principal Archaeologist for City of York Council.

Thanks are due to Lesley Collett, who drew all the figures and also prepared the drawings and plates for publication and designed and typeset the fascicule. Photographs were taken by successive YAT photographers and site directors: Mike Andrews scanned the photographs for publication. The summary was translated into French by Madeleine Hummler and into German by Hannah Linington and the index was prepared by Pam Scholefield. The text was edited by Frances Mee.

Index

by Pam Scholefield

A colon separates street numbers and page numbers. Page numbers with 't' are tables; figures are in italics; *f* shows insert facing at page 206.

i